Lecture Notes in Computer Science   9654

Commenced Publication in 1973
Founding and Former Series Editors:
Gerhard Goos, Juris Hartmanis, and Jan van Leeuwen

Editorial Board

David Hutchison
Lancaster University, Lancaster, UK
Takeo Kanade
Carnegie Mellon University, Pittsburgh, PA, USA
Josef Kittler
University of Surrey, Guildford, UK
Jon M. Kleinberg
Cornell University, Ithaca, NY, USA
Friedemann Mattern
ETH Zurich, Zürich, Switzerland
John C. Mitchell
Stanford University, Stanford, CA, USA
Moni Naor
Weizmann Institute of Science, Rehovot, Israel
C. Pandu Rangan
Indian Institute of Technology, Madras, India
Bernhard Steffen
TU Dortmund University, Dortmund, Germany
Demetri Terzopoulos
University of California, Los Angeles, CA, USA
Doug Tygar
University of California, Berkeley, CA, USA
Gerhard Weikum
Max Planck Institute for Informatics, Saarbrücken, Germany

More information about this series at http://www.springer.com/series/7409

Abdennour El Rhalibi · Feng Tian
Zhigeng Pan · Baoquan Liu (Eds.)

E-Learning and Games

10th International Conference, Edutainment 2016
Hangzhou, China, April 14–16, 2016
Revised Selected Papers

 Springer

Editors

Abdennour El Rhalibi
Computer Science
John Moores University
Liverpool
UK

Feng Tian
Science and Technology
Bournemouth University
Bournemouth
UK

Zhigeng Pan
Hangzhou Normal University
Hangzhou, Zhejiang
China

Baoquan Liu
Computer Science and Technology
University of Bedfordshire
Luton
UK

ISSN 0302-9743   ISSN 1611-3349   (electronic)
Lecture Notes in Computer Science
ISBN 978-3-319-40258-1   ISBN 978-3-319-40259-8   (eBook)
DOI 10.1007/978-3-319-40259-8

Library of Congress Control Number: 2016941081

LNCS Sublibrary: SL3 – Information Systems and Applications, incl. Internet/Web, and HCI

Printed on acid-free paper

This Springer imprint is published by Springer Nature
The registered company is Springer International Publishing AG Switzerland

Preface

Welcome to the proceedings of Edutainment 2016, the 10th International Conference on E-Learning and Games, which was held during April 14–16, in Hangzhou, China.

Edutainment stands for education and entertainment, and the Edutainment conference series covers not only the research issues of game-based learning, but also the issues of learning experiences that may be gained from entertainment. The series provides an international forum for researchers and practitioners in various disciplines to share and exchange experiences in the emerging research area combining education and entertainment. Initiated in Hangzhou, China, in 2006, the conference has been held in many places including Hong Kong (2007), Nanjing (China, 2008), Banff (Canada, 2009), Changchun (China, 2010), and Taiwan (2011).

This year, we sought contributions from academic researchers and industry players to advance the technology in all fields related to education and entertainment, aiming to address the various challenges currently faced by multi-disciplinary communities from pedagogy, mobile applications, computer graphics to multimedia, augmented/virtual reality and computer games. Edutainment 2016 received about 50 submissions. Each submission was reviewed at least two reviewers from our international Program Committee. In the end, 30 papers were accepted for presentation at the conference. The accepted submissions cover a very wide range of topics, including e-learning, digital culture heritage, computer games, computer graphics, and image processing. Parallel to the main track of the conference, the workshop on Intelligent Data Analytics and Visualization was also hosted, with eight submissions accepted and also included in these proceedings.

We would like to thank all the members of the Program Committee for their hard work in reviewing the papers and providing valuable feedbacks to the authors for the improvement and continuation of their research. Many thanks also go to our three keynote speakers, Prof. Feng Dong the from University of Bedfordshire (UK), Prof. We Chen from Zhejiang University (China), and Associate Prof. Robert S. Laramee from Swansea University (UK), for their inspirational plenary talks to the conference delegates. Last but not least, we would like to thank Hangzhou Normal University (Hangzhou, China) for hosting and organizing the conference.

April 2016
Feng Tian
Minghui Sun

Organization

Honorary Chairs

Jiaoying Shi — Zhejiang University, PRC
J.L. Encarnação — Technical University of Darmstadt, Germany

Conference General Chairs

Zhigeng Pan — Hangzhou Normal University, PRC
Abdennour El Rhalibi — Liverpool John Moores University, UK
Joaquim Jorge — Instituto Superior Tecnico, Lisbon, Portugal

Program Chairs

Maiga Chang — Athabasca University, Canada
Feng Tian — Bournemouth University, UK
Minghui Sun — Jilin University, China

Workshop and Special Sessions Chairs

Minhua Eunice Ma — University of Huddersfield, UK
Martin Goebel — Hochschule Bonn Rhein Sieg, Germany

Industry Chairs

Xiamao Wu — Smartisense GmbH, Germany
David Oyarzun — VICOMTech - Visual Interaction and Communication Technologies, Spain

Panel Chair

Dan Xu — Yunnan University, PRC

Poster/Demo Chair

Xubo Yang — Shanghai Jiaotong University, PRC

Publicity Chairs

Ying Song	Zhejiang University of Science and Technology, PRC
Tim Roden	Lamar University, USA
Kok-Wai Wong	Murdoch University, Australia

Publication Chair

Yuanquan Wang	Hebei University of Technology, PRC

Local Organization Chairs

Mingmin Zhang	Zhejiang University, PRC
Dandan Ding	Hangzhou Normal University, PRC

Conference Manager and Website Chair

Xinting Wang	Hangzhou Normal University, PRC

Technical Program Committee

Dhiya Al-Jumeily	Liverpool John Moores University, UK
Eike Anderson	Bournemouth University, UK
Anthony Brooks	Aalborg University, Denmark
Maiga Chang	Athabasca University, Canada
Yam-San Chee	National Institute of Education, Singapore
Thomas Connolly	University of the West of Scotland, UK
Dandan Ding	Zhejiang University, PRC
Rajae El Ouazzani	Ecole Supérieure de Technologie de Meknès, Morocco
Abdennour El Rhalibi	Liverpool John Moores University, UK
J.L. Encarnação	Technical University of Darmstadt, Germany
Liarokapis Fotis	Masaryk University, Czech Republic
Julien Gascon-Samson	McGill University, Canada
Martin Goebel	Hochschule Bonn-Rhein-Sieg, Germany
Martin Hanneghan	Liverpool John Moores University, UK
Yueh-Min Huang	National Cheng Kung University, Taiwan
Kin-Chuen Hui	The Chinese University of Hong Kong, SAR China
William Hurst	Liverpool John Moores University, UK
Marc Jaeger	CIRAD and University of Montpellier, France
Xiaogang Jin	Zhejiang University, PRC
Joaquim Jorge	Instituto Superior Tecnico, Lisbon, Portugal
Kashif Kifayat	Liverpool John Moores University, UK
Oscar Lin	Athabasca University, Canada
Minhua Ma	University of Huddersfield, UK
Katerina Mania	Technical University of Crete, Greece
Leonel Caseiro Morgado	Aberta University, Canada

Wolfgang Mueller	University of Education Weingarten, Germany
Andrés Navarro	Pontifica Universidad Javeriana, Colombia
Anton Nijholt	Twente University, The Netherlands
Claudio E. Palazzi	Università degli Studi di Padova, Italy
Zhigeng Pan	Hangzhou Normal University, PRC
Panagiotis Petridis	Aston University, UK
Jorge Posada	VICOMTech, Spain
Theresa-Marie Rhyne	North Carolina State University, USA
Tim Roden	Lamar University, USA
Yuanyuan Shen	Liverpool John Moores University, UK
Jiaoying Shi	Zhejiang University, PRC
Sud Sudirman	Liverpool John Moores University, UK
Mohd Shahrizal Sunar	Universiti Teknologi Malaysia, Malaysia
Minghui Sun	Jilin University, PRC
Mark Taylor	Liverpool John Moores University, UK
Rafiq Swash	Brunel University, UK
Ruck Thawonmas	Ritsumeikan University, Japan
Feng Tian	Bournemouth University, UK
Yuanquan Wang	Hebei University of Technology, PRC
Dunwei Wen	Athabasca University, Canada
Kok-Wai Wong	Murdoch University, Australia
Xiamao Wu	Smartisense GmbH, Germany
Dan Xu	Yunnan University, PRC
Xubo Yang	Shanghai Jiaotong University, PRC
Po Yang	Liverpool John Moores University, UK
Mingmin Zhang	Zhejiang University, PRC

Workshop Chairs

Baoquan Liu	University of Bedfordshire, UK
Wei Chen	Zhejiang University, China
Feng Dong	University of Bedfordshire, UK

Workshop International Program Committee

Youbing Zhao	University of Bedfordshire, UK
Manolis Tsiknakis	Foundation for Research and Technology, Greece
Kostas Marias	Foundation for Research and Technology, Greece
Emmanouil Spanakis	Foundation for Research and Technology, Greece
Horacio Saggion	Universitat Pompeu Fabra, Spain
Robert S. Laramee	Swansea University, UK
Alexandru C. Telea	University of Groningen, The Netherlands
Ik Soo Lim	University of Bangor, UK
Jiawan Zhang	Tianjin University, China
Yubo Tao	Zhejiang University, China
Zhao Geng	University of Leeds, UK

Xun Wang	Zhejiang Gongshang University, China
Fan Zhang	Zhejiang University of Technology, China
Lingyun Yu	Hangzhou Dianzi University, China
Xiangyang Wu	Hangzhou Dianzi University, China
Josef Kohout	University of West Bohemia, Czech Republic
Koji Koyamada	Kyoto University, Japan
Takayuki Itoh	Ochanomizu University, Japan
Issei Fujishiro	Keio University, Japan

Sponsors

1) Hangzhou Normal University

2) Hangzhou Science and Technology Association
3) Hangzhou Computer Federation for Committee of Digital Media and Human-Computer Interaction
4) Digital Media & Interaction Research Center of Hangzhou Normal University

Contents

Graphics, Imaging and Applications

Workshop on Intelligent Data Analytics and Visualization

E-Learning and Game

Visual Exploration of Virtual Lives
in Multiplayer Online Games

Zhiqi Liu[1], Yandi Shen[1], Junhua Lu[1], Dingke Kong[2], Yinyin Chen[1],
Jingxuan He[1], Shu Liu[1], Ye Qi[1], and Wei Chen[1(✉)]

[1] State Key Lab of CAD&CG, Zhejiang University, Hangzhou, Zhejiang, China
liuzhiqi91@gmail.com, shenyandisayid@gmail.com, elaine930127@gmail.com,
{akiori,qiye}@zju.edu.cn, he4444mingtian@gmail.com, njliushu@126.com,
chenwei@cad.zju.edu.cn
[2] Zhejiang Gongshang University, Hangzhou, Zhejiang, China
dinckong@gmail.com

Abstract. Analyzing the user behavior of multiplayer online games can
help understand the sociality and characteristics of players in the virtual world. The primary task is to characterize the game life and its
evolution within the game. We propose a novel network-based representation, EvolutionLine Graph, that illustrates the evolving behavior of
massive game players as a sequence of time-oriented transitions among
various status. We design and implement a novel visual analytics system,
GameLifeVis, that supports the visualization, exploration, and analysis
of multi-level user behaviors in an integrated visual interface. We exem-
plify the efficiency of our approach with case studies on a multi-faceted
dataset collected within a popular online game (15 million players) in 18
months.

Keywords: Game visualization · Time-oriented data visualization ·
Visual abstraction · Multiplayer online games

1 Introduction

With the rapid development of internet and electronic devices, online games have
become increasingly popular. Players are more diverse and they have access to
games in more places and at more times, and produce more data and content
for developers and researchers to leverage than ever before [1]. Modeling with
artificial societies provides a promising new mechanism for social computing,
especially for those involving human behaviors and social organizations [2]. The
players' playing styles may reflect their real interests and personalities to some
extent [3]. But the inner-relationship of players in virtual game world is likely to
be even more complicated than that in the real world. Typically, computer game
producers collect and store all information since the launching of the game. The
data collected in online games contain rich information about the social- and
cyber-related characteristics of massive game players. Apart from commercial

© Springer International Publishing Switzerland 2016
A. El Rhalibi et al. (Eds.): Edutainment 2016, LNCS 9654, pp. 3–14, 2016.
DOI: 10.1007/978-3-319-40259-8_1

values, online game data are of great importance for research in social, behavioral, and economic sciences, as well as human-centered computer science [4].

This paper presents our experience in analyzing and visualizing a data set that is collected by an online game company which operates a massively multiplayer online role-playing game (MMORPG). The game is set in ancient China. Players choose their own characters in the virtual world, and they are enabled to finish tasks, chat with friends, join leagues, trade with others, etc. For each game player, a record is generated everyday if the player logins on that day. Each record contains more than 40 attributes.

Given the available data set, we can now, more than ever, study how game players act in the virtual world. However, exploring and analyzing online game data is cumbersome because of the data's large size, heterogeneity, and time-varying characteristic. In addition, interesting patterns may be hidden behind the interleaved connections among players as well as their temporal evolutions. Based on the interviews with social science researchers and the chief designers of the game, we place our main focus on analyzing the user behaviors, and identify the following three objectives:

– **Identifying Behavior Types.** According to the gameplay theory, the game players can be classified into multiple categories [5]. We hope to examine the theory based on the data set, and identify different classes with respect to the behaviors of players.
– **Understanding Behavior Evolutions.** A virtual life of a game player evolves within two parallel worlds, the virtual world and the real world. We need to understand the temporal evolutions of user behaviors in a statistically meaningful way.
– **Discovering Overall Patterns.** Apart from the local patterns, we hope to uncover patterns which are shared by a majority of players.

Moreover, there are barely any integrated works that incorporate statistical methods, data mining and visualization techniques. In structuring and illustrating user behavior patterns and how game players shift from one status to another, we adopt a cluster-and-joint scheme: prior to modeling the transition of player behaviors, players are classified with respect to related attributes. We design and implement a visual exploration system, GameLifeVis, that supports pattern recognition, evolution tracking, and behavioral reasoning in an integrated visual interface. The main contributions of our study are two folds:

– A novel visual representation, Evolution Line Graph, that depicts the evolutions of virtual lives of massive game players;
– A visual exploration system that supports intuitive analysis of player behaviors and their evolutions.

The rest of the paper is organized as follows. Section 2 summarizes related work. We describe our raw data and preprocessing procedures as well as present interesting observations by means of statistical analysis in Sect. 3. We introduce our solution for visualizing and exploring game data in Sect. 4 and elaborate on our visualization system in Sect. 5. Case studies are given in Sect. 6 and followed by the conclusion in Sect. 7.

2   Related Works

2.1   Visualizing and Analyzing Game Data

Much attention has been drawn to the analysis of game data. Natkin et al. [6] made some effort to provide a narration model correlated to a user model in the design of mixed reality entertainment. Wang et al. [7] used a Latent Class Model to analyze the behavioral patterns of different players in different clusters. Due to the limited data quality, only a few attributes and a small part of data set were examined. Baukhage et al. [8] proposed a detailed mathematical model for game data clustering and analysis. Our work explored similar topics with an alternative solution.

MMORPGs are similar to sport in a way that they are both competitive games. Recently, an extensive amount of effort has been devoted to developing visualization methods for understanding and exploring sports [9,10].

To a certain degree, an online game can be regarded as social media. There has been a heated topic of analyzing and visualizing user behavior with the development of social media. Correa et al. [11] filtered complex networks structurally and semantically in order to help users discover clusters and patterns in the organization of social networks. LoyalTracker [12] is designed to track loyalty of users in search engines by leveraging the user log data. A new visualization technique is employed to summarize the dynamics of user loyalty over time. Similarly, the OpinionFlow system [13] leverages an opinion diffusion model to analyze information diffusion and propagation on Twitter.

2.2   Visualizing Time-Varying Multivariate Data

With the boosting of data acquisition devices and computing infrastructures, time-varying multivariate data become increasingly ubiquitous. In particular, visualizing online game log data remains a big challenge because the data are dynamic, multi-faceted and massive. Agrawal et al. [14] built the Badge and Network Traffic tool to create event animations and could report any abnormality noticed immediately to the user. The SDSS log viewer [15] is a visually assisted system to handle SQL log data. Though effective, previous works on log data visualization and analysis can not be applicable to visualizing game data. The main reason is that conventional log data visualization techniques focus on the evolutions of multiple dimensions, but fail to structure the inter-connections among different time points.

A particularly important task in visualizing time-varying multi-variate data is to illustrate the transition or evolution among different players' status in an explicit way. For instance, the Outflow approach [16] effectively depicts multiple sequences of events and their transitions. By abstracting the visual media as a sparse time-varying directed graph [17], a storyline graph representation [18] can be used to characterize a huge amount of image streams. Our approach targets a similar problem but emphasizes on the transition of different players' status in the virtual world.

3   Data Description and Preliminary Analysis

The dataset contains more than 10 billions records of 19 millions game players that are distributed in 54 game servers. We choose server 230 because of its relatively complete records.

3.1   Data Description

The raw data consists of more than forty attributes to describe the characteristics of game players. We remove the redundant and uninformative attributes (e.g. Player ID, IP address) and obtain 21 attributes. Most of attributes are time-varying.

- **Cyber.** This category includes four attributes in the virtual world. *Player ID* is the unique identification. *Role Gender* is the role gender. *Role Level* and *Role Age* denote the role level ($\in [0, 10]$) and the number of days since the first login time.
- **Physical.** *Login Time* denotes the date and time of a login. *Online Time Amount* denotes the total time spent on the game in the day of the record. *Login Times* denotes the count of login in the day.
- **Recreational.** A player holds a list of equipments like weapons, shields, and talismans, each of which has a specific function and a rating level. We assign a numeric value *Equipment* ($\in [0, 9]$) to rate the equipment list of the player. Likewise, two variables *Practice* and *Mastery* are defined and assigned to represent player's skills.
- **Economical.** There are four kinds of economic currencies: *Silver*, *Silver_note*, *Ingot* and *Ingot_note*. *Silver* can be obtained by accomplishing specific tasks, but *Ingot* can only be obtained by either paying money or trading with other players. *Silver_note* and *Ingot_note* are two special kinds of *Silver* and *Ingot*. Both these two currencies could only be obtained through official promotion activities and cannot be traded among players. Game players can make transactions between *Silver* and *Ingot* in the game. We select four attributes that are collected in each day: *Transaction_pnum* (the number of players who make transactions with the player), *Transaction_num* (the number of transactions), *Transaction_s* and *Transaction_i* (the number of *Silver* or *Ingot* obtained and disbursed in the transactions).
- **Social.** We extract two social networks with respect to the friendship and the league, and employ *Chat_send* and *Chat_receive* to denote the numbers of messages sent and received.

We count the total online time of each player, and cull those who played the game less than 20 h or remained at level 1 until their last login, leading to 1,461,013 records over 28,221 players. Players with total game time less than 20 h or final level of 1 are deemed as single-time or extremely inactive players, therefore are left out lest they should bias the overall evolution pattern.

3.2 Statistical Analysis

Before designing the visual analysis system, we conduct conventional statistical analysis to obtain an overview. The resultant observations inspire us to identify the objectives of visualization, which can be cross-validated with the findings from our case studies.

We use principle component analysis (PCA) to classify the collection of all players. The first three principal components account for 66.15 % of the overall variance, which are **Achievement** include *Role Age, Silver, Mastery*, etc.; **Social** including *Chat_send, Chat_receive, Recharging* and **Equipment** including *Equipment*. Based on the well-known player type theory [3], the motivation of players can be divided into four categories: Achievement-oriented players tend to set goals for themselves, which normally accompanies the accumulation of large amounts of virtual wealth; Exploration-oriented players keep on navigating to explore the virtual world by extending both the breadth and the depth of their expedition; Imposition-oriented players usually cause distress to other players by acquiring and utilizing equipments in the game and are often called killers; Social-oriented players like to make friends and leverage the communication system to socialize in the game. This preliminary analysis enlightens the visual design of our approach for characterizing the behavior and evolution of players.

4   The EvolutionLine Graph

Representing the evolutions of virtual lives of massive game players requires the characterization of both the patterns of the lives and their dynamic transitions. Informed by the discrete-time Markov process, we model the status of each player and its dynamics under a first-order Markovian assumption. This is reasonable because the status of a player at a time point is mainly dependent on the status of the last time point.

4.1   The Model

We uniformly segment the entire time period into M intervals $T = \{t_m, m = 1, 2, 3, ..., M\}$ (e.g., an interval contains 7 days in our implementation). We collect the attribute vectors of all players at all time intervals and classify them into K clusters. Let $\mathbf{X}_m = (X_1^{(m)}, X_2^{(m)}, ..., X_K^{(m)}) \in \mathbb{N}^K$ denotes the attribute vectors of players at the mth time interval, where $X_i^{(j)}$ represents the number of players in the ith cluster in the jth time interval. We compute a transition matrix $\mathcal{M}_m$ for each pair of $\mathbf{X}_m$ and $\mathbf{X}_{m+1}$, respectively.

4.2   Construction

Preprocessing. We denote the collection of attributes of players as S, with $\mathbf{v} = (v_1, v_2, ..., v_D) \in S$. Here D is the number of dimensions of $\mathbf{v}$. The data set described in Sect. 3 contains 21 attributes. Some of these attributes are employed in other components of our system (we neglect *Player ID* and *Logon Time* because they are identifications). Besides, the *Role Gender* of a player is unchanged since the role was created. Thus the final dimension of the attribute vectors is 18 ($D = 18$).

Each time a player logins, all of his attributes are recorded. Therefore attributes of a player can be regarded as varied over time. We aggregate all records of a player in a time interval t_m using different operations. In particular, the aggregation for accumulative attributes - *Role Age*, *Role Level*, *Equipment*, *Practice*, *Mastery* is *average*. The aggregation for other attributes is *summation*. The attribute vector after the aggregation is denoted as $\mathbf{v}_x^n = (\overline{x_1}, \overline{x_2}, ..., \overline{x_{18}})$, yielding a collection of vectors: $S^* = \bigcup_{x, 1 \leq n \leq M} \{\mathbf{v}_x^n\}$.

Clustering. We classify S^* into k clusters using the standard k-means algorithm. Our system is adaptive for different k; however, in the figures displayed in this paper, k is assigned to 15 for the best illustration after many experiments. For easy computation, we use the weighted-Euclidean distance parametrized by weights $\{\lambda_i\}_{i=1}^D (\sum_{i=1}^D \lambda_i = 1)$ as the distance metric. In our implementation, we choose a uniform weighting scheme: $\lambda_i = \frac{1}{D}$, $(1 \leq i \leq D)$. However, different weights could be chosen in favor of different purposes.

Transition Computing. It is quite common that a player x logs in the nth time interval but disappears in the following p time intervals. In this case, $\mathbf{v}_x^n$ and $\mathbf{v}_x^{n+p+1}$ are in S^*, but $\mathbf{v}_x^{n+1}, ..., \mathbf{v}_x^{n+p}$ are not. We compensate for the missing values by a simple interpolation scheme. Suppose that a player x enters this game in the m_0th time interval, we denote its records as $\mathbf{v}_x^{m_0}, \mathbf{v}_x^{m_1}, ..., \mathbf{v}_x^{m_j} \in S^*$. For every $n \geq m_0$, $m_i \leq n < m_{i+1}$, we assume that the player belongs to the cluster X_l in the m_ith time interval, and create a new vector $\mathbf{v}_x^n = \mathbf{v}_x^{m_i} \in X_l$. The completed data set is denoted $\overline{S^*}$. We define a time-varying transition matrix as: $\mathcal{M}_n = \{q_{ij}^{(n)}\}_{1 \leq i,j \leq K}$ as:

$$q_{ij}^{(n)} = \#\{x | \mathbf{v}_x^n \in X_i, \mathbf{v}_x^{n+1} \in X_j; \mathbf{v}_x^n, \mathbf{v}_x^{n+1} \in \overline{S^*}\}$$

Each entry $q_{ij}^{(n)}$ represents the number of players who transition from cluster X_i to X_j in the nth time interval.

4.3   Visualization

An evolution line graph is basically a node-link representation based on the axis layout of parallel sets [19], in which each node and link can be used to encode interested information. As shown in Fig. 1, the graph is placed from the root to the top, which implies the advance of time. We take the attributes that reveal the advance of time as the timeline, such as login date, accumulative online time amount, role age and role level. Each axis on the graph corresponds to a certain time point.

Along each axis, k boxes are placed, each of which represents a particular state. A state $N_l^{(n)}$ denotes a set of players which belong to certain cluster X_l at certain time point n. We define it as a *State*. A link connecting two states X_i and X_j refers to a transition T_{ij} between them. We adopt a transition band to describe the player state change T_{ij} that connects S_i and S_j. The widths of strips and boxes encode the type and number of transition. More specifically, we used the Bezier curve to scale down the middle part of the transition band to decrease the overlap area.

Since players may join or leave the game at different time points, we add several visual design elements to describe player's activeness. To express the state of players in different categories, each box is segmented into two sections: chromatic and gray. The length of chromatic section refers to the number of active players, while that of the gray section implies the number of extinct players. We also place a set of distribution histograms aside to represent the total number of new, active and extinct players, which are respectively colored in orange, green and gray.

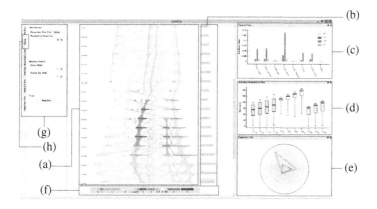

Fig. 1. The GameLifeVis interface: (a) evolution line view; (b) player distribution histogram; (c) centroid view; (d) attribute distribution view; (e) comparison view; (f) floating panel; (g) control panel; (h) filter. (Color figure online)

5   Visual Analysis

We design and implement a visual analysis system, GameLifeVis, based on the evolution line graph representation.

5.1   The Interface

The GameLifeVis incorporates many user exploration and interaction components: (a) a detailed evolution line graph view (main view), (b) a player distribution histogram, (c) a centroid view, (d) an attribute distribution view, and
(e) a comparison view. A suit of controlling panels are also provided, include a
floating panel (f) that shows the projection of the boxes, a control panel (g) that
configures the functions, and a filtering widget that allows for configuring user
preference (h).

Evolution Line View. The evolution line view presents the evolution of different clusters in a tree-like way. In particular, nodes and links are two fundamental
elements. A specific pattern is encoded in the sequences of transition bands. The
floating panel on the bottom of the main view is added to show the number
of players in each cluster at each time point, on which the boxes at the next
time point are projected. When the user drags the canvas, the floating panel is
automatically moving.

Coordinated Views. For the further exploration of each state in the main
view, we design three coordinated views as show in Fig. 1(c), (d) and (e). These
three views change with the main view when a cluster and a group of attributes
are selected in the Evolution Line View and control panel respectively.

- Centroid view uses histograms to directly express the statistical information
  of cluster centers. This view will display the normalized value of selected
  attributes of the target clusters. In addition, the bar color is set to be consistent with that of the corresponding cluster.
- Attribute Distribution View provides a set of box plots that demonstrate the
  distributive characteristics of the data records. It helps the user understand
  the mean, variance, minimum, and maximum of certain attribute.
- Comparison View supports the comparison of multiple attributes among different states. The selected information is presented in the radar chart, which
  clearly shows the discrepancy among the chosen states.

Control Panel. In order to better interact with each view, we set a control panel
on the left side of the main view. This control panel enables both scaling and
distortion of the visual elements in the main view. Meanwhile, we also add a data
filtering panel to facilitate data mining. In the coordinated views, we develop an
attribute selection panel so that users could choose attributes of interest at will.
For a more detailed description of the control panel, see Sect. 5.2.

5.2   Interactions

GameLifeVis supports several types of interactions.

Highlighting. When the mouse moves across the strips and boxes, their frames
will be highlighted for easy identification. Meanwhile, double-clicking a strip or
a box will highlight the elements within the corresponding two time intervals,

which facilitates the examination of local transitions. Moreover, to trace the transition of a certain cluster, users could double-click the floating panel to highlight the entire cluster and other related clusters.

Filtering. The filter allows the user to retrieve data of interest. Once the user sets a proper filter condition and presses on the button 'Filter', the evolution line graph in the main view will be reconfigured based on the filtering result.

Dragging and Adjusting. The widths of boxes and strips could be set dynamically regarding the different density of the Evolution Line. Users could also drag the boxes at each time point to observe the transition of density. Moreover, our system also supports the zooming function.

6   Case Study

We conducted two case studies to testify the efficiency of our approach.

6.1   Case 1

We cross validate our result from Sect. 3.2 using the filtering, which is shown in Fig. 2.

Imposition type. By visualizing the evolution of imposition-oriented players defined in Sect. 3.2, we have discovered that most imposition-oriented players are classified in cluster 3 (light purple), cluster 19 (dark blue) and cluster 7 (green). They only shift from cluster 3 to cluster 19 and finally arrive at cluster 7 without any backflow or skip. All three clusters have extremely high scores on the attribute *Equipment* but have low scores on other attributes. They only differ in that the average *Role Age* is in the order of cluster 3 < cluster 19 < cluster 7. From the interview with an experienced player, a reasonable speculation would be that these imposition-oriented players place high value on the *Equipment*. Despite their low *Recharging* and *Role Level*, they sustain themselves by enhancing their equipment levels and beating others in the virtual arena.

Achievement type. We can identify the achievement-oriented players in cluster 18 (blue), cluster 6 (light green) and cluster 1 (dark purple). All three clusters have high scores in *Role Level, Equipment, Silver, Silver_note, Mastery, OnlineTimeAmount* but have low scores on *Recharging*. These players usually set high achievement goals but do not resort to *Recharging*. The average *Role Level* of cluster 18 is lower than both cluster 6 and cluster 1 thus it could be seen as the precedent of the other two clusters. Transitions between cluster 6 and cluster 1 are extremely intertwined and frequent, indicating that players in these two clusters probably have the same predecessors but got diverged due to their different game habits.

Exploration type. Exploration-oriented players congregate in cluster 11 (red), where all attributes have below-average scores. Since they have no interest in upgrading, equipment, trading or socializing with other players, they are marginal players of the game but they like to take adventure.

Social type. No distinct pattern could be observed in the group of social-oriented players because there are very few of them. We can therefore deduce that this is not a social-oriented game and very few players focus on socializing with other players solely.

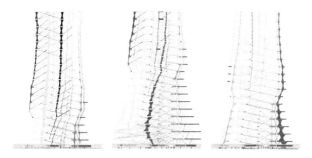

Fig. 2. Left: achieve-oriented; middle: exploration-oriented; right: imposition-oriented. (Color figure online)

6.2   Case 2

We first present the evolution of our game from a macroscopic perspective using both physical and virtual timelines.

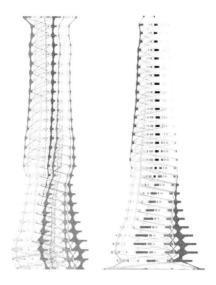

Fig. 3. Left: physical timeline; right: virtual timeline (Color figure online).

Physical Timeline. We provide the entire evolution line graph in the left half of Fig. 3, using physical time as the timeline and two weeks as the time interval. The total bar length at each time point represents the overall number of players who login at that time. We can see that the evolution line graph has an overall shape of a bottle, with two protrusions on in October, 2013 and June, 2014 corresponding to the two server merges. From the player distribution histogram, we can spot the continuous decreasing of new players and extinct players except during the first server merge.

Virtual Timeline. For comparison, we provide the Evolution Line graph in Fig. 3, using virtual *Role Age* as the time line and two weeks as the time interval. The entire graph has a shape of a tapering spire, which indicates the persistent loss of game players. Without resorting to specific attributes, we can identify the overall transitional patterns of certain clusters. For example, cluster 3 (light purple), cluster 4 (pink), cluster 19 (dark blue) are the majority groups in the beginning stage of the game, but die out quickly as the game develops. A reasonable explanation would be that players in these clusters lose interests in the game quickly. In contrast, cluster 1 (purple) and cluster 6 (light green) have few players in the beginning but gradually grow in size and become dominant. Players in these two clusters are believed to have lasting loyalty to this game.

7   Conclusion

This paper presents a preliminary effort on visual exploration of virtual lives evolution of massive game players. We conducted statistical analysis to obtain initial observations, and constructed a network-based representation to characterize the virtual lives of players as a temporally evolving graph. Visual exploration of the visualization supports an expressive and fine-grained understanding of the dynamics of player behaviors in a coordinated view of both the virtual and real worlds. The case studies demonstrate the effectiveness and efficiency of our approach.

Acknowledgements. This work is supported by NSFC (61232012, 61422211, 61303141), Zhejiang NSFC (Y12F020172), and the Fundamental Research Funds for the Central Universities

References

1. Riedl, M.O., Zook, A.: AI for game production. In: IEEE Conference on Computational Intelligence in Games, CIG 2013, pp. 1–8. IEEE (2013)
2. Wang, F.Y.: Social computing: fundamentals and applications. In: IEEE International Conference on Intelligence and Security Informatics, ISI 2008, pp. xxxv–xxxviii. IEEE (2008)
3. Bartle, R.: Hearts, clubs, diamonds, spades: players who suit muds. J. MUD Res. **1**(1), 19 (1996)

4. Bainbridge, W.S.: The scientific research potential of virtual world. Science **317**, 472–476 (2007)
5. Matsumoto, Y., Thawonmas, R.: MMOG player classification using hidden Markov models. In: Rauterberg, M. (ed.) ICEC 2004. LNCS, vol. 3166, pp. 429–434. Springer, Heidelberg (2004)
6. Natkin, S., Yan, C.: User model in multiplayer mixed reality entertainment applications. In: Advances in Computer Entertainment Technology, p. 74. ACM (2006)
7. Wang, S.T., Yang, J.C., S.Y., C., Kuo, W.C.: The clusters of gaming behavior in MMORPG: a case study in Taiwan. In: IIAI International Conference on Advanced Applied Informatics, IIAIAAI 2012, pp. 263–266 (2012)
8. Bauckhage, C., Drachen, A., Sifa, R.: Clustering game behavior data. IEEE Trans. Comput. Intell. AI Games **7**(3), 266–278 (2015)
9. Cox, A., Stasko, J.: SportVis: discovering meaning in sports statistics through information visualization. In: IEEE Symposium on Information Visualization, pp. 115–116. IEEE (2006)
10. Beck, F., Burch, M., Weiskopf, D.: Visual comparison of time-varying athletes' performance. In: Proceedings of the 1st Workshop on Sports Data Visualization (2013)
11. Correa, C.D., Crnovrsanin, T., Muelder, C., Shen, Z., Armstrong, R., Shearer, J., Ma, K.: Cell phone mini challenge award: intuitive social network graphs visual analytics of cell phone data using mobivis and ontovis. In: IEEE Conference on Visual Analytics Science and Technology, VAST 2008, pp. 211–212. IEEE (2008)
12. Shi, C., Wu, Y., Liu, S., Zhou, H., Qu, H.: Loyaltracker: visualizing loyalty dynamics in search engines. IEEE Trans. Vis. Comput. Graph. **20**(12), 1733–1742 (2014)
13. Wu, Y., Liu, S., Yan, K., Liu, M., Wu, F.: Opinionflow: visual analysis of opinion diffusion on social media. IEEE Trans. Vis. Comput. Graph. **20**, 1763–1772 (2014)
14. Agrawal, S., Sravanthi, K., Vadapalli, S., Karlapalem, K.: Vast 2009 traffic mini challenge: intuitive analytic information presentation. In: IEEE Conference on Visual Analytics Science and Technology, VAST 2009, pp. 271–272. IEEE (2009)
15. Zhang, J., Chen, C., Vogeley, M.S., Pan, D., Thakar, A., Raddick, J.: SDSS log viewer: visual exploratory analysis of large-volume SQL log data. Proc. Visual. Data Anal. **8294**, 1–13 (2012)
16. Wongsuphasawat, K., Gotz, D.: Exploring flow, factors, and outcomes of temporal event sequences with the outflow visualization. IEEE Trans. Visual. Comput. Graphics **18**(12), 2659–2668 (2012)
17. Song, L., Kolar, M., Xing, E.P.: Time-varying dynamic Bayesian networks. In: Bengio, Y., Schuurmans, D., Lafferty, J., Williams, C., Culotta, A. (eds.) Advances in Neural Information Processing Systems, vol. 22, pp. 1732–1740. Curran Associates Inc., Red Hook (2009)
18. Kim, G., Xing, E.: Reconstructing storyline graphs for image recommendation from web community photos. In: Proceedings of the IEEE Conference on Computer Vision and Pattern Recognition, CVPR 2014, pp. 3882–3889 (2014)
19. Kosara, R., Bendix, F., Hauser, H.: Parallel sets: interactive exploration and visual analysis of categorical data. IEEE Trans. Visual. Comput. Graphics **12**(4), 558–568 (2006)

Educational Folktale E-book with Collage Illustratable Tool

Dongwann Kang, Feng Tian$^{(\boxtimes)}$, and Reza Sahandi

Faculty of Science and Technology, Bournemouth University,
Fern Barrow, Poole, Dorset BH12 5BB, UK
{dkang,ftian,rsahandi}@bournemouth.ac.uk

Abstract. It is always challenging to teach children foreign languages, due to the difficulty of learning and their short attention span. To address the challenge and take advantage of the popularity of touchable tablets and smartphones, we propose an educational folktale e-book (EFE-Book) application with an interactive illustratable tool. EFE-Book is developed to teach pre-school children to learn foreign languages by telling folktales with illustrations. To encourage effective learning, EFE-Book provides an interactive collage tool that enables users to create collage-based illustrations by hand. To implement this, we propose a paper tile modeling method based on the Voronoi diagram. With EFE-Book, the user can create coloured paper tiles and attach them to the predesigned sketch through touch interface, such as Apple iPad.

Keywords: Mobile · E-learning · E-book · Collage · Stylization

1 Introduction

Many mobile applications in various fields such as games, e-books and e-learning have been developed in recent years, thanks to the advancement of mobile technology. Touchable screens are now widely used for display devices such as smartphones and tablet PCs, making interaction between users and applications much easier. Many drawing tools are now available through mobile applications, for example converting a photo into an image with artistic styles [2, 8]. In this paper we aim to discuss an educational e-book application which employs an interactive illustratable method. For e-learning applications, interactivity can enhance learning, especially when target users are children. In addition, using suitable stylization techniques can further improve learning.

In this paper, we propose an educational folktale e-book (EFE-Book) suitable pre-school children for learning foreign languages. The EFE-Book by using the collage art technique provides an interactive illustratable tool, thereby making learning foreign languages more effective and enjoyable.

The paper is organized as follows. Section 2, provides an overview of related work in mobile applications for e-learning and collage style rendering. Section 3 provides details of the EFE-Book with interactive illustratable tools. The results are discussed in Sect. 4. Finally, conclusion with a summary of our ideas and our future plans for further developments are discussed in Sect. 5.

© Springer International Publishing Switzerland 2016
A. El Rhalibi et al. (Eds.): Edutainment 2016, LNCS 9654, pp. 15–26, 2016.
DOI: 10.1007/978-3-319-40259-8_2

2   Related Work

Mobile devices have been considered as a good supplementary to support both students and teachers by providing services that facilitate teaching, learning and education related administrative tasks, e-book and e-learning [9]. Jacott [7] explained applications and effectiveness of mobile learning, which provides useful, authoritative and comprehensive guidance for professionals in education. With its wide use and popularity, the smartphone has become a powerful mobile device for e-learning and e-book. In Godwin-Jones's article [4], he explored the state of language learning applications, devices they run on, and how they are developed. Especially for language learning, Mori et al. [11] proposed an interactive e-book application on smartphone. Their application was based on a conversational agent that asks questions or makes comments about the current page, so that these features made the book significantly more interactive and engaging when compared to static e-books.

The collage stylization researches based on coloured paper have mainly focused on generating coloured paper tiles and placing them appropriately. Seo et al. [13] proposed a method that converts an input image into a coloured paper mosaic. In their method, the coloured paper tiles are generated by using the Voronoi diagrams [1]. To replicate the torn paper effect, they applied the random midpoint displacement method. Gi et al. [3] proposed a torn simulation-based coloured paper mosaic method. The method tears off paper tiles from given coloured papers, and places them on the most appropriate locations in an image. To locate tiles and minimize gaps and overlaps between tiles, they also proposed an energy function to avoid crossing edges in the image. By minimizing the energy function, a realistic coloured paper mosaic image is generated. In contrast, Han et al. [5] focused on the sequence in which tiles are placed, and proposed a method that sequentially places each tile according to a customizable rule defined by parameters. This method was the first to enable placement of tiles along an edge, or to place tiles that have a similar color to previous tiles, by adjusting the parameters. In this paper we partially employ some of the main ideas of the coloured paper tile stylization proposed in the above studies.

3   Development of EFE-Book with Interactive Illustratable Tool for Collage Art

In this section we give an overview of interfaces and functions of our e-book application for foreign language education, and propose an illustratable tool for collage art on the e-book.

3.1   The EFE-Book for Preschool Kids Learning Foreign Languages

An overview of the EFE-Book is presented in Fig. 1. The application consists of a cover page and several scenes. Since too many scenes may shorten the span of pre-school children, we limit the length of the scenes to 10. Each scene

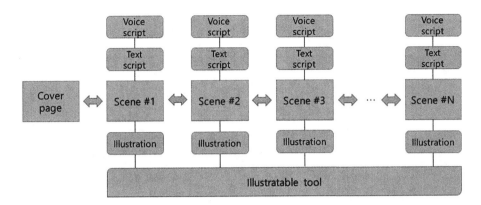

Fig. 1. Overview of the EFE-Book. The application consists of illustrated scenes with a short script. At each scene, a script is visually and auditorily played on the illustration. By using a menu on each scene, user can interactively create illustration through the proposed tool for collage art.

shows a representative illustration with a script which is a tale describing the scene. Figure 2 represents the layers of each scene. On the top layer, a menu bar and navigator buttons are located on the bottom and both sides of the scene, respectively. With navigator buttons, user can move to previous or next scene. The menu bar consists of several functions including replay which restarts the current scene, a table of contents that allows moving to a specific scene, an illustratable tool (more details in Sect. 3.2), and a movie function that plays all the scenes continuously. On the middle layer, a script is placed on a side of a scene. When a user enters a scene, a script is popped up. Then, a voice script is played with background music. At this time, the user may turn off the voice script to concentrate on reading. Moreover, the script can be replaced with another language using a language toggle button on the upper right corner of the scene. The EFE-Book provides scripts (both text and voice) with two languages, English and Korean. On the bottom layer, the illustration fills the entire scene. The illustrations in the EFE-Book are captured from original tale books, so they are static. However, we utilize fade in/out and zoom in/out effects to make the scenes dynamic when user enters each scene. At each scene, the user can create his/her own unique illustration with collage art through an illustratable tool from the menu. The detail of the illustratable tool is described in the next section.

3.2   Interactive Illustratable Tool for Collage Art

When a user selects the illustratable tool from the menu bar, the screen changes into the interactive illustratable mode, as shown in Fig. 3. The screen in this mode consists of two panels; a white canvas with a sketch on the right hand side panel, and a coloured paper including a colour selection tool on the left

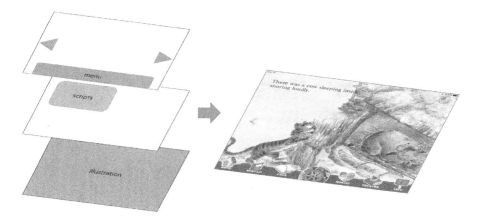

Fig. 2. Three layers of scenes. Menu bar and navigator buttons are located on the top layer; script is located on the middle; and illustration is located on the bottom.

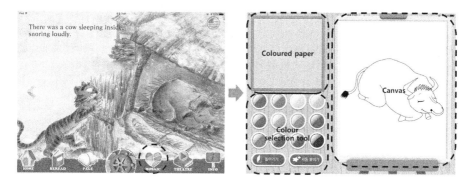

Fig. 3. Interactive illustratable mode.

hand panel. On the canvas, the predesigned sketch of an illustrated character in is located. The object is not filled with colours, so that user can fill it with coloured paper tiles. When user touches the coloured paper on the left hand panel and drags it to canvas, a small coloured paper tile is torn out from the coloured paper, and moves along to the trajectory of touched finger. Subsequently, the user can attach it to appropriate position on the canvas by keeping dragging. The colour selection tool may be used for changing colours.

Modeling Coloured Paper Tiles. When user enters the interactive illustratable mode, the coloured paper on the left panel is pre-divided into many small tiles. To divide the coloured paper into tiles, we employ the Voronoi diagram [6] as shown in Fig. 4. A Voronoi cell C_i is defined by using its pixel c, as shown in following equation.

$$C_i = \{c \in C_i | D(c, S_i) < D(c, S_j)\} \text{ for all } j, \qquad (1)$$

where S_i is the site of C_i and D is a Euclidean distance function.

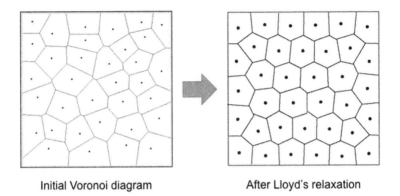

Initial Voronoi diagram   After Lloyd's relaxation

Fig. 4. Dividing coloured paper into small tiles with the Voronoi diagram and the Lloyd's relaxation method. Each cell of the Voronoi diagram is used to create coloured paper tiles.

For rectangular coloured paper on the left hand panel, we generate the initial Voronoi diagram by randomly inserting seed points, and relax the distribution of the seed points by using the Lloyd's method [10] to obtain uniform sized Voronoi cells. The coloured paper tiles are then created by converting each cell into polygon and filling them with selected colours. Although the coloured paper is divided into tiles, this is not visible on the panel, as each tile is seamlessly positioned without any gap between tiles.

Simulating Torn Paper Effect. In the coloured paper collage art, each tile has unique torn paper effects on their edges. We employ the random midpoint displacement method to simulate the torn effect. On each tile's edge, we select a midpoint, and subdivide the edge into two segments on that midpoint. The midpoint is then randomly displaced along a direction perpendicular to the edge. This is achieved by applying the following equation which calculates the randomly displaced midpoint:

$$f(p_1, p2) = \frac{1}{2}(p_1 + p_2) + r v_p \qquad (2)$$

$$v_p = R_{90}\overrightarrow{p_1 p_2}, \; R_{90} = \begin{bmatrix} 0 & -1 \\ 1 & 0 \end{bmatrix} \qquad (3)$$

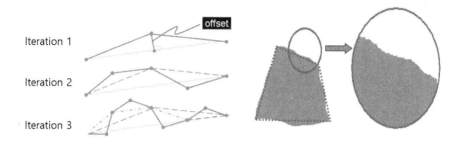

Fig. 5. Random midpoint displacement algorithm for torn paper effect.

where p_1 and p_2 are the points on both sides of an edge and r is a random value within $[-t : t]$ which adjusts the range of displacement offset. In this study, we use $t = 0.25$ as the value of t. Until the subdivided segments reach third iteration, we perform these steps iteratively. This approach generates an irregular torn shape on the edge of tile as shown in Fig. 5. However, in real torn paper, we can observe that the white tissue of paper is revealed. To mimic this effect, under the original Voronoi cell of the tile, we add another white Voronoi polygon which has the same shape with the original cell, and apply the random midpoint displacement algorithm separately. As a result, we can get a torn paper effect similar to that in real torn paper as shown in Fig. 6. When user starts dragging tiles from the coloured paper on the left panel, a torn paper effect is added to the edge of the tile.

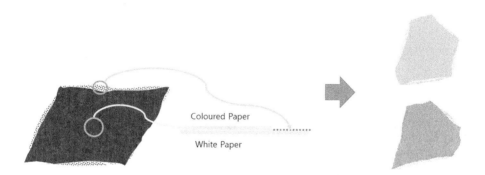

Fig. 6. Representation of the realistic torn paper effect. An additional white paper is added under the tile, and the random midpoint displacement algorithm is applied separately.

4   Results

We implemented EFE-Book by using OpenGL ES 2.0 [12] on Apple iPad's iOS environment, as shown in Fig. 7.

Figure 8 shows each step of illustration. User can navigate between scenes, and study a folktale with scripts written in a couple of languages including users' native language. Both text scripts and voice scripts are presented or played on each scene, so that user can learn the correct pronunciation of the foreign language such as English. At each scene, user can create illustrations through the illustratable tool. By touching and dragging tiles, the illustration of the paper collage art style can be generated. After the user finishes making collages, the result is displayed on the original scene of the EFE-Book, as shown in the Fig. 8, giving the impression that the user has created the illustration of the book. Figure 9 shows various collage results generated with the EFE-Book.

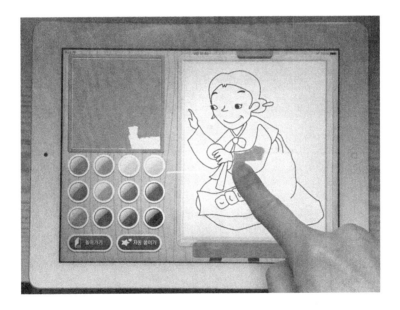

Fig. 7. EFE-Book on Apple iPad.

At the end of the application, we provided a link of webpage for a survey, as illustrated in Fig. 10(a), to evaluate EFE-Book's usability and usefulness. In total 32 users have responded. For the usability, we asked users how easy to use our application was. As shown in Fig. 10(b), most of users responded that our application was relatively easy. For the usefulness, the question is how well our

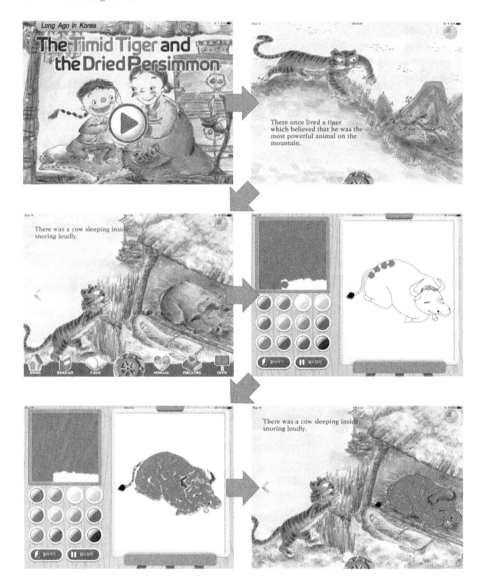

Fig. 8. Procedure of EFE-Book. While reading and listening to the book, user can create illustration through our interactive illustratable tool.

interactive illustratable tool on the EFE-Book helps in attracting children for studying foreign languages. As shown in Fig. 10(c), most of users agreed that the tool was useful for children's learning.

Fig. 9. Results generated with the EFE-Book. After the user finishes making collages, the result is displayed on the original scene of EFE-Book.

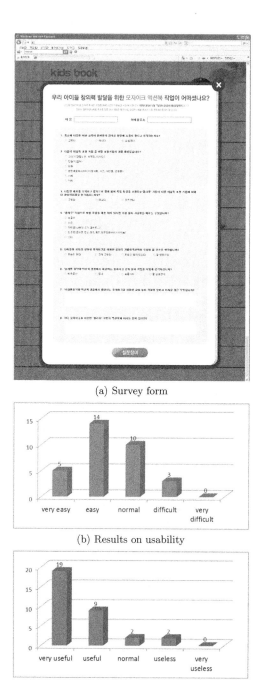

(a) Survey form

(b) Results on usability

(c) Results on usefulness

Fig. 10. Evaluation results of a survey on usability and usefulness.

5   Conclusion

In this paper we discussed our proposed e-book application (EFF-Book) to teach pre-school children foreign languages using devices such as smartphones or iPads. By utilizing the touch screen, our application provides an interactive illustratable tool for collage art. With folktale contents, our proposed illustratable tool can encourage the pre-school children to concentrate more while learning.

In future work, this will be extended to a book series by implementing a bookcase for additional books. We also intend to evaluate the effectiveness of the EFF-Book application from an educational perspective.

References

1. Aurenhammer, F.: Voronoi diagrams—a survey of a fundamental geometric data structure. ACM Comput. Surv. **23**(3), 345–405 (1991). http://doi.acm.org/10.1145/116873.116880
2. Capin, T., Pulli, K., Akenine-Moller, T.: The state of the art in mobile graphics research. IEEE Comput. Graph. Appl. **28**(4), 74–84 (2008)
3. Gi, Y.J., Park, Y.S., Seo, S.H., Yoon, K.H.: Mosaic rendering using colored paper. In: Proceedings of the 7th International Conference on Virtual Reality, Archaeology and Intelligent Cultural Heritage VAST 2006, pp. 25–30, Eurographics Association, Aire-la-Ville, Switzerland (2006). http://dx.doi.org/10.2312/VAST/VAST06/025-030
4. Godwin-Jones, R.: Emerging technologies: mobile apps for language learning. Lang. Learn. Technol. **15**(2), 2–11 (2011)
5. Han, M., Kang, D., Yoon, K.: Efficient paper mosaic rendering on mobile devices based on position-based tiling. J. Real-Time Image Process. **9**(3), 549–556 (2014). http://dx.doi.org/10.1007/s11554-013-0371-0
6. Hoff III, K.E., Keyser, J., Lin, M., Manocha, D., Culver, T.: Fast computation of generalized voronoi diagrams using graphics hardware. In: SIGGRAPH 1999 Proceedings of the 26th Annual Conference on Computer Graphics and Interactive Techniques, pp. 277–286. ACM Press/Addison-Wesley Publishing Co., New York, NY, USA (1999). http://dx.doi.org/10.1145/311535.311567
7. Jacott, L.: Mobile learning. A handbook for educators and trainers. Br. J. Educ. Stud. **57**(3), 337–339 (2009). Edited by Kukulska-Hulme, A., Traxler, J. http://dx.doi.org/10.1111/j.1467-8527.2009.437_6.x
8. Kang, D., Seo, S., Ryoo, S., Yoon, K.: A study on stackable mosaic generation for mobile devices. Multimed. Tools Appl. **63**(1), 145–159 (2013). http://dx.doi.org/10.1007/s11042-012-1065-5
9. Lehner, F., Nösekabel, H.: The role of mobile devices in e-learning - first experiences with a wireless e-learning environment. In: Proceedings IEEE International Workshop on Wireless and Mobile Technologies in Education WMTE 2002, pp. 103–106 (2002). http://dl.acm.org/citation.cfm?id=645964.674255
10. Lloyd, S.P.: Least squares quantization in PCM. IEEE Trans. Inf. Theor. **28**(2), 129–137 (2006). http://dx.doi.org/10.1109/TIT.1982.1056489

11. Mori, K., Ballagas, R., Revelle, G., Raffle, H., Horii, H., Spasojevic, M.: Interactive rich reading: enhanced book reading experience with a conversational agent. In: Proceedings of the 19th International Conference on Multimedia, MM 2011, pp. 825–826. ACM, NY, USA (2011). http://doi.acm.org/10.1145/2072298.2072478
12. Munshi, A., Ginsburg, D., Shreiner, D.: OpenGL ES 2.0 Programming Guide. Pearson Education, Upper Saddle River (2008)
13. Seo, S., Park, Y., Kim, S., Yoon, K.: Colored-paper mosaic rendering. In: Proceedings of SIGGRAPH 2001 Sketches and Applications in 28th Annual Conference on Computer Graphics and Interactive Techniques, p. 157. ACM, New York, NY, USA (2001)

The Design of Augmented Reality-Based Learning System Applied in U-Learning Environment

Jun Xiao[1(⊠)], Zhen Xu[1], Ye Yu[1], Shuo Cai[1], and Preben Hansen[2]

[1] Shanghai Engineering Research Center of Open Distance Education,
Shanghai Open University, Shanghai, China
{xiaoj,xuzhen,yuy,caishuo}@shtvu.edu.cn
[2] Department of Computer and Systems Sciences, Stockholm University,
Stockholm, Sweden
preben@dsv.su.se

Abstract. The easy and widely accessibility of Internet resources makes it possible to support learning almost anywhere at any time through powerful mobile technologies, and facilitate ubiquitous learning (u-learning) to grow in use and popularity. Augmented Reality (AR) can be recognized as a key technology that can be used in the U-learning environment to increase learning effect and improve learning experience. This paper designs an integrated model of U-learning, based on which we have also developed an augmented reality technology based learning system named as "Starry Sky Exploration—Eight Planets of Solar System"; an analysis on its implementation is reported and the AR learning system applicable for U-learning environment is found effective and practical.

Keywords: Augmented reality · U-learning · Integrated model

1 Introduction

In recent years, U-learning has become a mainstream way of learning driven by the development of technology. It integrates the advantages of both digital learning and mobile learning and aims to construct a learner-centered, intelligent and ubiquitous learning environment. The concept of U-learning originates from ubiquitous computing technology and it aims to construct a kind of intelligent and ubiquitous learning environment, where, the learners can use all kinds of terminals to access the required information in certain way regardless of time and place. Effective U-learning depends on the construction of technology-supported and intelligent seamless learning space [1]. Augmented reality is a key technology that can be used in the U-learning environment to increase learning effect and improve learning experience, and it can promote the optimal integration between learners and technology and prompt the transformation of existing learning paradigm so as to make U-learning realizable [2]. This paper puts forward the design model for U-learning as well as corresponding design principles, develops a learning system supported by augmented reality

A. El Rhalibi et al. (Eds.): Edutainment 2016, LNCS 9654, pp. 27–36, 2016.
DOI: 10.1007/978-3-319-40259-8_3

technology, and analyze the implementation of this learning system. The purpose is to provide more valuable reference for the improvement of learning effect and user experience in a U-learning environment.

2   Integrated Design Model

On the basis of the reference from the Keller's (1983) ARCS model and the mobile learning model [5] developed by Shih's (Shih & Mills, 2007), the comprehensive model in a U-learning environment was designed, as shown in Fig. 1.

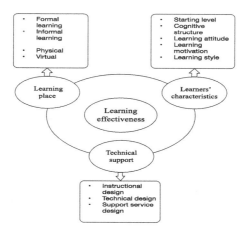

Fig. 1. Comprehensive model for the U-learning environment

The model focuses on the learner-centered design in a U-learning environment by carrying out analysis from three dimensions, such as the learners' characteristics, learning place and technological support in a bid to obtain the optimal learning achievement. The "ubiquity" of learning space and seamless switching of learning scenarios are realized by means of technical support. The designers can make use of the methods demonstrated by the model to integrate multi-disciplinary results into a comprehensive design mode to maximize the teaching capacity of learning space.

2.1   Learning Place

Learning place mainly refers to the specific location where the learners carry out learning activities. It is divided into formal learning place and informal learning place from the perspective of learning mode [3], and physical learning place and virtual learning place from the perspective of the form of place. Learners' learning content and design are restricted by the learning place. The switching of learning places can have direct influence on the learning consistency of learners.

2.2 Technical Support

The U-learning environment requires the technical support of teaching design concepts to integrate multi-dimensional learning modes, ranging from formal learning and informal learning to individualized learning and social learning, so as to meet different types of learning requirements. The increasing sophistication of new media technology featuring mobility and embedment greatly enhances the communication capacity, environmental perception and Internet connectivity. It also equips the learners with complete learning resources and records storage under the support of cloud computing technology. The learners' learning record will be analyzed and evaluated by means of learning analytics to provide effective feedback for learners. Meanwhile, data support will be used in the availability design of AR technology-based learning system applied in the U-learning environment so as to improve the design of the learning space and boost the user experience. Finally, the support service design shall be an important factor that goes through the whole learning process of learners to provide the learners with complete and improved support service and enhance the availability of the learning space so as to improve the learning efficiency.

2.3 Characteristics of Learners

Learners are the subjects of learning activities, and all their cognitive, emotional and social characteristics will exert influence on the information processing. To improve the learning efficiency, the teaching methods, media and technology must fit with the learners' characteristics. Therefore, the design and construction of the AR technology-based learning system applied in the U-learning environment must take into consideration the learners' characteristics. Under general conditions, the learners' characteristics are mainly categorized into five dimensions, namely, starting level, cognitive structure, learning attitude, learning objective and learning style [4]. By means of analyzing the learners' characteristics, we can figure out the stable and similar characteristics of learners so as to construct a favorable U-learning environment. By analyzing the variance and difference of learners, we can offer them better support service in a U-learning environment so as to offer learners an individualized learning environment.

2.4 Learning Effectiveness

Learning effectiveness is represented by the ratio between the comprehensive learning results and the comprehensive learning costs borne by the learners during the process of achieving the learning results, i.e., the synthesis of unit learning cost. The ultimate purpose of the effective design and implementation of AR technology-based learning system applied in the U-learning environment is to motivate the learners and maximize learning effectiveness. The learners' objective performance can be boosted by improving their subjective feeling. Thus, the "learner-centered" design principle shall be adopted when designing the comprehensive model for the U-learning environment.

2.5 Design Principles

In order to provide excellent learning experience and embody the power of technology, first, mobile technology, augmented reality technology and learning analytics, etc. shall be fully applied to promote the interaction between learners and learning environment, and offer learning support for U-learning and boost learners' passion for learning. Second, different groups of learners should be allowed to well integrate into the learning environment so that they can successfully fulfill their learning objectives and obtain good learning effectiveness. Third, the design of AR technology-based learning system applied in the U-learning environment shall be able to meet learners' learning requirements, equip them with full-range, humane and satisfying learning service support, fully embody the learner-centered concept and deliver a favorable U-learning environment.

3 Design of the Augmented Reality-Based Learning System in U-Learning Environment—"Starry Sky Exploration—Eight Planets of Solar System"

Based on the design model and principles, Shanghai Open Distance Education Engineering Technology Research Center of Shanghai Open University established a Digital Lab for Open Learning and designed a demonstrative U-learning learning system applied in a cross-media and multi-screen seamless interactive learning space— *Starry Sky Exploration—Eight Planets of Solar System* to enable the learners to experience the new learning space.

3.1 Learning Place Design

The Digital Lab for Open Learning is a learning space that integrates teaching, research, test, analysis and innovation as a whole. It incorporates advanced IT technology and practices advanced concepts of open and distance education. The purpose is to explore a way to realize the in-depth integration of information technology and open teaching. Also, digital effectiveness evaluation system is formed based on the teaching scenario simulation, energy consumption analysis, network analysis, brainwave analysis, behavioral sign analysis and online learning behavior analysis in the lab to furnish real-time and accurate learning response for the learners and effective and real-time evaluation data for the teaching test.

A demonstrative U-learning system–*Starry Sky Exploration—Eight Planets of Solar System* is designed to enable the teaching environment to better serve the teaching activities and further improve the performance of learning space. This learning system is applied in actual teaching activities to verify how this AR technology-based learning system can improve U-learning effectiveness and U-learning experience.

3.2 Technical Support

Starry Sky Exploration—Eight Planets of Solar System is a U-learning AR learning system and contains course featuring well-defined subject. Firstly, a video clip which lasts for about 5 min introduces the traits and orbits of the eight planets in solar system with clear and concise content as well as fine images. In teaching method design, the learning system relies on the learning environment of digital teaching lab where mobile learning, flipped classroom and MOOCs, etc. are supported to enable the learners to choose a learning mode that suits their respective need.

Meanwhile, the learning system also designs various ways of interaction with the teaching environment in the teaching link to integrate multiple new teaching technologies. Here, the learners can learn about the interesting planetary features and also have an interactive experience of the orbits and traits of various planets by means of 3D micro-class and augmented reality (AR) as well as other new digital multi-media methods. The technological support mode for the learning space involved in the U-learning learning system is as shown in Fig. 2.

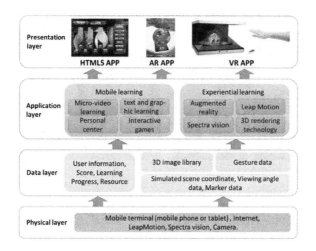

Fig. 2. The architecture of interactive mobile application system

3.2.1 The Architecture of Interactive Mobile Application System

Mainly based on mobile platform and devices, this system is integrated with various resources and applications, and establishes standard structural data for sharing to realize all kinds of interactive data integration, providing a total solution for learners using the U-learning learning system: *Starry Sky Exploration—Eight Planets of Solar System.*

(1) The physical layer at the bottom displays the required hardware for eight planets learning system, including the mobile terminal (mobile phone or tablet), Leap-Motion, camera, the spectra vision, as well as the access to the Internet.

(2) The data layer mainly includes data captured using the physical equipment; it also creates the learners' learning archives and 3D image library used for interaction.

(3) The application layer is divided into two categories, mobile learning and experiential learning. Mobile learning is carried out by accessing the micro-video, text and graphic, interactive games on the learning Cloud, and the individual learning information will be recorded at the same time. Experiential learning is realized by

combining the augmented reality technology, LeapMotion, spectra vision and other new technologies, with 3D rendering technology to enhance the learner's real experience and improve the interactive learning.

(4) The presentation layer, the final formation of the APP applications, can be installed on various mobile terminals to display the technological effects.

3.2.2   Demo Features of AR Learning System

Multi-mode Function. This learning system supports micro-course learning, mobile learning, learning analytics and MOOCs. It is compatible with the related software and hardware equipment in the digital lab, and it has ensured stable operation. See below: Interface screenshots Fig. 3.

Fig. 3. Interface screenshots

Planets Identification. The eight planets with their basic attributes can be displayed in the solar system in turn; thanks to AR interactive technology, learners can see a 3D planet by simply using their camera on the mobile device to capture the image on a symbol card. Figure 4.

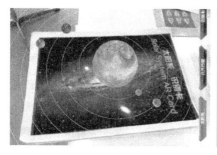

Fig. 4. Demo screenshots

3.3   Learners' Characteristics

This AR technology-based learning system applied in the U-learning environment is available a variety of modes of learning support for not only formal learners but also informal learners. Different from formal teaching in an ordinary classroom, the learners in U-learning environment have more diversified characteristics and the learners pay more attention to learning experience. According to the diversified characteristics of learners and the teaching environment of the digital lab, the learning system of Eight Planets of Solar System incorporates multiple learning modes in the teaching design to meet different learning requirements. The learning system design is divided into different versions to support the learning effectiveness in different learning environments. Meanwhile, the learning system is presented in a flexible, intuitive and participatory manner to provide the learners with excellent user-centered, individualized and socialized learning experience.

3.4   Learning Effectiveness

To verify learners' learning effectiveness in the U-learning environment, the research team makes use of the course of Eight Planets of Solar System as the case of application to carry out user experience test among the learners that have participated in the digital lab. The purpose is to verify the influence of AR technology-based learning system on learners' learning experience and evaluate the corresponding learning effectiveness. The data analysis results reveal that: In the U-learning environment, the seamless integration of formal learning and informal learning, multiple learning modes as well as the various cross-terminal supporting technologies bring excellent learning experience for learners and improve their learning effectiveness. The following specifies the implementation of learning effectiveness evaluation.

4   Assessment for the Effectiveness of Eight Planets of Solar System

We selected 7 high school students and 1 teacher to complete process-oriented teaching for the course of *Eight Planets of Solar System* in a teaching environment of digital lab. The teaching practice adopted new-technology-based hybrid teaching mode and made use of advanced equipment in the lab to carry out teaching activities, which comprise seven modules, namely "watching solar system survey (film), recognizing eight planets, observing eight planets, experiencing eight planets, interactive discussion, making concept map and carrying out interactive game". In the module of "observing eight planets", an AR identification card was made available for the learners and the learners could make use of the mobile terminals to scan the AR identification card to observe the characteristics of eight planets.

The module of "experiencing eight planets" made use of the holographic imaging system in the lab to present the position and running characteristics of the planets in a virtualized solar system to facilitate the students' independent observation. In the module of "interactive game", the learning effectiveness was tested in a question-answer form, and the correct rate was as shown in Fig. 5. The correct answer rate of the answering for the game-based learning can reflect the learning effectiveness of the learners objectively. Adopting a 100-point scoring mechanism, 7 leaners' average score reaches 96.5, proving a good learning effect.

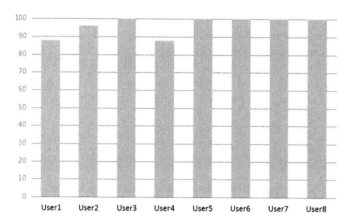

Fig. 5. Correct rate of game-based learning: User 1-User 8

Bioelectricity is one of the basic characteristics of life activities. When thinking, humans generate biological electrical signal, i.e. the brainwave, which can be collected by sensors placed on the scalp. Since the last century, people have increased the understanding of the brain to a large extent through the measurement, study and research of electroencephalograph (EEG) signals, and the related brainwave detecting and analysis systems are becoming more and more mature and reliable. Correspondingly, besides the subjective user experience survey data, we use NeuroEdu, a high-tech real-time brainwave analysis system based on the principle of bio-feedback, to give a systematic and complete record of the brainwave data of three learners as the supporting data of learner experience. NeuroEdu uses portable brainwave equipment as front-end electrical measuring equipment and can obtain EEG data and parameters that reflecting the psychological state of participants; it acquires and analyzes EEG signal generated from participants' brain activity, and produces a number of psychological parameters. By means of the EEG, the brainwave analysis can be measured in a real-time manner and the conscious state of each of the three learners can also be evaluated, such as mood, concentration, adaptability and response ability, etc. The conscious state of each learner was evaluated by means of multivariate evaluation without being interfered by any subjective factor. The learning analysis system of the lab mainly acquired the brainwave data of the three learners, analyzed their attention and emotion indicators and presented the learning experience effect of the learners from an object perspective. See Fig. 6 for the average attention and emotion indicators of the three learners.

With the advance of the teaching process, the learners' attention rises and peaks at the stage of observing and experiencing eight planets. During this period of time, the

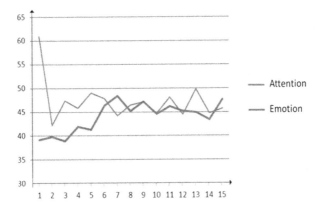

Fig. 6. Contrast Curve of Learner Attention Indicators blue line-attention, red line: emotion (Color figure online)

emotion indicators also increase gradually, indicating that the learning process has triggered interest in the learners. According to the results of the objective data analysis, the highest point of interest of the learners is consistent with learners' learning preference. In general, the learners are interested and pay high attention to the technology-supported teaching link. This indicates that the augmented reality effectively enables the learners to observe and experience eight planets. Obviously, this augmented reality-based learning system applied in U-learning environment can help the learners to acquire better learning experience and better learning effectiveness. Meanwhile, it is found through interview with learners that the user experience is closely related to the environment of wireless network technology during the process of carrying out teaching activities in the digital lab. The instability of the wireless network also restricts the learners' learning activities.

Based on the overall effectiveness evaluation for the learning system experience evaluation for Eight Planets in the Solar System, the learners generally show a strong interest in the experience-based environment constructed with new technologies, such as augmented reality. They also presented high satisfaction for the experience process. These results are consistent with the innovation design principle of emphasizing the application of technologies in U-learning environment. Meanwhile, the requirements for learning assessment and analysis raised by the students during their participation in the user experience survey also reflect the necessity of establishing a perfect learning support service system. Therefore, during the process of establishing augmented reality-based learning system applied in U-learning environment, we shall emphasize the integration of teaching and learning modes and emphasizing learner diversity so as to meet the diversified learning requirements of different groups of learners.

5 Conclusion

The development of new technology and its integration in educational sector bring great opportunity to the development of education. It also makes more diversified learning modes available for learners; how to apply such new technology as augmented reality to create good learning experience for U-learners and realize U-learning has become a matter of concern for the researchers.

This research aims to build a learner-centered augmented reality based learning system in U-learning environment to cater to U-learning needs, and put forward a comprehensive model of U-learning that can create maximum learning efficiency. However, we also realize that this model also needs to be tested and improved by more extensive and diversified participators so as to realize the optimal integration between learners and AR technology.

Acknowledgement. This paper is supported by "Shu Guang" award "MOOCs design and empirical research oriented Shanghai lifelong learning (13SG56)" from the Shanghai Municipal Education Commission and Shanghai Education Development Foundation. It is also supported by the 2014 Shanghai education scientific research key project "The Study of online learning mode for Shanghai lifelong learning (A1403)". Besides, thanks for the support of Science and Technology Commission of Shanghai Municipality research project "Shanghai Engineering Research Centre of Open Distance Education (13DZ2252200)".

References

1. Chan, T.-W., Roschelle, J., Hsi, S., Kinshuk, Sharples, M., Brown, T., et al.: One-to-one technology-enhanced learning: an opportunity for global research collaboration. Res. Pract. Technol. Enhanced Learn. **1**(1), 3–29 (2006)
2. Weidong, C., Xindong, Y., Jiping, Z.: Review of the studies on the smart classroom. Distance Educ. J. **4**, 39–45 (2011)
3. Xiangdong, C., Zhongwang, J.: The Application of Educational Augmented Reality Games. Distance Educ. J. **5**, 68–73 (2012)
4. Dimensions of Characteristics Analysis of Learners. http://peixun.lnjsjy.cn/courses/CZLS/html/module2/hd2/hd2_bz1_1.html
5. Shih, Y., Mills, D.: Setting the new standard with mobile computing in online learning. Int. Rev. Res. Open Distance Learn. **8**(2), 16 (2007)

ARDock: A Web-AR Based Real-Time
Tangible Edugame for Molecular Docking

Gaoqi He[1,2(✉)], Fei Sun[1], Dong Hu[1], Xingjian Lu[1], Yi Guo[1],
Shuhua Lai[3], and Zhigeng Pan[4]

[1] Department of Computer Science and Engineering,
East China University of Science and Technology, Shanghai 200237, China
hegaoqi@ecust.edu.cn
[2] State Key Laboratory of Virtual Reality Technology and Systems,
Beihang University, Beijing 100191, China
[3] School of Science and Technology, Georgia Gwinnett College,
Lawrenceville, GA 30043, USA
[4] Digital Media and Interaction Research Center, Hangzhou Normal University,
Hangzhou 310036, China

Abstract. Molecular docking is increasingly considered as a key tool for lead
discovery of structure-based drug design. While huge ligand-receptor combinations, intangible microcosmic molecular world and complex docking scoring
are the major challenges for modern molecular docking. In this paper, we present an edugame called ARDock, which is a web-based and interactive
molecular docking game. The web-based feature allows multiple participants to
engage in the game and provides solutions to complex scientific problems.
Augmented reality is imported and consequently molecular docking process
becomes tangible. The relative positions of two molecules are instantly updated
with the users' operation, enabling the spatial locating capabilities of humans.
The optimized scoring function is proposed to reduce the computation complexity, and the message-oriented middleware facilitates real-time communication between the browsers and the server. The overall framework and detailed
designs are illustrated. Some combination strategies make this edugame more
interesting, which in return can attract more users and enhance their continuous
participation. Sufficient user evaluations validate the usability of this game. This
work is a step to promote the popularization of molecular docking knowledge.

Keywords: Augmented reality · Molecular docking · Real-time
communication · Edugame · Interactivity

1 Introduction

In recent years, the complaints and concerns regarding computer games have increased
because of their popularity and potential harmful effects, particularly in educational
field. Accordingly, the theory of edutainment is developed rapidly and demonstrates the
educational value of computer games with proper handling. Edugame, which combines
entertainment forms and educational contents seamlessly, now is booming under this
situation as a kind of practice of edutainment. From the game design perspective,

© Springer International Publishing Switzerland 2016
A. El Rhalibi et al. (Eds.): Edutainment 2016, LNCS 9654, pp. 37–49, 2016.
DOI: 10.1007/978-3-319-40259-8_4

edugame must ensure gameplay and educational value compared with the general entertainment games or professional teaching software [1]. Various kinds of edugame have been studied and released, such as Virtual Leader for training leadership [2] and the Monkey Wrench Conspiracy for constructing weapons [3]. However, during the exploring of life and health issues in the microscopic world, edugame is encountering some challenges that include the expression of profound domain knowledge and real-time update of visual information.

Humans usually rely on drugs when suffered from disease. Determining how to identify an efficient drug against a certain disease attracts more attention from scientists as well as common persons. Molecular docking is an important method in structural molecular biology and computer-assisted drug design. This technique primarily aims to predict the predominant binding modes between a ligand and a protein with known 3D structures to discover the promising hit and lead compounds [4]. A number of docking software is frequently used, including DOCK [5], AutoDock [6] and Glide [7]. However, this set of software has certain limitations. First, interactivity is weak. Users can hardly participate in docking process directly, preventing them from understanding intuitively the intangible microscopic phenomenon. Second, matching is blind. Space matching at useless positions results in substantial computations and costs. Finally, the user is limited. Only people with professional backgrounds and rich experiences can operate them.

Thus, a real-time and web-AR based multiuser edugame, named ARDock, is presented in this paper. This work aims to promote the knowledge popularization of molecular docking through interactive augmented reality (AR), convenient browser-server pattern, and efficient docking score computation. The highlights of this work are as follows:

(1) Tangible interactivity is incorporated into molecular docking. Both the ligand and receptor are 3D modeled and rendered within the users' view. The relative positions of two molecules are instantly updated with the users' operation, allowing them to employ their spatial locating capabilities. The score is shown on the screen to evaluate the effect of current docking. Thus, ARDock can reduce the blindness of docking and provide a thorough understanding of the microscopic world of molecular docking through visual interaction.

(2) A web-AR based online edugame enables the active participation of multiple users and provides solutions to complex scientific problems. WebGL, rather than other plug-ins, achieves 3D molecular rendering in the browser. Even non-scientists have the opportunities to solve the issued problems and make their own contribute to molecular docking conveniently as a game player. Some combination strategies draw the attention of additional users and elicit their continuous participation, which is inspired by Foldit [8].

(3) Real-time computation guarantees the effectiveness of the game. The optimized scoring function reduces the computation complexity, and the message-oriented middleware (MOM) between the browser and the server enables real-time communication. The real-time position registration of virtual molecules is also achieved.

The rest of the paper is organized into six sections. Following the Introduction, Sect. 2 discusses the related work. Section 3 presents the overall framework and functionalities of ARDock. Section 4 introduces further details about the implementation of the game, and Sect. 5 evaluates the game performance. Finally, Sect. 6 summarizes the study and discusses future research directions.

2 Related Work

Molecular docking represents an important technology for structure-based drug design and has therefore been extensively looked into [9, 10]. This section highlights some of the most relevant studies about this method.

Molecular docking. Computer-aided drug design (CADD) methods have become an essential tool in the academia and pharmaceutical companies. And CADD has particularly played a major role in the discovery of therapeutically important small molecules for over three decades [11]. As more and more structures of proteins and nucleic acids become available, molecular docking is increasingly considered for lead discovery [12]. Molecular docking is conceived as an optimization task to identify the ligand conformation bound to the receptor with the most favorable binding energy. Such method is significantly efficient compared with the experimental approaches for screening a large number of potential compounds.

Interactivity in docking. Previous studies have focused on docking algorithms to improve either the accuracy or efficiency of scoring schemes [13, 14]. However, with the improvement of CADD and human–computer interaction techniques, more efforts have been exerted to raise the interactivity between the users and microscopic molecules during docking. An earlier work of gCOMBINE [15] can be considered a graphical user interface to conduct a structure-based comparative binding energy analysis on a set of ligand–receptor complexes. This approach evidently lacks considerable extent of interactivity and visibility. Innovations in computer science have recently led to the establishment of a new approach for extending the interactivity further. For example, Stalk [16] introduced an interactive system for virtual molecular docking using virtual reality technology. In this system, a user steps into the CAVE and uses a wand to translate, rotate, and fit the ligand into the cleft in the protein. Some scholars employed haptic display and device to explore and analyze molecular docking [17, 18]. However, some limitations remain, such as the expensive equipment, significant time lag, confusing context, and professional operations.

Edugame and AR. AR has been developed as a computer interface technology that combines real-world objects and computer-generated graphics. Considerable literature has investigated the usage of AR in molecular biology [19, 20]. For example, Art Olson presented an application that demonstrates the interactive computational docking of a drug molecule into the HIV protease target, which used auto-fabricated tangible models and AR for research and communication in molecular biology [19]. Furthermore, the use of web visualizers, which do not rely on slow software rendering drug molecules, has gained popularity [21]. For example, iSyn [22] is a WebGL-based solution that computationally synthesizes *de novo* drug compounds with click chemistry support through additional cutting reactions.

Edugame can offer players an engaging, immersive, and effective experience while providing them with knowledge about certain fields with pedagogical and educational considerations. Interactivity is the most basic feature of edugame, and the interactive process is parallel to the education process. New interfaces for AR have been widely utilized in edugame for several years, distributing in different fields [23–25]. However, previously developed edugame barely focuses on improving the interactivity and visibility of molecular docking during the past several years; hardly any of them incorporates AR and docking via the web.

3 Framework Design of ARDock

3.1 The Overall Workflow

This study presents a user-friendly edugame platform for interactive and visible molecular docking. Brower-server based multiuser online computer game design paradigm underlies the overall platform functionalities. This design strategy can make molecular docking more convenient and attractive for large amount of users. The functional framework of the proposed ARDock is shown in Fig. 1.

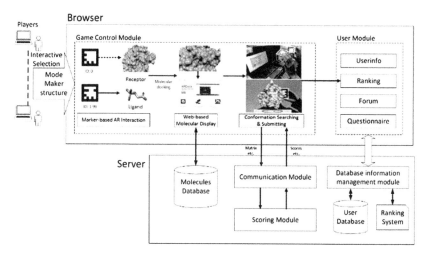

Fig. 1. Functional framework of ARDock; this platform utilizes a browser–server model. The human–computer interaction of the platform is mainly composed of AR.

In the browser-side, the player firstly chooses the marker patterns, molecular types, and interactive modes. ARDock consists of 100 markers, a molecules database, and two modes, namely, one-marker based or two-marker based mode. During one-marker interaction, the virtual ligand is mapped onto the moving marker, and the receptor in the docking is static. The experience of users is significantly improved naturally if the ligand and receptor are both controlled by separate markers. Thus, the two-marker mode is developed to control both the receptor and the ligand in a unified manner simultaneously. The dotted line in Fig. 1 indicates whether the receptor is controlled by a marker. Next, the AR function of marker-based is employed to access the camera of the browser as well as to capture and track the marker to obtain the transform matrix. The 3D drug molecule is then modeled and rendered on the web using WebGL technology instead of plug-ins. Users can observe the relative position of the ligand against the receptor to determine the potential binding sites by moving the marker. The transform matrix is transmitted to the server afterwards, providing information about the intermolecular location.

The scoring function at the server evaluates the matching conditions of the molecules. The scores are then returned to the web page in real-time because the docking is carried out on the front-end. Nonetheless, the scoring function cannot utilize the information from the front-end directly. This task depends on MOM technology, which is considered to be a bridge between the browser and the server in the real-time communication module. The user can submit his or her best score to the server for the ranking system.

To manage the user and evaluate the game, a user module is set up, which includes the ranking list, forum, questionnaire survey and user information management functions. Correspondingly, user management and data storage functions are also included in the server.

3.2   Summarized Features of ARDock

ARDock integrates the design methodology from both molecular docking and computer game. Thereby, it enables users to gain professional and complex knowledge about molecular docking while being entertained. As an interesting and instructive edugame for molecular docking, ARDock exhibits various features as shown in Table 1.

Table 1. Summarized features of ARDock.

Features	Associated operations
Diversity	Two modes; 100 markers; Existence of a molecular database
Interactivity & visibility	Marker-based AR interaction form; Intuitive understanding of the principle and microscopic world of molecular docking
Simplicity	Web online game; Independence of plug-ins for 3D modeling and rendering; Accessible marker as an interactive tool
Real-time	Real-time communication between browser and server; Real-time rendering of molecules; Real-time position registration of virtual molecules by controlling the marker
Interdisciplinary	ARDock integrates multiple disciplines, such as pharmaceutics and computer science, and attracts users of different backgrounds or ages to achieve the goal of science popularization

4   Key Techniques Design

A framework-based approach is used to design the system. Some key techniques are applied to the system, including 3D molecular modeling and rendering through the web, interactive docking based on AR, the modification of scoring function, real-time communication by MOM, and the combination strategy of crowdsourcing and game-play. All these techniques provide the advantages of tangible interfaces, real-time interaction, and playability.

4.1   Interactive Molecular Docking Based on Web-AR

Markers are the interactive and control tools for ARDock. The traditional concept of AR is to register a computer-generated virtual object on the real scene at the most appropriate position. ARDock adopts the technology of JSARToolKit for interaction on the page. The 3D molecular modeling and rendering through the web utilize WebRTC and the engine of Three.js. Two kinds of docking modes designed (i.e., one-marker and two-marker based) utilize AR technologies. Regardless of the number of markers used in the interaction, the primary interaction flow of ARDock is the same (see Fig. 2). The player holds and moves the markers in the view range of the camera after the docking mode and molecular structures are selected. The system captures the marker from the video frame after camera authorization is granted by the user. Then, the marker is picked out and the corresponding virtual molecule is imported and rendered through the web. Finally, the player can control the molecule by moving the marker respectively, and meanwhile the transform matrix is obtained. These tasks are conducted at the Game Controlling module shown in Fig. 1. The steering process of two docking modes is illustrated in Fig. 3.

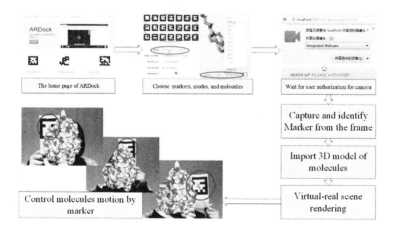

Fig. 2. Primary interaction flow based on Web-AR.

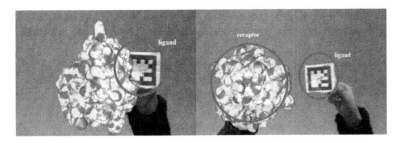

Fig. 3. Two modes of interaction. The left is one-marker based and the right is two-marker based. The difference is whether the marker used for receptor.

4.2   Real-Time Scoring and Communication

Molecular docking generally includes two primary processes, namely, the conformation search and the combining ability evaluation. For ARDock, the first process is accomplished by the player who controls the markers. Nevertheless, evaluating the combination conformation players obtained previously still depends on the scoring function similar to other software. ARDock evaluates intermolecular matching conditions through the scoring function at the server-side and achieves real-time communication between the browser and the server by utilizing MOM.

The Modification of the Scoring Function. Scoring function plays a critical role in docking. However, the binding free energy of the receptor and ligand can hardly be predicted accurately by calculation because of the high complexity of intermolecular interactions and identification processes [26]. To verify the dynamical and real-time molecular docking conveniently, this study selectively modifies a reliable and frequently used scoring function based on AutoDock, which uses the calculation method of semi-empirical binding free energy [6]. The binding free energy of AutoDock is a combination of five parts: van der Waals interaction energy, hydrogen bonding interaction energy [27], electrical energy, solvation effect energy, and torsional energy. The overall formula of the binding free energy for AutoDock is as follows:

$$\Delta G = \left(V_{bound}^{L-L} - V_{unbound}^{L-L} \right) + \left(V_{bound}^{P-P} - V_{unbound}^{P-P} \right) + \left(V_{bound}^{P-L} - V_{unbound}^{P-L} + \Delta S_{conf} \right).$$

Where L represents the ligand of the protein–ligand complexes, P is the corresponding protein, and ΔS_{conf} is the free energy of ligand. The formula is composed of three parts, which are the difference of the internal energy of ligand, the difference of internal energy of protein, and the interaction energy changes of the protein–ligand complexes before and after ligand binding [28].

Before docking, some improvements are realized in the following aspects: First, V_{bound}^{L-L} and V_{bound}^{P-P} are determined because of the nature of rigid docking. Second, $V_{unbound}^{L-L}$ and $V_{unbound}^{P-P}$ are constant because they are calculated in the pretreatment stage when the protein and ligand are selected. Third, two molecules are assumed to be far apart; thus, their interaction force can be disregarded, that is, $V_{unbound}^{P-L}$ is zero. Finally, the cutoff distance of 8Å is set between the molecules to further improve the calculation efficiency.

For ARDock, the internal energy remains the same after the molecule is imported. Thus, only the interaction energy is calculated because of the relative changes in the position of the ligand and protein in every docking rather than recalculate the energy of the entire compound. The modified scoring function, which is based on the local-scope search of the coordination site, can balance the speed and accuracy rate.

The Mechanism of Real-Time Communication. The scoring function cannot communicate with the browser directly because of the difference in programming languages. Thus, the communication module acts like a bridge that is responsible for data transmission. MOM is used for the game because it can achieves reliable, efficient, real-time, and cross-platform data transmission in the distributed system. This study utilizes a type of MOM called ActiveMQ, which is based on Java Message Service and can provide a standard and message-oriented application integration for multiple languages and systems. The process is mainly divided into two parts as shown in Fig. 4. Front-end communication is accomplished to communicate with the display program at the browser-side, such as obtaining the relative position information between molecules or accepting the assessment results from the server for the web display. Back-end communication aims to transmit data with the scoring function at the server. For example, passing the transposed matrix to the scoring procedure or receiving the energy value back is included.

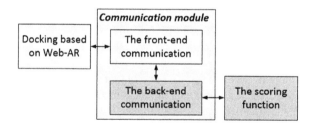

Fig. 4. Real-time communication process.

The Results. This phase primarily intends to assess the matching condition between the molecules using the scoring function and achieve the real-time communication between the browser and server through MOM for better and faster molecular docking prediction. The results are reprocessed to facilitate understanding for users. The docking scores, which are based on the one-marker mode, are shown in Fig. 5.

5   Evaluation Analysis

Game performance testing, which is an important part of game development, significantly affects user experience. ARDock is tested in terms of the aspects discussed in the subsequent paragraphs.

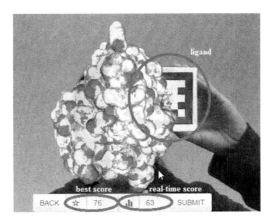

Fig. 5. Real-time scoring results displayed on the web; the left is the best score, and the right is the real-time score. The real-time scores will change with the marker moving accordingly and will replace the current best score if a higher one appears. Finally, the user can submit his or her own best results for ranking.

5.1   Environment Configuration

ARDock can run smoothly on a machine with Intel Core-i3 2.53 GHz CPU, 2G memory. The types and versions of the operation system are limitless in addition to the condition for the browser. The browser that supports WebGL technology must be used in the system, such as Chrome, Firefox, and IE. Furthermore, we suggest that the computer memory has better be to 2G because of the memory consumption of 3D molecule modeling and rendering on the web. Overall, the requirement for the computer performance of players is not high.

5.2   Scoring Function

The modified scoring function is used to test 128 different proteins and their corresponding ligands chosen from PDB. The computation time is shown in Fig. 6, and the scoring speed is improved by approximately 10 % than before. The computing speed of the scoring function can be improved effectively by removing the calculation of the constant energy and by adding the limitation of local scope during docking.

5.3   User Experience and Results

A total of 20 participants (5 females) aged 10 to 50 years with different professional backgrounds are recruited for the study. They include 12 undergraduates and postgraduate students, 4 middle school students, 2 college teachers, and 2 professional people. All participants are asked to submit their questionnaires, which include 12 questions to determine their socio-demographic information (i.e., age, gender, and profession), purposes of playing the game, and all aspects of game evaluations (see

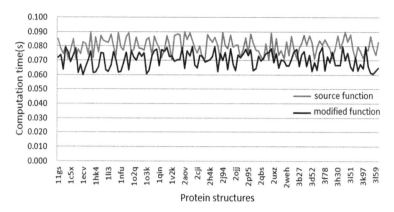

Fig. 6. Time comparison of the modified and source scoring functions.

Table 2. Question Design mapping to Feature Evaluation

Usability	Gameplay	Functionality
Q4: Obvious and useful prompts or not	Q7: Immersing interaction experience or not	Q10: Possibility of exploratory learning about docking
Q5: Easy operation or not	Q8: User-friendly interface or not	Q11: The completeness of user information management
Q6: Playing fluently or not	Q9: The incentive mechanism of ranking	Q12: Beneficial communication or not through forum

Table 2) according to their own gaming experience. The data from those questionnaires are collected and analyzed using statistical tools. All collected questionnaires are validated based on which the following conclusions are drawn:

(1) ARDock can popularize science for both AR technology and molecular docking to some extent. The purposes of people playing this game are different because of their individual and professional differences. People who do not have any background about molecular docking are attracted by the marker-based AR form. Professionals want to explore the micro-world of molecular docking by controlling the movement of markers although these experts become interested with this kind of interactive method as well. In any case, ARDock has a certain appeal and adaptability for individuals of different stages and backgrounds.

(2) The comprehensive assessment on the system is generally in a good condition. We have conducted game performance evaluation and user function evaluation through a questionnaire. The questions can be categorized into three aspects, namely, usability, gameplay, and functionality (see Table 2). The weighted summation to the answers of these questions is adopted to obtain the final result. Every feature contains three levels of dissatisfied, acceptable and excellent as indicated in Fig. 7.

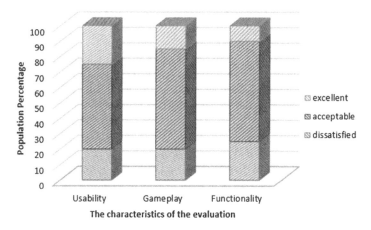

Fig. 7. Evaluation results of ARDock.

Overall, the participants are excited to engage in such an edugame and describe the experience as "interesting," "easy to use," and "novel and useful." With the aid of prompts and the forum communication, people can easily control the interactive tools and accordingly understand the principle and process of molecular docking. Also, the ranking mechanism serves as an incentive. The research results imply that ARDock combines the features of education and entertainment features successfully and that the system is usable. However, many flaws that some participants reported should be improved, such as the lack of aesthetic sense for the user interface. We plan to address these issues promptly. This work is a pilot study; thus, our ability to draw a more certain conclusion is restricted because of the limited number of participants. Many factors can affect the outcomes, such as the design of our survey question. In the future, further testing of our system is necessary.

6   Conclusions and Future Work

ARDock is an innovation that transcends the classic games and has great potential. This study makes three main contributions: First, we present the design for molecular docking as an edugame. Second, we implement the edugame called ARDock, which is based on this design framework. Through this platform, game users can experience the dynamic molecular interaction in a live environment. A realistic 3D visualization of docking not only facilitates the easy understanding of the operation mechanism at the molecular level but also explores the visual computing and cognition capabilities of humans. Finally, we set the function of user management and obtain some confirmation from a first-hand usability study of this system. Participants from different backgrounds can easily experience and operate this type of molecular docking in their own browsers at any place for education or entertainment.

In the future, we plan to optimize the scoring function further in terms of accuracy and application. The docking should not to be limited to rigid docking as well.

Additional user studies will be conducted to examine ARDock comprehensively, and our work will be extended to other edugame.

Acknowledgments. This work was funded by Natural Science Foundation of China (Grant No: 61332017 and 61300133), Open Research Funding Program of KLGIS (Grant No: KLGIS2015A05), the Fundamental Research Funds for the Central Universities (Grant No: 222201514331), the Opening Project of Shanghai Key Laboratory of New Drug Design (Grant No: 14DZ2272500).

References

1. Moreno-Ger, P., Burgos, D., Martínez-Ortiz, I., Sierra, J.L., Fernández-Manjón, B.: Educational game design for online education. Comput. Hum. Behav. **24**, 2530–2540 (2008)
2. Amon, T.: Simulations and the future of learning: an innovative (and perhaps revolutionary) approach to e-Learning. J. Educ. Technol. Soc. **7**, 149–150 (2004)
3. Prensky, M.: Digital game-based learning. Comput. Entertain. (CIE) **1**, 1–22 (2003)
4. Tang, Y.T., Marshall, G.R.: Virtual screening for lead discovery. Drug Des. Dis. 1–22 (2011). Springer
5. Ewing, T.J., Makino, S., Skillman, I.D., Kuntz, I.D.: DOCK 4.0: search strategies for automated molecular docking of flexible molecule databases. J. Comput.-Aided Mol. Des. **15**, 411–428 (2001)
6. Morris, G.M., Huey, R., Lindstrom, W., Sanner, M.F., Belew, R.K., Goodsell, D.S., Olson, A.J.: AutoDock4 and AutoDockTools4: automated docking with selective receptor flexibility. J. Comput. Chem. **30**, 2785–2791 (2009)
7. Halgren, T.A., Murphy, R.B., Friesner, R.A., Beard, L.L., Frye, W.T., Pollard, J.L.: Banks: glide: a new approach for rapid, accurate docking and scoring. 2. Enrichment factors in database screening. J. Med. Chem. **47**, 1750–1759 (2004)
8. Cooper, S., Khatib, F., Treuille, A., Barbero, J., Lee, J., Beenen, M., Leaver-Fay, A., Baker, D., Popović, Z.: Predicting protein structures with a multiplayer online game. Nature **466**, 756–760 (2010)
9. Mukesh, K.: Rakesh: Molecular docking: a review. Int. J. Res. Ayurveda Pharm **2**, 1746–1751 (2011)
10. Bortolato, A., Fanton, M., Mason, J.S., Moro, S.: Molecular docking methodologies. Biomol. Simul. **924**, 339–360 (2013)
11. Sliwoski, G., Kothiwale, S., Meiler, J., Lowe, E.W.: Computational methods in drug discovery. Pharmacol. Rev. **66**, 334–395 (2014)
12. Shoichet, B.K., McGovern, S.L., Wei, B., Irwin, J.J.: Lead discovery using molecular docking. Curr. Opin. Chem. Biol. **6**, 439–446 (2002)
13. Thomsen, R., Christensen, M.H.: MolDock: a new technique for high-accuracy molecular docking. J. Med. Chem. **49**, 3315–3321 (2006)
14. Gu, J., Yang, X., Kang, L., Wu, J., Wang, X.: MoDock: a multi-objective strategy improves the accuracy for molecular docking. Algorithms Mol. Biol: AMB **10**(8), 1 (2015)
15. Gil-Redondo, R., Klett, J., Gago, F., Morreale, A.: gCOMBINE: a graphical user interface to perform structure-based comparative binding energy (COMBINE) analysis on a set of ligand-receptor complexes. Proteins: Struct. Funct. Bioinf. **78**, 162–172 (2010)
16. Levine, D., Facello, M., Hallstrom, P., Reeder, G., Walenz, B., Stevens, F.: Stalk: an interactive system for virtual molecular docking. Comput. Sci. Eng. **4**, 55–65 (1997)

17. Lee, Y.-G., Lyons, K.W.: Smoothing haptic interaction using molecular force calculations. Comput. Aided Des. **36**, 75–90 (2004)
18. Lai-Yuen, S.K., Lee, Y.-S.: Interactive computer-aided design for molecular docking and assembly. Comput.-Aided Des. Appl. **3**, 701–709 (2006)
19. Gillet, A., Sanner, M., Stoffler, D., Olson, A.: Tangible augmented interfaces for structural molecular biology. Comput. Graph. Appl. IEEE **25**, 13–17 (2005)
20. Copolo, C.E., Hounshell, P.B.: Using three-dimensional models to teach molecular structures in high school chemistry. J. Sci. Educ. Technol. **4**, 295–305 (1995)
21. Li, H., Leung, K.-S., Nakane, T., Wong, M.-H.: iview: an interactive WebGL visualizer for protein-ligand complex. BMC Bioinform. **15**(56), 1 (2014)
22. Li, H., Leung, K.-S., Chan, C.H., Cheung, H.L., Wong, M.-H.: iSyn: WebGL-based interactive de novo drug design. In: IEEE, pp. 302–307 (2014)
23. Klopfer, E., Sheldon, J.: Augmenting your own reality: student authoring of science-based augmented reality games. New Dir. Youth Dev. **2010**, 85–94 (2010)
24. Eve, S.: Augmenting phenomenology: using augmented reality to aid archaeological phenomenology in the landscape. J. Archaeol. Method Theor. **19**, 582–600 (2012)
25. Ibáñez, M.B., Di Serio, Á., Villarán, D., Kloos, C.D.: Experimenting with electromagnetism using augmented reality: impact on flow student experience and educational effectiveness. Comput. Educ. **71**, 1–13 (2014)
26. Murcko, M.A.: Computational methods to predict binding free energy in ligand-receptor complexes. J. Med. Chem. **38**, 4953–4967 (1995)
27. Huey, R., Goodsell, D.S., Morris, G.M., Olson, A.J.: Grid-based hydrogen bond potentials with improved directionality. Lett. Drug. Des. Dis. **1**, 178–183 (2004)
28. Ruth, H., Morris, G.M., Olson, A.J., Goodsell, D.S.: A semiempirical free energy force field with charge-based desolvation. J. Comput. Chem. **28**, 1145–1152 (2007)

Research on Virtual Training System in Aerospace Based on Interactive Environment

Fang You[1], Yuxin Tan[1(✉)], Jinsong Feng[2], Linshen Li[2], Jing Lin[3], and Xin Liu[3]

[1] Tongji University College of Arts and Media, Shanghai 201804, China
498074482@qq.com
[2] Tongji University School of Software Engineering, Shanghai 201804, China
[3] Shanghai Tanwei Aerospace Media and Technology Co., Ltd.,
Shanghai, China

Abstract. There are precedents both at home and abroad to use virtual reality technology in the field of aerospace industries. The purpose is to improve the training efficiency of the device assembly and make the operators have more intuitive understanding of the safety and the logic of the assemble process. The virtual training system was presented on Zspace environment, which has strong sense of interaction and immersion. After confirming the requirements, designers determine the conceptual frame and iterative prototype of the system. At last, the article proposed the interactive features in terms of software and hardware under different requirements by giving an application example.

Keywords: Virtual reality · Virtual training · Virtual space interactive feature · Aerospace application

1 Introduction

VR (Virtual Reality, VR) also called as temporary environment or spiritual environment [1]. Computer and electronic technology generate the virtual world. The user can connect with virtual world by hearing, touching, smelling and a series of actions and the interaction causes a change to the objects in the virtual reality environment. Through the closed loop system users can have immersive, immediate feeling [2]. Virtual reality is a natural interaction technology [3]. It reflects the most advanced achievements in the fields of computer technology, computer simulation technology and parallel processing technology [4]. A standard virtual reality system consists of a computer, input/output devices, applications and databases [5].

Virtual training assembly system is a typical application of virtual reality, which has higher requirements of direct operation (DM) method. Through various input devices trainees can do prototype, verification, simulation, assembly path planning and training [6, 7]. Virtual reality technology was mainly used in the field of science education and display in domestic, while in abroad virtual reality were used in training, simulation, testing, and training.

© Springer International Publishing Switzerland 2016
A. El Rhalibi et al. (Eds.): Edutainment 2016, LNCS 9654, pp. 50–62, 2016.
DOI: 10.1007/978-3-319-40259-8_5

2 Background of Virtual Reality

2.1 Status Quo of Virtual Reality System

Virtual assembly environment can be divided into the following categories: desktop systems, helmet-mounted system, CAVE systems and large-screen projection systems [8]. Several types of systems were shown in Table 1.

Table 1. The virtual assembly environment

Virtual assembly environment	Operation	Hardware equipment	Experience	Cost
Desktop	Use mouse, keyboard to control objects	Common graphics processor, common monitor	Poor immersion, simple operation	Low
Helmet-mounted	Use external input devices to control objects	Data gloves, virtual reality glasses, Leap motion and other external input devices	Strong sense of immersion, a sense of dizziness, accuracy is not high	Middle
CAVE	Use a larger three-dimensional space (ceiling, floor, wall) as a display environment, manipulate objects by operating handle	Projectors, virtual reality glasses and various types of sensors	Strong sense of immersion, multi-user	High
Large-screen projection	Stitching the plurality of projection screen, manipulate objects by operating handle	Projectors, stereoscopic display glasses, operating handle	Strong sense of immersion, high technical difficulty	Low

The system uses Unity 3D to finish program part. Unity 3D is a integrated game development tool which supports the creation of a three-dimensional video or games, architectural visualization, real-time three-dimensional animation and other types of interactive content released in multi-platform and it's largely based on the programing.

The three-dimensional interactive display can be divided into the following categories according to the demand: (1) naked eye three-dimensional display and brands are Magnetic, SuperD, Alioscopy and so on, users don't need to wear 3D glasses to view three-dimensional images, but the resolution, viewing angle and aspects of visual distance still have many deficiencies; (2) polarizing stereoscopic display and brands are Zalman, TransviDeo, iZ3D and so on, users can enjoy 3D images with polarized stereoscopic glasses but the resolution is reduced by half and difficulty of technology is high; (3) inertial motion capture system and brands are Christie 3D, Perception, DepthQ DP and so on, it can projected to any screen, but the display space has limitations and the operator should have professional skills.

Usually there are two main factors to judge a virtual assembly training system, which are if the system correctly understands the user's intention and interaction semantics or not. To understand the user's intention can make human-computer interaction more natural and harmonious, and the semantic structure can facilitate information and well-structured knowledge. The former factor requires user behavior research, while the latter need to use DM method and multi-channel information input way [9–12]. To some degree, users' experience and professional knowledge limit their behavior and the interaction with virtual environment. So take the limitations of human perception into account, combined with interactive scenarios and actions to reach the target [13, 14].

2.2   Status Quo of Virtual Training System

The design and production of a model is a complicated systematic work in industrial production, which involves many specialties, complex system and special working space. These technical difficulties require workers have higher level of technology and experience. Original assembly training way is experienced operators using blueprint to teach new operators. But project file is not vivid enough; moreover operators are reluctant to look text.

The system mainly used for training and display. On one hand, to improve teaching efficiency and make the operators understand all aspects of device intuitively. The other hand, making the key technical points and features of the product looked more vividly and more easily for visitors to understand. Users will have curiosity of the system when they first use it because of the lack of experience. Designers take this for advantage to guide users to use stylus and infrared glasses to experience the characteristics of these input devices and set the tasks of scene and the functions of menu gradually.

2.3   Interactive Technology of Virtual Training Platform

Choosing Zspace as display platform because it's user-friendly operation. It can facilitate the exhibition and can be used in training, testing and simulation analysis. It was developed by Infinite Z. The system is an immersive, three-dimensional display platform which provides hardware and software solutions. It allows users and developers to use 3D holographic projection way to observe objects in virtual space.

Through tracking the markers on the polarized glasses to locate the transform and rotation, the system adjusts the screen angle according to the users' perspective in real time and alternates left and right perspective image at a rate of 60fps or 120fps. The two polarizing lenses of polarized glasses and the polarizer eye images have the same polarization direction, which ensure the separate of two images [15, 16]. Then the observer will have the illusion of depth like viewing the real thing. Polarized glasses are non-holographic 3D display technology, compared to the other style of glasses it has a high resolution, high contrast, high comfort, large range of viewing angles, low manufacturing cost.

From a hardware perspective, it has the advantage of desktop system, helmet and CAVE-style that is the cost is low, with strong sense of immersion and reduce the sense of vertigo. It also supports multi people watching. Comparing to the data gloves or operating handle stylus can manipulate 3D objects in a more accurately and quickly way. From a software perspective, it has software development kit for Unity3D, which reduced the difficulty to develop. It builds on the experience of human life, thus reducing the burden of learning and memory. One can use infrared stylus to pick up 3D objects to see the details with proprioception. It's the same when people want to observe an object in real life. This platform provides a natural unconsciously mode of operation (Fig. 1).

Fig. 1. Zspace

3   Design of Virtual Training System

3.1   The Interactive Task of System

The system uses the infrared stylus, polarized glasses to obtain operation information and output results via the monitor. The main action is the system determines whether to pick up the target object or not by collision detection; moving object to target position then assemble it in accordance with the requirements of logic and safety. The Fig. 2 shows the configuration of the system.

The needs are: (1) The system can simulate assemble scenarios. (2) Analyzing if the assembly sequence logic is correct or not. For instance, operation must follow a certain sequence, the battery will interfere with other components when user trying to remove or install it. (3) Feedback about erroneous operation. Based on the operational safety

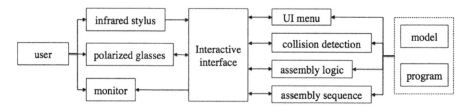

Fig. 2. Overall system description

principle, the system should simulate various operating result and the interference between different components.

Interactive behavior includes: (1) Operation between input devices and target object, UI, scene. (2) Interface interaction: presenting the appropriate menu depending on the selected model. (3) The state of 3D objects model state: move, crawl, release, and different color under state changes.

Extracting the task flow of installing the battery to the tooling plate as shown in Table 2.

Table 2. The task flow of installing the battery to the tooling plate

Task	Description	Target
Into the scene	Select "typical assembly" on homepage	Into the target scene
Check "working process"	Click "working process"	Check the flow directions then continues to operating instructions
Drag the battery into the scene	Click the thumbnail of the " Component Library" and dragged into the scene	Generate the target object
Disassemble the battery packaging	Put the battery model on the table according to the flow directions, the system determine if it touch the table, then trigger next event	The system determines if the user operate correctly then trigger next event
Install battery on the tooling plate	Picking up and moving the battery to the target installation location	By collision detection to determine if the object is moved to the target installation location
Install screws	Dragging the screw model into the scene to the target installation location, click on the "magnifying glass" button then moving to the target position	Use the "magnifying glass" feature

Extracting the character models based on the above segments task. As shown in Fig. 3. Users can smoothly understand the menu function in the process of completing the task.

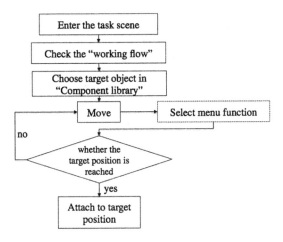

Fig. 3. Assembly tasks

3.2 The Design Flow of the System

Through expert interviews designer initially identified the needs of the assembly training systems and get to know the specific craft process. Focus on the main functions, interfaces and interactive, task flow of the existing software then summarizing the advantages and disadvantages. The Fig. 4 shows the low fidelity prototype of one scene.

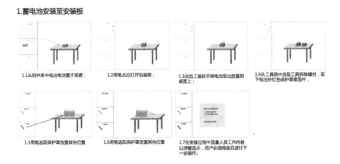

Fig. 4. Low fidelity prototype

In the second expert interview, designers verified the rationality of the framework of the prototype and confirmed the detail of software function. Discussing and select a typical assembly scene applied in display system. The third phase, confirming the user role, functional framework and interaction. Requirements of each module were shown in Table 3.

Table 3. Requirements of each module

Module	Description
Display	Check the appearance and internal structure of the model. Pick up the model; change angel of view; hide part of the model. Checking the video of satellite in working state
Typical assembly	Install the battery: according to the working flow, users install the battery on the tooling plate step by step Working flow: Assembling process must be fixed in accordance with the order of the installation process and irreversible Component Library: Select component from the library Safety Tips: Giving precautions when handling emergencies Switching perspective
Assessment	To complete the task without any prompting, and user will be timed and judged

System consists of two modules: the three-dimensional display part and interactive part. This article focuses on 3D interactive function module that is training and assessment system. Asking the trainees to operate the system in a correct flow sequence and remind trainees when occur to errors so that trainees can master techniques through repeated practice. The assessment system aims at testing the training effect.

Role of the scene: visitors can pick up and amplify the structure, observe it in a precise and interactive way. Open different module to different users, such as designers, operators and workers are able to test and operate. Figure 5 shows the information architecture of typical assembly module.

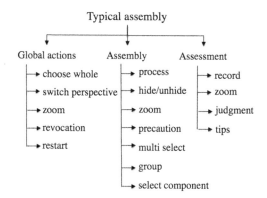

Fig. 5. The information architecture of typical assembly

Figure 6 shows the final interface of the system.

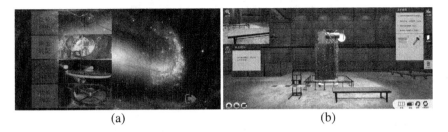

(a)   (b)

Fig. 6. (a, b) Final interface

4   The Definition and Implementation of Interaction of Virtual Training System

4.1   Interactive Feature of Virtual Training System in Terms of Software

In the real world, the convergence and focus are in the coupling state. However, when looking at the screen, the human eye needs to focus on the screen, while also converge at different depth look at 3D images. When depth of field of 3D image and the human eye's depth of field are same then the convergence and focus in coupling state, which is the main space when viewing 3D scenes. In order to see the 3D object in front of the screen or behind when it is not in coupled state, users need to separate convergence point and focal point to adapt to changes in the focal point of the depth of field; this situation will increase eye fatigue. 3D imaging and the decoupling between convergence point and focal point is proportional to some extent, but when the separation beyond a certain range, the three-dimensional illusion will be completely broken.

Three-dimensional image space is composed of the mutual of coupling and decoupling zone. It can be divided into within the screen, on-screen, off-screen three zones. To understand the advantages and disadvantages of each region will help to improve the experience of applications.

On-screen coupling region. When the object near the coupling region the human eye will be more comfortable. The scene should be placed in coupling region mostly to maximizing their stereoscopic effect. The surface of screen in the virtual world is fixed and it won't move with the glasses, so UI should also on this region. Decoupling area within the screen can be applied to strengthen the depth of background scene. Even the audience's attention remains in the coupling region; the depth of the background can make the background look broader especially the background is space. But in high-contrast areas should avoid display ghosting. As shown in Fig. 7, the background of display module is universe; the satellite will be placed in the space and in the state of operation that makes it looked more realistic.

Fig. 7. Display module

Decoupling off-screen area is the most amazing area. The object looks like floating in the air, it can break the shackles of the screen, jump out of the virtual world. Applications should be designed to encourage users to take the objects out of screen to experience this amazing 3D effect. As shown in Fig. 8, "take out" battery from screen to observe its structure, the red line is the radiation emitted by the infrared stylus.

Fig. 8. "Take out" the battery from the screen

The application can create a virtual world larger than the physical space, which allows users to explore the virtual space by moving the position of glasses [17]. As shown in Fig. 9, users use glasses or pen to view the virtual factory space.

(a)   (b)

Fig. 9. (a, b) The factory in typical assembly scene

4.2 Interactive Feature of Virtual Training System in Terms of Hardware

The virtual assembly training systems are mostly based on PC. The input includes mouse, keyboard and handle. The output includes the stereoscopic world within the screen, voice or other multi-media. Using mouse or keyboard to interactive with stereoscopic world is to emit a ray from a point in the screen, and control the object detected by the ray. It may results in most operation only valid for 2-dimensional space. When users need to move object vertically or rotate it, the interaction might be complex. Rare systems use the middle button to control object as a third source of information. Using operating handle as input can be used in scene roaming, however, there are limitations on the operation of a single object.

Platform consists of a computer, infrared stylus, polarized glasses and a monitor that can track the position and rotation of the glasses and stylus. Stylus has six dimensions that mean the virtual object can make movement in three directions. Meanwhile users can use stylus to "pick up", "flip" objects. The scene will automatic adjust its position based on the position of glasses. Compared to other assembly systems, the glasses not only as an output but also part of the input.

Monitor tracks the position of the glasses thus to control the left and right camera position in virtual scene and focal length. The interactions of infrared stylus are click, move, release corresponds to the operation of the pen is pressed, release, click. Stylus has three keys, taking into account the different functions assigned to each key will increase the difficulty of memory, so the system uses only one button. Operation target are target objects, UI components, static scene. As shown in Table 4.

Table 4. Interactive action and object state change

Operation of stylus	Operation target	Target	UI component	Static scene
Click		Choose multi objects in the multi-select mode, selected object will change color	Click to choose UI component to generate a model or have a function	
Long press		Long press to move the object		Long press to drag the scene and change angle of view
Release		Release the button, the object will attach to the target object or stop at current place		Get the current perspective

Extracting operation task flow according to the interaction as shown in Fig. 10. Clicking the button to select object, UI components, long press to move the object.

4.3   Realization of Function of Picking up the Virtual Object with Stylus

PC version was finished by Unity3D, controlled by the mouse and displayed on the normal screen. Then installed the SDK package, modify the input part of the program, so that it is adapted to the new display platform.

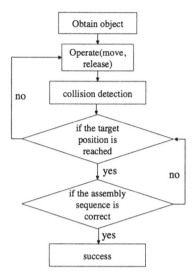

Fig. 10. Assembly process

The system changes the depth of the 3D image according to the distance between the plate and the human eye in real time. Input devices have four important variables which are the moving range and midpoint of the glasses and the moving range and midpoint of the stylus. The midpoint is the intermediate position from the position of glasses or stylus in real world to the position of object in virtual world, moving range is the effective operating range of glasses or stylus in the real world.

To control an object includes three parts, control stylus, rendering the ray emitted by the stylus, changing parameter of the camera. Stylus emits rays then collide with the object with specified class; pressing the stylus button when the ray come into an object, then pick it up and the object and ray remained relatively fixed; release the button then release the objects. The transform and rotation of stylus are p_s and r_s, through the point C of contact rays and the object and returns the position and direction of the length of the ray and the object T, as shown in Fig. 11.

The key value are:

p_c: the position of collision point (rays projected on a screen), p_t: target position of the object (output), p_s: the position of stylus (input), r_s: the rotation of Stylus, r_t: the rotation of target object (output), r_c: the rotation of the collision point, l: distance from nib to collision point, l_0: initial length (no target object) (Fig. 12).

$$\because p_c = p_s + \overrightarrow{SC} \ , \ \overrightarrow{SC} = p_c - p_s = r_c * l$$

$$\therefore l = \overrightarrow{SC} \ , l \leq l_0 为 p_t = p_c + r_c * \ CT$$

$$= p_c + r_c * (l + \overrightarrow{CT})$$

$$r_c = r_t = r_s \ .$$

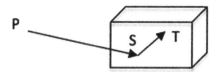

Fig. 11. Position of P, S, T

Fig. 12. Operation

5 Conclusion

Based on the virtual training system conclusions are as follows: compared to other 3D stereoscopic display device, the system has better solution for three-dimensional objects under certain demands. Users can interactive with virtual world in a breakthrough way. Polarized glasses used both as inputs and outputs, virtual objects have six degrees of freedom to control. Descripting the design process of the project. Summed up the interaction of glasses and stylus corresponding to different scenes. Explaining the principles of visual effects and interactive features of the platform.

References

1. 姜学智, 李忠华.国内外虚拟现实技术的研究现状. 辽宁工程技术大学学报 (02) (2004)
2. A survey on virtual reality. Science in China (Series F: Information Sciences), **03**, 348–400 (2009)
3. Zeng, J.C., Yu, Z.H.: Virtual Reality Technology and Its Application. Tsinghua University Press, Beijing (1996). (in Chinese)
4. 黄悦.浅谈虚拟现实技术. 科技信息(学术研究), (32), 203–205 (2008)
5. 徐娟.基于虚拟现实技术的铁道车辆运行仿真系统研究. 长沙: 中南大学 (2009)
6. Yuan, X.B., Yang, S.X.: Virtual assembly with biologically inspired intelligence. IEEE Trans. Syst. Man Cybern. C **33**, 159–167 (2003)
7. Smith, S.S.F., Smith, G., Liao, X.: Automatic stable assembly sequence generation and evaluation. J Manuf. Syst. **20**, 225–235 (2001)
8. 夏平均, 陈朋, 郎跃东, 姚英学, 唐文彦. 虚拟装配技术的研究综述. 系统仿真学报 **08**, 2267–2272 (2009)

9. Prendinger, H., Ishizuka, M.: Symmetric multimodality revisited: unveiling users' physiological activity. IEEE Trans. Ind. Electron. **54**, 692–698 (2007)
10. Zhang, J.W., Knoll, A.: A two-arm situated artificial communicator for human-robot cooperative assembly. IEEE Trans. Ind. Electron. **50**, 651–658 (2003)
11. Rodriguez, A., Basanez, L., Celaya, E.: A relational positioning methodology for robot task specification and execution. IEEE Trans. Robot. **24**, 600–611 (2008)
12. Chueh, M., Yeung, Y.L.W.A., Lei, K.P.C., et al.: Following controller for autonomous mobile robots using behavioral cues. IEEE Trans. Ind. Electron. **55**, 3124–3132 (2008)
13. Bedny, G., Karwowski, W., Bedny, M.: The principle of unity of cognition and behavior: implications of activity theory for the study of human work. Int. J. Cognit. Ergon. **5**, 401–420 (2001)
14. Kulyk, O.A., Kosara, R., Urquiza, J., Wassink, I.: Human-centered aspects. In: Kerren, A., Ebert, A., Meyer, J. (eds.) GI-Dagstuhl Research Seminar 2007. LNCS, vol. 4417, pp. 13–75. Springer, Heidelberg (2007)
15. 崔舜喆.三维图像投影装置.中国专利, 96110114.8, 16 November 1997
16. Stam, J.: Stable fluids. In: Proceedings of the 26th Annual Conference on Computer Graphics and Interactive Techniques, pp. 121–128. ACM Press, Los Angeles, California, USA (1999)
17. Real World vs. zSpace — Focus and Convergence. http://developer.zspace.com/docs/aesthetics/#Understanding_zSpace_Aesthetics/Focus_Convergence.php?TocPath=_____5
18. Baldonado, M., Chang, C.-C.K., Gravano, L., Paepcke, A.: The stanford digital library metadata architecture. Int. J. Digit. Libr. **1**, 108–121 (1997)
19. Bruce, K.B., Cardelli, L., Pierce, B.C.: Comparing object encodings. In: Ito, T., Abadi, M. (eds.) TACS 1997. LNCS, vol. 1281, pp. 108–438. Springer, Heidelberg (1997)
20. van Leeuwen, J. (ed.): Computer Science Today. LNCS, vol. 1000. Springer, Heidelberg (1995)
21. Michalewicz, Z.: Genetic Algorithms + Data Structures = Evolution Programs, 3rd edn. Springer, Berlin (1996)

Web3D Online Virtual Education Platform for Touring Huangyangjie Battlefield Scenario Over Internet

Chang Liu, Jinyuan Jia, Yibo Ge, and Ning Xie[✉]

School of Software Engineering, Tongji University, Shanghai 201804, China
ningxie@tongji.edu.cn

Abstract. This paper explores how the reconstruction of special history scenario will be applied in online education. After investigating various virtual reality techniques including design of virtual educational system, reconstruction of virtual scene, management of scene, AI, lightweighting for 3D model and light shadow rendering, we build an online education platform for touring a web3D virtual battlefield scenario called Huangyangjie in China. We firstly present the solution and scheme for rebuilding the web 3D battlefield Scenario using lightweight 3D models. Secondly, we present voxel of interesting (VOI) scene management strategy based terrain-voxel-model uniform structure. Finally, we optimize A* algorithm in AI management process and present Parallel-Split Variance Shadow Mapping (PSVSM) algorithm based on sparse voxelization in real-time Web-based rendering.

Keywords: Virtual reality · Virtual education · Scene management · Light weight 3D model · Shadow mapping

1 Introduction

With the rapid development of mobile internet and virtual reality technology, web3D technology is playing an important role in online education, especially in history education. In traditional course, teachers tell students the history scenario by words, oral introduction or pictures. It is difficult for students to be engaged. In order to create compelling virtual learning environment, we present online virtual education platform using web3D technology. In our Web3D platform, students enable experience 3D history scene online with high level of reality and immersive feeling so as to improve their interests on history. We demonstrate how to reconstruct the VR education scenario on the battlefield interactive visualization called Huangyangjie.

2 Related Works

Traditional VR application in education focuses on implement virtual roaming system research. One of typical representations is the panoramic roaming system by taking panoramic images or panoramic moving videos as input. The key positions of the real scene are shot as panoramic images using panoramic shoot technology, and all these

© Springer International Publishing Switzerland 2016
A. El Rhalibi et al. (Eds.): Edutainment 2016, LNCS 9654, pp. 63–76, 2016.
DOI: 10.1007/978-3-319-40259-8_6

images are mapped to 3D space using cube map method or environment map method. By moving the virtual camera in 3D space, this system can achieve the 3D scene real-time walkthrough [1–5]. Instead of users' eyes, panoramic camera shoots the entire panorama of real scene. In order to make audience experience a sense of immersion conveniently, panoramic moving videos taken by panoramic camera are displayed online [6, 7]. In traditional online roaming system, researchers take these two kinds of data as input data.

With the development of internet and grahpical hardware, a large-scale 3D model display has been proposed. The high quality 3D model data provides valuable resources available for online virtual reality, and these data are certainly taken as the main input data of the virtual roaming system. Alternatively, emergence of an excellent virtual reality data acquisition equipment, depth camera, provides new idea and means for virtual roaming system [8, 9]. Through specific RGB-D mapping, depth value of the RGB-D image can be shot by depth camera. Therefore, roaming system can produce excellent 3D simulated effect, especially for 3D indoor scene.

3   Overview of Our VR Platform

Our virtual education platform includes four modules: lightweight 3D model material library, scene management, AI and the illumination rendering (Fig. 1).

Fig. 1. Rendering performance of the scenario that offense march along mountain path.

Lightweight Material Library. In order to overcome the limitations of web browser loading capacity, we create Lightweight material library to store lightweight 3D models without reducing the quality of 3D model. It contains lightweight 3D models designed for web browser and these models' texture, light map, height map, material, animation and shade scripts.

Scene Management. Scene management considers not only limitations of web browser loading capacity, but also the diversity of battle scene elements. The scene management strategy is proposed based on terrain-voxel-model uniform structure of the scene improve resource loading efficiency, and increase the accuracy of AI interaction.

Humanoid Enemy AI. As the core module of this platform, the main AI algorithms based on multiple-sources and multiple-objects A* algorithm consider the intelligent interaction between player character and terrain, player character and static models, or player character and the non-player characters so as to improve our platform's playability, reality and interaction.

Illumination Rendering. In rendering module, we designed a special outdoor illumination solution by improving shadow-map algorithm, which achieves the high rendering performance (Fig. 2).

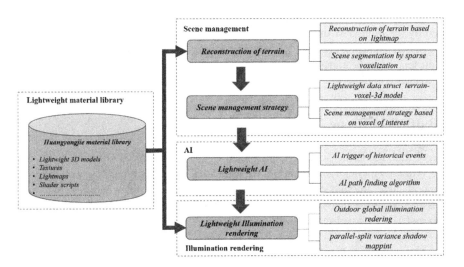

Fig. 2. Web 3D virtual education platform has four modules including lightweight 3D model material library, scene management, AI and the illumination rendering. Lightweight 3D model material library is data source. Scene manage responses how to load 3d models.

4 Lightweight Reconstruction of Battlefield Scene

4.1 Reconstruction of Terrain

The historical 3D model used is called Huangyanjie battle, which broke out in 1928. Firstly, through consulting history literatures and experts, this battle is located at

$26°$ north latitude, $114°$ east longitude, with an area of about 20 km^2. We achieve the data of terrain's height map and altitude. We normalize the 3D virtual terrain according to height map algorithm. As the local landscape has internally changed, we also rebuild terrain's texture of the year by historic images.

4.2 Lightweight 3D Modeling

Under the prior knowledge of 3D lightweight modeling guided by modeling experts, we convert the collected 3D models into the lightweight 3D model via a two-step process: reused-based lightweight and 3D model streaming.

The main idea of the lightweight processing is to find out similar parts of the model on the lightweight streaming mesh and make the similar parts steaming and reusable. The lightweight process has showed several advantages: Firstly, the bandwidth limitation has been reduced, which makes the 3D model transmission more effective. Secondly, it is not necessary to use any traditional uncompressing methods when uncompressing the model and this makes the example rendering technique being taken full advantages. Finally, the shape information of the model will not loss basically and the stored data amount will be reduced significantly.

In addition, the streaming transmission supported by Progressive Mesh (PM) coding and decoding technique can solve the 3D model transmission limitation problem caused by the limited of internet bandwidth. We use streaming format to store the 3D model streams and import them to a specific scene. By this way, the streaming model will present its appearance in general and becomes clearer gradually without being downloaded completely.

5 Battlefield Scene Management Strategy

The real time rendering scene is constructed of many various 3D models in a world space. After 3D model lightweighting, we found that it is still difficult for web browsers to support huge amounts of lightweighted 3D models' real-time rendering. To solve this issue, we present a new scene management method with voxel of interesting (VOI) and terrain-voxel-model uniform structure.

5.1 Sparse Voxelization of Terrain

As a special 3D model, terrain takes too much space. It replaces the space occupied by terrain with voxel unit. We split terrain with multiply levels performance. For example, if the level is 8, the terrain space will be divided into 83 voxels. Secondly, these voxels are used as little bounding boxes to judge whether the voxel space contain terrain mesh. Finally, we remain the voxels which contain terrain meshes, and delete others. In Fig. 3, when our terrain performance level is 8, only 78 voxels can be represented the terrain space, rather than 512 (Fig. 4).

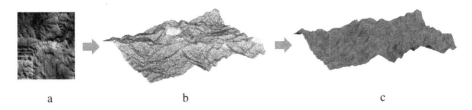

Fig. 3. a. The original height map achieved b. The 3D virtual terrain reconstructed by height map algorithm. c. The 3D virtual terrain mapped texture.

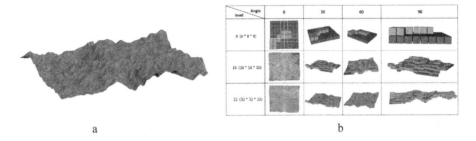

Fig. 4. a. The terrain divided into voxels. b. It illustrates different level of voxels which are divided from a. When level is n, the space will be divided to n^3.

5.2   Voxel-Centered Data Structure

After sparse voxelizing, we build relationship between terrain with voxel. In theory, the terrain can be segmented by the number of voxel. However, not all of terrains can be divided into many segments, especially mountainous terrains. If these complex terrains meshes are naively divided into tiny meshes, it may cause failure to generate many broken meshes. Therefore, we divided these terrains into a fixed number by default so as to guarantee a smooth transition between any two divided meshes at the same time. Secondly, we create new voxel data to rebuild the relationship between divided terrain meshes and voxels. Thirdly, it is known that 3D models except terrain are located to the terrain. If we use the voxels as little bounding boxes, these 3D models are included in one voxel or many voxels according to their locations. We put the bounded or partly bounded 3D models' index number, which are added into voxel data, and then build the relationship among terrain, voxel and 3D models.

5.3   Scene Management Strategy

During the process of web3D scene walkthrough, web browsers not only load 3D models in time but also achieve real-time rendering effect of these loaded 3D models. However, under the influence of network speed and computer hardware, it is very difficult for the web browsers to load huge amount of 3D models in real time. To solve this problem, researchers present the scene management strategy based on incremental loading, which make the application program load only the 3D models which may display in next moment. With this strategy, the problem of loading huge amount of 3D models in real time is solved by the similar strategy include AOI [10, 11] andSMLAOI [12, 13].

We present a new outdoor scene incremental loading strategy with AOI. In Fig. 5, we call the red frustum the present view frustum, while this blue frustum is marked the preloaded view frustum. In fact, field angle and length of the preloaded view frustum is enlarged based on the present view frustum. This method makes the web browser preload more 3D models for real-time translation and rotation of the present view frustum in next moment. When the frustum moves or rotates, the preloaded view frustum should add will-visible voxels and delete will-invisible voxels since the total quantity which the web browser can load is limited. Due to the relationship among terrain, voxel and models, voxels' increase or decrease represent the terrain meshes and 3D models' increase or decrease.

Fig. 5. The terrain is divided into many subspaces by voxels. These 3D models located on the terrain must be included in one voxel or many voxels.

6   AI Management in Battlefield Scenario

In order to enhance students' sense of participation, we implement a Role Playing Games (RPG) where the student play as the defense soldiers. From a soldier perspective, the student not only feel the battle's intense and brutal but also generate interest in history. The game playability is the key of the game's attraction, and it is closely related to AI management in battlefield scene. In this paper,we introduce two types of key AI methods.

6.1   AI Trigger of Historical Events

It is very important for historical facts' dynamic display to respect their truth and objectivity. Rather than showing all details, we select typical scenarios to display, and provide the historical facts' trigger logic. Triggering event by collision detection technology are as follow: offensive solider collide with bamboo sticks triggering event, offensive solider collide with roller element stone triggering event and so on. The detailed historical events' trigger logic is illustrated in Fig. 6.

6.2 Multiply Sources and Multiply Objects' Dynamic AI Path Finding Algorithm

In order to increase the game playability, we design an offensive path finding algorithm based on A* algorithm. As shown in Fig. 7a, we project terrain mesh on 2D plane constructed by M multiply by N grid group (M and N are integer greater than or equal to 1). We call these Fig. 7a as AI scene images, and call the grid node. As offensive solider moves from one node to the other node. They should pay a cost which means the value of danger, the aim is to find the path with the minimum cost. Color depth of node represents the value of danger, where darker color means much danger. The value of danger is determined by two factors. The first one is the time of going up to the mountain. The other is the distance between defense and offense. The more time of going up to the mountain and short of distance between defense and offense, the more dangerous. As roller element stone triggering event is triggered, we change the AI scene image as shown in Fig. 7b and all new values of danger should be calculated again. After a preset time, we change the AI scene image back. The entire progress is explained in Algorithm 1.

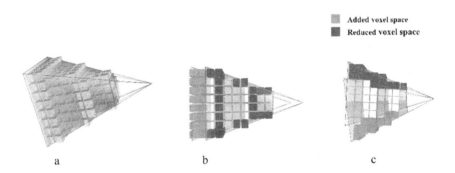

Added voxel space
Reduced voxel space

a   b   c

Fig. 6. a. The red frustum is the present view frustum, and the blue frustum is the preloaded view frustum. b. When the frustum moves, the preloaded view frustum should add will-visible voxels and delete will-invisible voxels. Green voxels are will-visible voxels and the blue voxels are opposite. c. When the frustum rotate, the preloaded view frustum will change as b.

Algorithm 1: Multiply sources and multiply objects' dynamic AI path finding algorithm

```
Input: the position of current node and the scene graph;
Output: The node series of best path under the current scene graph;

begin
    OpenArray = {STR};/*STR is starting node*/
    CloseArray =Null
    Int i = 0;
    G(OpenArray[0]) = 0;
    Y = STR.Y;
/* Y is the serial number of target node that in Y direction,the team who
tapping on the top of the mountain is the victory in the game, so if the
number n.y is greater than Y, it means reaching the top of mountain.*/
    While (OpenArray !=NULL):
        Sort by G(n) in OpenArray;
/*G(n) is the value of cost from the start node to n*/
        CUR = OpenArray[0];// CUR is the current node
        OpenArray delete OpenArray[0];
        CloseArray add CUR;
/*As the offense is close to defense, the cost ismainly determined by
distance by them.*/
        if (Y<CUR.Y)
            if (WDIS >=0.3)  WDIS - ΔW;
            if (WDG <=0.7)   WDG + ΔW;
    /* WDIS is the weight of costs for distance ;WDG is the weight of costs
for risk; ΔW: The weight of costs for dynamically changing ;*/
        Y = CUR.Y;
        For Neighbour of CUR
            If (Y <Y(Goal)) return CloseArray;
            DG(CUR, NEI) = Alpha/DIS(NEI, DEF);
    /* DG(n,n' )is the value of cost from the node n to n ', the node n '
is inversely proportional with the distance of the nearest offense' node
w , DG (n, n ') = Alpha/DIS (n, w); NEIis Neighbor nodes includingup, down,
left, right four neighbors of the current node;*/
            C(CUR, NEI) = WDIS * DIS(CUR, NEI) + WDG* DG(CUR, NEI);
    /* C(n,n' )is the value of cost from the node n to n ',  C (n, n') = WDIS
* DIS (n, n ') + WDG * DG (n, n '); DIS(n,n' )is the distance from the
nodes n to n ';*/
            Cost = G(CUR) +C(CUR, NEI);
            If(NEI in OpenArray & Cost<G(Neighbour)) OpenArray delete NEI;
            If(NEI in CloseArray & Cost<G(Neighbour)) CloseArray delet
                NEI;
            If(NEI not in OpenArray & Neighbor not in CloseArray)
                G(Neighbor) = Cost;
        OpenArray add NEI;
        NEI.Parent = CUR;
    end
```

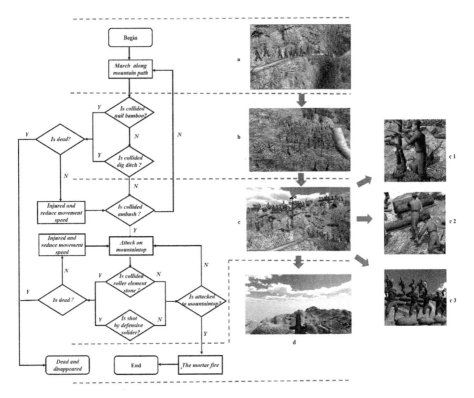

Fig. 7. The little games' total AI trigger logic. Right is the little games' performance. a. Offense march along mountain path. b. Nail bamboo. c. Offense attack on mountaintop. In this process, it includes c1. Offensive shot to defense, c2. offensive solider collide with roller Element stone, c3. defensive position. d. Mortar fire

7 Illumination Rendering

With the scene management strategy based on voxelization, we employ several rendering technologies for shadow. E.g. Phong Illumination model, hemispherical global illumination model, screen-space ambient occlusion (SSAO) and ShadowMap in which the quality and efficiency are both considered. Moreover, we assemble the advantages so as to make some further improvement.

We simulate the sun light by simply setting, spot light to cover the whole virtual scene. However, this method is just applicable to small scenes because of small attenuation radius. When used in large-scale scenes, we can observe that there is some bright area near the spot light while dark area far from the spot light. With this observation, there arises a new light model, named parallel light in which two attributions, light intensity and the direction can be used. But when used for some special effects, e.g. sunrise, sunset and obscured sun by clouds, the parallel light cannot meet the need, either. To overcome the above drawbacks, a combined light source of spot light and parallel light is implemented in this paper.

For rendering, we adopt WebGL as our online rendering technology. Meanwhile, considering the online rendering efficiency, we mainly improve Phong Illumination model and hemispherical global illumination model. The hard and soft shadows are realized with shadowmap, and then filtered by Parallel-Split Variance Shadow Mapping (PSVSM). At last, the self-occlusion is simulated with SSAO.

For real time large-scale scene rendering, we propose an efficient method by combining parallel-split variance shadow mapping and variance shadow map. PSSM [14] aims at the aliasing problem of shadow rendering in large-scale scenes. It improves the situation that only single shadow map existed in the former methods. In PSSM, the frustum is divided into many small sub-frustums along the direction of depth of field and a shadow map is saved for each sub-frustum. The Variance Shadow Maps [15] (VSM) is also a similar shadow method which is put forward by Donnelly on 2006. The drawbacks of these methods are the divided resolution is not explicitly defined. Our main idea is to initialize the sub-frustums count by a sparse voxelization procedure and divide the frustum in an ascending order from near to far, and the detail algorithm as follow.

Parallel-split variance shadow mapping based on sparse voxelization algorithm

```
Input: the current view frustum and voxels data in it
Output: pixel of the scene object texture
begin
    split(n);
/*split(n)function split the current view frustum into n parts, and split
parts' depth is equal; we create these parts data struct VF, and call them
VF1,VF2···VFn-1*/
    For (int i=1; i<=n; i++)
        AarrayVoxel[i] = Coutvoxels(VF_index);
  /*coutvoxel() function count the amount of voxels in every split frustum*/
    For (int i=1 ; i<=n ; i++)
      while(AarrayVoxel[i]> AarrayVoxel[i+1])
          if (VFi.far - VF3.near > Zn/2)
              VFi.far--, VF4.near--; //
          Else  VFi+1.near = VFi.near;
      Delete VFi;
      ············

      In Light View Space:
  /*ligh view space put the light position as view point*/
      RederDtoP();
  /*RenderDtoP() is a function that Render Depth To Texture(Depth) in Light
View Space*/
      f_DisRatio = Depth in Pixel / VF_Light
```

```
/*VF_Light is the light view frustrum*/
     Return  Vector3 pixel(f_DisRatio,f_DisRatio * f_DisRatio,0)
/*return the pixel in this texture*/
     ............

     In Current View Space:
     float f_ShadowRatio =0;
     float f_DisRatio = Depth in Pixel / far clip plane of VF[n];
 /*the split view frustrums are used here */
     float f_DepInLight_Squre  = g values of pixel in Texture(Depth);
     float f_DepInLight  = r values of pixel in Texture(Depth);
     float f_Variance = f_DepInLight * f_DepInLight -
                     f_DepInLight_Squre;
     float f_MD = f_DepInLight - fDistance;
     float f_MD_Squre = fMD * fMD;
     float f_P = f_Variance/(f_Variance + f_MD_Squre);
     f_ShadowRatio = max(f_p , f_DepInLight < f_DisRatio );
     the output color = pixel in current texture * f_ShadowRatio;
end
```

8   Experimental Results and Discussion

In order to validate the online performance of this platform, we use three different computers with different configurations. In test process, operation system is windows 8.1. Browser is Google Chrome browser. The configuration and related test results of these computers are shown in Table 1.

Table 1. Platforms' performance in computers with different configurations.

Name	Computer configuration			Platform performance		
	CPU	Memory	Graphics cards	Refresh rate	Memory usage	CPU usage rate
PC_1	Inter Core Quad CPU Q9400 2.66 GHz	2.0 G	NVIDIA GEFORCE GTX260	25 fps	320 M	27 %
PC_2	Inter Core i5-M460 CPU 3.20 GHz	4.0 G	NVIDIA GEFORCE GT620	33 fps	189 M	21 %
PC_3	Inter Core i7-3770 CPU 3.24 GHz	4.0 G	NVIDIA GEFORCE GTX760	37 fps	154.9 M	18 %

In Table 1, the display rate is more than 25 fps, the usage of memory is not more than 320 M, and usage rate of CPU is lower than 27 %. The experimental results demonstrate that this platform can fit for different computer configuration. The rendering effect of the total scene and shadow are illustrated in Figs. 8 and 9.

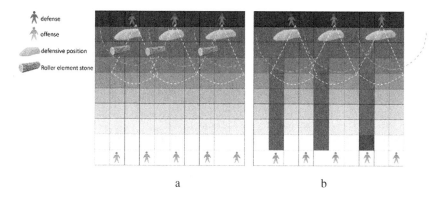

Fig. 8. a We project terrain mesh on 2D plane constructed by M multiply by N grid group (M, N are integer greater than or equal to 1), and call this type of image AI scene image. Green dotted border represents the defensive area of defensive position. Yellow dotted border represents the defensive area of defensive solider. Color depth of node represents the value of danger, where darker color, means much danger. b. As roller element stone triggering event is triggered, some code's color will be changed (Color figure online)

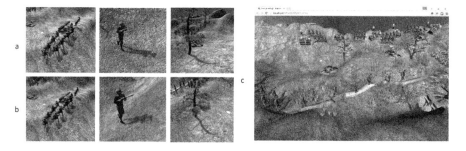

Fig. 9. a. Normal shadow using shadow map. b. Shadow using of high quality PSVSM algorithm. c. Rendering performance of the total scene.

9   Conclusion

We construct an online 3D virtual education platform in order to help students to engage the courses. Our contributions include virtual scene reconstruction, scene management, AI algorithm, 3D model lightweighting and illumination rendering. In the whole process, we present the solution and scheme for rebuilding the web 3D battlefield scenario, create voxel of interest (VOI) scene management strategy based terrain-voxel-model uniform structure, and optimize A* algorithm in AI management process and PSVSM algorithm.

Acknowledgments. National Natural Science Foundation (No. 61272276), National 12th five years Plan for Science Technology Support (No. 2012BAC11B00-04-03), The Research Fund for the Doctoral Program of Higher Education (No. 20130072110035), Changbai Valley Talent Plan of ChangChun National Hi-Tech Industrial Development Zone (NO.3-2013006), Key project in scientific and technological of Jilin province (NO. 20140204088GX) and Tongji University Young Scholar Plan (NO. 2014KJ074).

References

1. Boland, P., Johnson, C.: Archaeology as computer visualization: virtual tours of Dudley Castle c. 1550. In: Higgs, T., Main, P., Lang, J. (eds.) Image the Past: Electronic Imaging and Computer Graphics in Museums and Archaeology, vol. 114, pp. 227–233. British Museum Press, British (1996)
2. Horry, Y., et al.: Tour into the picture: using a spidery mesh interface to make animation from a single image. In: SIGGRAPH 1997, Proceedings of the 24th Annual Conference on Computer Graphics and Interactive Techniques, pp. 225–232. ACM Press/Addison-Wesley Publishing Co. (1997)
3. Kang, H.W., et al.: Tour Into the picture using a vanishing line and its extension to panoramic images. Comput. Graph. Forum **20**(3), 132–141 (2001)
4. Snavely, N., et al.: Photo tourism: exploring photo collections in 3D. ACM Trans. Graph. **25** (3), 835–846 (2006)
5. Haneta, T., Ohishi, H., Furuya, T., Takemoto, T.: Construction of 3-dimensional virtual environment based on photographed image (the acquisition and processing of the photographed image). In: Tino, A., Stephanidis, C. (eds.) HCII 2015 Posters. CCIS, vol. 528, pp. 683–689. Springer, Heidelberg (2015). doi:10.1007/978-3-319-21380-4_115
6. Kang, H.W., Shin, S.Y.: Tour into the video: image-based navigation scheme for video sequences of dynamic scenes. In: Proceedings of the ACM Symposium on Virtual Reality Software and Technology (VRST), pp. 73–80. ACM, Hong Kong, China (2002)
7. Deli, P., et al.: 3D modeling of architectural objects from video data obtained with the fixed focal length lens geometry. Geodesy Cartography **62**, 123 (2013)
8. Henry, P., Krainin, M., Herbst, E., Ren, X., Fox, D.: RGB-D mapping: using depth cameras for dense 3D modeling of indoor environments. In: Khatib, O., Kumar, V., Sukhatme, G. (eds.) Experimental Robotics. STAR, vol. 79, pp. 477–491. Springer, Heidelberg (2012)
9. Gupta, S., et al.: I1.4: invited paper: indoor scene understanding from RGB-D images. SID Symp. Dig. Tech. Pap. **46**(1), 87–90 (2015)
10. Li, F.W.B, Lau, R.W.H, Kilis, D.: GameOD: an internet based game on demand framework. In: Proceeding of ACM VRST 2004, pp. 129–136. ACM Press, Hongkong (2004)
11. Wang, W., Jia, J.: An incremental SMLAOI algorithm for progressive downloading of large scale WebVR scenes. In: Proceedings of Web3D2009, pp. 55–60, Germany (2009)
12. Wang, M., Jia, J., Zhongchu, Y., Zhang, C.: Interest-Driven Avatar Neighbors Organizing for P2P Transmission of Distributed Virtual World. Special Issue of Computer Animation and Virtual Worlds (2015)
13. Wen, L., Xie, N., Jia, J.: LPM: Fast Accessing Web3D Contents Using Lightweight Progressive Meshes, Computer Animation and Virtual Worlds (SCI) (2015, in Press)

14. Zhang, F., Sun, H., Xu, L., Lun, L.K.: Parallel-split shadow maps for large-scale virtual environments. In: Proceedings of Virtual Reality Continuum and Its Applications 2006, pp. 311–318, June 2006
15. Donnelly, W., Lauritzen, A.: Variance shadow maps. In: Proceedings of I3D 2006, pp. 161–165 (2006)

EDTree: Emotional Dialogue Trees for Game Based Training

Jay Collins, William Hisrt, Wen Tang$^{(\boxtimes)}$, Colin Luu, Peter Smith,
Andrew Watson, and Reza Sahandi

Department of Creative Technology, Faculty of Science and Technology,
Bournemouth University, Poole, Dorset BH12 5BB, UK
{wtang,Pjsmith,awatson,rsahandi}@bournemouth.ac.uk

Abstract. Immersion and interactivity are a major focus when creating gaming applications, as technology has improved and enabled the creation of larger and more detailed virtual environments the need for more engaging NPCs (non-playable characters) is also required. Many games utilise a form of dialogue tree when conversing with characters within a gaming application, allowing the user to choose their questions/responses. While this method does provide a dynamic conversation system, it is quite a one-sided level of interactivity with the NPC simply responding to the current question without it affecting the conversation on a whole. We present a novel dialogue system that explores the emotional state of the NPC to provide a more complex form of dialogue tree, termed EDTree (Emotional Dialogue Tree). Based on user actions, the interactions between the user and the NPC are enriched by the emotional state of the NPC. Utilising this system will provide an immersive experience based around improved believability of virtual characters. To demonstrate the effectiveness of our approach, we show an example of a training system that explores the use of gaming technology and the proposed EDTree.

1 Introduction

The use of dialogue trees within gaming environments has been around for several decades. Since the early 2000s it has seen major commercial use by large gaming companies such as Bethesda [1] and Bioware [2]. While the complexity of applications has been improved constantly with new technologies, the dialogue tree system remains the most advanced form of conversational interactivity between users and NPCs however has not seen much improvement since its inception. This is reflected in the lack of formal publication that has been placed on dialogue systems and as a result the systems currently in use remain conceptual and are not based on any scientific research. This paper aims to tackle some of the limitations observed in the current standard of dialogue methods whilst formally presenting a new system which advances current commonly used techniques.

Emotional response is one of the key factors in decision making and interactions between individuals [3,4], if realistic characters wish to be created the

A. El Rhalibi et al. (Eds.): Edutainment 2016, LNCS 9654, pp. 77–84, 2016.
DOI: 10.1007/978-3-319-40259-8_7

inclusion of emotions to dictate their actions would benefit their believability. One of the major issues presented with a dialogue tree is the lack of dynamic response from a virtual character, while the character will respond to any questions given by the user there is a lack of consistency during the conversation and the overall flow will remain static and unchanged regardless of actions being taken by the user. The goal of our proposed EDTree (Emotional Dialogue Tree) is to remove these limitations and improve the user experience by adding a more realistic form of interaction that taps into the emotional states of characters.

Due to the growing use of gaming applications in training simulations [5,6] there is a need to create realistic and intelligent virtual characters in systems that focus on human interaction. In this paper, we present the use of EDTree in a game-based training application. The objective is for professional training within the public sector, where engaging with conversations and dialogues are the norm. We have created a virtual training platform that realistically simulates interaction with the general public in order to train professionals in the police force. One of the primary requirements of the training applications was to teach users how to deal with potentially dangerous individuals in a safe environment where their decisions would emulate real life situations. The major challenges in creating such an application is to simulate realistically any actions taken by the user of the application, as a result, it should have a noticeable effect on the NPC, hence, the simulated effects will teach trainees how to appropriately handle a given situation.

2   Conversational Interactions

Conversational interactions between the player and an NPC are very important for an immersive virtual environment in order to engage the user with an application, a dialogue tree is the most commonly used technique to achieve this goal [7].

Dialogue trees are hierarchical data structures that allow the traversal of a conversational scene based on user inputs. Typically, users are presented with multiple conversational options for a question or response to engage with an NPC. After an option has been chosen, the NPC will respond in an appropriate manner. According to the users' conversational choices, the traversal of the dialogue tree will provide the responses, and new options for conversation become available. There are primarily two methods of implementing such dialogue trees, namely Hub and Spoke model and the Waterfall model [8].

2.1   Hub and Spoke Dialogue System

A Hub and Spoke system as shown in Fig. 1 features a central hub that will branch into different conversation options to facilitate dialogue interactions, each option leads to a set of NPC responses. After all options have been exhausted, the dialogue tree will return to the central hub and another option can be selected. The primary purpose of a Hub and Spoke system is to provide expositional information to the user, typically it only ends when a desired option has been selected or when the user has decided to end the conversation. This method of dialogue tree results in a very formulaic form of conversation where users are presented with repeated dialogue that does not emulate the real life interactions between two individuals.

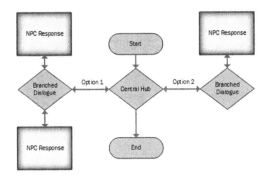

Fig. 1. Example of Hub and Spoke dialogue tree.

2.2   Waterfall Dialogue Tree

Figure 2 illustrates a waterfall dialogue tree that presents users with a series of choices that flow into new options and do not allow them to return to pick previous unchosen choices. A particular selection may be expanded to provide several dialogue options, but the overall flow remains the same, hence, there is a constant stream of new information.

While a dialogue tree that follows the waterfall technique provides a more realistic method of conversation than a Hub and Spoke system, it can be much more restrictive for the narrative of a game. For example, many applications require a very specific outcome to an interaction between the user and an NPC. As a result, many gaming applications that feature a waterfall style dialogue tree often end interactions with the same required outcome or response regardless of how the user has traversed the tree. Depending on the options the user has picked this can often lead to a very disjointed conversation where the response of an NPC doesn't seem to match the questions the user has asked, or responds in a way that can feel forced or irrelevant.

Due to the restrictions presented in both models, many modern applications choose a hybrid of both Waterfall and Hub and Spoke dialogue trees [8], allowing for the freedom of the Hub and Spoke style whilst maintaining the realism of the Waterfall method. While a combination of these methods provide a realistic interaction between the player and the NPC, there is little consistency between the previous conversation choices of the player and how the NPC responds. A player can often choose insulting conversation options and the NPC will not be affected by those choices in further conversations. As described by [1] dialogue

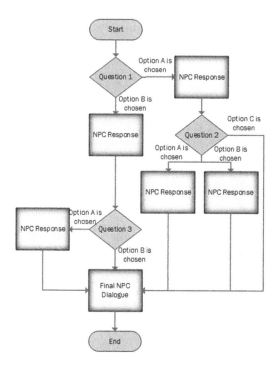

Fig. 2. Example of waterfall dialogue tree.

trees often feature hard coded responses even when user input is present. In order to achieve a higher level of realism, we propose a new method to incorporate emotional states of NPCs into the dialogue tree structures.

3   Emotional Dialogue Tree

In order to maintain consistency between user actions and NPC dialogue, a series of variables can be used to monitor the interaction with a given NPC. These values can encode various emotional states ranging from fondness, sympathy, respect or any arbitrary value based on the needs of the designer. Depending on the current emotional values of an NPC, they can be placed in a particular state and depending on the state the NPC will respond to the user based on their previous interactions.

As shown in Fig. 3, our EDTree structure can be added to any conventional dialogue tree as an extended component. While the EDTree is a powerful technique to enhance the interactions between users and NPCs, it should be noted that it is an addition to the current methods of dialogue tree design to add more importance to the actions and choices made by a user. Therefore, our proposed method can be easily used within an existing application system, without the need of redesign the core conversational system.

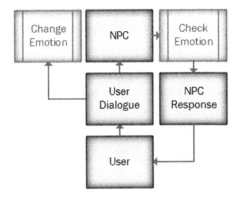

Fig. 3. Top level emotional dialogue tree structure and interaction loop.

3.1 EDTree Applications

We tested our EDTree technique primarily in a game-based training application. The application itself is aimed towards public sector staff learning different procedures to engage the general public with. Such applications also require realistic NPCs that will react in accordance to the decisions of the trainee. One important application is, for example, a police officer questioning a crime suspect as inappropriate actions could lead to dangerous outcomes. Within the application, the user is placed into a virtual environment and can interact with members of the public via conversational dialogues. As shown in Fig. 4, the emotional state of the NPC changes while being questioned from non-cooperative to co-operative.

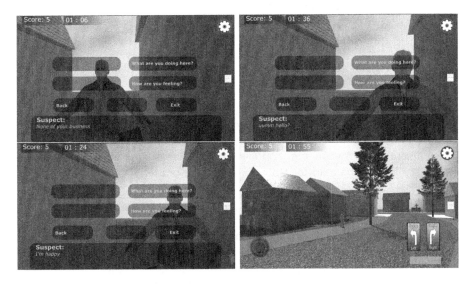

Fig. 4. Test scene: The NPC states of emotion changes during the conversation dialogues, from a state of disrespect (top left) to nervous (top right) to cooperative/happy (bottom left). The bottom right image shows a street scene.

To implement the EDTree each NPC were given variables for both nervousness and respect towards the player, as the user interacts with the NPC these values are modified based on the users actions, for example if the user performs a police background check on the NPC their nervousness value will be increased whereas engaging in general conversation such as asking how the NPC is feeling will increase respect. Each NPC is also given a multiplier to each emotion variable so that each action will have a potentially stronger result based on its "personality", for example a guilty suspect is much more likely to become nervous when performing a background check than an innocent one so this is reflected in the nervousness multiplier.

A directed graph traversal scheme for an emotional dialogue tree is shown in the following algorithm. This scheme constructs the emotional state into a graph. The *directed graph* G is a set of emotional states V and a set of state transfer E. The state transfers are of the form (i, j) where $i, j \in V$. A state of a graph G is a mapping $c : V \longrightarrow 1, 2, ..., s$ such that $e(i) \neq e(j)$ for all state transfers $(i, j) \in E$. $e(i)$ is referred to as the emotional value of the state that are displayed by the node i. Given a well structured set of states and links of each state, our proposed EDTree structure is able to propagate updates through the conversation dialogue efficiently.

The EDTree works by sequentially traversing algorithm the conversation dialogue graph as following:

Data: EDTree Algorithm
Result: Directed dialogue graph traversal
n = $|V|$;
Choose a start conversation dialogue state $d(1), ..., d(n)$ of numbers $1, ..., n$
$U := V$ **for** $i = 1$ to n **do**
$\quad\vert\quad v := d(i)\ E := EmotionalState\ e(v) := EmotionalValue$
$\quad\vert\quad U : the set of emotional values.$
end

Algorithm 1. Sequential dialogue graph algorithm

There are two important computation processes in the EDTree system. Firstly, setting the dialogue options from the user is important, which displays a series of questions/responses for the user to choose that will interact with the NPC. Secondly, each NPC has a text file that contains its entire dialogue. Based on the current conversation state, NPC's emotional state and what the user has selected the file can be read for the appropriate response.

3.2   Gamification of Training Scenario

The training system is developed based on the gamification of the training objectives and learning outcomes. Once the user engages in conversation with the NPC a group of options are presented to the user to exchange dialogues, each of these options would lead to different outcomes or steered towards a single outcome. Our training system utilises the EDTree and certain choices which will result in the NPC becoming more comfortable conversing with the trainee or more agitated by their actions. Primarily there are two variables in the proposed EMTree that dictate the state of the NPC, a nervousness value and a respect value, depending on these values, a NPC will be more cooperative towards the trainee. It is left to the discretion of the user how to deal with the NPC in order to achieve their goals and based upon how well a trainee can deal with the individual, he or she is scored appropriately at the end of the training session.

4   Results and Discussions

We tested our training system with the EDTree, which provides realistic interactions between users and NPCs. Each NPC was initially placed in one of four states being nervous-respectful, nervous-disrespectful, happy-respectful and happy-disrespectful, as the user interacted with a given NPC the nervousness and respect variables were modified based on player action changing the states of the NPC. As states were modified different dialogue scripts were read to produce different conversation options and outputs which reflected the NPC's emotional state resulting in a dynamic conversation system based on user action. With our system, users can be see how their actions and approach to a situation will affect an individual. The dynamic responses produced by our training system helps trainees to learn basic interaction skills and how to improve in the future.

Given that one of the main requirements of the application is teaching trainees how to deal with the public, this level of realism is a beneficial inclusion to the simulation and also allows supervisors to monitor the progress of their trainees by checking the emotional state of a particular NPC when the application is finished.

Another benefit of the EDTree is the ability to give each NPC more personality that is reflected in their interactions with the player. Attributes such as shyness, pride, jealousy etc. are also shown much more clearly and not just left to the narrative of the story.

5   Conclusion

We proposed a novel EDTree structure which adds many qualities to a virtual character within an application including personality, interactive immersion and engagement, all of which would greatly benefit an application that focuses strongly on character driven stories/narratives. Therefore, our EDTree enhanced gaming system is applicable to many applications that are built on conversations and dialogues.

While the benefits of the EDTree are clear, it requires a lot more work to implement than traditional methods of dialogue tree, because there are many states an NPC can have, there are many more conversational responses needed. In a purely textual based application this may not be an issue as it only requires more dialogue scripting which can be a relatively cheap resource to include. However, in more complex applications like those that require actors to voice NPCs, the proposed EDTree may not be practical.

In summary, our EDTree can be implemented into an application or in simulations similar to the one discussed in this paper that require accurate feedback based on user actions.

Acknowledgments. This project is supported by the HEIF-5+1 research grant. Authors would also like to thank Mr. Martin Taylor and his colleagues for valuable discussion on game-based training applications.

References

1. Sylvester, T.: Designing Games: A Guide to Engineering Experiences, pp. 108–110. O'Reilly Media, Sebastopol (2013)
2. Jrgensen, K.: Game characters as narrative devices. A comparative analysis of dragon age: origins and mass effect 2. Eludamos. J. Comput. Game Cult. **4**(2), 315–331 (2010)
3. Clore, G.L., Huntsinger, J.R.: How emotions inform judgment and regulate thought. Trends Cogn. Sci. **11**(9), 393–399 (2007)
4. Lerner, J.S., Li, Y., Valdesolo, P., Kassam, K.: Emotion and decision making. Annu. Rev. Psychol. 12–16 (2014)
5. Donovan, L.: The use of serious games in the corporate sector. In: The Irish Symposium on Game Based Learning, pp. 19–25, December 2012
6. Aldea, A., Iacob, M.-E., van Hillegersberg, J., Quartel, D., Franken, H.: Serious gaming for the strategic planning process. In: IEEE 16th Conference on Business Informatics, pp. 183–190, July 2014
7. Caiquan, X., Chunzhi, W., Qing, M., Xianbin, S.: An Argumentation-based interaction model and its algorithms in multi-agent system. In: The International Conference on Intelligent Computation Technology and Automation (ICICTA), pp. 493–496, May 2010
8. Freed, A.: Branching Conversation and the Working Writer, Part 2: Design Considerations (2014)

Survey: Development and Analysis of a Games-Based Crisis Scenario Generation System

Pisit Praiwattana$^{(\boxtimes)}$ and Abdennour El Rhalibi

Department of Computer Science, Liverpool John Moores University,
Byrom Street, L3 3AF Liverpool, UK
P.Praiwattana@2014.ljmu.ac.uk, a.elrhalibi@ljmu.ac.uk

Abstract. Crisis is an infrequent and unpredictable event which is challenging to prepare and resolve. Serious-game approach proved to provide potential support in training and simulating event of real-world crisis situation to different stakeholders. Yet in practice, the approach meets with difficulty on how to setup and utilize different core components such as asset management, crisis scenario generation, agent simulation, real-world constraints, and the evaluation process to yield beneficial information upon running the system. To address this issue, the key question is what can be done to propose a general crisis game-based framework providing necessary core components while generating evaluation result yielding potential analytical data for a crisis management process. Therefore, in this paper, we aim to review and consolidate the existing research on scenario generation techniques and related crisis simulation framework, then to propose novel solution to combine both processes and to derive a desirable scenario content which is also being validated in the simulation framework based on the JADE multi-agent architecture.

Keywords: Crisis simulation framework · Scenario generation · MAS

1 Introduction

Crisis can be defined as any event that is, or is expected to lead to, an unstable and dangerous situation affecting an individual, group, community, or the whole society. They can be caused by man-made actions or natural phenomenon or occasional accidents that are difficult to predict (i.e. earthquake, flooding, terrorism, hazardous outbreak, etc.). Crisis management organizations have to handle available resources and facilities to deal with the crisis disaster. These resources change over time in different situations, which causes challenges in preparing the right countermeasure plan, leading to unintentionally experiment via trial and error. Since crises are infrequent, Walker et al. [1] suggests that training from game with relevant real-world environment and well-defined scenario can be beneficial to crisis management personals to understand and prepare for any upcoming emergency situation due to its cost effectiveness in development compared to the setup-cost of real training practice.

Scenario may describe a hypothetical situation that provide a necessary environment setup, initial background of event and final goal to represent a sense of real-world

© Springer International Publishing Switzerland 2016
A. El Rhalibi et al. (Eds.): Edutainment 2016, LNCS 9654, pp. 85–100, 2016.
DOI: 10.1007/978-3-319-40259-8_8

situation in the practical training or test. As regard to of crisis scenario, the possible content structure can be separated into context and crisis. Context represents a pre-incident of crisis situation to enable the understanding of specific environment surrounding the area of event while crisis describes a set of specific events which may lead to dangerous, troubled and challenging situations, with potentially cascading effects. To test possible response, the script usually includes unpredictable or probabilistic chain of events that are out of control of any player.

Regarding the gaming technology, the advancement of widely accessible game engine systems such as Unity3D, Ogre3D, Unreal Engine and other related game development tools have improved the pipeline of game development where they reduce the barrier to entry for small team of developers to make games. Subsequently, increase in accessibility to game development application has encouraged many government departments and scientific organizations to apply game as a tool for non-entertainment purposes aiming to provide a mean to give learning experience using gameplay mechanisms such as visualization, interaction, competition, reward system, immersiveness, and so on. Zyda [2] introduced a classification of terms for edutainment game as serious game. By considering the field of crisis management and disaster planning, serious game offers great potential to address the visualization, interaction, communication and assessment of good practice via continuously improving user interface and environment simulation because of the fact that crisis is infrequent and infeasible to be fully demonstrated and experienced within the real world.

Although it is very common that modern serious games stay focus on generating an engaging experience of real crisis situation, developing of the crisis simulation framework for training or decision support system does require a plausible scenario which is often directed from domain experts. This process is time-consuming and often lacks of benchmarks to evaluate the quality of each different unique scenario. Bad design scenario will often lead to unpractical solutions with waste of computing time and training resources. There are several systems which aim to procedurally generate the scenario for training and simulation purpose with a variety of techniques. However, the problem is that the scenario generation system usually is more specific to a dedicated single simulation engine and, thus, is difficult to redeploy on a different system.

The another purpose of representing a crisis situation into a scenario is to be deployed into a simulation system to help answer a question of what is the best possible emergency response regarding to available resource parameters and procedures. A possible solution to the crisis incident is sometimes being represented as a problem of resource allocation and the deployment of crisis manpower. To focus on the process of defining and evaluating a scenario, development of a framework that facilitates the generation of different possible crisis scenario script while simulating its emergency response based on available resources will provide more elaborate understanding of crisis situation and also give a preliminary assessment of crisis scenario and its corresponding plan. The result will be beneficial to the decision support system and to transferring into practical crisis training.

In this paper, we propose a review of existing scenario generation techniques and discuss the context of related crisis simulation systems highlighting the important features of crisis simulation framework. Finally, we propose the development of an interactive game-based crisis scenario simulation framework developed on top of open multi-agent toolkits such as JADE. The reminder of the paper is organized as follows: In Sect. 2, we introduce some existing automated scenario generation systems; in Sect. 3, we review on emergency training and simulation systems; in Sect. 4, we discuss the important features of crisis simulation framework; in Sect. 5, we proposed our Crisis Scenario Generation System Framework Design; and, in Sect. 6, we conclude the paper.

2 Automated Scenario Generation Systems

Modern serious games do require a plausible scenario which is often directed from domain experts and it is a very time-consuming process. Automated scenario generation provides major benefits to the manual process by: (1) Content generation can quickly produce on demand scenario with setup and constraints; (2) Computer-generated scenario can be used to supplement human-based scenario quality. For Crisis Management domain, we initially focus on producing a sequence of crisis events while mainly considering: (1) resource management perspective; (2) stakeholder collaboration in solving an emergency situation.

Hullett and Mateas [3] apply a planning technique to generate a firefighter rescue training scenario in the collapsing building area. The system use HTNPlanner with building structure data as input while set a goal to create a situation that satisfy crisis final description, domain knowledge must be defined for planner to allow physical consistency and achieving better plausible result. As a result, the system generates a scenario by filling in content as a sequence of event or activities that are expected to occur and which usually manipulate world environment leading from initial state to the desired goal situation. The trainee is given a role and a set of specific skills to perform in the scenario. The variety of generated scenario is delivered in scale of small, medium and large world setting and it is argued to be better than random probabilistic distribution of element in case of fire situation, damage propagation, and comparable existing systems due to the provision of a domain knowledge consistency model. The main limitation of this system is that the work is tending to encounter a memory shortage during simulating the variation of levels in Medium and Large scale.

Grois et al. [4] developed a SceneGen algorithm for Navy DCTrain System using Noisy Bayesian Network (NOBNs) to search for key-event to satisfying scenario objective using data from knowledge-based in a form of belief network with a penalized likelihood and rejection test to discard non-plausible results. The process is aimed to provide offline-scenario generation. The authors also mention Case-based stochastic perturbation (CBSP) is used to acquire a seed scenario from experts then apply random distribution to manipulate more variation to the original which is likely to bring unreasonable or in-plausible result due to random nature without any testing for plausibility. ScenGen's strength lies in its ability to guarantee the "quality" of each and every scenario it generates through a carefully designed selection bias and it claims to be better in overall performance than Manual design by human subject matter experts (MDHE), Naïve random generation (NRG), and Case-based stochastic perturbation (CBSP) which produce lower-quality scenarios. It defines plausible quality by checking the occurrence of key events according to the desired learning objective. Some learning objective or key event can be occurred and added simultaneously at the same time step. The major drawback of this approach is to require a set of good base human generated scenario as a seed then manipulates them to obtain more variation in the automated results, and in addition the offline generation may lack efficiency in dynamic crisis simulation system when the setting is reflecting the complexity situation from real-world problem.

Martin et al. [5] proposed an automated scenario generation system which aims to be generic and applicable to any domain specific simulation system. The authors introduced a conceptual mapping approach which is based on (1) training objectives; (2) baseline scenario as a pre-defined ideal parameter scenario; and (3) scenario vignettes that is a complexity modification of scenario such as weather, light, and etc. The main objective and additional data such as weather condition (vignette) setting are composed in an XML file and generate the scenario variation using scripted functional L-system which are similar to shape grammar in procedural modelling but define the syntax rule to represent scenario elements. This system allows generic automated domain-independent scenario generation with different simulation framework. However, the disadvantage is that it requires extra work on developing a rule for FL-System but claimed that it is one-time requirement for new training domain and it is reusable in similar domain setting. The difficulty on generating a rule is also arguable.

Zook et al. [6] introduce a combinatorial optimization approach to scenario generation to deliver the requisite diversity and quality of scenarios while tailoring the scenarios to a particular learner's needs and abilities for military training in virtual environment which is opposite to the planning approach. The main scenario generation based is on a genetic algorithm to search for a best solution; reading in author-specified domain knowledge, the details and the type of possible events and requirement in scenario, and constraint order on events. The process works by considering instant event template for the scenario at random location; Mutating the parameter of random chosen scenario; Applying cross-over operation, to create new sequence of events to improve the quality of scenario for the next iteration. The authors proposed evaluation in an interesting and effective way: (1) quality of solution at run-time; (2) the diversity of scenario as function of running time, (3) performance of trainee and appropriateness of difficulty level when training on generated scenario. The result from their evaluation is to generate a unique scenario compared to planner generation approach, this technique based on a combinatorial optimization provides lower-quality solution initially, but explores multiple different regions in the solution space containing high-quality solutions and so refines multiple distinct scenario that meet provided learning objectives rather than explore variation on same high-quality scenario. In practice, planner is expected to yield a high-quality tailored scenario early and produce several scenarios of roughly equivalent quality that are very similar on a several high-quality scenario. The authors states the requirement of virtual technology for scenario training is vital to incorporates learner attributes and theoretically lead to more effective training as learner have greater opportunities to train more on relevant scenario. The major drawback is that the generation requires a predefined small element of events to be tailored into scenario and initial input of learner model for suitable evaluation fitness function for the genetic algorithm.

Different computational approaches have been proposed for scenario generation system. From the reviews, the combinatorial optimization search and planning techniques are efficient to produce a variety of quality scenario. The former is generic optimization approach working by evaluating a set of function to determine a necessary event elements of given scenario. It works best for a training aspect since these parameters such as scenario length, constrained sequence structure and a learner model are available to achieve a relevant and distinct result each time; the latter is deploying a planner to fill in between different key events based on the event precondition and constraints. The planner approach is simpler to design and control since the knowledge representation is concise using a formal planning domain definition language such as PDDL. The lack of variation by using planner is still arguable since there are several example system in digital story telling generation successfully applying such a method to order a story priori based on given setting element of dramatic arc [7]. While the seed approaches which blended a human-created element and automated searching process seem to be more effective in generating high-quality result, the lack of variation and time-consuming aspect make this technique less preferable in representing a general crisis simulation framework. For a heuristic approach, the creating of scenario is formed by evaluating a subcomponent of scenario to the given heuristic function. The given subcomponent will be kept in a final scenario if it passed the threshold although this method seems to deliver an effective scenario, it is computing inefficient. For our framework, we will employ the planning approach due to its simplicity in design for knowledge representation of crisis scenario rather than developing a learner model.

In this section, we have reviewed some of the proposed techniques on scenario generation system. We will continue discussing the crisis training and simulation system in the Sect. 3.

3 Crisis Simulation Systems

Following the review of the work on crisis generation, we propose in this section to review the related works on crisis simulation system.

The appropriateness of computer simulation for crisis emergency response can be observed by its category of usage: (1) to provide experience for training and entertainment using: (a) virtual equipment; (b) gaming simulation; and (c) combining a real system and simulation (to for e.g. enhance operational skill); (2) to perform experiments including education, understanding and decision support system (DSS) [8].

Agent-based simulation (ABS) has been used consistently with emergency response simulation due to the flexibility to model different situations with real-world complexity knowledge. An Agent is often considered as representation of human individual capable with a set of available skills involved in the domain, typically either civilian or rescuer, but sometimes it also represent non-human entity such as vehicles and building. An Agent is usually proactive and will be used to achieve some goal, and it is reactive in response of change in the environment [9]. An Agent is often scripted with different set of behavior depending on the given role and defined rules of system. The system is often designed to emulate how the events in the real-world unfold and then determine the appropriate response plan for the agents. ABS is best suited for modelling attack on transport, attack on crowded place, pandemic human disease and natural disaster such as flooding [10]. Several existing systems work around the concept of ABS for large scale emergency response and some aim to develop a serious game for crisis simulation system with modern gaming technology for practical training and also study the effective response of crisis plan.

Metello et al. [11] designed an emergency simulation game based on serious game technique aiming to represent observable crisis situations rather than just a representation of crisis in the learning game. This system helps to demonstrate an emergency plan in finding a flawed procedure during any given scenario such as oil leakage by allowing the trainee to interact with a simulation system which events has been fired to the world environment over time and providing a feedback by rendering the effect on the screen.

Schoenharl and Madey [12] demonstrated simulation of a multi-agent system WIPER (wireless integrated phone-based emergency response) corresponding to real GIS visualizing geographic terrain with each mobile phone users having a movement activities tracked by tower cellular segments in the area for a real-time response. A real-time data source provides real-time data regarding cell-phone usage from cell-phone providers. Using a historical data source (a repository of normal cell-phone usage), a detection and alert system detect possible anomalies in cell-phone usage patterns. The system also operates by taking a batch of different agent movement activities for simulation aiming to mimic the crisis event which are: (1) a flee event where every agent move away in disturbance; (2) a flock event where agent is trying to move as a mob (grouping); (3) a jam event where each agent is moving toward their specific goal but is constrained as in traffic jam. Their system can simulate a density of agents as population and measure traffic activity which represents the actual cell segment for a better understanding of the crisis situation.

Saoud et al. [13] describe a multi-agent based approach for modeling a simulation (SimGenis) to design optimal, efficient, and appropriate rescue strategies, based on the initial state of victims, number of rescuers, and method of communication between rescuers (electronic or paper). More precisely, the aim of the research was to determine how the response to a dynamic large-scale emergency depends on the use of a centralized and decentralized collaborative rescue strategy with applying heuristic algorithm on each agent and component of the simulator while testing using seven configurations with 300 agents for victims and rescuers. The optimal response for the simulation is derived from the total number of victims, initial state of the victims and the total number of rescuer (doctor, firefighter, and nurse). The results from the study states that there is no best unique rescue scenario and it is hard to predict depending on the disaster characteristic.

Takeuchi [14] introduced a Robocup Rescue which is using the 1995 Kobe earthquake as the original test scenario. The system is aiming to represent the disaster situation sensory information then to incorporate the agent-simulation system to mitigate disaster and encourage large scale research collaboration by holding an annual competition since 2001. The response is based on optimization of the design and implementation of better action selection method to maximize the objective function regarding the number of individual, proportion of remaining health to initial health point, and proportion of unburnt area of building. In addition, with the nature of multi-objective in crisis response, a vector-based score has been proposed to compare different responses strategies [15].

The AROUND project: Adapting robotic disaster response to developing countries [16] introduced the use of robots for observation task by the information gathered by robot is fed to spatial decision support system (SDSS), which uses agent-based model to predict the outcomes of possible course of action by human rescue teams. In AROUND, optimal agent behavior mimics that of the real-world rescuers they represent. The test scenario being used is modeled after an earthquake in the city of Hanoi (Vietnam) from 1935 and 1983. The project has some similarities to Robocup Rescue in the deploying a usage of robot in order to reducing a disaster damage in developing country. In AROUND, behavior is also modeled using a parameterized utility function, which is used for action selection and has similarity to real-life behaviors.

PLAN-C (planning with large agent-networks against catastrophes) is also another ABS developed to predict the behavior of individual and collectively in large-scale emergency such as terrorist attack [17, 18]. The simulation scenario is modeled after a possible terrorist attack which simulates the first 50 h following a Sarin chemical attack on Manhattan Island. The emergency response is represented as finding a solution to a multi-objective optimization problem (MOOP) since there is no best single optimum solution in the nature of disaster. The Pareto-optimal trade-off between different parameters is being discovered. The parameters being observed can be varied such as hospital resource level (consumable such as drug and medicine; recoverable such as bed and personals). The result is that increasing the number of resources will rapidly reduce the fatalities; however, up on passing some thresholds, the fatalities will not lessen even with more resources available. Still, the system provided an analysis result of civilian behavior on attending the nearby hospital regarding the effectiveness of hospital to admit and release the appropriate number of patient to reduce the most fatalities.

EpiSimS [19, 20] is also another ABS developed to study the optimized parameter of resource and procedures in a simulated SmallPox attack model and influenza outbreak. The analysis result from the simulation is that the rate of death is directly influenced by how quickly the infected patients can isolate themselves from the rest of population (society). Whereas, the study of deploying an official response such as mass evacuation, vaccination and quarantine to control the spread of smallpox is less effective on the rate of death.

From reviews, the proposed crisis simulation systems are aiming to train and study the effective result of deployed procedures during an emergency situation. The agent-based model is a core component to represent a complex and realistic system in the occurring crisis by modeling an agent with corresponding roles such as victim, crisis personal and facilities. The multi-objective optimization search is a common approach to investigate a best trade-off response to reduce the fatality or damage. The test scenario usually model after the large scale crisis occurred in the local region of the project. In this section, we have reviewed some of the proposed system on emergency simulation systems. We will continue discussing the overall of crisis framework in the Sect. 4.

4 Discussion on Crisis Simulation Framework

So far in the available literature, there are several similarities in the development of a crisis simulation framework regarding the preparation stage. The majority of the simulation system aim at representing the real-word knowledge then reproduces the crisis scenario based on historical records for devising a better decision support system and plan; and also to train the crisis personal for any upcoming event for a proper response.

During Real-time crisis situation, simulation framework such as WIPER applies the mobile network GIS information system to provide a realistic and real-time response for decision support simulation. Also for the preparation of study of crisis events by varying the different resource level, system such as PLAN-C can provide an analytical study of improved response on investigating some component of behavior. In addition, a new behavior which is not constrained to be human resemblance can be investigated as to maximize the evaluation function in Robocup Rescue. The similarities is that each simulation system is deployed using the agent-based model framework to simulate the behavior of individual such as victim and crisis personal (e.g. firefighter, doctor) then measure the parameter of objective function such as fatality rate as utility. The algorithm is often based on optimization of the objective function to derive a best trade-off practice of parameters on resource and procedures. The representation of world environment is often in a form of grid of cells such as in SimGenis and PLAN-C but later on the requirement to achieve realistic simulation it was necessary to incorporate GIS information input.

The simulation system can also benefit from deploying a scenario generation procedure. Each type of real-world complex situation requires a large and, sometimes, inaccessible information. In order to prepare and study a generic crisis and disaster situation from small-to-large scale, the procedural generation of scenario is desirable. In training, the procedural generation of scenario is still being an active study area. There are several common techniques on the process: *Seed approach* which blends the human generated sub-scenario with an automated system to append and manipulate the sequence of events for more variability such as SimGen, and is also a distinct method to derive a quality scenario. *Planning*, by using planner to fill in the in-between event from each key constrained events, is also a concrete method for generating consistent scenario since the domain knowledge is being scripted into the available condition of planner actions which also share similar usage in digital story telling system [7]; *Functional-L system*, with a requirement of developing a subsequent set of rule for conducting a scenario, the difficulty may rely on how to identifying rules that would produce a suitable set of scenario with varying result.; and *a generic optimization approach*, algorithms that apply mutation and cross-over to the human generated sub-key events to obtaining a unique scenario result based on the specific given parameter and learner model as fitness evaluation function.

Although, there is no distinct best solution on how to generate crisis scenarios, there are desirable components that the automated generation system should provide: (1) To allow scenario generation to operate with different simulation platform using a general data representation such as XML; (2) To incorporate an external simulation model knowledge such as fire, flood, epidemic and weather (e.g. tornado and earthquake); (3) To generate the scenario based on GIS vector information which would be sufficient to represent the environment of complex real-world problem; and (4) To allow interaction with user during a generation process and provide accurate desirable result during generation and evaluation of scenario.

While there are different techniques in generation of scenario and simulating of crisis situation, there is not much novel solution to combine both processes and to derive a desirable scenario content which is also being validated in the simulation framework. In next section, we propose a scenario generation framework based on the JADE multi-agent architecture which is aiming to incorporate the scenario generation technique and crisis simulation agent-based model into a unify system.

5   Crisis Scenario Generation System Framework Design

The crisis scenario generation framework is composed of many components. Figure 1 represents a high level architecture of our crisis scenario generation framework. In the following section, we will introduce these components respectively.

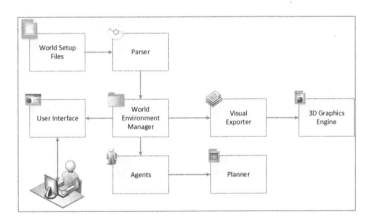

Fig. 1. Crisis scenario generation framework architecture

5.1   Parser Component

Setup information including different scope of scenario world location, available resources, possible set of actions, constraints, possible set of events' description, and related configuration keys. The purpose of this component is to parse the necessary files to initializing the base representation of the system world environment. Moreover, it is possible to create an API for importing a world-setup from different framework. This feature will be revisited in the later stage of development.

5.2   World Environment Manager Component

The world environment manager has the main task to handle the representation of centralized scenario world scene. It is responsible to maintaining the knowledge of the world stage based on any change from agents' actions or event triggering. It also allocates the information regarding the current situation in a scenario to agent manager with planner instance. Moreover, the world environments will coordinate and respond to agent's request for executing an action in the environment. Any conflict from agents' request will be resolved via this module rather than direct negotiation between each agent. In implementation detail, World Environment Manager may be operating as central agent which stores the world environment data structure and allow the execution of an action to manipulate the existing object variables in environment.

The sub-components of world environment manager are described as in the following:

- **World Scene:** The world scene component will hold the list of scenario knowledge and available resources in the current environment state of the world regarding the setup location and being updated by incrementing time steps. It is a central data structure which allows allocating of world stage knowledge into any requested component.
- **Event Manager:** The event manager component utilizes a pool of events with probabilistic model. It fires a sequence of events to conduct the scenario incident, which can be deterministic to representing a cascading effect of specific real-world situation depending on the proper setup files. This component will be directly monitoring the world scene and its incident world event will be allocated with corresponding world-scene information to the requested agent.
- **Time Manager:** This component handles keeping track of the time in the virtual simulation for conveniently synchronizing and calculating the action duration.
- **Action Capability:** All possible agent actions will be stored in this module with their specific precondition to execute such as requester role, available resource condition, and time duration.
- **Statistic and Evaluation Manager**: This component will keep statistic result data regarding each crisis incident in the generated scenario according with its executing plan providing a mean to evaluate the utility from outcome of different plan or decision.
- **Output Generator:** It generates the human readable representation of the current world state for being used in report and interacting with user
- **History Manager:** the history component will keep track of actions requested in each state of the world with meta-data for respective results in the world scene. This component served as an optional module to load/rollback the specific checkpoint of the world state which will contribute into framework novelty later on.
- **Conflict Manager:** The conflict resolver component will have an authority in resolving the conflict between agents' request. Currently, every action is not generated as a partial-order plan so there is likely to have no conflict. However, the necessity to have a dedicated component will become handy in extending the feature of framework.

5.3   User Interface

Current world information sent from the world manager output module will be displayed in this user interface component. User can observe the development of generating scenario step-by-step in a sequence of narrative log text. However, the current design does not focus on visualizing the virtual environment to the user via this channel directly. User may use this component to configure the option of the scenario setup before starting the actual simulation and also assign a preference choice for agent decision making if applicable.

5.4   Agent Component

The framework will elaborate the world scene and scenario by applying a multi-agent framework solution as each agent represents an actor in the scenario. In general, crisis management situation normally includes different tiers of decision making chain of command and, sometimes, crisis scenario can be represented in according to different scope of scenes whether a city-area event or in-a-building floor layout scene.

To address this model, agents may be allocated into separated level of abstract representation which can be defined as crisis manager, crisis facility/station, and crisis personal team. The hierarchy in chain of command will be deployed from manager to personal tier respectively. A simplify assumption will be made to indicate an actual sequence of agents' behavior, which greatly reduces system complexity.

The representation of agents' type is described as in the following:

- **Decision Making Agent (DMA):** This agent acts as a high-level decision making unit, crisis manager. In general, the decision-making agent, crisis manager, will be equipped with an instance of planner to generate plans according to the given world state and event notified from world environment manager. While using utility function preference, High-level plan will focus on allocation of resource, task assignment, optimization then being sent to control agents.
- **Control Agents (CA):** Control agent represents a facility unit, crisis facility. Being allocated the resource and task from DMA, this unit may evaluate resources with the given task in the case that the additional resource is required. If applicable, CA instantiate a field agent unit with setup of necessary resources and task.
- **Field Agents (FA):** This agent represents personal teams with resources. FA will perform direct request to execute an action with a world environment manager component.

Both CA and FA will use planner instance to perform planning with different level of scope from DMA, which focuses on essential actions that allow them to solve the given task. In addition, the agents will not directly negotiate between each other but directly report the result of current active action and its success or failure to the higher-tier agent then wait for further instruction. This allow the decision making agent to clearly monitor the assigned action's outcome. If there is a failure in the assigned action, it can evaluate the current situation and apply replanning algorithm if applicable.

Agents will be developed on top of JADE, multi-agent framework using standard agent communication language, ACL [21]. This technology will provide ease of message transferring and scalability as agents can be host on different machines on a distributed system.

5.5 Planner

Planner component allows the generation a plan consisting of sequence actions related to a given world state, allocated resources, and possible actions. This world information must be preprocessed into PDDL format then being stored in the local KBS of the Planner. The external planner instance will be deployed as in the current state to fasten the development of framework. We currently select a planner using forward chaining state space search to reach a goal with heuristic function, FF_Metric [22]. The constraint in resources, agent's actions, and goal's condition will be defined and solved as a constraint satisfaction solution [23].

It is important to note that there is no permanent decision on selecting a planner which can be revised in later stage. In the future work, this component may be designed with new algorithms providing better flexibility in creating a crisis plan with PDDL4 J Library. Monitoring algorithm and replanning algorithm are currently designed to handle execution of plan list resulted from a planner in general. Further design will include time duration boundary variable to provide more realistic replanning approach with dynamic and changing real-world situation. Figure 2 depicts the planner architecture.

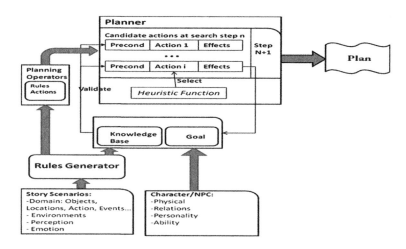

Fig. 2. Planner architecture

5.6 Visual Exporter

This component will be used for the frameworks with external graphics engine. The information of world representation must be formatted into a common data extension such as XML or COLLADA, which can be efficiently parsed for visualizing purpose later on. In the early state of current design, exporting data should contain a data structure representing each simulation step of world scene state. In future extension, the framework may import a world data then generate an incident event scenario with a sequence of solution plan. This information may be exported into game engine to use as a sequence of event simulation rather than one-time step of world scene.

5.7   3D Graphics Engine

This component aims to demonstrate how the frameworks can connect to external 3D graphics engines such as Unity3D and other similar engines. The crisis scenario simulation will be represented as 2D or 3D visual data in which the graphics representation of each element can be mapped from exported data of the world scene. This component is currently an optional extension upon completing the final implementation. Directly establish a socket communication with the 3D engine may be tested for real-time performance evaluation.

6   Framework Scalability Evaluation

Currently, the proposed framework is in an initial development stage, the core components involving world environment, agents, and planning have been implemented. We summarized an evaluation in this section.

To test a performance and scalability, we proposed increasing number of active agents in the system while measured a total duration to solve the given scenario tasks and a plan generation time For Testing scenario, we implemented a basic firefighter domain which describe fire situation where a world object is set *on-fire*. There are 4 basic operations which are *move-to*, *pick-up-a-supply*, *extinguish-a-fire* and *rest* while there are only one type of actor and facility, fireman and firestation.

The number of agents are instantiated with a scene of fixed size world objects in a single event. The time reported are run in a Laptop with Core i7-5500U @2.40 GHz, 2 Cores with RAM 16 GB (10 GB Available), and Window 10.

Our result are illustrated in Fig. 3. We test initially with single agent and then 2, 5, 10, 20, 30, 50, 100 respective in simultaneous instantiation to solve a world-event problem with 20 *on-fire* objects.

The result indicates that increasing the number of agents will require more time due to the fact that they generated more collision in action execution in the environment such as trying to execute an action on the same object. Only one agent will success while another fails triggering replanning process. This situation may lead to studying of opportunistic competition between each agent and invention of more efficient planning and replanning algorithm for multi-agent system.

Currently, the evaluation is based on a single machine rather than hosting an agent on different machines communicated on JADE environment which could improve stability and reduce execution time in larger world setup.

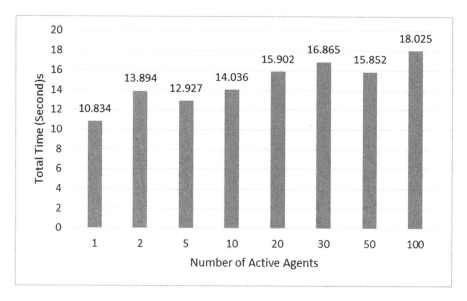

Fig. 3. Computation time of simultaneously solving a world event

The re-evaluation will perform after the implementation of command-tier agent such as fire station to simulate resource management environment in future version.

7   Conclusion

In this paper, we discuss a review on existing work regarding automated scenario generation technique and related crisis simulation framework then present a design of crisis scenario simulation framework developed on top of open multi-agent framework such as JADE to provide a new solution incorporating techniques based on planning in both area. This approach has a potential to provide a large variety of study and test environment to validate theory and plan in different situation on across domain especially crisis management. Further, it will allow the evaluation of trade-off between each decision on different perspective as stated in separated tiers of agent. While in regarding the scalability problem for simulation, the multi-agent framework enables a larger scale of computation with connecting more platforms as a container to the environment;

In the future work, we will continue the implementation of base simulation framework and provide more evaluation on result of different scenario setup with different tiers of agent. We will also develop an automated scenario generation on top of the simulation framework to validate and provide diversity of representation of crisis scenario.

References

1. Walker, W.E., Giddings, J., Armstrong, S.: Training and learning for crisis management using a virtual simulation/gaming environment. Cogn. Technol. Work **13**(3), 163–173 (2011)
2. Zyda, M.: From visual simulation to virtual reality to games. Computer **38**(9), 25–32 (2005)
3. Hullett, K., Mateas, M.: Scenario generation for emergency rescue training games. In: 4th International Conference on Foundations of Digital Games - FDG 2009 (2009)
4. Grois, E., Hsu, W.H., Voloshin, M., Wilkins, D.C.: Bayesian network models for generation of crisis management training scenarios. In: AAAI/IAAI, pp. 1113–1120 (1998)
5. Martin, G., Schatz, S., Bowers, C., Hughes, C., Fowlkes, J., Nicholson, D.: Automatic scenario generation through procedural modeling for scenario-based training. Hum. Factors Ergon. Soc. Annu. Meet. **53**, 1949–1953 (2009)
6. Zook, A., Riedl, M.O., Holden, H.K., Sottilare, R.A., Brawner, K.W.: Automated scenario generation: toward tailored and optimized military training in virtual environments. In: 7th International Conference on the Foundations of Digital Games (2012)
7. Porteous, J., Cavazza, M., Charles, F.: Applying planning to interactive storytelling: narrative control using state constraints. ACM Trans. Intell. Syst. Technol. **1**(2), 10 (2010)
8. Ören, T., Longo, F.: Emergence, anticipation and multisimulation: bases for conflict simulation. In: 20th European Modeling and Simulation Symposium (EMSS), pp. 546–555 (2008)
9. Wooldridge, M., Jennings, N.R.: Intelligent agents: theory and practice. Knowl. Eng. Rev. **10**(2), 115–152 (1995)
10. Challenger, R., Clegg, C.W., Robinson, M.A.: Understanding crowd behaviours: Simulation tools. U.K. Cabinet Office (2009)
11. Metello, M.G., Casanova, M.A., de Carvalho, M.T.M.: Using serious game techniques to simulate emergency situations. In: GeoInfo, pp. 121–182 (2008)
12. Schoenharl, T., Madey, G.: Design and implementation of agent-based simulation for emergency response and crisis management. J. Algorithms Comput. Technol. **5**, 4 (2011)
13. Saoud, N.B.B., Mena, T.B., Dugdale, J., Pavard, B., Ahmed, M.B.: Assessing large scale emergency rescue plans: an agent based approach. Int. J. Intell. Control Syst. **11**(4), 260–271 (2006)
14. Takeuchi, I.: A massively multi-agent simulation system for disaster mitigation. In: Ishida, T., Gasser, L., Nakashima, H. (eds.) MMAS 2005. LNCS (LNAI), vol. 3446, pp. 269–282. Springer, Heidelberg (2005)
15. Siddhartha, H., Sarika, R., Karlapalem, K.: Score vector: a new evaluation scheme for RoboCup Rescue simulation competition (2009)
16. Boucher, A., Canal, R., Chu, T., Drogoul, A., Gaudou, B., Le, V., Moraru, V., Van Nguyen, N., Vu, Q., Taillandier, P.: The AROUND project: adapting robotic disaster response to developing countries. In: IEEE Workshop on Safety, Security and Rescue Robotics, pp. 1–6, Washington, D.C. (2009)
17. Mysore, V., Narzisi, G., Mishra, B.: Agent modeling of a sarin attack in manhattan. In: First International Workshop on Agent Technology for Disaster Management, pp. 108–115 (2006)
18. Narzisi, G., Mysore, V., Mishra, B.: Multi-objective evolutionary optimization of agent-based models: an application to emergency response planning. In: Computational Intelligence, pp. 228–232 (2006)
19. Barrett, C.L., Eubank, S.G., Smith, J.P.: If smallpox strikes portland. Sci. Am. J. **292**(3), 54–61 (2005)

20. Mniszewski, S.M., Del Valle, S.Y., Stroud, P.D., Riese, J.M., Sydoriak, S.J.: EpiSimS simulation of a multi-component strategy for pandemic influenza. In: Proceedings of the 2008 Spring Simulation Multiconference, pp. 556–563 (2008)
21. FIPA Agent Communication Language (ACL) Specification. http://www.fipa.org/repository/aclspecs.html. Accessed 31 Jan 2016
22. Hoffmann, J.: The Metric-FF planning system: translating "ignoring delete lists" to numeric state variables. J. Artif. Intell. Res. 291–341 (2003)
23. Yokoo, M.: Constraint satisfaction problem. Distributed Constraint Satisfaction, pp. 1–45. Springer, Heidelberg (2001)

A Study of the Teaching Methods in the Course of the Programming of High-Level Language Based on Moodle Platform

Chun-Bo Bao[✉]

Faculty of Software Engineering, Fujian University of Technology,
Fuzhou, China
26865614@qq.com

Abstract. Programming of High-Level Language course is an important basic course for computer science and its related subjects; And Moodle [1, 2] is a well-known e-learning platform. This paper presents a teaching mode of programming based on Moodle platform. The method emphasizes problem inspiration and focus on the process of solving problems by using computer, during which the thinking methods, basic knowledge and skills were explored completely. Meanwhile, it also provides a scene of autonomic learning by means of Moodle platform which integrated the online judge, online test and other matched resources. Teaching practice shows the methods could stimulate the programming interests and motivate the learning enthusiasm. It is a very effective method.

Keywords: Moodle platform · Autonomic learning · Programming · Online judge · Problem-driven

1 Introductions

1.1 The Importance of Programming Course

Programming of High-Level Language (PHLL)is a core course of computer science and its related subjects in university. Generally it is the first course for undergraduate students in first semester, just as the CS50 [3], "Introduction to Computer Science", in Harford University; and the 6.00 [4], "Introduction to Computer Science and Programming", in MIT. For most undergraduate universities or the application- oriented colleges. The significance of PHLL course can be presented from the following four key aspects:

- It is the entrance to the computer industry and the enlightenment for computer science.
- It is the foundation of other major courses. If this course is not mastered, other major computer courses would never be understood thoroughly.
- It is well known that people in any industry should have some kind of basic skills. Therefore, for the students in computer industry, it is imperative to sharpen their basic skills in the PHLL course.
- As a Chinese saying goes, "interest is best teacher". So the PHLL course is also aimed at arousing students' interests in computer science.

© Springer International Publishing Switzerland 2016
A. El Rhalibi et al. (Eds.): Edutainment 2016, LNCS 9654, pp. 101–110, 2016.
DOI: 10.1007/978-3-319-40259-8_9

1.2   Traditional Teaching and Learning Methods

Traditionally the PHLL course is the center of classroom teaching. Focusing on syntactic phenomena, the lecture materials often consist of the basic syntax of programming and simple examples. In the classroom, students usually study passively and only use paper and pens to finish their homework. Generally, the homework consists of the choice question, the true or false question and few programming problems. Although student can get the higher score in the test, it can't deal with a real problem successfully, which is so called "high scores and low abilities".

1.3   Moodle Platform

Moodle [1, 2] is a well-known e-learning platform in tertiary institutions. Many universities and colleges use Moodle as the online learning system in their daily teaching and learning. Moodle is free open source software which means developer can make modification based on their needs. Moodle includes a lot of modules, such as online test, homework etc. It supports the flexible plug-in mechanisms. The plugging related with the programming is the online judge and the anti-plagiarism.

Moodle platform was developed based on the social constructionist learning theory, which emphasizes that learners (and not just teachers) can contribute to the educational experience. The constructionist learning theory thinks that the learning is a procedure of the meaning construction in some kind of scene by the collaboration human to human (including teacher and learning partner). So "the Scene", "Collaboration", "Conversation" and "Sense Making" are four crucial factors about learning environment [5]. Using these pedagogical principles, Moodle provides an autonomic learning environment, which is different from the traditional process of passively acquiring knowledge.

Constructionist learning involves students drawing their own conclusions through creative experimentation and the making of social objects. The constructionist teacher takes on a mediational role rather than adopting an instructional role. Teaching "at" students is replaced by assisting them to understand—and help one another to understand—problems in a hands-on way [6].

2   Methods

In our teaching practice of PHLL, we have implemented the four key points (see Sect. 1.1) based on Moodle platform. The framework of our method is described in Fig. 1. The details are given as below:

2.1   Objectives

Our PHLL course is forged all-directional and three dimensions stereo, which is aimed at cultivating the ability of analyzing and solving concrete problems, to train the professional skills/techniques in computer industry, to stimulate interests in computer

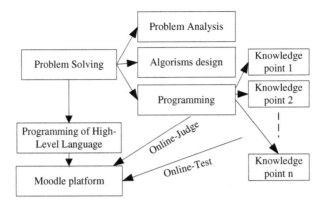

Fig. 1. Programming based on Moodle platform

learning and a sense of achievements that would help students build up their self-confidence. All of these could not be achieved by traditional methods. Therefore, we present this kind of method based on the Moodle platform. In this method, e-learning is combined with the class-room teaching. We want to build up a mechanism that makes student autonomic learning effective.

2.2 Problems-Driven

Our PHLL course is to solve problems. Methods and knowledge of programming, and skills of the designing program will be infiltrated into the solving procedure. So, we have designed elaborately more than 40 problems [4] from simple to some complicated. For examples, there are 6 problems included in Chap. 2, as shown below in Table 1.

Table 1. The problems in Chap. 2

Section	Problem name	Related knowledge points
2.1	Print information	Main function, comment, stand output, preprocessing, escape sequence
2.2	Sum and multiply for two fixed integer	Integer data type, variables and constant, arithmetic operation and expressions
2.3	Sum and multiply for two arbitrary integer	Standard input, test case, sequential structure
2.4	Calculate average	Float data type, transform between different data types
2.5	Temperature Transform	Initialization for variables, priority and associativity for operator
2.6	Area and perimeter	Symbolic constant

Every problem consists of the description and the sample case of input and output. We always solve a problem in the following steps. But before beginning, we will divide the students into 4 or 6 groups. Every group will contain 10 or 15 members. Teacher prior assigns a preparing duty related with solving problem to every group. We begin and perform our lessons through the form of lecturing and discussing.

- Problem analysis. This step is very important. It is a procedure of exploring answers. There might be multiple ways or schemes to solve a problem. So teachers should lead students to ponder as often as possible, which would gradually cultivate their computational thinking and raise their ability of analyze and solve problem. Notably, the students will be host in the procedure in the class. Teacher only plays the role of managing and guiding students.
- Algorism design. Every solving schemes, has corresponding an algorism. The algorism form may be a kind of pseudo code or a type of flow diagram. This step is aimed at training the abilities of abstract thinking by the algorism expressing, and the flow diagram drawing.
- Algorism implementation. This step is also called coding or programming. Here only notice the functional modules in the program, not concern the details of the modules.
- Running and testing. In this step, we'll compile and link the program to generate an executable application program firstly. Then we run the program respectively through the several input test case, checking whether the output result is what we want. This step aims at training the ability of the debugging.
- Knowledge points. In this step, discuss some related syntax in the solving program. This step is very distinctive because here only discuss the related knowledge point, which is different from others. Although every knowledge point seems to be alone but all knowledge points in different solving programs are dependable and present evolutionary and spiral.

2.3   Online Judge and Test

To realize our objectives of the PHLL course, another part of our method is the online judge based on Moodle platform. We designed more than 100 exercises [5] for online judge homework. This kind of homework has features as follows.

- Student can do his/her homework in any place as long as there is internet.
- Using e-learning environment instead of pen and paper, the operating ability of students can be trained very well.
- When a program is submitted to Online Judge platform, the program is judged automatically and the right or wrong will be presented immediately. So the student is happy and has a sense of achievement when he/she solved a problem or submitting program take on "Accept" status. Even if there were any errors, he/she would also check it carefully, which is necessary for the students of learning computer.

In Moodle platform, there are also other functions to meet the student automatic learning such as online test, various resources of course, interactive tool (blogs, message board) between teacher and student or student and student, and so on.

The Online Test is specially used to examine the basic concept of programming through the objective questions. The teacher will set up a test corresponding with the every chapter. Students proceed with their test by their own.

The Moodle platform also possesses abundant statistic-estimate functions. It can track the all activities of the students. Teachers can know every student according to the information and statistics provided by the Moodle platform.

2.4   Course Resources

We have brought out the publications – "Problem Solving and Programming" [7] and "Answers and Training Guide" [8] in Tsinghua University Press of China. The former is main textbook, another one is supplementary textbook. They are an important component of our PHLL course based on Moodle platform [9]. The publication, "Problem Solving and Programming", consists of 10 chapters as shown in Table 2.

Table 2. The contents of the main textbook

Chapter	Name	Time(hour)
1	Computer and Programming	2
2	Data Type and Variables – Introduction of Programming	4
3	Judgment and Decision – Selections Programming	4
4	Repeat and Iteration – Loop Programming	6
5	Divide and Conquer – Modular Programming	6
6	Data Batching – Array Programming	6
7	Address of Memory Unit – Pointer Programming	6
8	Object Prescription – Structure Programming	4
9	Data Permanent Storage – File Programming	4
10	Bit Operation – Low Levels Programming	2

The matched publication, "Answers and Training guide", comprises of 5 parts as shown in Table 3.

Table 3. The contents of the assist textbook

Part	Name
1	Solutions for Problem Set
2	Experiment Guide
3	Experiment Problem Set
4	Solutions of Experiment
5	Course Practice

These publications cannot be separated from the Moodle platform. They complement each other.

2.5   Teaching Case

Here we only take a problem in Sect. 3.3 of the main textbook [7] as the example of introducing our teaching methods. We will have a class teaching and learning through 90 min.

Problem description: Write a program which can divide the students into different groups through their grades. When you run the program, it asks you to input a grade one by one, it would answer with a comment and group name for every grade. Meantime a corresponding counter will add 1 automatically. When you want to finish the running, you just input Ctrl-Z, then it will output the statistics results. The grade ranges are "≥90, 80~90, 70~80, 60~70, <60"; The comments are "Good, Better, Middle, Pass, Fail"; And the group names are "A, B, C, D, F".

Input sample case: 45 55 77 88 99 98 78 67 Ctrl-Z

Output sample case: Fail F Fail F Middle C Better B Good A Good A Middle C Pass D

$$\text{aNum} = 2 \text{ bNum} = 1 \text{ cNum} = 2 \text{ dNum} = 1 \text{ fNum} = 2$$

Prior prepare: Teacher assigns the different duty to 4 groups and prompts students to review the learned knowledge points and methods. Teacher guides 3 groups using the single branch or double branch structure and 1 group use new method, multi-branch structure to solve this problem.

Analysis and design: In the class, the 4 students on behalf of their groups show their solutions in proper order respectively, and accompany the discussions.

The first solution shows the nested structure, which only use single branch choice structure to describe the judgment of falling in between two scores, such as more than or equal to 80 but less than 90. There is a sequential nested structure between the different judging ranges, as shown in the solution 1 in Fig. 2.

The second solution also shows the nested structure, but it is nested double branch choice structure. Whole solution only has one nested structure but it is a multi- levels nested structure, as shown in the solution 2 in Fig. 3.

The third solution is an optimized version for solution 2 as shown in solution 3 in Fig. 4. As we know, the score of a test should comply with normal distribution. In solution 2, there is a shortage. If one score is less than 60, the times of judgment will be 4. Then If one score is more than 90, the times of judgment will be 1. So if you could improve the sequence of judgment according to normal distribution, the times of judgment will decrease greatly.

All the above three solutions utilize the old knowledge sufficiently. But the fourth solution adopts a new scheme which is called multi-branch choices structure. In fact, it translates a score into an integer number first, then the program according the integer number goes through the adapted branch, as shown in the solution 4 in Fig. 5.

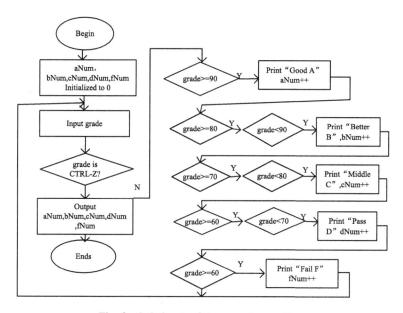

Fig. 2. Solution 1 of the grouping problem

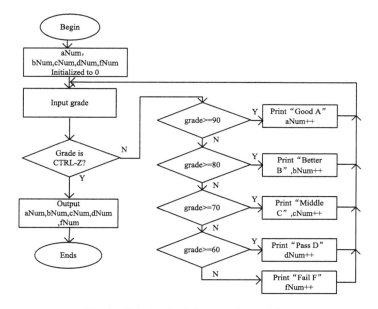

Fig. 3. Solution 2 of the grouping problem

Coding and Running: After a student shows his/her solution, he/she will show the implement codes. Here the teacher prompts and guides students to check program only through the module structure. Then running and testing the program, to verify the correctness through the given test cases. Input a group of scores and check the feedback information and statistic results.

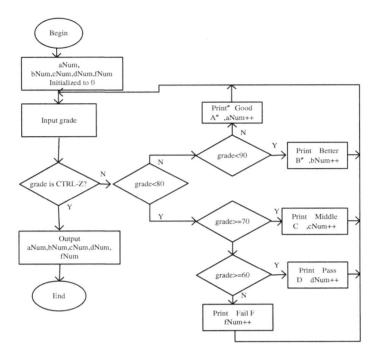

Fig. 4. Solution 3 of the grouping problem

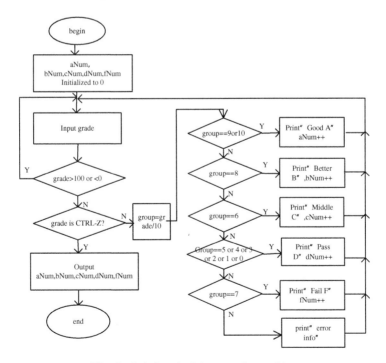

Fig. 5. Solution 4 of the grouping problem

Table 4. 2014 ACM freshman contest contrast

Method	Participating numbers	Finals numbers	%
New	90	18	20
Old	240	19	8

Table 5. 2015 ACM freshman contest contrast

Method	Participating numbers	Finals numbers	%
New	60	7	11.7
Other	60	3	5

Knowledge point: Here the teacher emphatically introduces the nested structure and lectures the details about the switch-case choice structure.

Home works: Lastly, the teacher will assign some autonomic learning materials, as below:

- Related online-judge problems
- Related online-test problems
- Assign autonomic learning duty to every group for next time.

3   Conclusions and Discussions

For recent years, we have made a comparison in two aspects. One is that the new method presented in this paper is compared with the traditional old method. Annually, our university holds the ACM contest of freshman. In 2014, participating object included 3 classes(90 students)they are trained by the new method and 8 classes (240 students) they are taught in old method. The result entered the final is shown as Table 4.

Another comparison is that 2 classes (60 students) they are trained in our method with another 2 classes (60 students) who are taught by other method but their using our textbooks. Similarly they are all take part in the 2015 ACM contest of freshman. The result entered the final is shown as Table 5.

The result shows the new method presented in this paper is superior to the old or other method in ACM clearly. Moreover the new method presented in this paper is superior to the old or other method in many aspects same clearly, such as the abilities of the analysis problem, the algorithm design, the team collaboration, the program debugging and the document writing, etc.

Certainly there are some students that could not adapt to this method because of their laziness or could not overcome the difficulty. The reason also may be their base is poor. So we must modify or enhance this method to meet the need of more students, to make more students adapt to the e-learning environment. Our problem is to make every student get better ability of programming. That is individualized teaching on e-learning. We are appending more e-learning materials such as short video, e-lecture, animation, interest story and so on for a given knowledge points except the online judging, online test, online problems set. I think the good future of this method is waiting ours, let us keep trying!

Acknowledgments. This work was supported by the Scientific Research Funds of Fujian University of Technology (E0600077).

References

1. https://moodle.org/
2. https://en.wikipedia.org/wiki/Moodle
3. http://open.163.com/movie/2010/6/D/6/M6TCSIN1U_M6TCSTQD6.html
4. http://open.163.com/special/opencourse/bianchengdaolun.html
5. http://baike.baidu.com/view/79065.htm
6. https://en.wikipedia.org/wiki/Constructionism_(learning_theory)
7. Bao, C.-B., Lin, F., Xie, L.-C.: Problem Solving and Programming. Tsinghua University Press, Beijing (2015)
8. Bao, C.-B., Lin, F., Xie, L.-C.: The Solutions and Training Guide for the Problem Solving and Programming. Tsinghua University Press, Beijing (2015)
9. http://cms.fjut.edu.cn/

Exploring Olfaction for Enhancing Multisensory and Emotional Game Experience

Lekai Zhang[1], Shouqian Sun[1], Baixi Xing[2(✉)], Jiaqi Fu[1], and Shixian Yu[3]

[1] College of Computer Science and Technology, Zhejiang University,
Hangzhou 310027, China
{zlkzhang,ssq,fujiaqi}@zju.edu.cn
[2] School of Computer Science and Technology, Hangzhou Dianzi University,
Hangzhou 310018, China
sisyxing@gmail.com
[3] Department of Psychology and Behavioral Sciences, Zhejiang University,
Hangzhou 310027, China
donnaysx@zju.edu.cn

Abstract. In recent years, an increasing amount of game players attribute importance to the perceived value of games, such as positive experiences and emotions, rather than functions in games. In contrast to the game itself, user experience is gradually becoming the main focus in the design of computer games. Therefore, a successful game should have a high perceived value and the capability of evoking positive emotions and experiences within the players through the five human senses. However, current games mainly depend on the visual, auditory and tactile experience, olfactory experience is very scarce. In order to explore the possibilities that the intervention of the sense of smell could enhance pleasantness experience of playing games. This study choose the Chinese folk music which is commonly used in Chinese games as background music, and some common odors as experimental stimuli. Three experiments were conducted. The first two experiments were used to classify the music clips and odors separately according to the evoked emotions. Results showed that most odors and music clips had a high effect on the arousal of emotion. The third experiment was used to verify whether congruent odors could increase the pleasantness of music significantly more than incongruent odors. Results showed that music-odor congruency played a key role in perceiving pleasantness of music. Congruent odor can increase pleasant perception of music while incongruent odor can decrease pleasant perception of music. These findings could be important not only for the theoretical understanding of multisensory and emotional feedback in game experience, but also for the optimization of game design.

Keywords: Olfaction · Chinese folk music · Emotion · Valence-arousal model · Pleasantness of game

1 Introduction

In recent years, an increasing demand for multi-modal systems and applications that are with multi-sensory has led to increased research interest in this area,

© Springer International Publishing Switzerland 2016
A. El Rhalibi et al. (Eds.): Edutainment 2016, LNCS 9654, pp. 111–121, 2016.
DOI: 10.1007/978-3-319-40259-8_10

especially in the field of video games. Therefore, purchasing decisions do not only depend on a product's usefulness and efficiency, but also closely relate to the perceived quality which attempts to provide positive experiences and emotions through the five human senses [1,2]. Schifferstein and Spence underlined the roles of the various senses and their interplay when people interact with different products [3]. In addition, emotions played a significant role in the mental process of decision making [4]. Thus a successful video game could evoke players' positive emotions and experiences through five human senses [5].

It is well known that current games mainly depend on the visual, auditory and tactile experience, olfactory experience is very scarce. However, several studies suggested that odors could enrich the user experience and perception of a multimedia application [6–8]. In addition, several cross-modal associations have been investigated by researchers between auditory sense and olfaction [9]. For example, Belkin et al. studied that pitch of an auditory tone could be matched with a stimulus odor [10]. Crisinel and Spence suggested that specific odors could be consistently matched to auditory musical notes [11]. Therefore, this study would explore the possibilities that the intervention of the sense of smell could enhance pleasantness experience of playing games. Because the background music of considerable Chinese games such as Fantasy Westward Journey and The Legend of Sword and Fairy are Chinese folk music, this research would study the association between Chinese folk music and odors by their emotion feature to explore whether olfaction could improve the happiness of music, thus enhancing the pleasantness of game experience.

However, researchers always paired music and odor in a semantic way, for example, Seo et al. paired Christmas carol and cinnamon, coffee and the sound of coffee advertisement [12]. Deroy et al. studied the associations between odors and contingent sensory features, namely odors, musical notes, and geometrical shapes [13]. It is difficult to relate music to one odor in a semantic way, so we can only choose many common odors to match the music in a emotional way. There are two widely used and dominant models for the description of emotions: the discrete categories and the dimensional model, for example, Ekman and Friesen proposed six basic discrete emotions [14], and Russell put forward a valence-arousal scale to describe emotions [15]. In this study, we employ Russells model for the evaluation of emotions. Through this method, emotions are evaluated in two dimensions: valence and arousal. Valence indicates whether an emotion (an experience, an event, etc.) is positive or negative to one person, and arousal indicates how strong this feeling is to one person. So each emotion can be located in the valence-arousal map to indicate its effect directly. This map is divided into 4 quadrants, and different emotions are placed on the plane in such a way that each emotion can be represented by a 2×1 vector.

In this study, we firstly classified music and odor using the scores on the valence-arousal coordinates. Next, we paired music and odor by their locations in the valence-arousal map. Finally, we conducted a music-odor perception matching experiment to test if the paired method was valid and if odor could influence the people's perception of music. Our findings revealed that music-odor congruency played a key role in perceiving pleasantness of music. Congruent odor could increase pleasantness of music, while incongruent odor could decrease pleasantness of music. These findings suggest that the intervention of the sense of smell could enhance pleasantness experience of playing games.

2   Experiment

This study is aimed at classifying Chinese folk music and odors by perceived emotions reported by participants, and to determine the interaction between music and odors (see Fig. 1).

Fig. 1. Music-Odor perception matching experiment: participants listened to the music clip while holding and smelling the matched odor or unmatched odor.

In this study, our experiment was divided into two parts:

In the first part, music clips and odors were separately classified according to the evoked emotions. Considering that the emotions evoked by odors are not so easy for evaluation or quantification, and ambiguous for its strong relation to individual preference, here we applied V/A model to evaluate emotions of music or odors. Through this way, music or odors were sorted by valence and arousal of the emotions they evoked.

In the second part, we planned to explore the relationship between odors and music. We believed that the perceived emotion can be influenced by the information input through other sensory channels. Thus we presumed that congruent odors could increase pleasantness of music significantly more than incongruent odors. If one perceived odors which conveyed the same emotion of the music he/she was listening to, the degree of the feeling perceived from the music would be enhanced, otherwise it would be reduced. The matching score could reflect the validity of the model when applied it to odors to some extant. So we reorganized experiment materials based on the results of our previous study (the method will be described concretely below) and used a 7-points Likert scale ranging from 1 (extremely unpleasant, absolutely mismatching) to 7 (extremely pleasant, absolutely matching) for subjective evaluation. Finally, we interviewed each participant to know more about detailed information during their evaluation process.

2.1 Music/Odor Emotion Classification Experiment

Participants. Twenty participants (9 females and 11 males) aged from 21 to 29 took part in music classification task and 15 participants (8 females and 7 males) aged from 20 to 30 took part in odor classification task. All of the participants were recruited from Zhejiang University, China. Participants olfactory or auditory dysfunction were assessed by asking them whether they had a history of disease about olfactory or auditory. Participants who declared no impairment on hearing or smelling were admitted to this study.

Auditory and Olfactory Stimuli. Regarding auditory stimuli, we applied Marsyas as the feature extraction tool [16]. According to Marsyas framework, we cut out 125 music clips from our Chinese folk music database [17,18], which were all instrument music to avoid the text content emotional influence. In the preliminary experiment, a period of 10 s of a key melody was extracted from the song to create the music clip. The extracted clip was .wav format with sampling rate of 16KHZ, which reserved most of the music information to insure a good listening experience. The process of music library building work is demonstrated as follows:

- Find a collection of 200 Chinese folk songs from internet and 40 albums, which included folk songs from different regions in China. A period of 10 s of music clip was extracted from the song. Thus 200 music clips were collected.
- Select 125 music clips from the collection of 200 clips by music experts. They voted to have the conclusion that each clip of song had the dominant emotion feature, if the emotion was hard to define, it would be discarded to avoid confusion in the following experiment. The extracted clip was stored and converted into .wav format, the sampling rate of 16 kHz, which reserves most of the music information.
- Build the music library.
  Regarding olfactory stimuli, it was hard to select, as we did not have a basic set of smell stimuli. The odors in the experiment were the result of an intense brainstorming process by four food major students. We would try to ensure that these odors could evoke different emotions that could be classified into four quadrants. The process of olfactory stimuli library building work is shown as follows:
- Find a collection of 30 odors from essences, perfumes and real objects which could evoke different emotions.
- For essence, we diluted it with water in a ratio of 5 % and sprayed it on fragrance blotter. For perfume, we sprayed it on fragrance blotter directly. They were placed in a 100 ml reagent bottles. In order to keep the accuracy of the sense of odors, we selected 20 odors from the collection.

Twenty odors were odor of tea, garlic, foeniculum vulgare, burnt smell, coffee bean, smoke, mildew, cream, almond, lemon, grass, menthocamphorate, rodent repellent, sandalwood, watermelon lollipop, lavender, soil, whiskey, roasted sweet potato and mothball. Odors were exuded by the 5 % diluted essence (garlic, foeniculum vulgare, burnt smell, Cream, Almond, rodent repellent, roasted sweet potato, Meilaixiang), selected perfume (mildew, grass, sandalwood, watermelon lollipop, lavender, soil, Scent Library) and the real objects (tea, coffee bean, lemon, menthocamphorate, whiskey, mothball).

Procedure. Experimental procedure was explained at the beginning, and an informed consent was signed before the experiment.

Participants who took part in the music classification task were required to listen to 125 music clips. They were arranged in separate cubic in a silent environment with no interruption. At the start of the session, the volunteers wore the headphone and set the music to the same degree of sound volume, the DB level was 60 and the head-phones were selected to be the same type to ensure the same sound effect. Experimenter played the music at random and participants were asked to do the emotion labeling work on the clips immediately in 1 to 10 scale for both arousal and valence dimensions according to their listening experience after listening session. Participants had a 2 min' break every 5 min.

In the odor classification task, participants were required to smell 20 different kinds of odors and then scored it. Experimenter played the bottle of odor at random and participants were asked to rate on the valence-arousal map scale of odor as soon as they finished smelling. They were asked to pick a bottle to smell the odor and then rate the scores on the valence-arousal map immediately in 1 to 10 scale for both arousal and valence dimension according to their smell experience after smelling session. During the evaluation process, since coffee beans was always used to restore sensitive sense of smell in the perfume shop, the participants were required to smell coffee beans to clear the remaining influence of the previous odor. In addition, participants could pause smelling the odor for a rest.

2.2 Music-Odor Perception Matching Experiment

Participants. Eighteen right-handed participants (8 females and 10 males) aged from 21 to 26 years took part in this study. All of the participants were recruited from Zhejiang University. Participants who declared no impairment on hearing or smelling in a selective questionnaire were admitted to this study. Experimental procedure was explained at the beginning, and an informed consent was signed before the experiment.

Auditory and Olfactory Stimuli. We selected 8 clips of music according to the results from prior experiment. All of the participants had high valence and high arousal (in the first quadrant). Furthermore, we divided them into 2 groups, each containing 4 songs. 1 min sound of rain was served as white noise.

Then we selected 8 odors from first (lemon/cream/coffee bean/grass) and second (garlic/burnt smell/mildew/Foeniculum Vulgare) quadrants.

Four different pairs of 2 music groups and 2 odor groups were presented in a within-subject way. The order was counterbalanced between subjects.

Procedure. Each participant would first listen to the 8 clips of Chinese folk music, each lasting 10 s, and then rated their pleasantness on a 7-point Likert scale ranging from 1(extremely unpleasant) to 7(extremely pleasant). Following 1 min white noise, they listened to the music clip while holding and smelling the paired odor. After that, they had to rate the pleasantness of the music as well as indicating the congruency between the music and odor on a 7-point Likert scale ranging from 1(extremely weak) to 7(extremely strong). The whole experiment lasted about 5 min.

There were two experiment conditions: the match condition, in which the odor and music were both rated as high valence and high arousal; the mismatch condition, in which the music was rated as high in both valence and arousal while the odor was rated as having high arousal but low valence. Half of the participants received the matching condition first, the other half of them oppositely. We proposed that exposing to incongruent odor would compromise the people's pleasant perception of music.

3   Results and Discussion

3.1   Results of Music/Odor Emotion Classification Experiment

Results of Classification. After gathering the data from participants, we tried to present it on the coordinate system (valence as the horizontal axis, arousal as the vertical axis). Thus the music clips and odors were divided into four quadrants roughly, then we analyzed their distribution. Here we applied such standard to determine their distribution: if more than 60 % of participants classified one music clips into one same quadrant or more than 50 % participants classified one odor into the same quadrant, this music clip or odor was classified in this category, otherwise it would be removed as the emotion it evoked was too ambiguous. Follow this criterion, 71 music clips were identified in the first quadrant, 18 music clips were identified in the second quadrant, no music clip was identified in the third quadrant, 1 music clip was identified in the fourth quadrant while the others were too ambiguous to identify. What's more, 6 odors (coffee beans, cream, lemon, grass, menthocamphorate and watermelon lollipop) were identified in the first quadrant, 8 odors (garlic, burnt smell, foeniculum vulgare, smoke, mildew, almond, rodent repellent, sandalwood) were identified in the second quadrant, 1 odor (tea) was identified in the fourth quadrant while the other odors (mothball, roasted sweet potato, whiskey, lavender) were too ambiguous to identify.

We can see directly from the Fig. 2 that most music clips from Chinese folk music and odors were classified into the first or second quadrant, which implied that among our experimental materials, most odors and music clips had a high arousal of emotion.

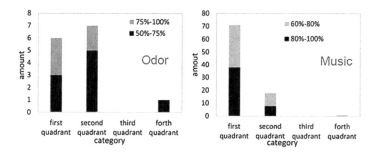

Fig. 2. Distribution of ordor/music clips in different quadrants (x% means x% partic-ipants agreed to classify a music clips or odor into one quadrant).

Materials Selection for Music-Odor Perception Matching Experiment. We selected the materials for further study from the 100 %-agreed music clips (which meant 100 % participants had classified this music clip into the same quadrant, see Fig. 3) in the first quadrant. But due to the number of participants and the number of odors, we chose 50 %-agreed odors (which meant more than 50 % par-ticipants had classified this odor into the same quadrant, see Fig. 4) in the first and second quadrant. In the future, we will expand the sample size to gain a better result.

Based on the data gathered, we selected the music clips and odors for further study. For music, we selected No. 61 and No. 41, No. 64 and No. 51, No. 46 and No. 55, No. 45 and No. 39 (the clips in each pair had a shortest distance between them). For odors, we selected Garlic, Foeniculum Vulgare, Burnt Smell, Mildew (as the mismatch group) and Coffee Bean, Cream, Lemon, Grass (as the match group).

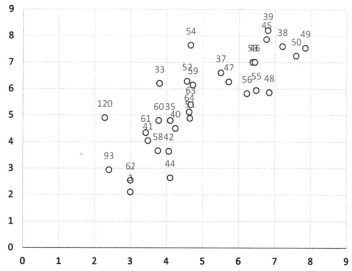

Fig. 3. Valence-arousal map (first quadrant) for 100 %-agreed music clips

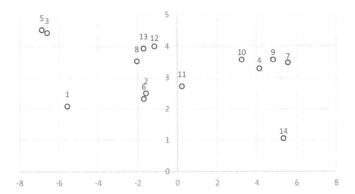

Fig. 4. Valence-arousal map (first and second quadrant) for 50 %-agreed odors (1-Garlic; 2-Foeniculum Vulgare; 3-Burnt Smell; 4-Coffee Bean; 5-Smoke; 6-Mildew; 7-Cream; 8-Almond; 9-Lemon; 10-Grass; 11- Menthocamphorate; 12-Rodent repellent; 13-Sandalwood; 14-Watermelon Lollipop)

3.2   Results of Music-Odor Perception Matching Experiment

Validation of the Paired Method. First, we tested whether paired odor and music using the scores in the valence-arousal coordinate was appropriate. Paired t-tests revealed that participants rated the music and odor in the match condition (4.4± 0.3) as more congruent than those in the mismatch condition ($2.5 \pm 0.3, t_{17} = 6.589, p < .01$) (see Fig. 5). In other words, music and odor, which fell into the same quadrant, were perceived as more congruent than those that did not.

Odor Congruency on Sound Pleasantness. Repeated measures of ANOVA showed a main effect of match condition on rated sound pleasantness $F(1.39, 23.66) = 15.54, p < .01, \eta_p^2 = .48$, computed using Greenhouse-Geisser correction. Pairwise comparison revealed that sound was more pleasant when a congruent odor was present (5.0 ± 0.2) than no smell was present (4.5 ± 0.2), $p < .01$. But an incongruent odor (3.7 ± 0.2) could reduce the pleasantness of a music compared with

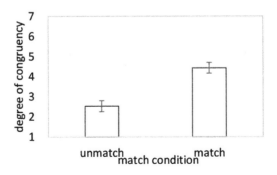

Fig. 5. Degree of congruency in different match conditions ($mean \pm SE$).

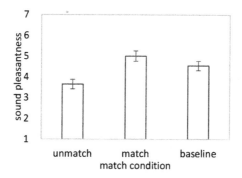

Fig. 6. Mean rated sound pleasantness of different match condition ($mean \pm SE$).

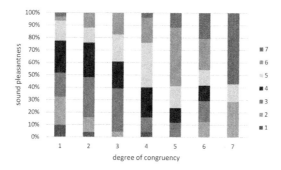

Fig. 7. Correlation between music-odor congruency and sound pleasantness

the baseline condition, $p < .01$ (see Fig. 6), which implied that odor congruency could, to some extent, enhance the pleasantness of a music.

Correlations Between Degree of Congruency and Odor Pleasantness. Pearson correlation analysis showed that a positive relationship existed between degree of congruency and sound pleasantness $r_{144} = 0.42, p < .01$. As shown in Fig. 7, with the congruency between odor and music going up, the music received higher scores in pleasantness.

4   Conclusion

This study conducted three experiments to explore whether congruent odors could increase the pleasantness of music significantly more than incongruent odors. Results shows that scents played a significant role in music perception. Our findings revealed that congruent odor could increase the pleasantness of music, while incongruent odor could decrease the pleasantness of music. The research results can be applied in designing of multi-modal video games through releasing congruent odor to increase players' pleasantness. Furthermore, as a basic research, this research find some odors which can improve the emotional experience of Chinese folk music.

In future studies, we will collect real background music of games and more kinds of odors to explore the relationships between sensory modalities and players' experience of games. In addition, physiological response may be synchronized with brain wave signals and behavior observation methods such as video records to measure players' emotions, through which we can know how users' physiological signals' changes when playing the games.

Acknowledgments. This study is partly supported by the National Natural Science Foundation of China (No. 61303137, 61402141, 61562072), the Department of Science and Technology of Zhejiang Province (No. 2015C31051), the Foundation of Zhejiang Educational Committee (No. Y201430757).

References

1. Prei, T.: Qualitätsorientierte Unternehmensführung. P3-Ingenieurges. für Management und Organisation (2003)
2. Köhler, M., Schmitt, R.: Systematic Consumer Evaluation Measurement for Objectified Integration into the Product Development Process (2012)
3. Schifferstein, H.N.J., Spence, C.: Multisensory Product Experience - Product Experience - 5. Product Experience, pp. 133–161. Wiley, New York (2008)
4. Schmitt, R., Dur, J.V., Diaz-Pineda, J.: Objectifying user attention and emotion evoked by relevant perceived product components. J. Sens. Sens. Syst. **3**(2), 315 (2014)
5. Bordegoni, M., Cugini, U., Ferrise, F.: Multisensory user experience design of consumer products. In: Fukuda, S. (ed.) Emotional Engineering, vol. 2, pp. 219–242. Springer, London (2013)
6. Ghinea, G., Ademoye, O.: A User perspective of olfaction-enhanced mulsemedia. In: Proceedings of International ACM Conference on Management of Emergent Digital EcoSystems, pp. 277–280 (2010)
7. Ademoye, O.A., Ghinea, G.: Information recall task impact in olfaction-enhanced multimedia. ACM Trans. Multimedia Comput. Commun. Appl. **9**(3), 167–186 (2013)
8. Ghinea, G., Ademoye, O.: The sweet smell of success: enhancing multimedia applications with olfaction. ACM Trans. Multimedia Comput. Commun. Appl. **8**(1), 213–224 (2012)
9. Spence, C.: Crossmodal correspondences: a tutorial review. In: Attention, Perception and Psychophysics, vol. 73, no. 4, pp. 971–995. Springer, Heidelberg (2011)
10. Belkin, K., Martin, R., Kemp, S.E., Gilbert, A.N.: Auditory pitch as a perceptual analogue to odor quality. Psychol. Sci. **8**(4), 340–342 (1997)
11. Crisinel, A.S., Spence, C.: A fruity note: crossmodal associations between odors and musical notes. Chem. Senses **37**(2), 151–158(8) (2012)
12. Seo, H.S., Lohse, F., Luckett, C.R., Hummel, T.: Congruent sound can modulate odor pleasantness. Chem. Senses **39**(3), 215–228 (2014)
13. Deroy, O., Crisinel, A.S., Spence, C.: Crossmodal correspondences between odors and contingent features: odors, musical notes, and geometrical shapes. Psychon. Bull. Rev. **20**(5), 878–896 (2013)
14. Ekman, P., Friesen, W.V., O'Sullivan, M.: Universals and cultural differences in the judgments of facial expressions of emotion. J. Pers. Soc. Psychol. **53**(4), 712–717 (1987)

15. Russell, J.A.: A circumplex model of affect. J. Pers. Soc. Psychol. **39**(6), 1161–1178 (1980)
16. Tzanetakis, G., Cook, P.: Marsyas: a framework for audio analysis. Organ. Sound **4**(3), 169–175 (2000)
17. Xing, B., Zhang, K., Sun, S., Zhang, L., Gao, Z., Wang, J., Chen, S.: Emotion-driven Chinese folk music-image retrieval based on DE-SVM. Neurocomputing **148**, 619–627 (2015)
18. Zhang, K., Sun, S.: Web music emotion recognition based on higher effective gene expression programming. Neurocomputing **105**, 100–106 (2013)

Graphics, Imaging and Applications

Real-Time Weighted Median Filtering with the Edge-Aware 4D Bilateral Grid

Hanli Zhao[1], Dandan Gao[1], Ming Wang[1], and Zhigeng Pan[2(✉)]

[1] Intelligent Information Systems Institute, Wenzhou University,
Wenzhou 325035, China
[2] Digital Media and HCI Research Center,
Hangzhou Normal University, Hangzhou 311121, China
zhigengpan@gmail.com

Abstract. Weighted median filtering is a fundamental operator in a great variety of image processing and computer graphics applications. This paper presents a novel real-time weighted median filter which smoothes out high-frequency details while preserving major edges. We define a new 4D bilateral grid by incorporating the 3D bilateral grid with an additional range dimension. The edge-aware weights and the weighted median values are computed in the 4D space. The proposed algorithm is highly parallel, enabling real-time GPU-based edge-aware implementation. Experimental results show that our algorithm can be run efficiently in real-time on modern GPUs. Applications including JPEG artifact removal and image stylization are demonstrated to verify the feasibility of the proposed weighted median filtering algorithm.

Keywords: Median filter · Bilateral filter · Bilateral grid · GPU

1 Introduction

Edge-preserving smoothing filters aim at reducing image noises while preserving meaningful structures. The research on developing new effective edge-preserving smoothing filters have been conducted for decades. The median filter [13] has been proven to be more effective than a linear smoothing filter in preserving edges. Each neighbor pixel contributes to equal weight to the filtered central pixel in the standard median filter. Therefore, it still cannot preserve high-contrast boundaries. The bilateral filter [11] is a widely used edge-preserving filter in image processing and computer graphics community and many improvements have been made in recent years. However, due to the nature of weighted mean of neighboring pixels, noises are also used for weighting the output value of the filtered pixel. On the other hand, the weighted median filter directly selects the neighbor pixel with a weighted median intensity value to substitute the intensity of the filtered pixel. Consequently, weighted median filtering can produce better edge-preserving smoothing results than bilateral filtering in many applications.

In recent years, many algorithms have been proposed in order to improve the filtering efficiency. Zhang et al. [17] proposed a few efficient schemes to achieve

© Springer International Publishing Switzerland 2016
A. El Rhalibi et al. (Eds.): Edutainment 2016, LNCS 9654, pp. 125–135, 2016.
DOI: 10.1007/978-3-319-40259-8_11

a linear computation complexity $O(r)$ with regard to the kernel size r. However, their algorithm is designed for fast CPU implementation but not suitable for GPU parallelization. Ma et al. [6] proposed a constant time weighted median filtering algorithm by elevating the computation in the 3-dimensional space. The constant time guided filter [3] is employed to filter the data in the 3D volume with edge-preservation. Similarly, Yang et al. [15] formulated both the median and bilateral filtering as a unified constant-time cost volume aggregation framework. Their algorithm implements the bilateral filter using recursive schemes and uses it in the constant time edge-preserving smoothing in the 3D space. In this paper, we would like to further improve the performance by exploiting the computation on an even higher dimension.

Driven by the insatiable market demand for real-time processing, the programmable GPU has evolved into a highly parallel manycore processor with great computational power. Currently, the GPU has been worked as a co-processor of the CPU to address problems that can be expressed as data-parallel computations [7]. In particularly, a 2D image contains regularly aligned pixel matrix and the processing on each pixel is inherently highly parallel.

In this paper, we elevate the computation domain into a 4D space to even improve the performance of weighted median filtering. This is achieved by taking advantage of the bilateral grid [1]. The original bilateral grid is used to approximate the bilateral filtering in a 3D space. It is highly efficient that the time complexity is linear with respect to the computation grid. In our work, we adapt the original bilateral grid and scatter the pixel data into our new 4D bilateral grid. As a result, the edge-aware weights and the weighted median values are computed in the 4D space. Extensive experimental results are presented at the end of the paper to demonstrate the effectiveness of our GPU-accelerated implementation.

The remainder of this paper is organized as follows. Section 2 briefly reviews some of previous work. Section 3 describe our approach in detail, while experimental results and applications are presented in Sect. 4. Finally, we conclude the paper in the last section.

2   Related Work

A variety of edge-preserving image smoothing filters have been proposed for decades. In this section, we only briefly review some related work of median filters.

We first review the unweighted median filter which was first introduced by Tukey [12]. Then Hang et al. [4] presented a $O(r)$ median filtering algorithm based on storing and updating the gray level histogram of the picture elements in the window. Weiss [13] introduced a vectorable $O(\log r)$ median filtering algorithm based on distributed histograms. Cline et al. [2] presented a constant time 8-bit median filter implementation based on a separable argument while Perreault and Hébert [9] proposed a constant time median filter by reducing the update of the column and kernel histograms as well as the computing of the median. Kass and Solomon [5] computed accurate derivatives and integrals of locally-weighted histograms over large neighborhoods and enables a constant time isotropic median filter. These unweighted median filtering algorithms are well suited for CPU implementation and thus cannot be parallelized using GPU. In addition, the median filter may fail to preserve high-contrast image boundaries.

There also have been some weighted median filters by taking into account high-contrast edges. A comprehensive tutorial paper was written by Yin et al. [16]. Rhemann et al. [10] employed the GPU-based weighted median filter as a post-processing step to remove streak-like artifacts in the disparity map while preserving the object boundaries. Bilateral filtering weights are used for the median filter weights. Zhang et al. [17] proposed a joint-histogram representation, median tracking and a new data structure that enables fast data access. Although their approach reduces computation complexity to $O(r)$, the acceleration schemes are highly serial and cannot be implemented on the GPU. The algorithm of Yang et al. [15] computes the range distance for all cell with the same spatial coordinate for each pixel and formulates the weighted median filter as a cost aggregation problem followed by a winner-take-all selection. Yang further employ the recursive bilateral filtering [14] for constant time edge-preserving median weights. Unfortunately, the GPU parallelization is not involved in their algorithm. Ma et al. [6] developed the first constant time algorithm for the previously time-consuming weighted median filter. All cells of the 3D volume is initialized as zero, and each image pixel is scattered into corresponding cell based on its spatial coordinate and range coordinate. The constant time guided filter [3] is adopted to compute the edge-aware median weights. Ma et al. implemented their weighted median filter using CUDA to improve the performance. We observe that the performance of the weighted median filter can be further optimized.

3   Our Algorithm

First of all, let us introduce the definition of weighted median filter. The weighted median filter is a nonlinear rank order based filter that smoothes an image while preserving edges. For a box filter window $N(\mathbf{p})$ centered at the pixel $\mathbf{p}$ in an image I, a non-negative weight $w(\mathbf{p}, \mathbf{q})$ is assigned to each neighbor pixel $\mathbf{q} \in N(\mathbf{p})$. Let M be the filtered output, the weighted median of $N(\mathbf{p})$ is defined as the value $M(\mathbf{p})$ minimizing the following sum expression [16]:

$$M(\mathbf{p}) = \arg \min_{b} \sum_{\mathbf{q} \in N(\mathbf{p})} w(\mathbf{p}, \mathbf{q})|I(\mathbf{q}) - b| \qquad (1)$$

where $b \in [0, 255]$ which contains a total of 256 integral numbers for an input 8-bit digital image. If the value of $w(\mathbf{p}, \mathbf{q})$ corresponds to the weight of an edge-preserving smoothing filter, the weighted median filter can produce an edge-preserving smoothing output. In particularly, the bilateral filter [11] is the commonly used filter to compute the weight. From the definition of weighted median filter, the output of the filter is calculated by sorting the values inside $N(\mathbf{p})$ and then adding up the weights from the beginning of the sorted set until the sum being equal to half of the total sum of weights.

Ma et al. [6] and Yang et al. [15] have proposed their respective constant time implementations of the weighted median filter by elevating the computation domain into a 3D volume. In our approach, we aim to compute the weighted median filter in an even higher dimension to obtain more performance gain. In the following, we will describe our GPU-based implementation for the edge-preserving weighted median filter in detail.

The bilateral grid [1] is a fast GPU-based implementation for bilateral filtering. The original bilateral grid is defined as a 3D array, where the first two dimensions (x, y) respect to 2D spatial coordinates in the image while the third dimension z corresponds to the image intensity range. In this paper, we extend the original bilateral grid to define a new 4D data structure for our weighted median filtering. Specifically, we add an additional range dimension a into the original bilateral grid.

In general, our new 4D bilateral grid is used in three steps. First, we create a grid from the input image. Then, the data inside the grid are weighted and smoothed. Finally, the weighted median values are computed by grid slicing and accumulating.

3.1 Grid Creation

Given an input image I and an edge image E normalized to $[0, 1]$, the sampling rate of x and y axes s_s, the sampling rate of z axis s_r and the sampling rate of a axis s_a, we construct our 4D bilateral grid Γ as follows:

1. For all grid cells (x, y, z, a):

$$\Gamma(x, y, z, a) = 0 \tag{2}$$

2. For each pixel at position (x, y):

$$\Gamma([\frac{x}{s_s}], [\frac{y}{s_s}], [\frac{E(x, y)}{s_r}], [\frac{I(x, y)}{s_a}]) + = 1 \tag{3}$$

where $[\cdot]$ denotes the closest-integer operator. Note that we only count the number of pixels into each grid cell during the construction of our 4D bilateral grid. This is quite different from Chen et al.'s bilateral grid [1] which accumulate both the image intensity and the number of pixels using homogeneous coordinates.

3.2 Grid Smoothing

The grid smoothing is performed to obtain aggregated weights in each intensity level. Ma et al. [6] employed the guided filter [3] to smooth each slice of their 3D histogram volume while Yang et al. [15] suggested to employ constant time bilateral filters in their method. Benefitting from the edge-aware bilateral grid, a 3D separable Gaussian smoothing is applied to the x, y and z axes where the variance along the spatial and range dimensions are σ_s and σ_r respectively [1]. Note that the a axis remains unfiltered.

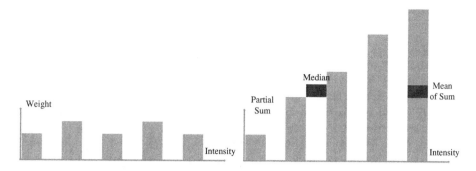

Fig. 1. Illustration of median computing: (left) sliced Γ weights based on the a level (right) the corresponding partial sum of weights and the interpolated median value.

3.3   Grid Slicing

The partial sum of weights for each pixel is calculated by adding up each slice based on the a level:

$$S(x, y, a) = \sum_{a_m=0}^{a} \Gamma\left(\frac{x}{s_s}, \frac{y}{s_s}, \frac{E(x,y)}{s_r}, a_m\right) \tag{4}$$

Let $A = \lceil 1/s_a \rceil$ be the number of a levels, then the value of a ranges from 0 to $A-1$ with a total of A integral numbers. Consequently, we can find the weighted median intensity $\bar{a}$ from the mean sum: $S(x, y, \bar{a}) = S(x, y, A-1)/2$. The values of x/s_s, y/s_s, $E(x,y)/s_r$ and $\bar{a}$ are usually not integral numbers and thus the slicing and interpolation of the bilateral grid are required.

Our 4D bilateral grid can be viewed as a sequence of 3D bilateral grids based on a levels. Given the 4D bilateral grid Γ and the edge image E, we slice the grid at $(x/s_s, y/s_s, E(x,y)/s_r, a)$ for each level a. The grid slicing operation is actually a simple trilinear interpolation which is implemented with a linear interpolation of two bilinear interpolations from the grid cells. Note that each cell of the grid only stores a scalar value. Therefore, our slicing does not need to divide Γ with homogeneous values which is happened in Chen et al.'s bilateral grid [1]. Since we cannot find the exact value of $\bar{a}$, we estimate it by slicing S with a linear interpolation followed by a scaling:

$$M(x, y) = s_a \cdot \left(\lfloor \bar{a} \rfloor + \frac{S(x, y, \bar{a}) - S(x, y, \lfloor \bar{a} \rfloor)}{S(x, y, \lfloor \bar{a} \rfloor + 1) - S(x, y, \lfloor \bar{a} \rfloor)}\right) \tag{5}$$

where $\lfloor x \rfloor$ denotes the largest integer not greater than x. For an 8-bit digital image, the maximum value of A is 256 and the minimum sampling rate of a is $s_a = 1/256$. If we use the minimum sampling rate of a, no interpolation is required and the accessed result is the exact weighted median value. If a coarser sampling rate of a is used, the linear interpolation will produce approximate median values. Note that higher order interpolations [1,15] can be used to produce a better fitting result but may need more computations. We illustrate the process of median computing in Fig. 1.

4   GPU Implementation

In this section, we present the implementation details on the GPU parallelization which enables a real-time weighted median filtering.

Chen et al. [1] have implemented their bilateral grid using the vertex shader and the pixel shader in the graphics rendering pipeline. Currently, NVIDIA CUDA [7] provides highly parallel supports for arbitrary data scattering and data collection using GPUs. CUDA C is a standard C programming language with some ornamentations to allow the programmer to specify which code should run on the GPU. In our work, we have implemented the proposed weighted median filter using the easy-to-use yet powerful CUDA.

The 4D bilateral grid is stored as a 2D texture by tiling both of z levels and a levels across the texture plane. Since our bilateral grid does not contain homogeneous coordinates, we only use a 32-bit floating point for each pixel. Assume the width and height of an image is W and H respectively, then a grid in general requires $(4 \times W \times H)/(s_x^2 \times s_r \times s_a)$ bytes of video memory in this format. For typical values of $s_s = 16$, $s_r = 1/16$ and $s_a = 1/16$, our 4D bilateral grid requires about 4 megabyte of video memory per megapixel.

For the grid creation, we launch CUDA *threads* based on the numbers of x and y levels of the grid. As a consequence, we can take advantage of the CUDA *shared memory* for the collection of in-cell pixel numbers. The efficient *atomic addition* on the shared memory is used for accumulating the number of pixels into each grid cell.

During the grid smoothing, the sampling rates s_s and s_r correspond to the variance of the Gaussian σ_s and σ_r as suggested in [8]. The 3D separable Gaussian filter is applied to x, y and z axes respectively with a 5-tap 1D Gaussian kernel. Again the shared memory is used to avoid duplicated loading of the grid data among different threads in each CUDA *block*.

Finally, the weighted median is computed with two loops. The first loop accumulates the partial sums S. For the trilinear interpolation used in computing S, we perform two bilinear interpolations for the two nearest z levels and linear interpolate between them. The second loop finds the two consecutive intensity levels based on the sum of S and then linear interpolate between them to output the filtered result.

5   Experimental Results

We have implemented our novel weighted median filter using highly parallel NVIDIA CUDA kernels. In order to verify the efficiency of the proposed algorithm, we tested it on a PC with a 2.5 GHz Intel Core i3-2100T CPU (12 GB main memory) and an NVIDIA GeForce GTX Titan X GPU (3072 streaming processors and 12 GB graphics memory).

Figure 2 show a various smoothing effects with gradually increasing sampling rates of s_a. We first transform the input RGB color space into CIE-Lab color space and perform the proposed weighted median filtering on the luminance

Fig. 2. Various smoothing effects with increasing sampling rates of σ_a (left to right and top to bottom): input, $s_a = 1/256$, $s_a = 1/128$, $s_a = 1/64$, $s_a = 1/32$, $s_a = 1/16$, $s_a = 1/8$, $s_a = 1/4$. We set $s_s = 16$, $s_r = 1/16$ for all images.

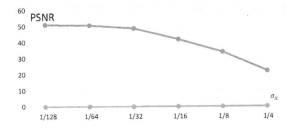

Fig. 3. PSNR statistics of Fig. 2 as compared with the result of $s_a = 1/256$.

channel and then transform it back to RGB color space. An 8-bit luminance channel contains maximum 256 intensities and thus the minimum sampling rate is $1/256$. With the minimum sampling rate, we obtain the exact median result as shown in the top-left image of Fig. 2. With the gradually coarser sampling rate, linear interpolation is used to approximate the median value. From Fig. 2, we can see that the approximation error is gradually increased with the increase of sampling rate. For the bottom-right two images, unwanted quantization artifacts are visible. We give the corresponding quantified PSNR (peek signal-to-noise ratio) values for these approximate results as compared with the exact one in Fig. 3. The minimum PSNR value is always over 40 dB with $s_a \leq 1/16$ which means that the approximate result is quite similar to the exact one. The PSNR value is low with $s_a > 1/16$ and visible artifacts arise as approved in Fig. 2.

In order to verify the capability of edge-preservation corresponding to s_r, we show different smoothing effects with different sampling rates of s_r in Fig. 4. More edges are preserved with smaller s_r, whereas less edges are preserved with

Fig. 4. Different smoothing effects with increasing sampling rates of s_r (left to right). $s_r = 1/16$, $s_r = 1/8$, $s_r = 3/16$, $s_r = 1/4$. We set $s_s = 16$, $s_a = 1/16$ for all images.

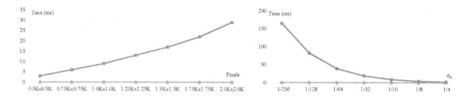

Fig. 5. Performance statistics: (left) the running times for different sized grayscale images with the same $s_a = 1/16$, (right) the running times for a 1-megapixel grayscale image with different s_a. We set $s_s = 16$, $s_r = 1/16$ for all images.

large s_r. When the value of s_r is too large, some meaningful edges are also smoothed.

We have recorded the running times in Fig. 5 to test the performance of the proposed weighted median filter on a grayscale image. If we set constant values for all parameters (i.e., s_s, s_r and s_a), the performance is linear with respect of the image size. As shown in Fig. 5 left, our algorithm requires less than 30ms even for a high-resolution image with 2.0K × 2.0K pixels. Therefore, real-time performance can be achieved for high resolution images with our novel weighted median filter. We have also give the performance statistics for a 1-megapixel grayscale image with different values of s_a in order to test the impact of the parameter s_a. As shown in Fig. 5 right, the performance is gradually improved with the increase of s_a. It should be noted that larger values of s_a will result in approximate median values as illustrated in Fig. 3. In comparison, Zhang et al.'s 100+ times faster weighted median filter [17] requires 0.450s to filter an image with 1920 × 1080 pixels and the kernel size of 10 × 10 using an Intel i7 3.4 GHz CPU. Zhang et al.'s CPU-based algorithm can only achieve near real-time performance for QVGA-sized images and cannot be parallelized on the GPU directly. Yang et al. [15] did not show the performance of their weighted median filter in their paper and the CPU performance of 83ms per megapixel was reported for their median filter with $s_a = 1/16$.

We have applied our weighted median filter to remove artifacts from the JPEG compression. The frequency quantization of JPEG compression may introduce unwanted artifacts near edges, as show in Fig. 6. These artifacts are

Fig. 6. Removal of JPEG Cartoon artifacts.

Fig. 7. Image stylization effects based on our weighted median filter.

smoothed and the underlying edges are preserved with our edge-aware weighted median filter. As shown in Fig. 7, we have also used our edge-aware filter to perform vivid image stylization. Image details are smoothed while important edges are emphasized in image stylization. We first perform our edge-aware filter to generate a piecewise smoothing image and then draw coherent lines [18, 19] onto salient edges.

6   Conclusions and Future Work

In this paper, we have presented a novel real-time weighted median filtering algorithm by substantially exploit the parallelism of modern GPUs. A new edge-aware 4D bilateral grid is defined by elevating the computation domain of the traditional 3D bilateral grid into an even higher dimension. The use of 4D bilateral grid makes the computation complexity of weighted median filtering be less relevant to the size of input image but depend on the coarsely sampled bilateral grid. Experimental results have shown that our new algorithm can be run efficiently in real-time. In addition, the applications have demonstrated the feasibility of the proposed algorithm.

When small sampling rates are used to perform the filtering operation, large memory and computational costs are required because of the large resolution of the bilateral grid. In the future, we would like to reduce the required memory by exploring a compact representation of the bilateral grid. Another future direction is to exploit various real-time image processing applications related to the weighted median filtering.

Acknowledgements. This work was supported by the National Natural Science Foundation of China (Grant No. 61100146), the Zhejiang Provincial Natural Science Foundation of China (Grant No. LY15F020019), the Science and Technology Planning Project of Wenzhou, China (Grant No. G20150019), and the Open Project Program of the State Key Lab of CAD&CG (Grant No. A1610), Zhejiang University. We gratefully acknowledge the support of NVIDIA Corporation with the donation of the GeForce GTX Titan X GPU used for this research.

References

1. Chen, J., Paris, S., Durand, F.: Real-time edge-aware image processing with the bilateral grid. ACM Trans. Graph. **26**(3), 103 (2007)
2. Cline, D., White, K.B., Egbert, P.K.: Fast 8-bit median filtering based on separability. In: ICIP (2007)
3. He, K., Sun, J., Tang, X.: Guided image filtering. In: Daniilidis, K., Maragos, P., Paragios, N. (eds.) ECCV 2010, Part I. LNCS, vol. 6311, pp. 1–14. Springer, Heidelberg (2010)
4. Huang, T., Yang, G., Tang, G.: A fast two-dimensional median filtering algorithm. IEEE Trans. Acoust. Speech Sig. Process. **27**(1), 13–18 (1979)
5. Kass, M., Solomon, J.: Smoothed local histogram filters. ACM Trans. Graph. **29**(4), 100 (2010)
6. Ma, Z., He, K., Wei, Y., Sun, J., Wu, E.: Constant time weightedmedian filtering for stereo matching and beyond. In: Proceedings of 2013 IEEE International Conference on Computer Vision, ICCV 13, pp. 49–56. IEEE Computer Society, Washington, DC, USA (2013)
7. NVIDIA Corp.: CUDA Programming Guide, Version 7.5 (2015). https://developer.nvidia.com/cuda-toolkit
8. Paris, S., Durand, F.: A fast approximation of the bilateral filter using a signal processing approach. In: Proceedings of European Conference on Computer Vision (2006)
9. Perreault, S., Hébert, P.: Median filtering in constant time. IEEE Trans. Image Process. **16**, 2389–2394 (2007)
10. Rhemann, C., Hosni, A., Bleyer, M., Rother, C., Gelautz, M.: Fast cost-volume filtering for visual correspondence and beyond. In: CVPR (2011)
11. Tomasi, C., Manduchi, R.: Bilateral filtering for gray andcolor images. In: Proceedings of 6th International Conferenceon Computer Vision, ICCV 98, pp. 839–846. IEEEComputer Society, Washington, DC, USA (1998)
12. Tukey, J.W.: Exploratory Data Analysis. Addison-Wesley, Reading (1977)

13. Weiss, B.: Fast median and bilateral filtering. ACM Trans. Graph. **25**, 519–526 (2006)

14. Yang, Q.: Recursive bilateral filtering. In: Fitzgibbon, A., Lazebnik, S., Perona, P., Sato, Y., Schmid, C. (eds.) ECCV 2012, Part I. LNCS, vol. 7572, pp. 399–413. Springer, Heidelberg (2012)

15. Yang, Q., Ahuja, N., Tan, K.H.: Costant time median and bilateral filtering. Int. J. Comput. Vis. **112**, 307–318 (2015)

16. Yin, L., Yang, R., Gabbouj, M., Neuvo, Y.: Weighted median filters: a tutorial. IEEE Trans. Circuits Syst. II **43**(3), 157–192 (1996)

17. Zhang, Q., Xu, L., Jia, J.: 100+ times faster weighted medianfilter (WMF). In: Proceedings of 2014 IEEE Conference on Computer Vision and Pattern Recognition, CVPR 14, pp. 2830–2837. IEEE Computer Society, Washington, DC, USA (2014)

18. Kang, H., Lee, S., Chui, C.K.: Coherent line drawing. In: Proceedings of NPAR 2007, pp. 43–50. ACM, New York (2007)

19. Zhao, H., Jin, X., Shen, J., Mao, X., Feng, J.: Real-time feature-aware video abstraction. Vis. Comput. **24**(7–9), 727–734 (2008). (Special Issue of CGI 2008)

Nose Tip Detection and Face Localization from Face Range Image Based on Multi-angle Energy

Jian Liu[✉], Quan Zhang, and Chaojing Tang

College of Electronic Science and Engineering,
National University of Defense Technology, Changsha, China
jianliu@nudt.edu.cn

Abstract. In this paper, we propose a novel method to detect nose tip and localize face from face range image. The nose tip detection procedure of the method is based on the idea of Multi-angle Energy (ME) and works in scale-space. The face localization procedure of the method is based on the position of the nose tip and a modified version of Multi-angle Energy. The scale-space is established by robust smoothing the input face range image. In the nose tip detection procedure, for each scale of the scale-space, we compute the Multi-angle Energy for each point of the face range image. For the points whose values of ME are not equal to zero, hierarchical clustering method is used to cluster them into several clusters. In the obtained first h largest clusters, we can find a nose tip candidate by using a cascading scheme. For all scales of the scale-space, we get a series of nose tip candidates. We apply hierarchical clustering again for them. Nose tip can be found in the largest cluster. In the face localization procedure, we present a modified version of ME. With the modified ME, we use a similar cascading scheme to detect one endo-canthion for the input face range image. Based on the distance between nose tip and endocanthion, face localization is achieved by using a sphere which is centered on the nose tip to crop the face region. We evaluate our method on two well-known 3D face databases, namely FRGC v2.0 and BOSPHORUS, and compare our method with other state-of-the-art methods. The experimental results show that the nose tip detection rates of our method are higher than those of the state-of-the-art methods. The face localization results are fine and can adapt to the face scale variance.

Keywords: Nose tip · Endocanthion · Multi-angle energy · Face localization · Scale-space · Face range image

1 Introduction

In the 3D facial studies, 3D facial landmarks play a significant role, which can facilitate many 3D facial studies tasks. In these 3D facial landmarks, nose tip has the most distinct feature [24], which is at the center of the facial surface and is commonly the highest protruding local point [10]. Nose tip plays a very

© Springer International Publishing Switzerland 2016
A. El Rhalibi et al. (Eds.): Edutainment 2016, LNCS 9654, pp. 136–147, 2016.
DOI: 10.1007/978-3-319-40259-8_12

important role in face localization, face recognition, facial features extraction, face alignment, etc. For example, in [3], the mean and Gaussian curvature maps are first computed. Based on the signs of mean and Gaussian curvature, a *HK* classification method is used to extract nose and eyes candidates. These candidates are combined to form a series of face triangles. Face localization can be achieved by processing these face triangles through a PCA-based classifier. In [14], before performing face recognition, the nose tip is detected firstly using a coarse to fine approach. Then a sphere with a radius r is centered at the nose tip to crop out the required facial area, which will reduce the computational cost and facilitate face recognition dramatically. In [6], in order to annotate the landmarks automatically, the nose tip is first identified as the most robust and prominent landmark. The nose tip is located by fitting a sphere for each facial point. All points within 50 mm of the nose tip are used to align the face pose via the Hotelling transformation. After that, other landmarks can be easily annotated. In [12], all 3D face convexities are detected as the nose tip candidates from the Emerging from Sphere (EfS) algorithm. In these candidates, histograms of oriented gradients and SVM classifier are applied to identify the nose tip and its orientation. Face can be automatically aligned based on the spherical depth map representation.

In this paper, we propose a method to detect nose tip and localize face from face range image based on Multi-angle Energy. Our method is an extension of earlier work [11]. Compare with our earlier work [11], the main differences are: (1) We present an improving definition of Multi-angle Energy. (2) We improve the nose tip detection rate by using a new cascading scheme with the improving Multi-angle Energy. (3) We present a new way to detect the endocanthion with a modified version of Multi-angle Energy. (4) Based on the distance between nose tip and endocanthion, we localize the face from the input face range image.

2   Nose Tip Detection

Xu et al. [24] observed that nose tip is the highest local point and Guo et al. [6] observed that the area around the nose tip can be approximated as a semi-sphere. Inspired by their ideas, we propose a novel nose tip detection method which works in scale-space. We first give the definition of Multi-angle Energy (ME). For each point $\mathbf{p}_i$ in a range image, we can get a series of points $\{\mathbf{p}_{i_j}\}$ which fulfill $R_1 \leq \|\mathbf{p}_{i_j} - \mathbf{p}_i\| \leq R_2$ (In the experiment, we set $R_1 = 18\,mm, R_2 = 19\,mm$). As showed in Fig. 1, $\{\mathbf{p}_{i_j}\}$ reside in the ring area colored by green. The multi-angle energy of $\mathbf{p}_i$ is

$$\mathrm{ME}_i = \begin{cases} \dfrac{\sum_{j=1}^{k} |\arccos d_{i_j}|}{k} & \forall d_{i_j} < 0 \\ 0 & \exists d_{i_j} \geq 0 \end{cases} \tag{1}$$

where k is the number of points $\{\mathbf{p}_{i_j}\}$, d_{i_j} is as follow

$$d_{i_j} = \frac{(\mathbf{p}_{i_j} - \mathbf{p}_i) \cdot \mathbf{N}_i}{\|\mathbf{p}_{i_j} - \mathbf{p}_i\|} \tag{2}$$

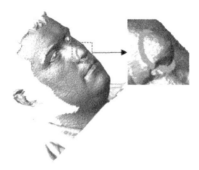

Fig. 1. Points which are used to compute ME.

Fig. 2. *Left*: Multi-angle energy feature. *Middle*: Gaussian curvature. *Right*: Mean curvature.

where $\mathbf{N}_i$ is the normalized normal of $\mathbf{p}_i$, which can be computed by the *PlanePCA* method of [7]. The geometric meaning of $\arccos d_{i_j}$ is the angle between vector $(\mathbf{p}_{i_j} - \mathbf{p}_i)$ and $\mathbf{N}_i$. Equation (1) means that if all angles between $\mathbf{N}_i$ and each vector $(\mathbf{p}_{i_j} - \mathbf{p}_i)$ are larger than $90°$, point $\mathbf{p}_i$ will be a local protruding point. A value of ME is assigned to it. Otherwise, point $\mathbf{p}_i$ will not be treated as a local protruding point. A zero value of ME will be assigned to it. Figure 2 (*Left*) shows the multi-angle energy feature. Compared with the Gaussian curvature feature (Fig. 2 (*Middle*)) and mean curvature feature (Fig. 2 (*Right*)) which are used in many works [1,3,10,22], the multi-angle energy feature is more distinctive and more suitable for the detection of nose tip. To establish scale-space, we use the method of Garcia [5] to robust smooth the range image with a series of smoothing parameters. Then in each scale of the scale-space, we use Eq. (1) to compute the Multi-angle Energy (ME) of each point in one range image. After that, for the points whose values of ME are not equal to zero, we use hierarchical clustering method [20] to cluster them into several clusters. For each of the first h largest clusters, we can find one point with the largest value of ME in that cluster. Thus we get h such points $(\mathbf{p}_k, k = 1, 2, ..., h)$ for these h clusters. Then for each of these h points, we fit a sphere to its neighboring points in the least square sense and get the radius r and the sphere fitting error E of the fitted sphere [6]. Finally, we apply a cascading filtering scheme to find the nose tip candidate. The steps are as follows: (1) For points $(\mathbf{p}_k, k = 1, 2, ..., h)$,

---

Algorithm 1. Nose tip detection

Input:

A face range image: I: $\mathbf{P} = \{\mathbf{p}_1, \mathbf{p}_2, ..., \mathbf{p}_n\}, \mathbf{p}_i \in \mathbb{R}^3$

Output:

Nose tip: $\mathbf{p}_{\mathrm{nosetip}}$

1: Establish scale-space.

2: **for** each scale in scale-space $\mathbb{S}$ **do**

3:   **for** $i = 1 : n$ **do**

4:     Compute multi-angle energy ME_i of point $\mathbf{p}_i$ using Equation (1).

5:   **end for**

6:   Apply hierarchical clustering to the points whose values of ME are not equal to zero.

7:   **for all** the first h largest clusters **do**

8:     Find one point with the largest value of ME in each of these h clusters.

9:     In the points just found, find the ones whose radii r of the fitted spheres are close to a value r_0.

10:     Find the points whose fitting errors E of the fitted spheres are below a threshold value.

11:     In the resulting points, find one point with the largest value of ME, which is the nose tip candidate $\mathbf{p}_s$.

12:   **end for**

13: **end for**

14: **for all** $\mathbf{p}_s, s \in \mathbb{S}$ **do**

15:   Find the largest cluster using hierarchical clustering and compute the mean value of ME.

16:   find the point $\mathbf{p}_{\mathrm{nosetip}}$ whose ME is closest to the mean value.

17: **end for**

---

find the ones whose radii r of the fitted spheres are close to a value r_0 (in the experiments, we set $r_0 = 11\,mm$); (2) In the points just found, find the ones whose fitting errors E of the fitted spheres are below a threshold value; (3) In the resulting points, find the one who has the largest value of ME, which is the nose tip candidate.

In each scale of the scale-space, we get one nose tip candidate. For all these nose tip candidates, we apply hierarchical clustering again and get several clusters. In the largest cluster, we compute the mean value of ME, then choose the point whose ME is closest to the mean value as nose tip. The method is detailed in Algorithm 1.

3   Endocanthion Detection and 3D Face Localization

Endocanthions are the two points which lie in the left and right inner eye corners. Endocanthion is the local most concave point. To detect endocanthion, we modify Eq. (1) as follow:

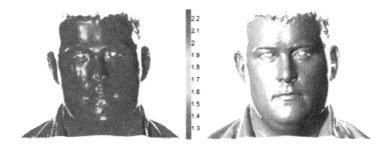

Fig. 3. *Left*: The value of ME$'$. *Right*: The endocanthion detection result (red dot indicates the endocanthion) (Color figure online)

$$\text{ME}'_i = \begin{cases} \dfrac{\sum_{j=1}^{k} |\pi - \arccos d_{i_j}|}{k} & \forall d_{i_j} > 0 \\ 0 & \exists d_{i_j} \leq 0 \end{cases} \qquad (3)$$

Figure 3 (*Left*) shows the value of ME$'$ (The face range image has been smoothed to reduce the noise.). We can see that the points near inner eye corners have large value of ME$'$ and form large clusters. The steps to detect endocanthion are as follows:

(1) For each point $\mathbf{p}'_i$ which fulfills $R'_1 \leq \|\mathbf{p}'_i - \mathbf{p}_{\text{nosetip}}\| \leq R'_2$ (these points form the endocanthion search region), compute their values of ME$'_i$ by using Eq. (3);
(2) For the points whose values of ME$'$ are not equal to zero, apply hierarchical clustering method [20] to cluster them into several clusters;
(3) For the first h largest clusters, find the clusters whose standard deviations of distribution are smaller than a threshold value;
(4) In the clusters just found, find one point with the maximum value of ME$'$, which is the endocanthion we just want.

Figure 3 (*Right*) shows the endocanthion detection result. We should point out that we only detect one endocanthion. The reason is that when the yaw angle of the head is large, sometimes we can only see one endocanthion due to self-occlusion. Besides, since we have detected nose tip, using only one endocanthion is sufficient to localize 3D face. To localize the 3D face, we just center a sphere on the nose tip. The radius of the sphere is $2.5l_n$, where l_n is the Euclidean distance between nose tip and endocanthion. 3D face localization is accomplished by using the sphere to crop the face region.

4   Experimental Results

The datasets, the evaluation experiments and experimental results are described in this section. The experiments are tested on a standard PC with Intel Core i5-3470 3.20 GHz CPU, 4 G memory in the Windows 7 operating system and the simulate tool is Matlab 2014a.

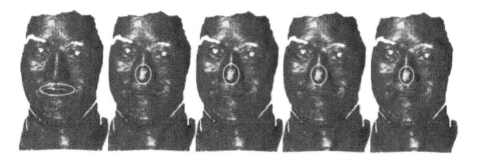

Fig. 4. Range images in scale-space with ME features. From left to right: scale parameter $s = 1$, $s = 2$, $s = 3$, $s = 4$, $s = 5$.

4.1   Databases

Two different 3D face databases are used to test our proposed method. The first one is the FRGC version 2.0 data set [19]. Face range images in FRGC v2.0 are taken by the Vivid 900/910 sensor, which is a structured light sensor that takes a 640 by 480 range image. The database consists of training set and testing set. There are 943 range images in the training set which are from 275 different subjects. The testing set contains 4007 range images which are from 466 different subjects. Subjects faces are frontally or near frontally posed and present different artifacts such as facial expressions, noise, image distortion, spikes, and surface holes. The second is BOSPHORUS database which is a multi-expression, multi-pose 3D face database enriched with realistic occlusions [21]. Facial data in BOSPHORUS database are acquired by Inspeck Mega Capturor II 3D digitizer. In the database, there are 4666 range images from 105 different subjects which are aged between 25 and 35 in various poses, expressions and occlusion conditions.

4.2   Experimental Results of Nose Tip Detection

Experimental Results on FRGC V2.0. In the experiments, we set the parameters as follows: the parameter s which controls the degree of smoothing is within the range of $[1, 5]$ in a step size of 1, the two radii of the ring $R_1 = 18\,mm$ and $R_2 = 19\,mm$, the hierarchical clustering criterion is Euclidean distance and the cutoff value of step 6 in Algorithm 1 is $1.5\,mm$, the cutoff value of step 15 in Algorithm 1 is $13.5\,mm$, the radius threshold value $r_0 = 11\,mm$, the fitting error threshold value $E = 0.5$. In some cases, the multi-angle energy feature may locate false nose tip, but in the scale-space, with the scale increasing, the locating point will finally converge to the true nose tip position. Figure 4 shows the fact. To evaluate the nose tip detection rate of our method, we manually annotate the nose tip in the testing range images of FRGC v2.0 and use these nose tip positions as benchmarks. During annotating, we find the nose region data of sample 04505d222 and 04814d22 in Fall2003 set are missing, so we exclude these

Table 1. Nose tip localization errors of FRGC

Localization errors (mm)	≤ 5	≤ 10	≤ 20
Percentage of the total (%)	78.23	99.93	100

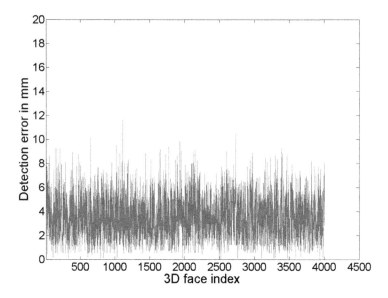

Fig. 5. Nose tip detection errors for FRGC v2.0.

two samples. We accept the 20 mm error threshold for successful detection of nose tip as it can be tolerated in the Iterative Closest Point (ICP) algorithm which is widely used in face recognition [2,10,17]. The nose tip detection rates of our method on FRGC v2.0 are shown in Table 1. The nose tip detection errors are drawn in Fig. 5. Figure 6 shows some successful nose tip detection examples.

Experimental Results on BOSPHORUS. Figure 7 shows that for BOSPHORUS, in some cases the multi-angle energy feature may locate false nose tip in certain scales in the scale-space, but with the scale increasing, the locating point will finally converge to the true nose tip position. The BOSPHO-RUS 3D face database contains the ground truth position of nose tip of each range image, so we can use these positions as benchmarks. The nose tip detection rates of our method on BOSPHORUS 3D face database are shown in Table 2. The nose tip detection errors are drawn in Fig. 8. Figure 9 shows some successful nose tip detection examples. Compared with the nose tip detection results in FRGC v2.0, the nose tip detection rates are lower in BOSPHORUS. The main reason is that some range images in BOSPHORUS have an extreme head pose rotation such as the yaw angle $\approx \pm 90°$.

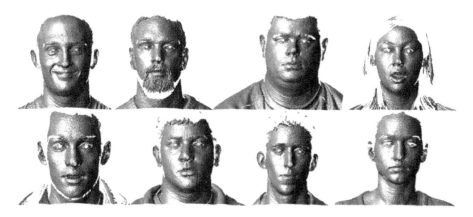

Fig. 6. some successful nose tip detection examples in FRGC v2.0 (red dot indicates the nose tip) (Color figure online).

Fig. 7. Range images under large expression in scale-space with ME features. From left to right: scale parameter $s = 1$, $s = 2$, $s = 3$, $s = 4$, $s = 5$.

Table 2. Nose tip localization errors of BOSPHORUS

Localization errors (mm)	≤ 5	≤ 10	≤ 20
Percentage of the total (%)	29.36	90.81	98.84

Comparison with State-of-the-art Techniques. Table 3 shows the comparative results of our nose tip detection method against other state-of-the-art methods in 10 mm and 20 mm precision. From the table we can see that our method of nose tip detection achieves the highest detection rate for both 10 mm and 20 mm precision. We also notice that there are no methods can handle both rotation and occlusion conditions except ours. Besides, our method need not training, and can also handle large facial expressions.

4.3   Experimental Results of Face Localization

The common technique to localize the 3D face is to center a sphere with a fix radius at the nose tip and crop the face area [4,8,14,15]. This technique is

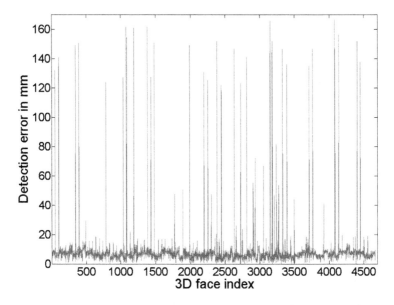

Fig. 8. Nose tip detection errors for BOSPHORUS.

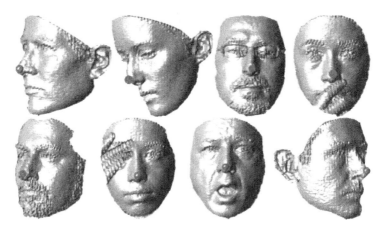

Fig. 9. some successful nose tip detection examples in BOSPHORUS (red dot indicates the nose tip) (Color figure online).

sensitive to face scale variance [23]. Our method also uses a sphere to crop the face area by centering it at the nose tip. But the radius of the sphere is not fix, which is dependent on the distance between the nose tip and endocanthion. Thus the sphere can adapt to the face scale variance. Figure 10 shows the fact.

In the top row of the figure, the radius of the sphere is 80 mm. With the face scale changing, method [14] leads to an over-cropping. In the bottom row of the figure, the radius of the sphere adapts to the face scale variance, which leads to a satisfactory cropping result. Some face localization results are shown in Fig. 11. We can see that the results of face localization are very satisfactory.

Table 3. Comparison with other state-of-the-art methods

Methods	Databases	Training	Rotation	Occlusion	Detection rate (10 mm)	(20 mm)
Xu et al. [24]	3DPEF+MPI	yes	yes	no	-	99.3 %
Peng et al. [17]	FRGC v2	no	yes	no	95.98 %	99.43 %
Perakis et al. [18]	FRGC v2+Ear	yes	yes	no	98.56 %	-
Faltemier et al. [4]	FRGC v2	no	no	no	98.20 %	-
Mian et al. [13]	FRGC v2	no	no	no	-	98.3 %
Pears et al. [16]	FRGC v2	no	yes	no	99.92 %	-
Li and Pedrycz [9]	FRGC v2	no	no	no	98.16 %	99.84 %
our method	FRGC v2	no	yes	yes	99.93 %	100 %

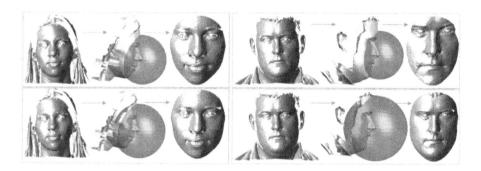

Fig. 10. *Top row*: Face localization results using method [14]. *Bottom row*: Face localization results using our method.

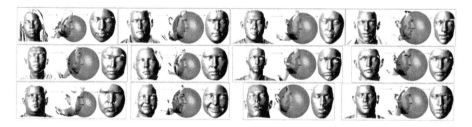

Fig. 11. Some face localization results.

5   Conclusion

In this paper, we have proposed a novel method to detect nose tip and localize face in face range image. The proposed method consists of nose tip detection procedure and face localization procedure. The nose tip detection procedure is robust to noise, does not rsire any training and any particular model, can handle large rotations, occlusions and facial expressions. The face localization procedure can adapt to the face scale variance with a fine face localization result.

We test our method in two well-known 3D face database, namely FRGC v2.0 and BOSPHORUS 3D face database, and compare our method with other state-of-the-art methods. The experimental and comparative results show that the nose tip detection rates of our method are higher than those of the state-of-the-art methods, the face localization results are satisfactory and can adapt to the face scale variance.

References

1. Chang, K.I., Bowyer, W., Flynn, P.J.: Multiple nose region matching for 3D face recognition under varying facial expression. IEEE Trans. Pattern Anal. Mach. Intell. **28**(10), 1695–1700 (2006)
2. Colbry, D., Stockman, G., Jain, A.: Detection of anchor points for 3D face verification. In: 2005 IEEE Computer Society Conference on Computer Vision and Pattern Recognition-Workshops, CVPR Workshops, p. 118. IEEE (2005)
3. Colombo, A., Cusano, C., Schettini, R.: 3D face detection using curvature analysis. Pattern Recogn. **39**(3), 444–455 (2006)
4. Faltemier, T.C., Bowyer, K.W., Flynn, P.J.: A region ensemble for 3-D face recognition. IEEE Trans. Inf. Forensics Secur. **3**(1), 62–73 (2008)
5. Garcia, D.: Robust smoothing of gridded data in one and higher dimensions with missing values. Comput. Stat. Data Anal. **54**(4), 1167–1178 (2010)
6. Guo, J., Mei, X., Tang, K.: Automatic landmark annotation and dense correspondence registration for 3D human facial images. BMC Bioinform. **14**(1), 232 (2013)
7. Jordan, K., Mordohai, P.: A quantitative evaluation of surface normal estimation in point clouds. In: 2014 IEEE/RSJ International Conference on Intelligent Robots and Systems (IROS 2014), pp. 4220–4226. IEEE (2014)
8. Ju, Q.: Robust binary neural networks based 3D face detection and accurate face registration. Int. J. Comput. Intell. Syst. **6**(4), 669–683 (2013)
9. Li, D., Pedrycz, W.: A central profile-based 3D face pose estimation. Pattern Recogn. **47**(2), 525–534 (2014)
10. Li, Y., Wang, Y., Wang, B., Sui, L.: Nose tip detection on three-dimensional faces using pose-invariant differential surface features. IET Comput. Vis. **9**(1), 75–84 (2014)
11. Liu, J., Zhang, Q., Zhang, C., Tang, C.: Robust nose tip detection for face range images based on local features in scale-space. In: 2015 International Conference on 3D Imaging (IC3D), pp. 1–8. IEEE (2015)
12. Liu, P., Wang, Y., Zhang, Z.: Representing 3D face from point cloud to face-aligned spherical depth map. Int. J. Pattern Recogn. Artif. Intell. **26**(01), 1255003 (2012)
13. Mian, A., Bennamoun, M., Owens, R.: Automatic 3D face detection, normalization and recognition. In: Third International Symposium on v3D Data Processing, Visualization, and Transmission, pp. 735–742. IEEE (2006)
14. Mian, A.S., Bennamoun, M., Owens, R.: An efficient multimodal 2D–3D hybrid approach to automatic face recognition. IEEE Trans. Pattern Anal. Mach. Intell. **29**(11), 1927–1943 (2007)
15. Nair, P., Cavallaro, A.: 3-D face detection, landmark localization, and registration using a point distribution model. IEEE Trans. Multimedia **11**(4), 611–623 (2009)
16. Pears, N., Heseltine, T., Romero, M.: From 3D point clouds to pose-normalised depth maps. Int. J. Comput. Vis. **89**(2–3), 152–176 (2010)

17. Peng, X., Bennamoun, M., Mian, A.S.: A training-free nose tip detection method from face range images. Pattern Recogn. **44**(3), 544–558 (2011)
18. Perakis, P., Passalis, G., Theoharis, T., Kakadiaris, I.A.: 3D facial landmark detection under large yaw and expression variations. IEEE Trans. Pattern Anal. Mach. Intell. **35**(7), 1552–1564 (2013)
19. Phillips, P.J., Flynn, P.J., Scruggs, T., Bowyer, K.W., Chang, J., Hoffman, K., Marques, J., Min, J., Worek, W.: Overview of the face recognition grand challenge. In: IEEE Computer Society Conference on Computer Vision and Pattern Recognition, 2005. CVPR 2005, vol. 1, pp. 947–954. IEEE (2005)
20. Rokach, L., Maimon, O.: Clustering methods. In: Maimon, O., Rokach, L. (eds.) Data Mining and Knowledge Discovery Handbook, pp. 321–352. Springer, Berlin (2005)
21. Savran, A., Alyüz, N., Dibeklioğlu, H., Çeliktutan, O., Gökberk, B., Sankur, B., Akarun, L.: Bosphorus database for 3D face analysis. In: Schouten, B., Juul, N.C., Drygajlo, A., Tistarelli, M. (eds.) BIOID 2008. LNCS, vol. 5372, pp. 47–56. Springer, Heidelberg (2008)
22. Segundo, M.P., Silva, L., Bellon, O.R.P., Queirolo, C.: Automatic face segmentation and facial landmark detection in range images. IEEE Trans. Syst. Man Cybern. B Cybern. **40**(5), 1319–1330 (2010)
23. Werghi, N., Rahayem, M., Kjellander, J.: An ordered topological representation of 3D triangular mesh facial surface: concept and applications. EURASIP J. Adv. Sig. Process. **2012**(1), 1–20 (2012)
24. Xu, C., Tan, T., Wang, Y., Quan, L.: Combining local features for robust nose location in 3D facial data. Pattern Recogn. Lett. **27**(13), 1487–1494 (2006)

A Class of Variable Degree Trigonometric Polynomial Spline and Its Applications

Min Sheng[1,2(✉)], Benyue Su[2,3], and Liping Zou[1]

[1] School of Mathematics and Computational Science, Anqing Normal University,
Anqing 246133, China
msheng0125@aliyun.com
[2] The University Key Laboratory of Intelligent Perception
and Computing of Anhui Province, Anqing Normal University,
Anqing 246133, China
[3] School of Computer and Information, Anqing Normal University,
Anqing 246133, China

Abstract. A class of variable degree trigonometric polynomial spline is presented for geometric modeling and industrial design. The corresponding generalized Hermite-like interpolating base functions provide bias and tension control facilities for constructing continuous interpolating curves and surfaces. The constructed curves and surfaces by the new spline can represent some conic and conicoid segments very approximately. The new interpolation spline, which need not solve m-system of equations, provides higher approximation order for data fitting than normal cubic Hermite interpolation spline for proper parameters. The idea is extended to produce Coons-like surfaces. Moreover, the new spline can be used for trajectory planning of manipulators in industrial design, which provides a continuity of position, velocity and acceleration, in order to ensure that the resulting trajectory is smooth enough. The variable degree trigonometric polynomial spline can be used to fit the sequence of joint positions for N joints. This new method approve to be practicable by the experimental results, and can meet the requirements of smooth motion of the manipulator.

Keywords: Curves and surfaces modeling · Hermite-like interpolation · Variable degree interpolation spline · Trajectory planning · Manipulator

1 Introduction

It is well known that Hermite interpolation and cubic spline interpolation are powerful tools for image processing and geometric modeling by interpolating curves and surfaces. However, they sometime can not exactly represent some conic and conicoid segments. Moreover, curve shapes cannot be adjusted except by their corresponding tangent vectors at the end points based on cubic Hermite interpolation model. On the other hand, as mentioned by Peña [11], the importance of trigonometric polynomials is well known in electronics, medicine,

© Springer International Publishing Switzerland 2016
A. El Rhalibi et al. (Eds.): Edutainment 2016, LNCS 9654, pp. 148–162, 2016.
DOI: 10.1007/978-3-319-40259-8_13

geometric modeling and the area of industrial design [6,7,12]. A number of recent papers deal with properties of trigonometric polynomials and their applications: Mainar et al. [8] found some bases for the spaces $\{1, t, \cos t, \sin t, \cos 2t, \sin 2t\}$, $\{1, t, t^2, \cos t, \sin t\}$ and $\{1, t, \cos t, \sin t, t \cos t, t \sin t\}$. Mazure [9] characterized extended Chebyshev spaces by Hermite interpolation and Bernstein bases. Morigi [10] considered a class of generalized polynomials consisting of the null spaces of certain differential operators with constant coefficients which contain ordinary polynomials and appropriately scaled trigonometric polynomials. Su and Tan presented a class of C^2 generalized B-spline like quasi-cubic blended interpolation spline by trigonometric polynomials in [15] and discussed the geometric modeling for interpolation surfaces based on blended coordinate system in [14].

Note that these existing methods can deal with some free-form curves and surfaces (FFC/FFS) and transcendental curves precisely due to the blending bases of polynomial and trigonometric functions, but suffer from complicated procedures in constructing interpolating curves and surfaces.

In 1966, Schweikert [13] introduced a generalization of the classical C^2 cubic interpolation spline. For each interval of the knot sequence $x_0 < x_1 < \cdots x_N$, the pieces that formed this new class of splines were taken from the four dimensional space

$$span\{1 - t, t, \frac{1}{\rho_i^2}(\frac{sinh(\rho_i(1-t))}{sinh(\rho_i)} - (1-t)), \frac{1}{\rho_i^2}(\frac{sinh(\rho_i t)}{sinh(\rho_i)} - t)\}, t = \frac{x - x_i}{x_{i+1} - x_i},$$

where ρ_i are tension parameters and as $\rho_i \to +\infty$, the space tends to the space of linear polynomials. Costantini [3] presented variable degree polynomial spline (VDPS) given by $span\{(1-t)^\mu, P_{n-2}, t^\mu\}$.

In the area of industrial design, we know that manipulator trajectory planning plays an important role in modern industrial production. The aim of trajectory planning is to generate a geometric path without collision in robot motion space, which is expressed as a sequence of discrete points. In order to ensure that manipulator can move smoothly when it makes high operating speed, we need to design a continuous trajectory to interpolate the given points. So many interpolation curves and corresponding optimal problem have been designed and presented for these discrete given points, such as normal cubic spline curve, B-spline curve, NURBS curve, and so on [2,5,12,16]. We now introduce the new interpolating spilne for the manipulator trajectory planning.

The main purpose of this paper is to develop a new method for constructing interpolating curves and surfaces based on generalized Hermite-like interpolation polynomials. This approach has the following features:

- The introduced generalized Hermite-like base functions possess the properties similar to those of cubic Hermite base functions. The introduced new interpolation spline is C^2 continuous, and the degree of introduced interpolation spline is variable with tension parameters μ_i and μ_{i+1}.
- The shapes of interpolating curves and surfaces by the introduced generalized polynomials can be adjusted by both tension parameters μ_i and μ_{i+1}, and corresponding tangent vectors at the end points.

– With the tension parameters and interpolation points chosen properly, the trigonometric polynomial curves can be used to represent straight lines, parabola, circular arcs and some transcendental curves precisely, the corresponding tensor product surfaces can also represent sphere and some quadric surfaces exactly.

The rest of this paper is organized as follows: Sect. 2 discusses the construction and properties of generalized Hermite-like interpolation polynomials. In Sect. 3, we present a new class of variable degree trigonometric polynomial spline, and analyze the related propositions. The applications via introduced spline in the curves and surfaces modeling and manipulator trajectory planning are demonstrated in Sect. 4. Finally, we conclude the paper in Sect. 5.

2   Quasi-Cubic Hermite-Like Interpolation Polynomials

As we know, normal cubic Hermite base functions of interpolation in the space $P_3([0,1]) := span\{1, t, t^2, t^3\}$ are defined by

$$F_0(t) = 2t^3 - 3t^2 + 1, \ F_1(t) = -2t^3 + 3t^2, \ G_0(t) = t^3 - 2t^2 + t, \ G_1(t) = t^3 - t^2, \quad (1)$$

where $t \in [0,1]$; $F_i(t), G_i(t), (i = 0,1)$ are cubic polynomials satisfying $F_0(t) + F_1(t) = 1$ and $G_0(t) = -G_1(1-t)$.

The four base functions have end points properties:

$$\begin{aligned}
&F_0(0) = 1, \ F_1(0) = 0, \ F_0(1) = 0, \ F_1(1) = 1, \\
&G_0(0) = 0, \ G_1(0) = 0, \ G_0(1) = 0, \ G_1(1) = 0, \\
&F_0'(0) = 0, \ F_1'(0) = 0, \ F_0'(1) = 0, \ F_1'(1) = 0, \\
&G_0'(0) = 1, \ G_1'(0) = 0, \ G_0'(1) = 0, \ G_1'(1) = 1.
\end{aligned} \quad (2)$$

These results motivate us to construct blending Hermit-like bases in generalized spaces.

In the following we discuss the cubic Hermite-like interpolation models based on base functions from $span\{1, cos\frac{\pi}{2}t, sin\frac{\pi}{2}t, cos\pi t, (cos\frac{\pi}{2}t)^{\mu_0}, (sin\frac{\pi}{2}t)^{\mu_1}\}$ and $span\{1, t^{\mu_0}, (1-t)^{\mu_0}, cos\pi t, (cos\frac{\pi}{2}t)^{\mu_1}, (sin\frac{\pi}{2}t)^{\mu_1}\}$, $t \in [0,1]$, $\mu_0 \geq 2, \mu_1 \geq 2$.

Definition 1. *For two arbitrarily selected real values of μ_0, μ_1 with $\mu_i \in R$, $\mu_i \geq 2, (i = 0,1)$, the following four functions in t are defined as trigonometric Hermite polynomials (THP):*

$$\begin{aligned}
&TF_0(t) = (cos\frac{\pi}{2}t)^2, &&TF_1(t) = (sin\frac{\pi}{2}t)^2, \\
&TG_{0,\mu_1}(t) = \frac{2}{\pi}(sin\frac{\pi}{2}t - (sin\frac{\pi}{2}t)^{\mu_1}), \ &&TG_{1,\mu_0}(t) = -\frac{2}{\pi}(cos\frac{\pi}{2}t - (cos\frac{\pi}{2}t)^{\mu_0}),
\end{aligned} \quad (3)$$

where $t \in [0,1]$.

Simple calculations verify that

$$
\begin{aligned}
&TF_0(0) = 1, \quad TF_1(0) = 0, \quad TF_0(1) = 0, \quad TF_1(1) = 1, \\
&TG_{0,\mu_1}(0) = 0, \, TG_{1,\mu_0}(0) = 0, \, TG_{0,\mu_1}(1) = 0, \, TG_{1,\mu_0}(1) = 0, \\
&TF_0'(0) = 0, \quad TF_1'(0) = 0, \quad TF_0'(1) = 0, \quad TF_1'(1) = 0, \\
&TG_{0,\mu_1}'(0) = 1, \, TG_{1,\mu_0}'(0) = 0, \, TG_{0,\mu_1}'(1) = 0, \, TG_{1,\mu_0}'(1) = 1,
\end{aligned} \tag{4}
$$

and $TF_0(t) + TF_1(t) = 1$, $TG_{0,\mu_1}(t) = -TG_{1,\mu_0}(1 - t)$ for $\mu_0 = \mu_1$.

Definition 2. *For two arbitrarily selected real values of μ_0, μ_1 with $\mu_i \in R$, $\mu_i \geq 2, (i = 0, 1)$, the following four functions in t are defined as generalized trigonometric Hermite polynomials (GTHP):*

$$
\begin{aligned}
&GTF_0(t) = (\cos\tfrac{\pi}{2}t)^2, \qquad\qquad GTF_1(t) = (\sin\tfrac{\pi}{2}t)^2, \\
&GTG_0(t) = -\tfrac{1}{\mu_0}((1 - t)^{\mu_0} - (\cos\tfrac{\pi}{2}t)^{\mu_1}), \, GTG_1(t) = \tfrac{1}{\mu_0}(t^{\mu_0} - (\sin\tfrac{\pi}{2}t)^{\mu_1}),
\end{aligned} \tag{5}
$$

where $t \in [0, 1]$.

Simple calculations verify that

$$
\begin{aligned}
&GTF_0(0) = 1, \, GTF_1(0) = 0, \, GTF_0(1) = 0, \, GTF_1(1) = 1, \\
&GTG_0(0) = 0, \, GTG_1(0) = 0, \, GTG_0(1) = 0, \, GTG_1(1) = 0, \\
&GTF_0'(0) = 0, \, GTF_1'(0) = 0, \, GTF_0'(1) = 0, \, GTF_1'(1) = 0, \\
&GTG_0'(0) = 1, \, GTG_1'(0) = 0, \, GTG_0'(1) = 0, \, GTG_1'(1) = 1,
\end{aligned} \tag{6}
$$

and $GTF_0(t) + GTF_1(t) = 1$, $GTG_0(t) = -GTG_1(1 - t)$.

These properties, like those of normal cubic Hermite polynomials, can be used for two-point Hermite-like interpolating curves with parameters μ_0 and μ_1, which are defined by

$$
TH_{\mu_0,\mu_1}(t) = p_0 TF_0(t) + p_1 TF_1(t) + p_0' TG_{0,\mu_1}(t) + p_1' TG_{1,\mu_0}(t), \tag{7}
$$

$$
GTH_{\mu_0,\mu_1}(t) = p_0 GTF_0(t) + p_1 GTF_1(t) + p_0' GTG_0(t) + p_1' GTG_1(t), \tag{8}
$$

where $\mu_0, \mu_1 \in R$, $\mu_0, \mu_1 \geq 2$, $t \in [0, 1]$ and p_0, p_1, p_0', p_1' are position and derivative vectors on both ends of the segment $[0, 1]$.

For any selected μ_0, μ_1 and vectors p_0, p_1, p_0', p_1', $TH_{\mu_0,\mu_1}(t)$ and $GTH_{\mu_0,\mu_1}(t)$ all represent a unique curve and

$$
\begin{aligned}
&TH_{\mu_0,\mu_1}(0) = GTH_{\mu_0,\mu_1}(0) = p_0, \, TH_{\mu_0,\mu_1}(1) = GTH_{\mu_0,\mu_1}(1) = p_1, \\
&TH_{\mu_0,\mu_1}'(0) = GTH_{\mu_0,\mu_1}'(0) = p_0', \, TH_{\mu_0,\mu_1}'(1) = GTH_{\mu_0,\mu_1}'(1) = p_1'.
\end{aligned}
$$

Especially, if $\mu_0 = \mu_1 = 2$, we can get

$$
TH_{2,2}(t) = (1, \cos\tfrac{\pi}{2}t, \sin\tfrac{\pi}{2}t, \cos\pi t)
\begin{pmatrix}
\frac{1}{2} & \frac{1}{2} & -\frac{1}{\pi} & \frac{1}{\pi} \\
0 & 0 & 0 & -\frac{2}{\pi} \\
0 & 0 & \frac{2}{\pi} & 0 \\
\frac{1}{2} & -\frac{1}{2} & \frac{1}{\pi} & \frac{1}{\pi}
\end{pmatrix}
\begin{pmatrix}
p_0 \\ p_1 \\ p_0' \\ p_1'
\end{pmatrix},
$$

and

$$
GTH_{2,2}(t) = (1, t, t^2, \cos\pi t)
\begin{pmatrix}
\frac{1}{2} & \frac{1}{2} & -\frac{1}{4} & -\frac{1}{4} \\
0 & 0 & 1 & 0 \\
0 & 0 & -\frac{1}{2} & \frac{1}{2} \\
\frac{1}{2} & -\frac{1}{2} & \frac{1}{4} & \frac{1}{4}
\end{pmatrix}
\begin{pmatrix}
p_0 \\ p_1 \\ p_0' \\ p_1'
\end{pmatrix}.
$$

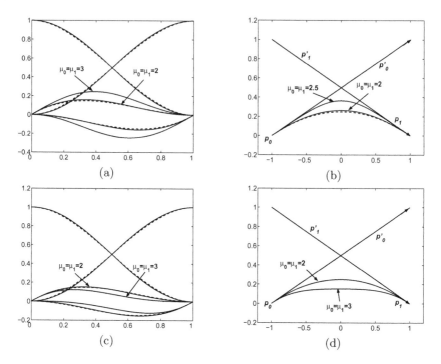

Fig. 1. The (a) and (c) show the families of four THP and GTHP base functions respectively, dashed lines represent normal cubic Hermite base functions. The (b) and (d) indicate the families of THP and GTHP curves for given p_0, p_1, p_0', p_1' respectively.

3   The Variable Degree Spline via Trigonometric Polynomials

Definition 3. *Given a knot vector* $U : x_0 < x_1 < \cdots < x_N$. *Let* $\boldsymbol{TS}_3^\mu = \{s(x) \in C^2[x_0, x_N] \ s.t. \ s(x) \in \boldsymbol{TP}_3^{\mu_i, \mu_{i+1}} \ for \ x \in [x_i, x_{i+1}], i = 0, 1, \cdots, N-1\}$, *where* $\boldsymbol{TP}_3^{\mu_i, \mu_{i+1}} := span\{1, \cos\frac{\pi}{2}t, \sin\frac{\pi}{2}t, \cos\pi t, (\cos\frac{\pi}{2}t)^{\mu_i}, (\sin\frac{\pi}{2}t)^{\mu_{i+1}}\}, t = \frac{x-x_i}{x_{i+1}-x_i};$ $\mu_i \geq 2, \mu_{i+1} \geq 2, \mu_i, \mu_{i+1} \in R.$

If $s(x) \in \boldsymbol{TS}_3^\mu$ *and* $s(x_i) = y_i$, *we call* $s(x)$ *trigonometric Hermite-like interpolation spline(THIS).*

Definition 4. *Given a knot vector* $U : x_0 < x_1 < \cdots < x_N$. *Let* $\boldsymbol{GTS}_3^\mu = \{s(x) \in C^2[x_0, x_N] \ s.t. \ s(x) \in \boldsymbol{GTP}_3^{\mu_i, \mu_{i+1}} \ for \ x \in [x_i, x_{i+1}], i = 0, 1, \cdots, N-1\}$, *where* $$\boldsymbol{GTP}_3^{\mu_i, \mu_{i+1}} := span\{1, t^{\mu_i}, (1-t)^{\mu_i}, \cos\pi t, (\cos\frac{\pi}{2}t)^{\mu_{i+1}}, (\sin\frac{\pi}{2}t)^{\mu_{i+1}}\}, t = \frac{x-x_i}{x_{i+1}-x_i}, \mu_i \geq 2, \mu_{i+1} \geq 2, \mu_i, \mu_{i+1} \in R.$$

If $s(x) \in \boldsymbol{GTS}_3^\mu$ *and* $s(x_i) = y_i$, *we call* $s(x)$ *generalized trigonometric Hermite-like interpolation spline (GTHIS).*

Let $h_{j-1} = x_j - x_{j-1}$, $\lambda_{j-1} = \frac{h_j}{h_{j-1}+h_j}$, $j = 1,2,\cdots,N$.

From Definitions 3 and 4, we set

$$TH_{j,3}^{\mu_i,\mu_{i+1}}(x(t)) = y_{j-1}TF_0(t) + y_j TF_1(t) + h_j(m_{j-1}TG_{0,\mu_1}(t) + m_j TG_{1,\mu_0}(t)),$$
$$GTH_{j,3}^{\mu_i,\mu_{i+1}}(x(t)) = y_{j-1}GTF_0(t) + y_j GTF_1(t) + h_j(m_{j-1}GTG_0(t) + m_j GTG_1(t)),$$
$$j = 0,1,\cdots,N-1. \tag{9}$$

Note: In the different interval, we can replace μ_0 and μ_1 in the above base functions in Eq. (9) respectively. Correspondingly, $TG_{0,\mu_1} \triangleq TG_{0,\mu_{i+1}}, TG_{0,\mu_0} \triangleq TG_{0,\mu_i}$.

We now know that $TH_{j-1,3}^{\mu_{j-1,0},\mu_{j-1,1}}(x(t))$ and $GTH_{j-1,3}^{\mu_{j-1,0},\mu_{j-1,1}}(x(t))$ are C^1 continuous. But if we suppose that $TH_{j-1,3}^{\mu_{j-1,0},\mu_{j-1,1}}(x(t))$ and $GTH_{j-1,3}^{\mu_{j-1,0},\mu_{j-1,1}}(x(t))$ are C^2 continuous, then $m_j, (j = 0,1,\cdots N)$ must be solved. We can suppose

$$\frac{d^2}{dx^2}TH_{j-1,3}^{\mu_{j-1,0},\mu_{j-1,1}}(x_j^-) = \frac{d^2}{dx^2}TH_{j,3}^{\mu_{j,0},\mu_{j,1}}(x_j^+), \tag{10}$$

$$\frac{d^2}{dx^2}GTH_{j-1,3}^{\mu_{j-1,0},\mu_{j-1,1}}(x_j^-) = \frac{d^2}{dx^2}GTH_{j,3}^{\mu_{j,0},\mu_{j,1}}(x_j^+), \tag{11}$$

$j = 1,2,\cdots,N-1.$

(1) Now we discuss the functions of $TH_{j-1,3}^{\mu_{j-1,0},\mu_{j-1,1}}(x(t))$.
If $\mu_0 = \mu_1 = 2$, we get

$$\lambda_j m_{j-1} + 2m_j + (1-\lambda_j)m_{j+1} = \pi[\frac{1-\lambda_j}{h_{j+1}}(y_{j+1}-y_j) + \frac{\lambda_j}{h_j}(y_j - y_{j-1})], j = 1,2,\cdots,N-1.$$

Given initial values $m_0 = y_0'$, $m_N = y_N'$, we can solve the Eq. (10) for m_j, $(j = 1,2,\cdots,N-1)$. Especially, if $h_j = h_{j+1} = 1$, $j = 0,1,\cdots,N-1$, then we get:

$$\begin{pmatrix} 1 & 0 & 0 & \cdots & 0 & 0 & 0 \\ 1 & 4 & 1 & \cdots & 0 & 0 & 0 \\ \vdots & \vdots & \vdots & \ddots & \vdots & \vdots & \vdots \\ 0 & 0 & 0 & \cdots & 1 & 4 & 1 \\ 0 & 0 & 0 & \cdots & 0 & 0 & 1 \end{pmatrix} \begin{pmatrix} m_0 \\ m_1 \\ \vdots \\ m_{N-1} \\ m_N \end{pmatrix} = \begin{pmatrix} y_0' \\ \pi(y_2 - y_0) \\ \vdots \\ \pi(y_N - y_{N-2}) \\ y_N' \end{pmatrix}$$

(2) For the functions of $GTH_{j-1,3}^{\mu_{j-1,0},\mu_{j-1,1}}(x(t))$ from Eq. (11), we have
(i) If $\mu_{j-1,0} = \mu_{j-1,1} = 2$, then

$$(\frac{\pi^2}{4}-1)\lambda_j m_{j-1} + (\frac{\pi^2}{4}+1)m_j + (\frac{\pi^2}{4}-1)(1-\lambda_j)m_{j+1} = \frac{\pi^2}{2}[\frac{1-\lambda_{j-1}}{h_j}(y_{j+1}-y_j) + \frac{\lambda_{j-1}}{h_{j-1}}(y_j - y_{j-1})],$$

$j = 1, 2, \cdots, N - 1$.

(ii) If $\mu_{j-1,0} = 2$, $\mu_{j-1,1} > 2$, then

$$\lambda_{j-1}m_{j-1} + k_j m_j + (1-\lambda_{j-1})m_{j+1} = \frac{\pi^2}{2}[\frac{1-\lambda_{j-1}}{h_j}(y_j - y_{j+1}) + \frac{\lambda_{j-1}}{h_{j-1}}(y_{j-1} - y_j)],$$

where $k_j = -\frac{\pi^2}{8}[(1 - \lambda_{j-1})\mu_{j,1} + \lambda_{j-1}\mu_{j-1,1}] - 1$, $j = 1, 2, \cdots, N - 1$.

(iii) If $\mu_{j-1,1} = 2$, $\mu_{j-1,0} > 2$, then

$$\frac{\pi^2}{2\mu_{j-1,0}}\lambda_{j-1}m_{j-1} + k_j m_j + \frac{\pi^2}{2\mu_{j,0}}(1-\lambda_{j-1})m_{j+1} = \frac{\pi^2}{2}[\frac{1-\lambda_{j-1}}{h_j}(y_{j+1} - y_j) + \frac{\lambda_{j-1}}{h_{j-1}}(y_j - y_{j-1})],$$

where $k_j = \lambda_{j-1}[(\mu_{j-1,0} - 1) + \frac{\pi^2}{2\mu_{j-1,0}}] + (1 - \lambda_{j-1})[(\mu_{j,0} - 1) + \frac{\pi^2}{2\mu_{j,0}}], j = 1, 2, \cdots, N - 1$.

Also with the initial values of m_0, m_N, we can solve the $m_j (j = 1, 2, \cdots, N-1)$ from the above equations.

(iv) If $\mu_{j-1,0} > 2$, $\mu_{j-1,1} > 2$, we get

$$m_j = \frac{\pi^2}{2k_j}[\frac{1-\lambda_{j-1}}{h_j}(y_{j+1} - y_j) + \frac{\lambda_{j-1}}{h_{j-1}}(y_j - y_{j-1})],$$

where $k_j = \lambda_{j-1}[(\mu_{j-1,0} - 1) + \frac{\pi^2}{4}\frac{\mu_{j-1,1}}{\mu_{j-1,0}}] + (1 - \lambda_{j-1})[(\mu_{j,0} - 1) + \frac{\pi^2}{4}\frac{\mu_{j,1}}{\mu_{j,0}}], j = 1, 2, \cdots, N - 1$.

Note: In this conditions of **(iv)**, we do not need to solve the linear system for $m_j, (j = 0, 1, \cdots, N)$ to construct the cubic Hermite-like interpolation spline $GTH_{j-1,3}^{\mu_{j-1,0},\mu_{j-1,1}}(x(t))$

Example 1: Given $g(x) = \frac{\sin x}{x}$, knot vector $U := (0, \frac{\pi}{2}, \pi, \frac{3\pi}{2})$ and corresponding derivative values $g'(x_j) := (0, -\frac{4}{\pi^2}, -\frac{1}{\pi}, \frac{4}{9\pi^2}), (j = 0, 1, 2, 3)$. If we interpolate the values of function $g(x)$ and corresponding derivative values $g'(x_j)$ at the

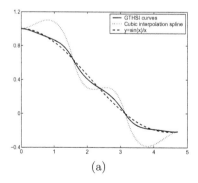
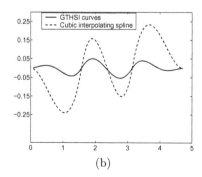

(a)   (b)

Fig. 2. (a) The figures of function $g(x)$, normal cubic interpolation spline curves and GTHIS curves with $\mu_0 = \mu_1 = 3$. (b) The figure describes the interpolation errors associated with GTHIS curves and normal cubic interpolation spline curves.

knots, we can obtain a GTHIS curve by choosing $\mu_0 = \mu_1 = 3$ without solving m-system of equations (See: Fig. 2(a)). Figure 2(b) indicates the error function of interpolation spline associated with the GTHIS spline and cubic polynomial spline, which shows that the GTHIS spline has a better approximation order than cubic interpolation spline.

4   The Applications by Introduced Variable Degree Spline

4.1   The Applications of Introduced Spline in the Curves and Surfaces Modeling

Let us suppose that $p_0' = k_0 u_0$ and $p_1' = k_1 u_1$, where $u_0 := \frac{p_0'}{||p_0'||}, u_1 := \frac{p_1'}{||p_1'||}$. By varying k_0 and k_1, we can obtain an infinite family of curves, all of which have the same end points and slopes, but entirely different interior shapes.

Given four points q_0, q_1, q_2 and q_3 with $(q_i \in R^n, n \in \mathrm{N}, i = 0, 1, 2, 3)$, we can obtain a trigonometric model for $p_0 := q_0, p_1 := q_1, p_0' := q_2 - q_0, p_1' := q_3 - q_1$. In this case, a new class of geometric forms is obtained by

$$TH_{\mu_0,\mu_1}(t) = q_0 TB_{0,\mu_0,\mu_1}(t) + q_1 TB_{1,\mu_0,\mu_1}(t) + q_2 TB_{2,\mu_0,\mu_1}(t) + q_3 TB_{3,\mu_0,\mu_1}(t), \quad (12)$$

$$GTH_{\mu_0,\mu_1}(t) = q_0 GTB_{0,\mu_0,\mu_1}(t) + q_1 GTB_{1,\mu_0,\mu_1}(t) + q_2 GTB_{2,\mu_0,\mu_1}(t) + q_3 GTB_{3,\mu_0,\mu_1}(t), \tag{13}$$

where $\mu_0, \mu_1 \in R$, $\mu_0, \mu_1 \geq 2$, $t \in [0, 1]$.

Proposition 1. *Using the above notations, we have:*

$$TB_{0,\mu_0,\mu_1}(t) = \cos^2 \tfrac{\pi}{2} t - \tfrac{2}{\pi} \sin \tfrac{\pi}{2} t + \tfrac{2}{\pi} \sin^{\mu_1} \tfrac{\pi}{2} t, \; TB_{1,\mu_0,\mu_1}(t) = \sin^2 \tfrac{\pi}{2} t + \tfrac{2}{\pi} \cos \tfrac{\pi}{2} t - \tfrac{2}{\pi} \cos^{\mu_0} \tfrac{\pi}{2} t,$$
$$TB_{2,\mu_0,\mu_1}(t) = \tfrac{2}{\pi}(\sin \tfrac{\pi}{2} t - \sin^{\mu_1} \tfrac{\pi}{2} t), \qquad TB_{3,\mu_0,\mu_1}(t) = -\tfrac{2}{\pi}(\cos \tfrac{\pi}{2} t - \cos^{\mu_0} \tfrac{\pi}{2} t),$$
$$\tag{14}$$

$$GTB_{0,\mu_0,\mu_1}(t) = \cos^2 \tfrac{\pi}{2} t + \tfrac{1}{\mu_0}(1-t)^{\mu_0} - \tfrac{1}{\mu_0}\cos^{\mu_1}\tfrac{\pi}{2}t, \; GTB_{1,\mu_0,\mu_1}(t) = \sin^2 \tfrac{\pi}{2}t - \tfrac{1}{\mu_0}t^{\mu_0} + \tfrac{1}{\mu_0}\sin^{\mu_1}\tfrac{\pi}{2}t,$$
$$GTB_{2,\mu_0,\mu_1}(t) = -\tfrac{1}{\mu_0}(1-t)^{\mu_0} + \tfrac{1}{\mu_0}\cos^{\mu_1}\tfrac{\pi}{2}t, \qquad GTB_{3,\mu_0,\mu_1}(t) = \tfrac{1}{\mu_0}t^{\mu_0} - \tfrac{1}{\mu_0}\sin^{\mu_1}\tfrac{\pi}{2}t.$$
$$\tag{15}$$

Parabola, circular arcs and some transcendental curves can be represented precisely by choosing proper q_0, q_1, q_2, q_3 and μ_0, μ_1. Denote $TH(t) := TH_{\mu_0,\mu_1}(t)$, $GTH(t) := GTH_{\mu_0,\mu_1}(t)$ and $TB_i(t) := TB_{i,\mu_0,\mu_1}(t)$, $GTB_i(t) := GTB_{i,\mu_0,\mu_1}(t), (i = 0, 1, 2, 3)$ in the remainder of the paper. For example:

(i) Let $q_0 = q_2$ and $q_1 = q_3$. Then $TH(t) = GTH(t) = q_0 \cos^2 \tfrac{\pi}{2} t + q_1 \sin^2 \tfrac{\pi}{2} t = q_1 + (q_0 - q_1) \cos^2 \tfrac{\pi}{2} t$. So $TH(t)$ and $GTH(t)$ all represent a line segment precisely in these conditions.

(ii) Let $q_0 = \tfrac{2}{\pi}(q_1 - q_3), q_1 = \tfrac{2}{\pi}(q_2 - q_0)$ and $\mu_0 = \mu_1 = 2$, $\qquad (*)$

or let $q_1 - q_0 = \frac{2}{\pi}(q_3 + q_2 - q_1 - q_0)$ and $\mu_0 = \mu_1 = 2$. $\hspace{2cm}$ (**)

Then $TH(t)$ represents a segment of elliptic arc for proper q_0, q_1, q_2, q_3.

In fact, under the conditions of (*), we can get $TH(t) = q_0 cos\frac{\pi}{2}t + q_1 sin\frac{\pi}{2}t$. Especially, if $q_0 = (1,0), q_1 = (0,1)$, then $q_2 = (1,\frac{\pi}{2}), q_3 = (-\frac{\pi}{2},1)$. So $TH(t) = (cos\frac{\pi}{2}t, sin\frac{\pi}{2}t)$.

Under the conditions of (**), we can get $TH(t) = q_0 + \frac{2}{\pi}(q_3 - q_1) + \frac{2}{\pi}(q_1 - q_3)cos\frac{\pi}{2}t + \frac{2}{\pi}(q_2 - q_0)sin\frac{\pi}{2}t$. So we know that $TH(t)$ can represent a segment of circular and elliptic arc precisely (See: Fig. 3(a)).

(iii) Let $\mu_0 = \mu_1 = 2$. By simple calculations, we know that both $TH(t)$ and $GTH(t)$ represent quadratic polynomial curves. In fact, from (14) and (15), we have

$$1 = TB_0(t) + TB_1(t) + TB_2(t) + TB_3(t),$$
$$sin\frac{\pi}{2}t = TB_1(t) + TB_3(t) + \frac{\pi}{2}TB_2(t), \hspace{2cm} (16)$$
$$sin^2\frac{\pi}{2}t = TB_1(t) + TB_3(t).$$

$$1 = GTB_0(t) + GTB_1(t) + GTB_2(t) + GTB_3(t),$$
$$t = GTB_1(t) + GTB_2(t) + 2GTB_3(t) \hspace{2cm} (17)$$
$$t^2 = GTB_1(t) + 3GTB_3(t).$$

(iv) If $q_0 - q_2 = q_1 - q_3$, $q_0 = -q_1$ and $\mu_0 = \mu_1 = 2$, then $GTH(t) = \frac{1}{2}(q_0 - q_2) + (q_2 - q_0)t + \frac{1}{2}(q_0 + q_2)cos(\pi t)$. So $GTH(t)$ can represent a segment of sine or cosine curve for proper q_0, q_2. Especially, if $q_0 = (1,1), q_2 = (-1,1)$, then $GTH(t) = (x(t), y(t)) = (1 - 2t, cos(\pi t)), t \in [0,1]$. So $GTH(t)$ represents a segment of sine curves (See: Fig. 3(b)).

(v) If $q_0 = -q_2$, $q_3 = 3q_1$ and $\mu_0 = 2, \mu_1 = 2$, then $GTH(t) = q_0(1 - t)^2 + q_1t^2$. So $GTH(t)$ can represent the curve $\sqrt{x} + \sqrt{y} = 1$ precisely for proper q_0, q_1. Especially, if $q_0 = (1,0), q_1 = (0,1)$, then $GTH(t) = (x(t), y(t)) = ((1 - t)^2, t^2)$, $t \in [0,1]$. So $\sqrt{x} + \sqrt{y} = 1$ (See: Fig. 3(c)).

We can generalize the methods, which are used to construct THP and GTHP curves, to bicubic Coons-like surfaces.

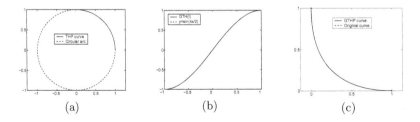

(a) $\hspace{3cm}$ (b) $\hspace{3cm}$ (c)

Fig. 3. (a) A segment of circular arc is represented precisely by THP curves. (b) A segment of sine curves is represented precisely by GTHP curves. (c) A segment of curves with $\sqrt{x} + \sqrt{y} = 1$ is represented precisely by GTHP curves.

Definition 5. *If $H(u,v)$ is a bivariate continuous vector function defined in the parameter domain of $[0,1] \times [0,1]$, we can construct a bicubic Hermite-like interpolating surface $SH(u,v) = H(u) \cdot M \cdot T(v)$ which interpolates the end points and corresponding tangent vectors:*

$$H(u) = (TH_0(u), TH_1(u), TH_2(u), TH_3(u)); T(v) = (TH_0(v), TH_1(v), TH_2(v), TH_3(v))^T$$

$$C = \begin{pmatrix} H(0,0) & H(0,1) & H'_v(0,0) & H'_v(0,1) \\ H(1,0) & H(1,1) & H'_v(1,0) & H'_v(1,1) \\ H'_u(0,0) & H'_u(0,1) & H''_{uv}(0,0) & H''_{uv}(0,1) \\ H'_u(1,0) & H'_u(1,1) & H''_{uv}(1,0) & H''_{uv}(1,1) \end{pmatrix}.$$

Given the values of function $H(u,v)$, corresponding tangent vectors and up to second partial derivatives at the end points, we can construct THP surfaces and GTHP surfaces by corresponding THP polynomials (3) and GTHP polynomials (5).

Figure 4(a1) offers a segment of sphere and interpolating surfaces, Fig. 4(b1) indicates the error function of original surface and interpolating surface associated with bicubic Hermite interpolation polynomials, Fig. 4(c1) shows the error function associated with original surface and THP surface.

Figure 4(a2) offers another original function of $H(u,v) = (x(u,v),$ $y(u,v), z(u,v))$ associated with $x(u,v) = e^{u+v}$, $y(u,v) = e^{u-v}$, $z(u,v) = uv$ and interpolating surface, Fig. 4(b2) indicates the error function of original surface $H(u,v)$ and interpolating surface associated with bicubic Hermite interpolation polynomials, Fig. 4(c2) explains the error function associated with GTHP surface and surface $H(u,v)$.

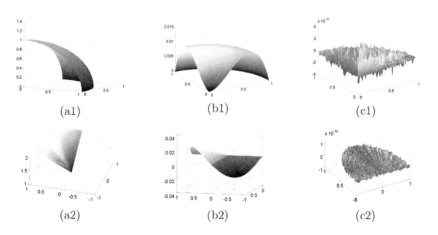

Fig. 4. The figures of original surface, interpolating surface, and corresponding error functions by THP and GTHP interpolation respectively.

From these figures we know that the interpolating surfaces associated with the THP surface for the first original function and the GTHP surface for the second original function have a better approximate order than the interpolating surface associated with bicubic Hermite interpolating polynomials.

4.2   The Applications of Introduced Spline in the Manipulator Trajectory Planning

In this section, we consider the applications of introduced spline in the manipulator trajectory planning. Our goal is to find a path which connects the given start point and the target point, and make the manipulator move smoothly between the two end points while avoiding all obstacles in the motion. In our approach, the variable degree spline interpolation based method is applied to construct the trajectory. Moreover, the generated trajectories have continues values of the accelerations without solving equations system, and thus ensures the smoothness of the trajectory. The generation process of trajectories with the variable degree spline possess the lower computational complexity than the one via normal polynomial spline method.

Given a sequence of data points $q_i, (i = 0, 1, \cdots, N)$ in joint space of manipulation, planning manipulator trajectory with the variable degree interpolation spline. The input data point has been taken to be the same as in [16], in order to make a comparison with the results obtained from the experiment. Let four data points in joint space, $q_0(0, 60), q_1(1, -50), q_2(3, 80), q_3(4, 100)$, the time is used as the X-axis and the joint angle is used as the Y-axis. Given the initial conditions, acceleration is zero in start and end points. Here, we compare the acceleration curves via the variable degree interpolation spline with the one by cubic spline and the cubic triangular Bézier spline [16] in Fig. 5.

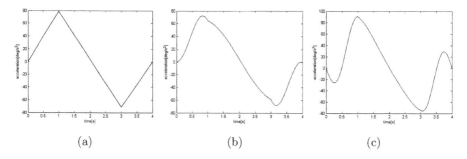

Fig. 5. The acceleration curves via the cubic spline (a), the cubic triangular Bézier spline [16] (b), and the variable degree interpolation spline (c)

As stated in the foregoing, we described the trajectory of manipulator. However, in modern industrial production, the speed of operation directly affects the productivity. If the manipulator can achieve the maximized the speed of operation, the traveling time must be minimized. Therefore, the optimization problem is to adjust the time intervals between via-points such that the total traveling time is minimum. There are N joints which must be considered. Now, for the joint j $(1 \leqslant j \leqslant N)$, let $q_1, q_2, \cdots, q_n$ be the via-points in joint space and $t_1, t_2, \cdots, t_n$ be the sequence of time instants corresponding to the via-points; let $h_i = t_{i+1} - t_i$ $(i = 1, 2, \cdots, n-1)$ be the time interval between two consecutive via-points and a_i be the acceleration of the interpolation q_i, $S_{j,i}(t) \triangleq GTH_{j,3}^{\mu_{j,0},0,\mu_{j,1}}(x(t))$ be the variable degree interpolation spline for the jth joint defined on the interval $[t_i, t_{i+1}]$. It is assumed that the position, velocity, acceleration are continuous on this time interval. $S_{j,i}(t), S'_{j,i}(t), S''_{j,i}(t)$ and $S'''_{j,i}(t)$ $(t \in [t_i, t_{i+1}])$ are the position, velocity, acceleration and jerk between the via-points q_i and q_{i+1} respectively. The v_1 and v_n, a_1 and a_n are joint velocities and joint accelerations at the initial time $t = t_1$ and at the terminal time $t = t_n$. According to the definition of quasi-cubic Hermite-like interpolation polynomials, we have:

$$S_{j,i}(x(t)) = q_{j,i}GTF_0(t) + q_{j,i+1}GTF_1(t) + h_i(v_{j,i}GTG_0(t) + v_{j,i+1}GTG_1(t))$$
$$S'_{j,i}(x(t)) = \frac{1}{h_i}(q_{j,i}GTF'_0(t) + q_{j,i+1}GTF'_1(t)) + v_{j,i}GTG'_0(t) + v_{j,i+1}GTG'_1(t)$$
$$S''_{j,i}(x(t)) = (\frac{1}{h_i})^2(q_{j,i}GTF''_0(t) + q_{j,i+1}GTF''_1(t)) + \frac{1}{h_i}(v_{j,i}GTG''_0(t) + v_{j,i+1}GTG''_1(t))$$
$$S'''_{j,i}(x(t)) = (\frac{1}{h_i})^3(q_{j,i}GTF'''_0(t) + q_{j,i+1}GTF'''_1(t)) + (\frac{1}{h_i})^2(v_{j,i}GTG'''_0(t) + v_{j,i+1}GTG'''_1(t))$$
$$j = 1, 2, \cdots, N, i = 1, 2, \cdots, n-1$$

$$(18)$$

From Eq. (11), let $\mu = 3$, we have:

$$v_{j,i} = \frac{2\pi^2}{8+\pi^2}[\frac{1-\lambda_{i-1}}{h_i}(q_{j,i+1} - q_{j,i}) + \frac{\lambda_{i-1}}{h_{i-1}}(q_{j,i} - q_{j,i-1})], i = 2, \cdots, n-1, j = 1, 2, \cdots, N$$

$$(19)$$

In order to apply the mathematic model, the kinematics constraints should be formulated, for convenience, let

$$VC_j = velocity\ constraint\ for\ the\ jth\ joint$$
$$WC_j = acceleration\ constraint\ for\ the\ jth\ joint$$
$$JC_j = jerk\ constraint\ for\ the\ jth\ joint$$

The optimal problem is formulated mathematically as follows.
Objective function:

$$Minimize \quad T = \sum_{i=1}^{n-1} h_i \tag{20}$$

Constraints:

$$\begin{cases} |S'_{j,i}(x(t))| \leqslant VC_j, \\ |S''_{j,i}(x(t))| \leqslant WC_j, j = i, \cdots, N, i = 1, \cdots, n \\ |S'''_{j,i}(x(t))| \leqslant JC_j, \end{cases} \tag{21}$$

Table 1. Input data for trajectory planning

Joint	Via-points(deg)			
	1	2	3	4
1	120	90	45	0
2	−10	60	40	100
3	0	−20	30	70

Table 2. Kinematics limits of the joints

Joint	Velocity(deg/s)	Acceleration(deg/s2)
1	100	70
2	95	75
3	100	75

Table 3. Simulation results

Method / Time	Proposed method	Cong's Method([2])
$h_1(s)$	0.256	2.321
$h_2(s)$	0.768	1.811
$h_3(s)$	0.323	2.165
Total times	1.347	6.297

The above constraints can be expressed in explicit forms by Eqs. (18) and (19) as follows: Objective function:

$$Minimize \quad T = \sum_{i=1}^{n-1} h_i$$

s.t.

$$
\begin{cases}
max\{|v_{j,i}|, |v_{j,i+1}|\} + \frac{\pi}{2h_i}|p_{i+1} - p_i| + \frac{\pi}{4}\sqrt{v_{j,i}^2 + v_{j,i+1}^2} \leqslant VC_j, \\
\frac{\pi^2}{2h_i^2}|p_{i+1} - p_i| + \frac{2v_{j,i+1}}{h_i} + \frac{3\pi^2}{8h_i}\sqrt{v_{j,i}^2 + v_{j,i+1}^2} \leqslant WC_j, \\
\frac{\pi^3}{2h_i^3}|p_{i+1} - p_i| + \frac{2(v_{j,i}+v_{j,i+1}))}{h_i^2} + \frac{9\pi^3}{16h_i^2}\sqrt{v_{j,i}^2 + v_{j,i+1}^2} \leqslant JC_j, \\
h_i \geqslant max \frac{|q_{j,i+1} - q_{j,i}|}{VC_j},
\end{cases}
\quad j = 1, \cdots, N, i = 1, \cdots, n
$$

$$(22)$$

since h_i are the time parameters, and should be subject to a lower bound. Here, we briefly described the optimization algorithm and will achieve the experiment in simulation for manipulator. The input data has been taken to the same as in [2] (Table 1).

5 Conclusions and Discussions

We have proposed a new class of Hermite-like interpolation polynomials and a variable degree trigonometric polynomial interpolation spline. The technique enhances the control capability of curves and surfaces with the control points and parameters μ_0 and μ_1. In addition, we can replace parameters μ_0 and μ_1 by different parameters μ_i and μ_{i+1} in the different interval. So the new curves are locally-controllable via the different parameters μ_i and μ_{i+1}. Moreover, the introduced curves can represent straight lines, polynomial curves, conics and some transcendental curves precisely (Tables 2 and 3).

For CAD field, the four points form a control polygon and these control points can be used to adjust curve shape in a predictable and natural way. The form of generalized interpolation model is a good candidate for use in an interactive environment to design curves for CAD system and in computer graphics applications.

The new interpolation methods can offer higher approximation order than normal Hermite polynomial interpolation method, but do not need to solve m-system of equations for proper parameters.

Experiment results show the new presented spline can be introduced in the area of industrial design. It has a better approximation order with GTHIS spline than the case with the cubic interpolation spline in the curves and surfaces modeling, and we can design a continuous trajectory to interpolate the given points in the trajectory planning to ensure that manipulator can move smoothly when it makes high operating speed. The generation process of curves and surfaces modeling and trajectories planning with the variable degree spline possess the lower computational complexity than the one via normal polynomial spline method.

Acknowledgments. Project supported by the National Natural Science Foundation of China (No. 11471093) and in part by the Natural Science Research Funds of Education Department of Anhui Province (No. KJ2014A142).

References

1. Baltensperger, R.: Some results on linear rational trigonometric interpolation. Comput. Math. Appl. **43**, 737–746 (2002)
2. Cong, M., Xu, X.: Time-jerk synthetic optimal trajectory planning of robot based on fuzzy genetic algorithm. Int. J. Intell. Syst. Technol. Appl. **8**, 185–199 (2010)
3. Costantini, P., Lyche, T., Manni, C.: On a class of weak Tchebycheff systems. Numer. Math. **101**, 333–354 (2005)
4. Du, J.Y., Han, H.L., Jin, G.X.: On trigonometric and paratrigonometric Hermite interpolation. J. Approx. Theory **131**, 74–99 (2004)
5. Gasparetto, A., Zanotto, V.: A technique for time-jerk optimal planning of trajectories. Robot. Comput.-Integr. Manuf. **24**, 415–426 (2008)
6. Han, X.: Piecewise trigonometric Hermite interpolation. Appl. Math. Comput. **268**, 616–627 (2015)
7. Juhász, I., Róth, Á.: A scheme for interpolation with trigonometric spline curves. J. Comput. Appl. Math. **1**, 246–261 (2014)

8. Mainar, E., Peña, J.M., Sánchez-Reyes, J.: Shape preserving alternatives to the rational Bézier model. Comput. Aided Geom. Des. **18**, 37–60 (2001)
9. Mazure, M.L.: Chebyshev spaces and Bernstein bases. Constr. Approx. **22**, 347–363 (2005)
10. Morigi, S., Neamtu, M.: Some results for a class of generalized polynomials. Adv. Comput. Math. **12**, 133–149 (2000)
11. Peña, J.M.: Shape preserving representations for trigonometric polynomial curves. Comput. Aided Geom. Des. **14**, 5–11 (1997)
12. Romani, L., Saini, L., Albrecht, G.: Algebraic-Trigonometric Pythagorean-Hodograph curves and their use for Hermite interpolation. Adv. Comput. Math. **40**, 1–34 (2014)
13. Schweikert, D.G.: Interpolatory tension splines with automatic selection of tension factors. J. Math. Phys. **45**, 312–327 (1966)
14. Sheng, M., Su, B.Y., Zhu, G.Q.: Sweeping surface modeling by geometric Hermite interpolation. J. Comput. Inf. Sys. **3**, 527–532 (2007)
15. Su, B.Y., Tan, J.Q.: A family of quasi-cubic blended splines and applications. J. Zhejiang Univ. Sci. A **7**, 1550–1560 (2006)
16. Wang, Y., Wenlong, X., Sun, N.: Manipulator trajectory planning based on the cubic triangular Bézier spline. In: Proceedings of the World Congress on Intelligent Control and Automation, pp. 6–9 (2010)

Visualization of Multi-dimensional Information of Electromagnetic Environment Based on Three Dimensional Spheres

Ying Gao, Hongshuai Han[✉], Fei Ge, and Shuxia Guo

School of Marine Science and Technology,
Northwestern Polytechnical University, Xi'an 710072, China
2530012324@qq.com

Abstract. In the current research of visualization technology, most visualization methods based on 2D or 3D appearance of the layer (such as trees, maps etc.). Only a few methods have fully used the three-dimensional space. Aiming at the complex, Multi-dimensional and time-varying characteristics of electromagnetic, and this paper shows the visual display of multiple dimensions, allows users to obtain the corresponding Multi-dimensional information attribute characteristics from different angles. By using the idea of VisDB and the color scheme of the visual database, the multi dimension value of 2D information is set up. The Mercator projection of the inverse function to a pixel mapping to the sphere of a point, the two-dimensional panel abstract data into 3D visual sphere, realize the complex electromagnetic environment of multi-dimensional information to three-dimensional sphere mapping. The method can reflect the different types of visual effects in the visual results, and improve the performance of Multi-dimensional information visualization.

Keywords: Three-dimensional sphere · Multi-dimensional information visualization · Electromagnetic environment · Complexity

1 Introduction

Simple information visualization techniques, such as line images and scatter plots, have been widely used for decades [1–3]. With the help of the line chart, the reader can easily understand the one-dimensional information, such as the variables function. Similarly, 3D line and scatter charts can describe the relationship among the three variables [4, 5]. When the number of variables is four or five, you may use animation techniques and virtual environments to convey more essential relationship among variables. For relationships with more than five variables, standard geometric projection technology and human perception system no longer offer help [6, 7]. Therefore, we studied the Multi-dimensional information visualization method, which can be summarized as: "How to quickly understand a lot of information in a set of standards". It requires that the method can describe the complex information and make people at a glance. So we need to design a new method of Multi-dimensional information visualization.

© Springer International Publishing Switzerland 2016
A. El Rhalibi et al. (Eds.): Edutainment 2016, LNCS 9654, pp. 163–172, 2016.
DOI: 10.1007/978-3-319-40259-8_14

2   Evaluation of Electromagnetic Environment Complexity

2.1   The Concept of Complex Electromagnetic Environment

The complexity of the electromagnetic environment is relative [8, 9]. On the one hand, the same electromagnetic environment is different from the objects it affects, which have an impact on the electronic equipment in a certain frequency channel; however it may have no effect on the other channel of the electronic device. On the other hand, it related to the ability to adapt to the object. In the same environment, it's complex for the weak adaptation capacity, but it may be easy for the strong adaptation capacity. With the development of technology and equipment, something looks intricate now that may be uncomplicated in the future. And that the electromagnetic environment is in the dynamic changes, even for the same electronic device, the feeling and reaction of complexity is not alike at the different frequency channel, time, location and direction, etc. Therefore, the complexity of the assessment of complex battlefield electromagnetic environment is particularly important.

2.2   Electromagnetic Environment Complexity Assessment Index

Electromagnetic signals of the time-domain, frequency-domain, spatial, energy-domain representation as to select complex battlefield electromagnetic environment metric based indicators. It selected electromagnetic signal pattern, frequency occupation, frequency of coincidence rate, electromagnetic signal density and power density as metric for battlefield electromagnetic environment complexity. The concrete structure is shown in Fig. 1 [10].

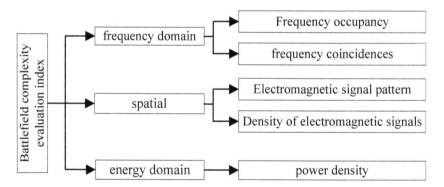

Fig. 1. Battlefield electromagnetic environment complexity evaluation index. After selecting the measure indexes, we need to quantify the metrics, and then we can get the five correlation coefficient by using the related indexes of the electronic countermeasure equipment as the reference.

2.3   The Weight Distribution by Hierarchy Analysis Method

Each electromagnetic environment parameters calculated after at a fixed position and fixed time, according to the fuzzy analytic hierarchy process for the establishment of fuzzy complementary judgment matrix weight calculation method to determine the weight of each information. Based on analytic hierarchy analysis method and combining with the equipment work site and other practical conditions get $0.1 \sim 0.9$ rating scale method results are shown in Table 1:

Table 1. Fuzzy complementary judgments matrix of weight of each index

	Electromagnetic signal pattern	Frequency occupancy	Frequency coincidence	Electromagnetic signal density	Power density
Electromagnetic signal pattern	0.5	0.6	0.6	0.6	0.4
Frequency occupancy	0.4	0.5	0.5	0.6	0.4
Frequency coincidence	0.4	0.5	0.5	0.6	0.4
Electromagnetic signal density	0.4	0.4	0.4	0.5	0.3
Power density	0.6	0.6	0.6	0.7	0.5

The weighted of fuzzy complementary judgments matrix is obtained according to the table A is:

$$A = \begin{bmatrix} 0.5 & 0.6 & 0.6 & 0.6 & 0.4 \\ 0.4 & 0.5 & 0.5 & 0.6 & 0.4 \\ 0.4 & 0.5 & 0.5 & 0.6 & 0.4 \\ 0.4 & 0.4 & 0.4 & 0.5 & 0.3 \\ 0.6 & 0.6 & 0.6 & 0.7 & 0.5 \end{bmatrix}$$

According to type $W_i = \left(\sum_{j=1}^{n} a_{ij} + \frac{n}{2} - 1 \right) \Big/ (n(n-1)) \quad i = 1, 2, \cdots, n$

Get result:

$$W_1 = \left(\sum_{j=1}^{5} a_{1j} + \frac{5}{2} - 1 \right) \Big/ (5 \times (5-1))$$
$$= ((0.5 + 0.6 + 0.6 + 0.6 + 0.4) + \frac{5}{2} - 1) / (5 \times 4) = 0.21$$

In like manner,

$$W_2 = 0.195, W_3 = 0.195, W_4 = 0.175, W_5 = 0.225,$$
$$W = (0.21, 0.195, 0.195, 0.175, 0.225).$$

So get the weight of each index distribution bar graph as shown in Fig. 3, pie chart is shown in Fig. 4 (Fig. 2):

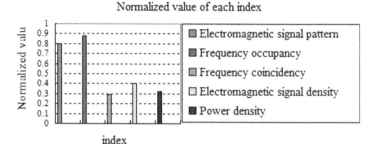

Fig. 2. Normalized index coefficients

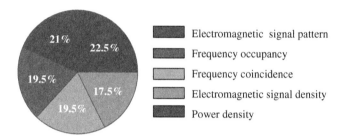

Fig. 3. The weight distribution of the five indexes

Fig. 4. 3 cases with surface function

3   Visualization of Multi-dimensional Information Based on Three Dimensional Sphere

3.1   Area Distribution Function

Regional distribution function: The position of latitude and longitude corresponding to each parameter on the sphere is determined by the regional distribution function. In this paper, the three-dimensional distribution function is used, because of its two characteristics. First, ADF returns a specific area for each parameter. Secondly, the ADF function makes the human perception and sphere corresponding parameters can be mapped to the information sphere of longitude and latitude [11].

$$a = ADF(lo, la) = \left\{ \begin{array}{l} [2\pi * lo/LO_{NO}, 2\pi * (lo+1)/LO_{NO}] \\ [\pi * la/LA_{NO}, \pi * (la+1)/LA_{NO}] \end{array} \right\} \tag{1}$$

Where lo is the weight grade; la is each parameter in the weight of each level; LO_{NO} is the highest level in weight; LA_{NO} is the number of parameters for each grade in weight.

Figure 5 shows the three features that can be used. ADF function can be assigned to a valid expression method. Ratchet, cross and peak valley is assigned by the user specific standard features.

Fig. 5. A randomly generated planar information set

3.2 From 2D to 3D the Inverse Function of Mercator Projection

Shown in Fig. 5 the two-dimensional arrangement of randomly generated flat information and color scheme, using VisDB (visualization of dimensional data) color scheme: from yellow to green, blue and green to blue and magenta to red, in decreasing approximation, color of longitude and latitude region are obtained.

We use the Mercator projection 2D panel into the inverse function of 3D field. The Mercator projection inverse function in Eq. 7 can be set for each pixel mapping plane above the sphere to the corresponding position.

$$\varphi = 2\tan^{-1}(e^y) - \frac{\pi}{2} = 2\tan^{-1}(\sinh(y))$$
$$\lambda = x + \lambda_0 \tag{2}$$

The x and y coordinates of 2D pixel representation, and representation of longitude and latitude.

Figure 6 is a visualization result of a six dimensional information set. Each dimension of the set from minimum to maximum parameters is relevant. By a quickly glance, you can see the similarity of Fig. 6.

Fig. 6. Visualization result of a six dimensional information set

4 Multi-dimensional Information Visualization of Electro-Magnetic Environment Complexity

4.1 Multi-dimensional Information of Electro-Magnetic Environment Complexity

The complexity of electromagnetic environment is described with five parameters. Each parameter refers to the expression of a dimension in specific electronic equipment and a specific time, space. Therefore, in a moment of electromagnetic environment parameters are calculated, and then through the fuzzy analytic hierarchy process to obtain the weight can be for each parameter using ADF and Mercator projection to solve corresponding latitude regions and each region size and the color scheme for drawing.

4.2 Multi-dimensional Information Representation of Electromagnetic Environment Complexity

On the basis of the above work, we designed the Multi-dimensional information visualization flow of electromagnetic environment based on 3D sphere, as shown in Fig. 7.

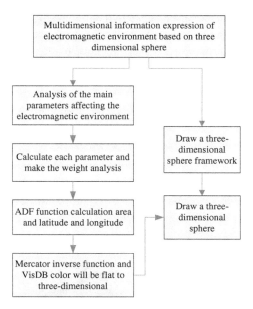

Fig. 7. Visualization of Multi-dimensional information of EME based on 3D sphere

The specific steps of Multi-dimensional information visualization of electromagnetic environment based on 3D sphere are as follows:

Step 1: Analysis and characterization of the spatial distribution characteristic parameters of electromagnetic environment signal: signal type, spectrum occupation degree, signal density, frequency overlap coefficient, power density coefficient, etc. Spatial distribution characteristics' modeling of electromagnetic signals establishes the above parameters model which reflects characteristics of the spatial distribution of electromagnetic signals.

Step 2: Analysis of the electromagnetic environment of each information weights, according to the fuzzy analytic hierarchy process for the establishment of fuzzy complementary judgment matrix weight calculation method to determine the weight of each message. In the fuzzy analytic hierarchy process, factors of pair wise comparison judgment by a factor than the importance of other factors such as a $0.1 \sim 0.9$ standard degree method to quantitative said. Then the fuzzy judgment matrix is obtained, such as the formula 3. For the selected indicators, according to its effect on monitoring equipment, to get the weight relationship of Describe indicators of the electromagnetic environment and to Establish weight fuzzy complementary judgment matrix. Finally, a common formula 4 and Eq. 5 to calculate the weight value of each index.

$$
A = \begin{bmatrix}
\alpha_{11} & \alpha_{12} & \cdots & \alpha_{1n} \\
\alpha_{21} & \alpha_{22} & \cdots & \alpha_{2n} \\
\vdots & \vdots & & \vdots \\
\alpha_{n1} & \alpha_{n2} & \cdots & \alpha_{nn}
\end{bmatrix} = A(a_{ij})
\tag{3}
$$

Compared and judged the element *in* the matrix A to show the importance of the element on the element, the formation of the A matrix can be found to be of the following properties:

$$
\alpha_{ij} > 0
$$

$$
\alpha_{ij} = 1/\alpha_j (i \neq j)
$$

$$
\alpha_{ij} = 1 (i, j = 1, 2, \cdots, n)
$$

(1) The product of each line element of a matrix of computation

$$
M_i = \prod_{j=1}^{N} \alpha_{ij} \quad i = 1, 2, \cdots, n
\tag{4}
$$

(2) Calculation of n root mean square:

$$
\bar{W}_i = \sqrt[n]{M_i},
$$

Normalized processing of vector $\bar{W} = [\bar{W}_1, \bar{W}_2, \cdots, \bar{W}_n]^T$:

$$W_i = \frac{\bar{W}_i}{\sum\limits_{j=1}^{n} \bar{W}_j} \tag{5}$$

$W = [W_1, W_2, \ldots, W_n]^T$ is the desired feature vector. Thus, complexity measure based on the analytic hierarchy process method of comprehensive evaluation system has been analyzed, and the mathematical model is established, this qualitative and quantitative method is suitable for the evaluation of electromagnetic environment parameters. Using fuzzy complementary judgment matrix to obtain the weight vector of values, still need to undertake comparative judgment consistency test, only through the consistency test before they can think the weight value is reasonable. According to the weight in the three-dimensional sphere surface distribution of the position of longitude, latitude and table size, and each parameter of the size of three-dimensional sphere of different processes.

Step 3: Using the area distribution function make every parameter of electromagnetic environment is projected onto the surface of the sphere. In this paper, using the regional distribution function of reason is because of its two characteristics. First, ADF return a return a specific area for each parameter. Secondly, ADF function makes human perception corresponds with the ball; you can map the parameter information to the sphere of latitude and longitude.

Step 4: Use the VisDB (Visualization of Dimensional Data) after the color scheme, using the Mercator projection formula (Mercator) inverse function of the two-dimensional panel projected onto a three-dimensional sphere.

Step 5: Using OpenGL VC++ to program the constructed model, draw up the basic sphere, for each parameter using ADF and Mercator projection to solutions corresponding latitude regions and each region size, and depict it by its color scheme.

4.3   Visualization of the Process of Parameter Variation

As shown in Fig. 8, after the three-dimensional sphere and Multi-dimensional message combined, each part of the three-dimensional sphere is characterized by complex electromagnetic environment parameters.

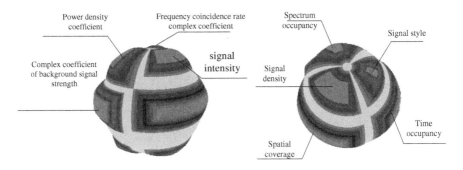

Fig. 8. Significance of each part of the three dimensional sphere

Fig. 9. The three dimensional sphere changes with different fields

As shown in Fig. 9, with the change of spatial domain, time domain, and energy domain, the electromagnetic environment parameters of multi dimension sphere is changed.

5 Conclusion

According to the statistical analysis, Analysis of information is established and easy to analyze with the help of an online graph in a certain dimension. Modern Multi-dimensional information visualization generally involves higher coding dimension, is rarely compare with more advanced and intuitive images and information. This is considered to be a direction of development of modern analysis may need to in the coming years. Actually, in the application of visualization of electromagnetic environment parameters prove, using Multi-dimensional information visualization method is feasible, realistic scenarios and the interactive operation with high efficiency. Hope this research can inspire more research in this field.

References

1. Wang, X., Zhang, L., Dong, C.-W., Rui, X.-P.: A multi-dimensional visualization method combining MDS and SVM. In: 2012 8th International Conference on Natural Computation, pp. 436–439 (2012)
2. Moon, S.-J., Pyeon, M.-W., Eo, Y.-D., Kang, N.-G., Kim, J.-R.: Analysis of current technologies for real time multi-dimensional map service, pp. 665–668 (2012)
3. Liang, F.L., Huang, M.L., Chen, Y.W., Liang, J., Nguyen, Q.V.: Clutter reduction in multi-dimensional visualization of incomplete data using sugiyama algorithm. In: 2012 16th International Conference on Information Visualisation, pp. 93–99 (2012)
4. Okada, Y.: Network data visualization using parallel coordinates version of time-tunnel with 2D to 2D visualization for intrusion detection. In: 2013 27th International Conference on Advanced Information Networking and Applications Workshops, pp. 1088–1093 (2013)
5. Thai, V.T., Handschuh, S., Decker, S.: Tight coupling of personal interests with multi-dimensional visualization for exploration and analysis of text collections. In: 12th International Conference Information Visualisation, pp. 221–226 (2008)

6. Yamazawa, M., Itoh, T., Yamashita, F.: Visualization and level-of-detail control for multi-dimensional bioactive hemical data. In: 12th International Conference Information Visualisation, pp. 11–16 (2008)
7. Rui, X., Zhang, L.: Research on visualization of multi dimension information based on SOM. J. Appl. Sci. Eng. **1**(3), 379–388 (2011)
8. Chen, J., Zhang, D.: Prediction of electromagnetic environment in battlefield based on complexity transform. Microw. J. **27**(1), 91–96 (2011)
9. Zhang, B., Hu, X., Hu, R.: Complex electromagnetic environment simulation uncertain space construction. J. Comput. Simul. **26**(2), 11–13 (2009)
10. Zhi, P., Gao, Y., Ge, F.: Research on algorithm of quantitative evaluation of battlefield electromagnetic environment complexity **35**(3), 40–44 (2014)
11. Hao, J.: Multi-dimensional information visualization. Design of information visualization and case studies. Dissertation of the University of Texas at Dallas (2010). UMI Number: 3421498

Remote Rendering for Mobile Devices Literature Overview

Chanchan Xu, Guangzheng Fei$^{(\boxtimes)}$, and Honglei Han

School of Animation and Digital Arts,
Communication University of China, Beijing, China
gzfei@cuc.edu.cn

Abstract. Mobile device such as mobile phone, PDA (Personal Digital Assistants), HPC (Handheld Personal Computer) and so on has become a prevalent commodity and also a significant influence power that dominates people's daily life. Remote rendering over these platforms is a continuous research subject that still attracts many people's attention. It is also a promising topic for its extensive usage in applications for mobile devices. It is still a challenging issue for the limitation of the wireless network and the process ability of the client side. Here we introduce the state of the art remote rendering techniques over mobile devices and analyze them in order to get a clear perception and a better understanding of this topic.

Keywords: Remote rendering · Mobile and personal devices · Compression

1 Introduction

Due to the light-weight, handheld-size, portability and availability to the internet, mobile device such as mobile phone, PDA (Personal Digital Assistants), HPC (Handheld Personal Computer) and so on has become a prevalent commodity and also a significant influence power that dominates people's daily life. More applications are ported to it and more powerful hardware devices are developed for these applications. This brings not only entertainment, excitement and convenience to people, but also requirement for more complex applications such as 3D games which perform the same quality as the video games on the computer.

Despite the growing process ability of the CPU, it is still unfeasible for 3D graphic applications to run directly on those lightweight platforms. First, their CPU is not so powerful enough to handle large sums of data. Second, they lack the specific graphics hardware for GPU-based solutions to accelerate the computation process. Third, their limited memory and lower resolution restrict the running programs and the storable data size. Moreover, their battery usually can't last for long. The exponential growth in data storage capacity and collection of applications such as 3D digital museum display, large terrain navigation and so on pushes the exploiting of the hardware capabilities to the edge.

Remote rendering is a common and also effective solution to tackle this issue. The idea is early introduced by Schmalstieg [1]. The application runs on a dedicated workstation (called the server-side or server) with sufficient computation ability and

A. El Rhalibi et al. (Eds.): Edutainment 2016, LNCS 9654, pp. 173–181, 2016.
DOI: 10.1007/978-3-319-40259-8_15

network resources. The workstation bears most of the computation burden while only a little computation work needs to be done on a not so powerful device (called the client-side or client). Communication between the server and the client goes through the internet, transferring commands of the user or results of images, video, geometry data or other media data. In this way, the client can ease lots of workloads and can also display relatively high quality results, which makes 3D graphics application rendering viable for lower-end computers or mobile platforms. This stimulated the research on remote walkthrough, remote visualization, 3D cloud games and so on lower-end devices such as mobile devices.

However, the remote rendering also confronts with many challenging issues, such as response latency during an interactive operation, compression for decreasing the transmitted data amount, rendering quality at multiple resolutions of end devices, and finally, workload distribution between the server and the client.

We survey the state of the art research techniques related to remote rendering, especially on mobile devices, summarize and analyze them in order to get a clear perception and a better understanding for further study. We arrange the rest of our paper as follows: first we list state of the art techniques, classify them according to the rendering side and analyze the quality of different categories (Sect. 2). Then the main issues involved in remote rendering are discussed in Sect. 3. In the end, we discuss and conclude the whole article in Sect. 4.

2 Categories of the Remote Rendering

Considering the rendering side that happens, the remote rendering can be divided into client-side rendering, server-side rendering and hybrid rendering.

2.1 Client-Side Rendering

Rendering on the client side demands an adequate computation capability for the hardware. Models of the scene need to be downloaded from the server and rendered on the client. The aim is to keep the graphics which the client should render as simple as possible while the client still can achieve satisfactory performance. Usually the transmitted data are geometry information, including the meshes, triangles, indices, textures and so on. That causes a high occupation of the bandwidth and a heavy render burden for the client.

A number of approaches can be identified to tackle these problems. The classical method of culling, including view-frustum culling, occlusion culling and back-face culling can skip the rendering of unsighted geometry. A LOD (Level of Detail) method can greatly simplify the complex structure of the graphics. Lluch et al. [2] designs a multi-resolution method for diverse resolution of handheld devices by using a view-dependent LOD strategy. For further decreasing the data that should be trans-mitted, sending line primitives which represent the outline of the graphics [3] or point clouds [4] for non-photorealistic rendering (NPR) will do help.

2.2   Server-Side Rendering

For server-side rendering methods, an ad hoc computer, i.e., the server, which possesses sufficient resources, both on computation ability and network, takes charge of the graphics rendering and interaction with the clients. The rendering results which formed in 2D images, videos and so on are sent to the client through the internet. Usually, the server side uses cluster PCs or graphics accelerators to enhance the performance. The aim of this approach is to make the 2D raster image get their best performance in a 3D interactive virtual scene. This can be achieved by decreasing the frequency of transmitting images [5, 6] and decreasing the size of the images or videos which have to be transmitted [7, 8].

Demand driven is a common used strategy to reduce the transmission times. Only when a demand is sent to the server for updates, will new frames be rendered for the client. The use of image warping can generate new frames from some reference images, which can also decrease the frequency of sending. Shi et al. [5] employs a reference prediction algorithm to find the viable reference images which also covers the largest area according to some predefined motion patterns. Paper [9] compares the quality of three main image warping methods: point splat image warping, quad splat image warping and mesh-based image warping.

As for cutting down the images' or videos' size, compression and video coding method need to be used before the transmission [10]. The server-side rendering does a great job in remote walkthrough applications [6] and medical uses [11].

2.3   Hybrid Rendering

The hybrid rendering approaches combine both the computation resources of client-side and server-side, aiming to limit the transferred data amount and enhancing the rendering quality of the client. It is very suitable for digital cultural heritage models display [12, 13] and large terrain navigation [14].

In order to protect the privacy of the original cultural heritage models from misuse yet still provide the viewers a proper interaction for navigation, the server sends sparse 3D mesh patches [13], simplified models [15] or even point models [12] to the client for interaction. When the interaction is over, the high-resolution map can be transmitted to the client for display. For large terrain navigation, paper [14] divides the scene into two parts: the one closes to the users' position and the one far away from the user's position. The closer part is rendered on the client with chunks which delivered from the server, while the far-off part is rendered on the server as impostor for the background of the client. The efficiency relies heavily on both sides and workload distribution algorithms need to be used to improve it. For more details of hybrid rendering, search paper [16].

2.4   Analysis of the Three Methods

Below we analyze the three kinds of remote rendering in Table 1.

Table 1. Analysis of client-side/server-side/hybrid rendering

	Client-side rendering	Server-side rendering	Hybrid rendering
Render side	C	S	C & S
Data transmission	**Geometry data** Partial model Simplified model Line primitives Point cloud	**Images or video** Image for mapping Image for impostor Video for interaction	**Images and geometry data** Images for reference Geometry for interaction
Aim	Keep graphics simple enough Satisfactory performance	Make 2D image fit 3D scene Satisfactory performance	Limit transferred data amount Enhance the rendering quality
OBW[a]	High	Low	Medium
Limitations	High occupation of BW Hard-/software compatibility Limited resource on the client Risk of model data leaking	Unnatural interaction Artifacts on image mapping Artifacts on image warping Threshold of updating	Hard-/software compatibility Limited resource on the client
Improve approach	LOD method Line extraction Prefetching and prediction	Image warping Video compression Video coding	Image warping Workload distribution Video compression and coding
Application	**Small graphics and interaction** NPR Multi-resolution rendering	**Static or almost static scene** Large virtual city navigation Remote walkthrough Medical display	**Scene with simple interaction** Remote walkthrough Large terrain visualization Heritage model display

[a] OBW is short for Occupied Bandwidth

The client-side rendering methods are mainly limited by the capability of the client hardware. The high occupation of the bandwidth further slows down the download and interaction. These approaches are suitable for those in which the generation of 3D meshes takes a far more computational amount than the rendering process. Improvement methods focus on minimizing the size of the transferred data which is rendered on the client side: LOD methods, Culling methods, Line rendering methods, Point rendering methods and so on. The server-side rendering approaches ease the rendering burden of the client side and lower down the bandwidth occupation so that the system can run more complicated applications without considering the hardware capacity and the hardware/software compatibility on the client-side. Image mapping and image warping are common methods in server-side rendering techniques. However, this comes at the expense of trade-offs, which may cause unnatural user experience in the interaction and artifacts in the display. Compensation is a crucial method in solving the artifacts. For more fluent interaction, a threshold of updating frames and compression methods should also be used. The hybrid rendering methods inherit both the limits of the former two types: the limitation of the client resources; the high occupation of the internet; the artifacts of the display during interaction. Model simplification methods, image warping with depth images, video compression can greatly improve the performance of the system.

3   Main Issues Involved in Remote Rendering

In this section, we summarize some of the main issues involved in remote rendering approaches, and list them below for detailed illustrations.

3.1   Compression for Transmission

The size of data which transmitted through the internet, and further processed by the client is crucial for the performance of the whole remote rendering pipeline. Limited by the capacity of the client devices and the bandwidth of the network, a good compression method is needed to decimate the volume of the data. According to the data type which should be compressed, we divide the compression method into geometry compression and image compression.

For cutting down the size of the geometry, surfaces decimation algorithms and view-dependent strategies can help a lot. LOD methods are effective ways in getting simplified models. Partial models lying in an interesting area/region can be extracted and lower down the bandwidth occupation [14] according to the users' position. What's more, the reconstruction of the whole scene with artistic representation like feature lines or point clouds can reduce the volume of the data while still maintaining the virtual environment's nature.

As for image compression, main stream codecs lead the way. The JPEG compression method can greatly decrease the size of the image (see $0.8\% \sim 2.1\%$ of the original BMP image [12]). With interaction, the server will send a short video to the client for display. Paper [10] proposes an adaptation algorithm to optimize the video encoding quality with an ROI based partitioning according to the depth map of the original image. Paper [17] also applies the ROI method in video encoding. In paper [18], a wavelet based PTC (Progressive Transform Coder) codec is used to compress the residue of the tiles. Paper [19] uses a warping-based motion estimation method in augmenting compression of the video on the server side with the depth information of the external and internal camera parameters.

3.2   Quality in Display

The quality of performance on the client mainly relies on the capacity of the hardware and the resolution of the models or images. The representation of geometry models is independent of the client's resolution. The qualities mainly depend on the resolution of the model itself, i.e., the LOD. Multi-resolution of the geometry which represents different densities of geometry cells and also different approximations of the shape can be achieved by the LOD method and used for multiple client devices [2].

However, the quality of image-based rendering method depends heavily on the resolution of the client [7]. Extra information of images with high-resolution will be ignored by the client with relatively low resolution on the screen. Paper [20] uses two types of streaming according to the target resolution of the end devices: graphics commands for high resolution devices and graphical output for relatively low resolution devices.

3.3   Latency in Interaction

Dealing with latency in interaction is an inevitable problem with the graphics applications with which the user interact frequently. It is defined as "the time from the generation of user interaction request till the appearance of the first updated frame on the mobile client" [5]. The interaction latency has a great influence on the user's experience, especially in games. Due to [21], the tolerable latency limit in a first person shooting game is 100 ms, but most of the remote rendering systems possess more than that: 700+, 300+, and 200+ ms latencies in GPRS, EDGE, and UMTS cellular networks [22]. Ways to reduce the interaction latency can be image warping, compression of the data, protocols for transmission and prefetching strategies.

Image warping methods can generate new view frames from some reference images and depth images. An essential issue of image warping is minimizing the frequency and amount of the reference images. Paper [5] proposes a novel algorithm to find the most proper references with which the view positions of warped images cover the largest area. Image warping method are at the price of trade-offs. Holes or sampling artifacts can have great impacts on the image. Approaches have come out to solve the occlusion exposure and insufficient sampling. Paper [2] reduces the latency by only sending geometry updates to the client with a synchronization process to keep the geometry coherence of the server and the client. Video compression codecs used for real-time display can also be helpful in decrease the sending time of the data.

A prefetching method is very useful in the interaction of walkthrough [18, 23]. With the Grid-Lumigraph method, the arbitrary views can be reconstructed [13], still with the help of sampling images.

3.4   Workload Distribution and Acceleration

The efficiency of remote rendering relays heavily on the both side devices' capacities. An efficacious splitting of workload will do a lot help in improving the performance of the remote rendering system. This includes a splitting of the rendering burden and an arrangement of the rendering tasks on the multiple rendering nodes or clusters.

Paper [14] splits the workload between the client and the server with scenes in close up views rendered on the client and scenes in medium or far range in sight rendered on the server. For serving multi-client synchronously, Neven [11] employs an algorithm based on the current frames' noise and choose the proper render node according to a probability density function.

As for the acceleration method, GPU based acceleration methods are normally used for hardware acceleration, such as the Doellner's Render Worker [6]. Paper [24] uses a parallel rendering strategy for real time rendering.

3.5   Level of Detail (LOD)

The aim of LOD technique is to decrease the complexity of the geometry, and then further reduce the size of data which should be computed. The kernel of LOD is how to create the LOD, how to select the proper LOD and how to transit between two LODs. A LOD model can be generated through a structure of Octree. Different levels of primitives represent different levels of details. Edge collapse operation can create a continuous change in geometry's resolution. A simply way to select the proper LOD is according to the distance of the viewer's position or the projected area on the screen. Lluch et al. [2] proposes a method to efficiently compute the difference between two given level of details.

Strictly speaking, the LOD method is not the main issues in remote rendering, but it is an important strategy for data compression [7, 18], progressive rendering [25], adaptively display in resolution for the client [2]. In paper [18], the LOD method is used with a tile-based division and stitching in the terrain rendering, and successfully achieved a real-time frame rate (about 20–40 fps for low end client with low bandwidth). Quillet et al. [7] uses a line-based rendering with LOD and reduces the data size as about 2 Mb smaller than the method with textures in storage. In paper [25], a smooth level of detail selection is provided for progressive rendering.

4   Conclusion

For a better understanding and a clear conception of remote rendering, we illustrate the state of the art techniques, especially those over mobile devices. We then divide these techniques into several groups according to the rendering side that happens, and then introduce them with further analysis. Moreover, we list some main issues which involved in remote rendering, including data compression for quicker transmission, adaptable display quality for multiple end devices, lower interaction latency of instant response, and workload distribution for more efficient performance of the remote rendering system.

With the prevalent usage of mobile devices, demands to display more complex graphics on these platforms will become more urgent. However, the insufficiency of these platforms' hardware and the wireless network resources will still remain unchanged for quite a long time. Regardless of the hardware updates, future research works will focus on the reducing latency method of interaction, the simplification method of graphical models, compression method for more effective compression rates, workload balance between the client side and server side for more sufficient use of the hardware in both sides.

Acknowledgments. This work is supported by the National Key Technology R&D Program under Grant No. 2012BAH62F02.

References

1. Schmalstieg D.: The remote rendering pipeline: managing geometry and bandwidth in distributed virtual environments. Ph.D. Vienna University of Technology, Vienna (1997)
2. Lluch, J., Gaitán, R., Escrivá, M., Camahort, E.: Multiresolution 3D rendering on mobile devices. In: Alexandrov, V.N., van Albada, G.D., Sloot, P.M.A., Dongarra, J. (eds.) ICCS 2006. LNCS, vol. 3992, pp. 287–294. Springer, Heidelberg (2006)
3. Diepstraten, J., Gorke, M., Ertl, T.: Remote line rendering for mobile devices. In: Computer Graphics International, pp. 454–461 (2004)
4. Ji, G., Shen, H.W., Gao J.: Interactive exploration of remote isosurfaces with point-based non-photorealistic rendering. In: Visualization Symposium, pp. 25–32 (2008)
5. Shi, S., Nahrstedt, K., Campbell, R.: A real-time remote rendering system for interactive mobile graphics. ACM Trans. Multimedia Comput. Commun. Appl. (TOMM) 8 (2012)
6. Doellner, J., Hagedorn, B., Klimke, J.: Server-based rendering of large 3D scenes for mobile devices using G-buffer cube maps. In: Proceedings of the 17th International Conference on 3D Web Technology pp. 97–100 (2012)
7. Quillet, J.C., Thomas, G., Granier, X., Guitton, P., Marvie, J.E.: Using expressive rendering for remote visualization of large city models. In: The 11th International Conference on 3D Web Technology, Columbia, Maryland, USA, pp. 27–35 (2006)
8. Tizon, N., Moreno, C., Preda, M.: ROI based video streaming for 3D remote rendering. In: 2011 IEEE 13th International Workshop on Multimedia Signal Processing (MMSP), pp. 1–6 (2011)
9. Smit, F., van Liere, R., Beck, S., Froehlich, B.: An image-warping architecture for VR: low latency versus image quality. In: Virtual Reality Conference, pp. 27–34. IEEE (2009)
10. Tizon, N., Moreno, C., Cernea, M., Preda, M.: MPEG4-based adaptive remote rendering for video games. In: The 16th International Conference on 3D Web Technology, pp. 45–50 (2011)
11. Neven, D.M.: Interactive remote rendering. Master of Science, Computer Science, Delft University of Technology (2014)
12. Su, C., Ping, J., Yue, Q., Xukun, S.: Protected-3DMPS: remote-rendering based 3D model publishing system in digital museum. J. Comput. Inf. Syst. 2, 277–283 (2006)
13. Okamoto, Y., Oishi, T., Ikeuchi, K.: Image-based network rendering of large meshes for cloud computing. Int. J. Comput. Vis. 94, 12–22 (2011)
14. Noguera, J.M., Segura, R.J., Ogáyar, C.J., Joan-Arinyo, R.: A scalable architecture for 3D map navigation on mobile devices. Pers. Ubiquit. Comput. 17, 1487–1502 (2013)
15. Koller, D., Turitzin, M., Levoy, M., Tarini, M., Croccia, G., Cignoni, P.: Protected interactive 3D graphics via remote rendering. ACM Trans. Graph. (TOG) 23, 695–703 (2004)
16. Schoor, W., Hofmann, M., Adler, S., Benger, W., Preim, B., Mecke, R.: Remote rendering strategies for large biological datasets. In: Proceedings of the 5th High-End Visualization Workshop, Baton Rouge, Louisiana (2009)
17. Makhinya, M.: Performance challenges in distributed rendering systems. Department of Informatics, Computer Science, Knowledge and Systems, University of Zürich, Zürich (2012)

18. Deb, S., Bhattacharjee, S., Patidar, S., Narayanan, P.J.: Real-time streaming and rendering of terrains. In: Kalra, P.K., Peleg, S. (eds.) ICVGIP 2006. LNCS, vol. 4338, pp. 276–288. Springer, Heidelberg (2006)
19. Giesen, F., Schnabel, R., Klein, R.: Augmented compression for server-side rendering. In: Vision Modeling and Visualization, pp. 207–216 (2008)
20. Eisert, P., Fechteler, P.: Remote rendering of computer games. In: SIGMAP, pp. 438–443 (2007)
21. Claypool, M., Claypool, K.: Latency and player actions in online games. Commun. ACM **49**, 40–45 (2006)
22. Marquez, J., Domenech, J., Gil, J., Pont A.: Exploring the benefits of caching and prefetching in the mobile web. In: Proceedings of WCITD p. 8 (2008)
23. Lazem, S., Elteir, M., Abdel-Hamid, A., Gracanin, D.: Prediction-based prefetching for remote rendering streaming in mobile virtual environments. In: IEEE International Symposium on Signal Processing and Information Technology, pp. 760–765 (2007)
24. Yoo, W., Shi, S., Jeon, W.J., Nahrstedt, K., Campbell, R.H.: Real-time parallel remote rendering for mobile devices using graphics processing units. In: IEEE International Conference on Multimedia and Expo (ICME), pp. 902–907 (2010)
25. Callahan, S.P., Bavoil, L., Pascucci, V., Silva, C.T.: Progressive volume rendering of large unstructured grids. IEEE Trans. Visual. Comput. Graph. **12**, 1307–1314 (2006)

Research of Mesh Layout Algorithm Based on Greedy Optimization Strategy

Ziting Lou[✉] and Yaping Zhang

College of Computer Science and Information Techniques,
Yunnan Normal University, Kunming City 650500, Yunnan Province, China
louziting@163.com

Abstract. In view of low rendering performance of complex data set which is caused by the limited memory bandwidth and data access speed, this paper presents a mesh layout algorithm based on greedy optimization strategy, by rearranging triangle sequences to improve spatial and temporal locality. Firstly, according to the improved cost function, we choose the vertex with the minimum cost as the focus vertex. Then render its all adjacent unrendered triangles by pushing their bounding vertices into buffer. The above steps are executed iteratively until adjacent triangles of all vertices are rendered. Finally, we get the reordered triangle sequence. Experimental results show that the algorithm provides a higher vertex cache hit ratio with less running time, which can effectively solve the problem of data access speed lagging behind the processing speed of GPU seriously.

Keywords: Cache optimization · Mesh layout · Greedy optimization strategy · Average Cache Miss Ratio · 3D mesh models

1 Introduction

Although in recent years the processing ability of CPU and GPU has been greatly improved, but the poor rendering performance of complex data set still exist, which is mainly due to the limited memory bandwidth and data access speed lagging behind the processing speed of CPU and GPU seriously. Data input and output has become the primary bottleneck in the large-scale data processing.

In order to improve the speed of data exchange between CPU and GPU, reduce the bandwidth requirement of CPU, GPU uses vertex caching mechanism and texture caching mechanism to avoid duplication of vertex computation to improve cache performance [1]. There are a variety of algorithms to optimize the texture cache access ratio [2], but the algorithm to improve the speed of the vertex cache access is very few. Access performance of the vertex cache is usually measured by the Average Cache Miss Ratio (ACMR), which is the ratio of the number of cache misses and the amount of triangles during rendering. ACMR is in the range of [0.5, 3.0], because each vertex misses at least once, at most three times. Note that, ACMR can't reach the minimum, mainly because of limitation of the vertex cache capacity. If the vertex cache can hold all vertices, the triangle can be organized in any way to make ACMR close to 0.5. However the cache capacity is very small, it is difficult to contain all of vertices.

© Springer International Publishing Switzerland 2016
A. El Rhalibi et al. (Eds.): Edutainment 2016, LNCS 9654, pp. 182–192, 2016.
DOI: 10.1007/978-3-319-40259-8_16

Assuming the cache size is k, the number of vertices is n, and k is often less than n. In an ideal situation, the minimum ACMR can be $k/2(k-1) = 0.5 + \Omega(1/k)$, and $\Omega(1/k)$ is a linear function of $1/k$ [3]. In addition, the shape of the mesh will also lead to additional overhead of ACMR. Therefore, to improve the efficiency of the vertex cache access, it is necessary to reduce ACMR and optimize the cache access.

2 Mesh Layout Optimization

Cache access optimization has direct relations not only with the hardware performance, but also with the way of data access and data layout. For the latter, reordering techniques can be used to improve the performance of cache access. Reordering techniques include computation reordering and data layout optimization [4]: (1) Computation reordering usually uses compiler or application with specific hand-tuning to reorder instruction sequences of application to improve the instruction access locality. (2) Data layout optimization reorders the data in memory so that its layout matches the expected access pattern, and improves the spatial locality and temporal locality of the data.

Currently cache access optimization techniques based on mesh layout (hereinafter referred to as mesh layout optimization techniques) are one of the key research directions in computer graphics and visualization, which belongs to data layout optimization. According to the different assumptions of the cache, mesh layout optimization techniques can be classified as either cache-oblivious or cache-aware [4]. Cache-oblivious algorithms do not assume any knowledge of cache parameters. While in cache-aware algorithms cache replacement strategy and cache size are known. The replacement strategies are LRU (Least Recently Used), FIFO (First Input First Output) and controllable mode. Today, most graphics cards use FIFO cache replacement strategy. According to the different means of reordering, mesh layout optimization techniques can be classified four categories: graph and matrix layouts, rendering sequences, space-filling curves and processing sequences [5]. According to the different memory organizations for representing triangle meshes, meshes can be classified five categories [1, 5]: independent triangles, triangle strips, indexed triangle strips, indexed triangles and edge-based representations. Because index representation only needs small amount of data space and transmission expense, which makes it the most common representation at present, but the random access to vertices also brings an increase of ACMR.

Hoppe [1] proposed a greedy strip-growing algorithm for reordering the faces, the basic strategy is to incrementally grow a triangle strip, and to decide at each step whether is better to add the next face to the strip or to restart the strip. Bogomjakov and Gotsman [6] divided mesh into multiple triangle clusters by using a graph partitioning software package Metis [7]. By ensuring that ACMR of each cluster is the best, thus they can realize ACMR optimization of the whole mesh. Lin and Lindstrom [8] also proposed an algorithm for generating a sequence of triangles(hereinafter referred to as LinSort), which uses heuristic condition to guide global search for mesh vertices, and also gets a very low ACMR. Sander et al. [9] presented an algorithm that optimizes the order in which triangles are rendered, to improve post-transform vertex cache efficiency as well as for view-independent overdraw reduction. Nehab et al. [10] proposed an automatic preprocessing algorithm that produces a view-independent ordering of mesh triangles. In addition to the above algorithms, Hua Xiong proposed cache optimization algorithm based on triangle layout [11, 12], which is similar to the greedy algorithm and uses cost metric related to ACMR to reorder triangle sequence. Chen et al. [3] presented a mesh layout optimization method based on triangle strip. By checking up the problems in vertex cache missing, they setup a seed strip in the model mesh, and select the vertices associated with multiple edges in the seed strip to form a new strip called derived strip. Through the establishment of the seed strip and derived strip repeatedly, they generate an optimized triangle sequence of the model mesh. Qin and Shi [5] proposed an algorithm that employs hybrid model to generate triangle strips which have the minimal vertex cache miss rate. It adopts last-in-first-used (LIFU) vertices cache replacement policy. Moreover, it redefines a novel primary cost function. Measured by the cost function, the triangle strip can grow in either counter-clockwise or clockwise direction.

3 Mesh Layout Algorithm Based on Greedy Optimization Strategy

3.1 Algorithm Analysis and Comparison

Except Bogomjakov's algorithm, which is based on space filling curve, the rest of the above algorithms are based on the optimization strategy. Those algorithms proposed by Hoppe, Siyuan Chen and Aihong Qin respectively are based on the triangle strips. As shown in Fig. 1, it can be seen that ACMR is the best for LinSort and Hoppe. The algorithms proposed by Sander et al., Neheb et al. and Xiong Hua respectively which are slightly higher than LinSort and Hoppe in ACMR, and the rest of the algorithms are not optimized.

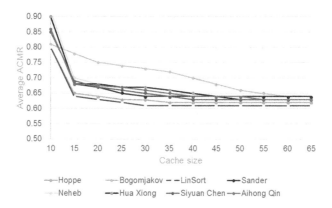

Fig. 1. The average ACMR under different cache sizes (Color figure online).

As shown in Fig. 2, this paper uses these ply models to test the related algorithms. Table 1 shows the number of vertices, triangles and the size of the mesh file in ASCII format.

| (a) Cow | (b) Bunny | (c) Armadillo | (d) Dragon | (e) Buddha |

Fig. 2. Ply mesh model

Table 1. Mesh model data sets

3D Mesh	Vertices	Triangles	Data
Cow	2903	5804	174 KB
Bunny	35947	69451	2.894 MB
Armadillo	172974	345944	6.599 MB
Dragon	437645	871414	32.265 MB
Buddha	543652	1087716	40.646 MB

Tables 2 and 3 show ACMR and running time on six test models with LinSort. All tests were carried out using a Windows PC with Intel Core i7-2600 @ 3.40 GHz, NVIDIA GeForce GTX 460 (1 GB), and 4 GB of memory. As can be seen from the following tables, the algorithm can get the optimal ACMR when the cache size is 12, the running time is reasonable, and it's proportional to the model size and cache size. So in this paper, we improve the algorithm of LinSort to make ACMR better and reduce the running time of the algorithm.

Table 2. ACMR of LinSort

3D Mesh	ACMR					
	$K = 10$	$K = 12$	$K = 16$	$K = 24$	$K = 32$	$K = 64$
Cow	0.682	0.654	0.910	1.007	1.055	1.139
Bunny	0.668	0.653	0.960	1.076	1.098	1.151
Armadillo	0.680	0.662	0.924	1.041	1.095	1.184
Dragon	0.684	0.663	0.822	0.935	0.990	1.095
Buddha	0.681	0.660	0.813	0.922	0.973	1.073

Table 3. Running time of LinSort

3D mesh	Running time (second)					
	$K = 10$	$K = 12$	$K = 16$	$K = 24$	$K = 32$	$K = 64$
Cow	0.508	0.573	0.763	1.139	1.703	4.641
Bunny	7.642	8.415	11.114	16.671	23.558	64.978
Armadillo	57.501	59.503	72.812	98.534	133.337	334.35
Dragon	119.76	121.815	142.759	194.822	267.364	709.117
Buddha	155.360	153.055	183.460	238.379	330.618	808.000

3.2   Triangle Layout Optimization Algorithm Based on Greedy Optimization Strategy

In this paper, in order to ensure efficiency of the algorithm and optimization of results, we improved the algorithm LinSort for generating a sequence of triangles. The core idea of LinSort is to colorcode any vertex of the input mesh in the following three colors: ①White represents the vertex is not in the buffer. Some or all of its connecting faces have not yet been rendered. Therefore, it will need to be pushed into the buffer at subsequent rendering stages. ②Gray shows the vertex is currently in the buffer. ③Black shows the vertex has no more adjacent triangles that have not been rendered. The vertex can be either in or out of the cache. Once it left the cache, it will not be needed or come back again during the subsequent rendering procedure [8].

At each iteration of the algorithm, a gray or white (in the case of empty buffer) vertex is selected as the focus, and its all adjacent unrendered triangles are rendered by pushing theirs white bounding vertices into buffer. Once all the triangles connecting to the focus vertex have been rendered, we turn it into black. The basic idea of the algorithm is to ensure that the algorithm is local optimization, which reduces the number of cache misses per vertex. Therefore, it is needed to decide which vertices are used as the focus at each stage of rendering, which also determines the order of the final rendering sequence.

In order to achieve optimal rendering efficiency and reduce cache miss ratio, the algorithm associates each vertex v with a cost value, denoted $C(v)$. According to the cost function, the vertex with the minimum cost is chosen as the focus vertex. In LinSort, the cost metric of v is expressed as

$$C(v) = k_1 C_1(v) + k_2/C_2(v) + k_3 C_3(v) \tag{1}$$

$C_1(v)$ represents the total number of vertices to be pushed into the buffer when all triangles connecting to v are rendered. $C_2(v)$ indicates that the number of triangles can be rendered during the vertex v turning black; $C_3(v)$ indicates the position of the black vertex v in the cache. k_1, k_2, k_3 are weighting coefficients. In the algorithm proposed by Lin et al., when $K = 12$, $k_1 = 1$, $k_2 = 0.5$, $k_3 = 1.3$, ACMR is the minimum. The explanation is that the number of triangles is usually two times the number of vertices. Therefore, it sets $k_1 \approx 2k_2$ to treat the first two factors C_1 and C_2 equally, and k_3 should be close to k_1 and k_2. Table 2 is measured in this condition.

Through experiments, we find that the empirical value of LinSort, can get the optimal ACMR, but ACMR deviation is within 0.1 when $K = 12$, $k_1 = 1$, $k_2 = 0.5 \sim 6.5$,

$k_3 = 0.1 \sim 2.7$. For the FIFO replacement policy, we need to set k_3 greater than 1 in order to give priority to the vertex in the front-most position of the buffer, to prevent the vertex being pushed in the buffer again.

As shown in Fig. 3(a)–(d), solid dots indicate vertices already in the buffer; hollow dots indicate vertices have not been rendered [13]. According to the cost function of Lin et al., given K = 12, $k_1 = 1$, $k_2 = 0.5$, $k_3 = 1.3$, the cost values are $1.25 + 1.3C_3(v)$, $1.5 + 1.3C_3(v)$, $2.5 + 1.3C_3(v)$, $3.17 + 1.3C_3(v)$ for Fig. 3(a), (b), (c) and (d) respectively. According to the current cache position and the cost value, we select the scheme (a) for rendering, which can make ACMR of this iteration minimum, thereby reducing the total ACMR.

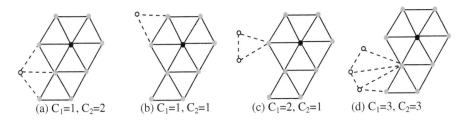

(a) $C_1=1$, $C_2=2$ (b) $C_1=1$, $C_2=1$ (c) $C_1=2$, $C_2=1$ (d) $C_1=3$, $C_2=3$

Fig. 3. C1 and C2

If only having two cases (c) and (d), according to the minimum cost metric function, we need select scheme (c) to render. However in order to ensure that ACMR is optimal, the priority should be given to the vertex that leads to more rendered triangles. The more triangles rendered, the lower ACMR would have. In Fig. 3(a), if the hollow dot is pushed into the buffer, it can render two triangles, and ACMR is 1/2. In Fig. 3(b), if the hollow dot is pushed into the buffer, it can render a triangle, ACMR is 1. For Fig. 3(c) and (d), their corresponding ACMR are 2 and 1, respectively. So in only two cases (c) and (d), we should choose scheme (d) to make ACMR optimal. Therefore, we add the average cache miss rate $C_1(v)/C_2(v)$ into the cost function which is proposed by Lin et al.. The improved cost function is expressed as

$$C(v) = k_1 C_1(v) + k_2/C_2(v) + k_3 C_3(v) + C_1(v)/C_2(v) \tag{2}$$

According to the improved cost function, the cost metric of scheme (c) and (d) are $4.5 + 1.3C_3(v)$ and $4.17 + 1.3C_3(v)$, respectively, which means we should choose scheme (d) to render. Actually, the later experimental results show that it can get lower ACMR.

Table 4 shows the pseudo code description of the algorithm, where V is vertex set of model and F is face set, M is a fixed-size FIFO cache model, V_w, V_g, V_b represent white, gray and black vertex set, respectively, V_g indicates that vertex set of the current cache zone, F_{output} represents the resulting triangle rendering sequence. When $V_g \neq \varnothing$, the algorithm selects vertex with the minimum cost in V_g as the focus vertex v_{focus}. If the cache is empty, i.e., $V_g = \varnothing$, any one of the white vertices will be picked as v_{focus} to push into the cache, and marked as gray.

Table 4. Pseudo code of triangle layout optimization algorithm based on greedy optimization strategy

Procedure K-Cache-Reorder(V, F, M)
1.   Initialization: $V_w \leftarrow V$, $V_g \leftarrow \varnothing$, $V_b \leftarrow \varnothing$, $F_{output} \leftarrow \varnothing$
2.   While$\|V_b\| < \|V\|$ /*iteratio until all vertices turn into black*/
3.   if $V_g = \varnothing$ /*cache is empty*/
4. $v_{focus} \leftarrow$ any white vertex
5.   else
6. $v_{focus} \leftarrow$ minimum cost vertex in V_g
7. $F'(v_{focus}) \leftarrow \{f \in F \setminus F_{output}: v_{focus}$ is a vertex of $f\}$
8.   for each $f \in F'(v_{focus})$
9. $V'(f) \leftarrow \{$white vertices of $f\}$
10.   for each $v \in V'(f)$
11.   if$\|V_g\| = K$ /*cache is full*/
12.   pop_one(M, V_g, f), $v \leftarrow$ first vertex of V_g
13.   Push v: $V_w \leftarrow V_w \setminus \{v\}$, $V_g \leftarrow V_g \cup \{v\}$
14.   Output any renderable faces except f
15.   Output f: $F_{output} \leftarrow F_{output} \cup \{f\}$
16.   Turn v_{focus} black: $V_b \leftarrow V_b \cup \{v_{focus}\}$. if $V_g \neq \varnothing$, $V_g \leftarrow V_g \setminus \{v_{focus}\}$
17.   Checking each $v \in V_g$ for the possible turning black and leaving the cache

3.3   Data Structures

Firstly, the data structure of the algorithm is given:

```
typedef struct VertCachRec{    // The adjacent vertex record of the current vertex
    unsigned int nVertIdx;          // vertex index
    byte bFlag;                     // vertex tag
}VertCachRec;
typedef struct WhiteVertRec{    // white vertex record
    unsigned int nVertIdx;          // white vertex index
    WhiteVertRec* pNextRec;     // point to the next white vertex
}WhiteVertRec;
class CVertexConnRecord{       // the adjacent information of the vertex
    std::deque<unsigned int>m_pFaceIdx; // all triangles connecting to the vertex
    byte m_bFlag;                   // vertex tag
};
    // CVertexConnRecord object list
    CVertexConnRecord* m_pVertexConnRec;
    // white vertex list
    WhiteVertRec** m_pWhiteVertHashMap;
    // the current vertex cache list
    std::deque<unsigned int> m_pVertCacheQue;
```

3.4   Runtime Algorithm

Here are the key steps of the algorithm:

(1) **Extract the adjacent triangles of the vertex.** The algorithm traverses the original triangles list to get the adjacent triangles of the vertex. In the traversal, we push the triangle index into m_pFaceIdx of the adjacent vertices. When traversing all the triangles, we can get the adjacent triangles of all the vertices. Then traversing the CVertexConnRecord object list and calculating the number of adjacent triangles of each vertex, if the number is zero, it indicates that the vertex is an isolated vertex and we should label it as the black vertex, otherwise the vertex is labeled as the white vertex and put into the white vertex list.

(2) **Initialize mesh layout optimization.** At this time, the vertex buffer is empty. If the white vertex list is not empty, the algorithm selects any one of the white vertex as the focus and pushes it into the cache and labels it as the gray.

(3) **Select the focus vertex to render.** The algorithm traverses vertex buffer, and calculates the cost metric for each gray vertex, then selects the vertex with the minimum cost of the cost function as the focus. When all faces connecting to the vertex have been rendered, it is labeled as black.

To calculate the number of vertices that need to be pushed into the buffer, the algorithm traverses the queue m_pFaceIdx of the focus vertex to get its all adjacent triangles. If vertex of the adjacent triangle is labeled as white, we pop it from the list of the white vertices, and then push it into the vertex buffer and label it as gray. When all the adjacent triangles have been processed, the number of vertices pushed into the buffer is obtained. If the FIFO vertex buffer is full, the algorithm pops the top from buffer, and pushes the white vertices of unrendered triangles adjacent to the focus into the vertex buffer. If there are some unrendered adjacent triangles of the top vertex, it will be labeled as white again, and pushed into white vertex list. If all triangles connecting to the top vertex have been rendered, it will be turned into black, popped from the buffer, and no longer need to be pushed into the buffer.

(4) If all vertices are turned into black, it is shown that all triangles have been rendered, and then the rendering sequence of the triangle is obtained.

4   Experiment and Comparison

Table 5 shows the results of our optimization algorithm and LinSort, in which the cache size is 12, $k_1 = 1$, $k_2 = 0.5$, $k_3 = 1.3$, the ACMR of our algorithm is lower than that of LinSort. Figure 4(a) represents the original mesh layout, Fig. 4(b) represents the optimized mesh layout. Different colors indicate the different rendering order of mesh triangles. Figure 4(c) and (d) represent that cache misses before and after the mesh layout, red indicates cache miss, green indicates cache hit.

Table 6 Statistics the running time of LinSort and our algorithm with six test models. As shown in Table 4, compared to LinSort, ACMR of our algorithm is lower, running time is also relatively reduced. The main reason is that LinSort picks the vertex

Table 5. ACMR of mesh layout optimization

3D Mesh	Original	LinSort	Our algorithm
Cow	1.835	0.654	0.649
Bunny	2.085	0.653	0.635
Armadillo	2.630	0.662	0.649
Dragon	1.723	0.663	0.658
Buddha	1.653	0.660	0.656

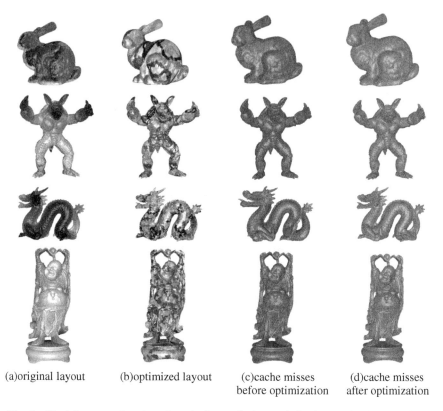

(a)original layout   (b)optimized layout   (c)cache misses   (d)cache misses
                                                     before optimization   after optimization

Fig. 4. Mesh layout and cache misses before and after optimization (Color figure online)

with the minimum degree, i.e., number of its white neighbors as the initial focus vertex, while our algorithm selects any white vertices as the focus randomly. When calculating the cost metric, our algorithm considers not only the number of adjacent unrendered triangles, the number of vertex pushes required for rendering all unrendered triangles connecting to the current vertex, and its position in buffer, but also the weight for the first two factors. Therefore, our algorithm can ensure quality of mesh optimization and reduce the running time.

Table 6. The running time of mesh layout optimization

3D mesh	LinSort (second)	The new algorithm (second)
Cow	0.607	0.547
Bunny	8.933	8.328
Armadillo	60.997	59.171
Dragon	130.823	116.493
Buddha	165.992	153.782

In order to show the relationship between ACMR of optimized model and the rendering performance, we test interactive rendering rate for the above five models with LinSort and our algorithm. The test results are shown in Table 7. We can find that interactive rendering rate of the model is linearly inversely proportional to model size closely; it decreases as the model size increases. Interactive rendering rate of single model is inversely proportional to ACMR, and increases as ACMR decreases.

Table 7. Test of interactive rendering rate

3D mesh	LinSort		The new algorithm	
	ACMR	Interactive rendering speed (ten thousand triangles/s)	ACMR	Interactive rendering speed (ten thousand triangles/s)
Cow	0.654	921	0.649	921
Bunny	0.653	871	0.635	897
Armadillo	0.662	796	0.649	798
Dragon	0.663	798	0.658	813
Buddha	0.660	718	0.656	731

5   Conclusion

In this paper, we propose an improved mesh layout algorithm based on greedy optimization strategy. Experiments show that the algorithm yields better ACMR compared to other existing methods and the running time is also reduced. But it only applies to less than 100 MB mesh models, and the reduction in running time is not obvious. Therefore, the next work is to find the optimal rendering sequence for large-scale mesh model. We intend to segment large-scale mesh into several sub-meshes, and then implement parallel cache optimization for each sub-mesh, which can realize mesh layout and ensure the optimal rendering performance for large-scale 3D model.

Acknowledgments. This work was supported by Key Laboratory of Educational Informatization for Nationalities Ministry of Education, Yunnan Normal University and the National Natural Science Funds (61262070, 61462097).

References

1. Hoppe, H.: Optimization of mesh locality for transparent vertex caching. In: Proceeding of SIGGRAPH 1999, pp. 269–276. ACM, New York (1999)
2. Dai, X., Xiong, H., Gong, J.: Automatic merging method of texture in a 3D city model. J. Wuhan Univ.: Inf. Sci. Ed. **40**(3), 347–352 (2015)
3. Chen, S., Shi, G., Wang, Q.: Data optimization for 3D model rendering by triangle strip deriving. J. Comput.-Aided Des. Comput. Graph. **21**(8), 1155–1163 (2009)
4. Yoon, S.-E., Lindstrom, P.: Mesh layouts for block-based caches. IEEE Trans. Vis. Comput. Graph. **12**(5), 1213–1220 (2006)
5. Qin, A., Shi, J.: Cache-friendly triangle strip generation based on hybrid model. J. Comput.-Aided Des. Comput. Graph. **23**(6), 1006–1012 (2011)
6. Bogomjakov, A., Gotsman, C.: Universal rendering sequences for transparent vertex caching of progressive meshes. Comput. Graph. Forum **21**(2), 137–148 (2002)
7. Karypist, G., Kumart, V.: Multilevel k-way partitioning scheme for irregular graphs. J. Parallel Distrib. Comput. **48**(1), 96–120 (1998)
8. Lin, G., Lindstrom, P.: An improved vertex caching scheme for 3D mesh rendering. IEEE Trans. Vis. Comput. Graph. **12**(4), 640–648 (2006)
9. Sander, P., Nehab, D., Barczak, J.: Fast triangle reordering for vertex locality and reduced overdraw. In: Proceedings of SIGGRAPH 2007, pp. 89–98. ACM, New York (2007)
10. Nehab, D., Barczak, J., Sander, P.: Triangle order optimization for graphics hardware computation culling. In: Proceedings of ACM SIGGRAPH Symposium on Interactive 3D Graphics and Games, pp. 207–211. ACM, New York (2006)
11. Xiong, H.: Research of Rendering Acceleration Techniques for Parallel Environments, pp. 71–80. Zhejiang University, Hangzhou (2008)
12. Shi, J.: Distributed Parallel Graphics Rendering Techniques and Its Application, pp. 189–274. Science Press, Beijing (2010)

An Interactive 2D-to-3D Cartoon Modeling System

Lele Feng[✉], Xubo Yang[✉], Shuangjiu Xiao, and Fan Jiang

School of Software, Shanghai Jiao Tong University, Shanghai, China
lelefeng1992@gmail.com, yangxubo@sjtu.edu.cn

Abstract. In this paper, we propose an interactive system that can quickly convert a 2D cartoon painting into a 3D textured cartoon model, enabling non-professional adults and children to easily create personalized 3D contents. Our system exploits a new approach based on solving Poisson equations to generate 3D models, which is free from the limitations of spherical topology in prior works. We also propose a novel method to generate whole textures for both sides of the models to deliver colorful appearances, making it possible to obtain stylized models rendered with cartoon textures. The results have shown that our method can greatly simplify the modeling process comparing with both traditional modeling softwares and prior sketch-based systems.

Keywords: Modeling interface · Deformation · Texture · Interactive modeling

1 Introduction

The demand for personalized 3D models is rapidly growing with the increasing applications of emerging technologies like 3D printing and augmented reality. However, for novice users, it is difficult to build 3D models using professional modeling systems. Traditional 3D modeling tools, such as Maya [1] and 3ds Max [2] require users to learn a complicated interface, which are daunting challenges for novice users. In order to simplify the 3D modeling pipeline, sketch-based modeling systems, such as Teddy [3] and its follow-up works [4–8] presented approaches to create 3D models from 2D strokes. However, these systems have some common limitations. First, most of these systems require users to sketch from a large number of different views, making it difficult for novice users to complete their tasks. Second, these systems cannot generate models from 2D cartoon images directly and only use them as the guide images. In order to create desired models, users have to draw carefully to make their sketch match with the silhouettes in guide images. As a result, the silhouettes of the final shape may differ from the input sketch, which may be undesired. Third, shapes that can be handled by these systems are also limited. For example, they do not allow cycles of connection curves. Surfaces with edges or flat surfaces also cannot be generated directly. Finally, models generated by these systems lack texture information, thus the rendering of these models cannot take advantage of the original paintings. Unlike sketch-based systems, Ink-and-Ray [9] involves Poisson equations to produce bas-relief meshes, which can support global illumination effects for hand-drawn characters. However, the resulted

© Springer International Publishing Switzerland 2016
A. El Rhalibi et al. (Eds.): Edutainment 2016, LNCS 9654, pp. 193–204, 2016.
DOI: 10.1007/978-3-319-40259-8_17

meshes are not full 3D models, which limit their usage and artifacts may appear when rendered with a perspective camera or from different views.

The goal of our work is to design a system that allows creating full three-dimensional models from two-dimensional cartoon images directly without requiring much input. Our system makes it possible to quickly create a consistent 3D model with full textures.

Contributions. We introduce an interactive system to help non-professional users to build their own personalized 3D contents, where a full 3D textured cartoon model can be created easily from a single 2D cartoon image. First, our system employs an automatic segmentation method to reduce the difficulty of sketching silhouettes in the previous works. Second, the algorithm of mesh generation used by our system can handle a large range of models, including holes and sharp edges. We also introduce a method to generate textures for full models, which is not supported by prior works. Our results show that our system makes it an easy task for novice users to create personalized 3D models from cartoon paintings.

2   Related Work

Many efforts have been made in constructing 3D models from 2D images. Previous systems can be classified into three groups: sketch-based modeling systems, single-view modeling systems and pseudo 3D modeling systems.

2.1   Sketch-Based Modeling System

Sketch-based 3D modeling has been a popular research field. Systems such as Teddy [3] and its descendants ShapeShop and [4] FiberMesh [5] approached the problem by asking users to sketch from many views, leveraging users' 2D drawing skills. A good survey can be found in [10]. RigMesh [8] presented an approach to modeling and rigging in contrast to the traditional sequential. However, their system cannot generate a desirable shape when the input sketch does not have an obvious symmetry axis. Moreover, all of these methods cannot deliver textured models, unless users draw colorful strokes on the models directly. In addition, due to their modeling methods (limited to spherical topology), the range of models that these systems can handle is limited. Surfaces with edges or flat surfaces cannot be generated directly. And they do not allow cycles of connection curves. Another drawback of their methods is requiring users to sketch from a large number of different views. Schmidt et al. [11] found that novice users were unable to complete their tasks and became frustrated very easily with the change of views.

2.2   Single-View Modeling System

In order to solve the problems in multi-view sketch-based systems, many single-view modeling systems are proposed. In Gingold et al. [7], structured annotations were introduced for 2D-to-3D modeling. In their implementation, the user can add some primitives and annotations, which are structured and semantic. The system then generates 3D models from inconsistent drawings. However, adding annotations from a single view demands decent 3D perspective understandings, which is difficult and time-consuming for novice users. A similar work using annotations is Naturasketch [12]. The system is a sketch-based modeling system per se, but it solved the problems in sketch-rotate-sketch workflow by introducing multiple annotations. Karpenko and Hughes [13] proposed a system that can generate 3D models from single-view contours. A common drawback of these methods is that they require tedious specification of the inputs to produce the desired results.

2.3   Pseudo 3D Modeling System

Other researches focus on producing pseudo 3D models rather than full 3D models. Rivers et al. [14] proposed an approach which using 2D input to generate 2.5D models which can be rotated in 3D. Instead of generating a 3D polygonal mesh, they generate a 2.5D cartoon, which naturally supports a stylized drawing style. However, the system demands artists to draw different views (at least three), and some effects we take for granted with a 3D model, such as lighting and collision detection, are not natively supported. TexToons [15] is a system that uses depth layering to enhance 3D-like effects to texture-mapped hand-drawn cartoons, where the overall appearance feels synthetic due to the lack of full 3D details. Sýkora et al. [9] presented a system to produce bas-relief meshes. The approach preserved the look-and-feel of the two-dimensional domain and delivered a similar look compared with a full three-dimensional model. However, the meshes created by the system cannot be rotated due to their bas-relief topology. When rendered with a perspective camera or viewed from different angles, their system may cause some artifacts because the meshes are not full 3D models.

In this paper, we introduce a system for 3D modeling and deformation from 2D cartoon images. Compared with sketch-based systems, our system does not require the user to model from different views. When provided a cartoon image, our system can segment it into several regions automatically. We design a few user interface elements to help users refine the result. Inspired by the inflation method in Ink-and-Ray [9], our system employs a new approach based on solving Poisson equations to generate full 3D models, which is free from the limitations of spherical topology in prior works. We also propose a method to generate whole textures for both sides of the models to deliver colorful appearance, which is unsupported in the above systems. The user can add point handles to deform models to achieve desired poses. The results have shown that our method can take advantage of the original 2D images as much as possible, while requires a little user input.

3   User Interface

Our interface is shown in Fig. 1. The interface includes three parts: the leftmost palette, which contains all the tools supported by our system, a window displaying the user inputs, and a window displaying the generated 3D models. The user starts by selecting a cartoon image and then performs several operations to generate models. The process can be divided into five steps:

Fig. 1. The user interface of our system.

- Segmentation. After the user selects a cartoon image, our system first extracts the regions from the image. Each area enclosed by dark edges forms a region. The result is the initial segmentation and the user can perform some optional operations to correct the result, such as background selection, merging and splitting regions. After the user has done with these segmented regions, our system will grow these regions to eliminate edge pixels and then find contours for them.
- Boundary operations. Region boundaries are then extracted from the segmentation result. The user can select a boundary and modify it optionally, such as filling holes and specifying flat boundaries.
- Mesh generation. Different 3D models are generated based on these boundaries and their types. Our system supports three kinds of meshes: inflated meshes, concave meshes and half inflated meshes. Figure 2 shows an example of generating three kinds of meshes based on the same boundary.
- Texture operations. Our system can synthesize textures for the generated meshes automatically. The original paintings are used as textures of front faces directly and the back textures are synthesized based on the front textures. Our system uses a heuristic rule that the farther an area is away from the region boundary, the more likely this area should not be reused in the back texture. The user can use tools to modify the results to decide whether or not to reuse an area in the back texture.
- Shape deformation. By default, the centers of generated meshes are all located at the same depth where $z = 0$. The relative depth order may be undesired. The user can

add some point handles on the mesh, and deform the meshes in order to get a satisfactory depth order. The deform operations supported by our system include translation, rotation and scaling. We find that this tool gives a chance for the user to obtain more imaginative 3D models.

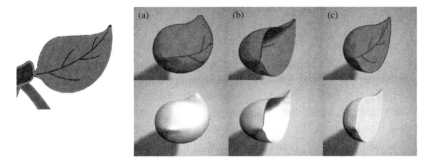

Fig. 2. Three kinds of meshes supported by our system. The left image shows the input boundary. Our system can generate three kinds of meshes based on this boundary. (a) the inflated mesh. (b) the concave mesh. (c) the half inflated mesh.

4 Implementation

In this section, we will describe more details about the above steps.

4.1 Segmentation

Given a cartoon image as input, our system first extracts regions from the image automatically. Our segmentation uses the curve structure extraction method in [16]. The method first calculates curve points by applying non-maximal suppress on secondary derivative of cartoon images, and then links them together to form structure curves. For many cartoon images, this method can extract usable outlines immediately. However, when the input images contain noises, the result is not as neat as desired. To detect final outlines from the initial result, we employ an adaptive algorithm [17] on the initial result. Our system then performs a seed fill algorithm to find enclosed regions.

4.2 Mesh Generation

Our system will find boundaries for each region. These boundaries are used to generate meshes according to their types. We first apply conforming constrained Delaunay triangulation [18] to each boundary, obtaining a discrete region ω. The triangulation uses the Triangle package [19]. We then use the inflation algorithm in [9]. The algorithm takes advantage of solving a Poisson equation:

$$-\nabla^2 f(x) = c, \forall x \in w \tag{1}$$

subject to:

$$f(x) = 0, \forall x \in B_D \tag{2}$$

$$\frac{\partial f(x)}{\partial n} = 0, \forall x \in B_N \tag{3}$$

The function $f(x)$ corresponds to the inflated heights of the region and c is a positive number specifying how much the region is inflated. The equation should subject to two types of boundary constraints, Dirichlet or Neumann boundary constraints. By default, all of the boundary vertices are subject to Dirichlet boundary constraints. The resulting $f(x)$ produces a parabolic-like cross-section. Our system then uses a function $f'(x) = \sqrt{f(x)}$ to convert it into a more smooth mesh. These heights are used by both front and back faces. For regions that need to remain flat, Neumann boundary conditions can be used. This inflation method may produce sharpness along the meshes' cross-sections. Local Laplacian smoothing methods [20, 21] are then employed to smooth the edges.

Three kinds of meshes are supported by our system. For inflated meshes, we just use the inversed heights for back faces and glue them to front faces with a small shift. For concave meshes, the heights of front faces are scaled by a scalar smaller than one and then inversed to produce a concave effect. In the case of half inflated meshes, the heights of front faces are simply set to zero. This method is simple but delivers satisfactory results in our experiments.

4.3   Texturing

Our system will generate both front and back textures for each region. We use the [x, y] coordinates as texture coordinates for front faces and attach the original image to them directly. For back faces, the system should generate proper back textures. The essential idea is that areas that are far away from the boundary of the region are more likely not reused on the back texture. Given a region, our system first selects a main color which contributes the most along the boundary. This main color is used to initialize the back textures. Our system then applies marker-based segmentation using watershed algorithm to separate areas in the original texture. The algorithm begins with the binarization of the input image. Then we apply the distance transform on the binary image. We threshold this distance image and perform some morphology operations to extract areas from the image. For each area we create a seed for the watershed algorithm by extracting its contour. Then we apply the watershed algorithm and combine adjacent areas. In order to compare their distance from the region boundary, we apply the distance transform on the whole region and use this distance map to calculate the nearest path from each area to the boundary. If the distance is smaller than a threshold (we use 5 in our implementation), then we suppose this area should be reused in the back texture.

The user can use tools provided by our system to modify the results (whether or not to reuse an area). If an area is not reused according to a user input, the pixels of this area will be filled with the main color selected at the beginning.

4.4   Shape Deformation

Shape deformations can help the user to get correct depth orders between different regions and to deform the generated models to obtain desired poses. The user can first add some point handles on the region in the 2D cartoon image. Then our system will calculate skin weights for each point handle and assign to each vertex a set of skin weights for each handle. The weights are computed using bounded biharmonic weights [22]. The method defines the weights w_j as minimizers of the Laplacian energy subject to constrains that enforce interpolation of the handles and other desirable properties, such as smoothness, shape-awareness locality and sparsity. When the user drags the point handle, the system then uses the linear blend skinning function [23] to deform the model.

4.5   Rendering

Every mesh generated by our system is attached with a texture, which is the combination of two textures, one for front faces and one for back faces. In order to render them on the mesh correctly, we assign each vertex a texture coordinate [u, v]. For front faces, these coordinates are simply the [x, y] coordinate of this vertex. For back faces, the v component in [u, v] is still the value of y, but the u component is the sum of x and 1. So any texture coordinate larger than 1 indicates this vertex belongs to some back face. When rendering the mesh, the system will use this information to decide which part of the texture to sample.

Once the mesh is generated, our system uses a tone-based shading [24] to deliver a stylized look. More complicated lighting effects are also supported. When rendering the scenes shown in Fig. 3, we employ the method in [25] to add stylized specular effects on the models.

5   Results

We tested our system on a 2.6 GHz Intel Core i7 under OS X 10.9.5, running at interactive rates. To demonstrate the versatility of our method, we selected a set of cartoon images with different types, including characters, fruits, animals, plants and so on. These are shown in Figs. 3 and 6.

In Fig. 3, we show two sample scenes, in which all of these models (except the walls) were created from cartoon images using our system. Most of them took less than 5 min to create, and some just took a few seconds, such as the oranges and mangoes. In Fig. 6, we illustrate some examples with different poses and structural complexity. In each example, we show the original cartoon image, the result of the segmentation

Fig. 3. Sample scenes created using our system. Most of the models took less than 5 min to create, and some just took a few seconds. Top: the scenes constructed by these models. Below: the original cartoon images used in the scene.

phase, the annotations including region operations and point handles made by the user, the front view and side view of the generated and deformed 3D models.

6   Evaluation

The results have shown that our system can handle a variety of cartoon images. We compared our system with the prior works. Sketch-based modeling systems [3–8] can only handle tubular organic shape (limited to spherical topology). Surfaces with edges or concave silhouettes (see the grasses and trees in Fig. 3) and cycles of connection curves (such as the letter "B") cannot be created by these systems. Our system is free from these limitations and can create models with almost the same silhouettes in the original images. Moreover, flat surfaces (see the mushrooms in Fig. 3, the sleeves of the Boy and Bear in Fig. 6) and concave meshes (see the grasses in Fig. 3, the ears of the Boy and Bear in Fig. 6) can also be created easily.

One of the main advantages of our system is that we don't require the user to rotate from different view during modeling. Because our system can segment the input images by their silhouettes accurately and automatically, the user doesn't need to sketch a lot like other sketch-based systems do. We created two models similar to those in [7]. With their system, one required 20 min and the other required 13 min to create, which only took 8 min and 5 min with our system.

7   User Study

To test the usability of our system, we performed an informal user study consisting of fifteen children whose average age was twelve. These children were divided into three groups, each using a different system among our system, RigMesh [8] and the system with structured annotations [7]. After a 20 min training of each system, the children were allowed to create their own models. We also encouraged them to draw their own cartoon images with color pens and to use these paintings as the inputs of each system. Figure 4 shows a young girl was drawing a yellow star and the resulted model she created with our system which took about 3 min. We then collected their feedback of each system. Many children noted that the system with structured annotations [7] was not easy to produce desired models. They had to deform from certain basic primitives and the annotations provided by the system were somewhat complicated. The screen was easily messed up with these primitives and annotations. Some children using RigMesh struggled with creating models with holes and complained the system cannot create models with the exactly same silhouettes they sketched. In contrast, children using our system gave positive feedback of the simple and convenient annotations provided by our system. They remarked that the automatic segmentation and inflation was very helpful. Many children, including those using the other two systems, were excited with the textured models created by our system and would like to have this in the other two systems.

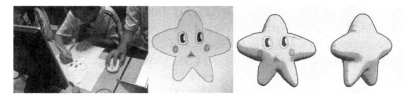

Fig. 4. A young girl was drawing a yellow star and the model she created with our system (Color figure online).

8 Conclusions and Future Work

We have implemented an interface for 3D modeling from cartoon images to simplify the modeling process, making it convenient for novice users to obtain their own 3D models. Compared with the prior sketch-based systems, our system can handle a large range of models, such as cycles of connection curves, surfaces with edges and flat surfaces. The models generated by our system also contain texture information, which can deliver a similar look to the original cartoon images as much as possible. The deformation employed by our system gives a chance for the user to get a better pose for their models. Our results show that our system makes it possible to create personalized 3D contents from cartoon images effectively.

Our system can be applied to many related areas, such as education and augmented reality. In applications such as Magicbook [26], children can see three-dimensional virtual models appearing out of the book pages through a handled augmented reality display. However, those applications demand developers to prepare models in advance, which is time-consuming. Instead, our system focuses on modeling from 2D cartoon images rapidly, and enables children to author their own models, giving full play to their creativity. We build our demo based on Vuforia SDK [27]. Figure 5 demonstrates such an ideal Augmented Reality example using our system. The child can first draw a

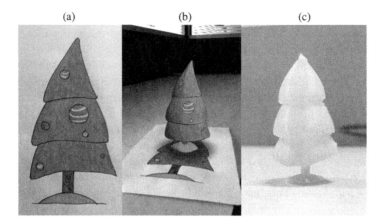

Fig. 5. Applications. (a) the picture of a hand-drawn cartoon image. (b) the scenario in augmented reality. (c) the substance printed by a 3D printer.

cartoon image, and then take a photo of it (Fig. 5a). The picture is provided as the input of our system. Next, our system generates the desired model based on a few user inputs. The model is then added to the database. Finally, children can see their own three-dimensional virtual models standing on the cartoon images through a display (Fig. 5b). The time that the entire process takes is just a few minutes. The resulted 3D models can also be printed by 3D printers (Fig. 5c).

Fig. 6. More complex models created using our system. (a) the original cartoon images. (b) the results of the segmentation phase. (c) the annotations including region operations and point handles made by the user (gray: region boundaries, red: Neumann boundary conditions, blue: point handles). (d) the front views. (e) the side views (Color figure online).

Our system still has its limitations. First, the user needs to modify region boundaries to model occluded parts. In the future, we plan to employ more intelligent methods [28, 29] to complete these regions automatically. Second, the textures of occluded areas are simply filled with the main color selected by our system. However, in some cases the method does cause some artifacts. This drawback can be fixed by using more advanced texture analysis methods such as [30].

Acknowledgments. We are grateful to all the volunteers who participated in our user studies. This work is supported in part by the National Natural Science Foundation of China (nos. 61173105 and 61373085) and the National High Technology Research and Development Program of China (no. 2015AA016404).

References

1. AUTODESK Maya (2015). http://www.autodesk.com/products/maya/overview
2. AUTODESK 3ds Max (2015). http://www.autodesk.com.cn/products/3ds-max/overview
3. Igarashi, T., Matsuoka, S., Tanaka, H.: Teddy: a sketching interface for 3D freeform design. In: ACM SIGGRAPH 2007 Courses, p. 21. ACM (2007)
4. Schmidt, R., Wyvill, B., Sousa, M.C., et al.: Shapeshop: sketch-based solid modeling with blobtrees. In: ACM SIGGRAPH 2007 Courses, p. 43. ACM (2007)
5. Nealen, A., Igarashi, T., Sorkine, O., et al.: FiberMesh: designing freeform surfaces with 3D curves. ACM Trans. Graph. (TOG) **26**(3), 41 (2007). ACM
6. Cordier, F., Seo, H., Park, J., et al.: Sketching of mirror-symmetric shapes. IEEE Trans. Vis. Comput. Graph. **17**(11), 1650–1662 (2011)
7. Gingold, Y., Igarashi, T., Zorin, D.: Structured annotations for 2D-to-3D modeling. ACM Trans. Graph. (TOG) **28**(5), 148 (2009). ACM
8. Borosn, P., Jin, M., DeCarlo, D., et al.: Rigmesh: automatic rigging for part-based shape modeling and deformation. ACM Trans. Graph. (TOG) **31**(6), 198 (2012)
9. Sýkora, D., Kavan, L., Čadík, M., et al.: Ink-and-ray: bas-relief meshes for adding global illumination effects to hand-drawn characters. ACM Trans. Graph. (TOG) **33**(2), 16 (2014)
10. Olsen, L., Samavati, F., Sousa, M.C, et al.: A taxonomy of modeling techniques using sketch-based interfaces. In: Eurographics State of the Art Report (2008)
11. Schmidt, R., Isenberg, T., Jepp, P., et al.: Sketching, scaffolding, and inking: a visual history for interactive 3D modeling. In: Proceedings of the 5th International Symposium on Non-photorealistic Animation and Rendering. ACM, pp. 23–32 (2007)
12. Olsen, L., Samavati, F.F., Jorge, J.A.: NaturaSketch: Modeling from images and natural sketches. IEEE Comput. Graph. Appl. **31**(6), 24–34 (2011)
13. Karpenko, O.A., Hughes, J.F.: SmoothSketch: 3D free-form shapes from complex sketches. ACM Trans. Graph. (TOG) **25**(3), 589–598 (2006). ACM
14. Rivers, A., Igarashi, T., Durand, F.: 2.5 D cartoon models. ACM Trans. Graph. (TOG) **29**(4), 59 (2010). ACM
15. Sýkora, D., Ben-Chen, M., Čadík, M., et al.: TexToons: practical texture mapping for hand-drawn cartoon animations. In: Proceedings of the ACM SIGGRAPH/Eurographics Symposium on Non-photorealistic Animation and Rendering, pp. 75–84. ACM (2011)
16. Cheng, M.M.: Curve structure extraction for cartoon images. In: Proceedings of the 5th Joint Conference on Harmonious Human Machine Environment, pp. 13–25 (2009)

17. Sýkora, D., Buriánek, J., Žára, J.: Colorization of black-and-white cartoons. Image Vis. Comput. **23**(9), 767–782 (2005)

18. Shewchuk, J.R.: Delaunay refinement algorithms for triangular mesh generation. Comput. Geom. **22**(1), 21–74 (2002)

19. Shewchuk, J.R.: Triangle: engineering a 2D quality mesh generator and Delaunay triangulator. In: Lin, M.C., Manocha, D. (eds.) Applied Computational Geometry Towards Geometric Engineering. LNCS, vol. 1148, pp. 203–222. Springer, Heidelberg (1996)

20. Field, D.A.: Laplacian smoothing and Delaunay triangulations. Commun. Appl. Numer. Methods **4**(6), 709–712 (1988)

21. Vollmer, J., Mencl, R., Mueller, H.: Improved laplacian smoothing of noisy surface meshes. Comput. Graph. Forum **18**(3), 131–138 (1999). Blackwell Publishers Ltd.

22. Jacobson, A., Baran, I., Popovic, J., et al.: Bounded biharmonic weights for real-time deformation. ACM Trans. Graph. **30**(4), 78 (2011)

23. Magnenat-Thalmann, N., Laperrire, R., Thalmann, D.: Joint-dependent local deformations for hand animation and object grasping. In: Proceedings on Graphics Interface 1988 (1988)

24. Gooch, A., Gooch, B., Shirley, P., et al.: A non-photorealistic lighting model for automatic technical illustration. In: Proceedings of the 25th Annual Conference on Computer Graphics and Interactive Techniques, pp. 447–452. ACM (1998)

25. Anjyo, K., Hiramitsu, K.: Stylized highlights for cartoon rendering and animation. IEEE Comput. Graph. Appl. **23**(4), 54–61 (2003)

26. Billinghurst, M., Kato, H., Poupyrev, I.: MagicBook: transitioning between reality and virtuality. In: CHI 2001, Extended Abstracts on Human Factors in Computing Systems, pp. 25–26. ACM (2001)

27. Developer, V.: SDK, Unity extension Vuforia–2.8 (2014)

28. Geiger, D., Pao, H., Rubin, N.: Salient and multiple illusory surfaces. In: Proceedings of the 1998 IEEE Computer Society Conference on Computer Vision and Pattern Recognition, pp. 118–124. IEEE (1998)

29. Orzan, A., Bousseau, A., Barla, P., et al.: Diffusion curves: a vector representation for smooth-shaded images. Commun. ACM **56**(7), 101–108 (2013)

30. Elad, M., Starck, J.L., Querre, P., et al.: Simultaneous cartoon and texture image inpainting using morphological component analysis (MCA). Appl. Comput. Harmonic Anal. **19**(3), 340–358 (2005)

Monet-Style Images Generation Using Recurrent Neural Networks

Yili Zhao[1,2(✉)] and Dan Xu[1]

[1] School of Information, Yunnan University, Kunming 650091, Yunnan, China
ylzhao@vip.sina.com, danxu@ynu.edu.cn
[2] School of Computer and Information, Souwest Forestry University,
Kunming 650224, Yunnan, China

Abstract. An automatic Monet-style images generation method using long short term memory recurrent neural network is proposed in this paper. The method shows that long short term memory recurrent neural network can learn the structure and characteristics of Monet's paintings properly by demonstrating its ability to generate impressionism-style images. With Monet's paintings as input, similar style of images can be constructed using the proposed method iteratively. The experiment results indicate that the trained recurrent neural networks were able to generate Monet-style images with a small amount of training data.

Keywords: Recurrent neural network · Style transfer · Long short term memory · Non-photorealistic rendering

1 Introduction

Algorithmic painting-style image generation is a difficult and hot task that has been actively explored in non-photorealistic rendering field. Many common methods for algorithmic painting-style generation consist of constructing carefully engineered painting style features and rely on simple generation schemes, such as Markov models or graph-based energy minimization techniques. While these approaches are sometimes able to produce interesting compositions, the resulting painting pieces usually consist of repetitive sequences and lack painting style structures that are common in most art works. With the increase in computational resources and recent advancements in recurrent neural network (RNN) architectures, novel generation method may now be practical for large-scale painting-style generation. The most common recurrent neural network used for modeling long-term dependencies is the long short term memory (LSTM) network, introduced by Hochreiter and Schmidhuber [1]. LSTM is an RNN architecture designed to be better at storing and accessing information than standard RNN, and has recently given state-of-the-art results in a variety of sequence processing tasks, including text generation [2], speech recognition [3] and handwriting recognition [4]. The main goal of this paper is to demonstrate that RNN network can use its memory to generate complex, realistic sequences containing long-range structure. More specifically, LSTM network is used for the task of automatic Monet-style images generation.

© Springer International Publishing Switzerland 2016
A. El Rhalibi et al. (Eds.): Edutainment 2016, LNCS 9654, pp. 205–211, 2016.
DOI: 10.1007/978-3-319-40259-8_18

2 Related Work

In this paper, we try to render new images with a given style, and this problem is usually approached in a branch of computer vision called non-photorealistic rendering (NPR) [5]. Conceptually most closely related are methods using texture transfer to achieve artistic style transfer [6, 7]. These previous approaches mainly rely on non-parametric techniques to directly manipulate the pixel representation of an image.

In contrast, deep neural networks operate in the feature spaces that explicitly represent the high level content of an image. Mordvintsev et al. [8] proposed Deep-Dream which uses a convolutional neural network to find and enhance patterns in images via algorithmic pareidolia, thus creating a dreamlike hallucinogenic appearance in the deliberately over-processed images. They used gradient ascent to generate images that maximized activity on particular hidden neurons, and fed the generated output back into the input to create feedback loops that acted to amplify activity. Combined with image transformations each iteration, this created endless fractal-like animations and hallucinations of abstract but subtly recognizable imagery.

Karpathy and Fei-Fei [9] presents a model that generates natural language descriptions of images and their regions, and their approach leverages datasets of images and sentence descriptions to learn about the inter-modal correspondences between language and visual data. Angeliki et al. [10] introduces a language-driven image generation method which can generate an image visualizing the semantic contents of a word embedding. Their method is based on two mapping functions. The first takes as input a word embedding and maps it onto a high-level visual space which is defined by one of the top layers of a convolutional neural network (CNN). The second function maps this abstract visual representation to pixel space, in order to generate the target image.

Gatys et al. [11] extracts the artistic style of an image, for example, a painting by Van Gogh or Edvard Munch, and applies it to another image, such as a photograph. In their research, the authors use convolutional neural networks to separate the content and the style of the image, and store different representations for each image. Doing so enabled them to apply different transformations or even mix and match representations from different images.

While the works listed above have applied deep neural networks to the task of image caption and image generation, most of these sources attempted to solve the task of transferring a specific style from one painting to another image. By contrast, this paper main focus is using RNN and LSTM to perform Monet-style image generation directly.

3 LSTM Network and Models

Figure 1 illustrates the basic recurrent neural network prediction architecture. An input vector sequence $\mathbf{x} = (x_1, \cdots, x_T)$ is passed through weighted connections to a stack of N recurrently connected hidden layers to compute first the hidden vector sequences $\mathbf{h}^n = (h_1^n, \cdots, h_T^n)$ and then the output vector sequence $\mathbf{y} = (y_1, \cdots y_T)$.

In most RNNs the hidden layer function is an elementwise application of a sigmoid function. The LSTM architecture, which uses purpose-built memory cells to store

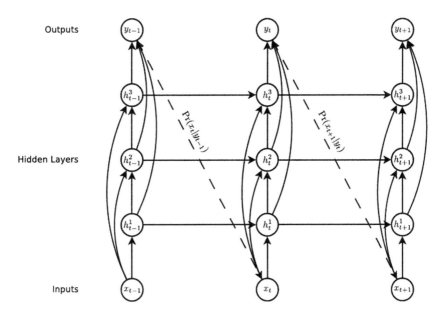

Fig. 1. Deep recurrent neural network prediction architecture.

information, is better at finding and exploiting long range dependencies in the data. A single LSTM memory cell structure is illustrated in Fig. 2.

We define our problem of impressionism painting sequence modeling formally as follows: Given a set of vectors $P_0, P_1, \cdots, P_T$, representing impressionism paintings at the intervals t, we would like to generate the most likely vector P_{t+1} representing an impressionism painting at the next interval $t + 1$. In essence, this is a sequence modeling task in which we are trying to estimate the next sequence conditioned on the previous sequences. In the case of our problem, the inputs are already continuous and hence we can frame the problem of estimating P_{t+1} as a sequence generation task. We can perform this task by using a recurrent network in which each feed-forward computation results in a new estimate $t + 1$ representing our best guess for P_{t+1}. By training the recurrent neural network on various already known Monet-style painting sets, we can learn useful priors to aid in future impressionism paintings generation tasks. The loss function is L_2 loss which is given by

$$\ell(\theta) = \frac{1}{T} \sum_t (P_t - \hat{P}_t)^2 \tag{1}$$

One of the benefits of phrasing the image generation problem as a generation task across the painting sequence is that we can feed the recurrent network any manner of painting data we have available for training purposes. In order to simplify training, we first load the list of images as an array and convert each image into a mono-channel vector by concatenate all the rows on each image into one single row. Then we perform color quantization by using K-Means algorithm to achieve clustering aim. It also serves as a means of reducing the dimensionality of the training data.

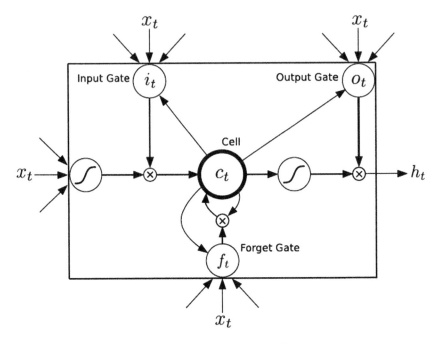

Fig. 2. Long short-term memory cell structure.

The recurrent neural network is consisted of 2 stacked LSTM layers with dropout layer, and the dropout layer consists in randomly setting input units to 0 at each update during training time, which helps prevent overfitting. The network also includes a dense full connected layer and an output layer with softmax activation. RMSProp is used as the learning optimizer in the training procedure. This optimizer is usually a good choice for recurrent neural networks. Each LSTM unit maintains a memory c_t at interval t. The output h_t is given by

$$h_t = \sigma_t \tanh(c_t) \tag{2}$$

where σ_t is an output gate that modulates the amount of memory content exposure. The output gate is computed by

$$\sigma_t = \sigma(W_0 x_t + U_0 h_{t-1} + V_0 c_t) \tag{3}$$

where V_0 is a diagonal matrix. The memory cell c_t is updated by partially forgetting the existing memory and adding new memory content $\hat{c}_t$

$$\hat{c}_t = \tanh(W_c x_t + U_c h_{t-1}) \tag{4}$$

We trained the LSTM networks on about one hundred Monet's impressionism style paintings. The LSTM networks were trained each iteration for 2000 epochs, and the network consisted of 2048 hidden dimensions. The number of hidden dimensions has a direct impact on the quality of image generation, and having hidden dimensions of size 2048 seemed to produce the best results and provided a reasonable compromise between GPU memory footprint and training time.

4 Experiments and Results

After training the network, we can generate new Monet-style images by providing a seed sequence $S_0, S_1, \cdots, S_{t-1}, S_t$, representing seed paintings at the intervals $0, 1, \cdots, t-1, t$. The first step is to perform a feed-forward computation on the seed sequence. After the feed-forward computation is complete, we are left with a new set of vectors $P_1, P_2, \cdots, P_t, P_{t+1}$, representing the predicted paintings at the intervals $1, 2, \cdots, t, t+1$. We call this collection of vectors the generation sequence. In the second step, we then perform another feed-forward pass with the entire generation sequence as input and append the last vector estimate to the generation sequence. For example, assuming our generation sequence was from $P_1, P_2, \cdots, P_{t+k-1}, P_{t+k}$, we would append the estimate for P_{t+k+1} to the generation sequence at the end of the second step. We then iteratively perform the second step until we have generated a sufficiently long sequence as specified by the user. The LSTM network implemented in this paper is based on Theano library [12, 13], and Nvidia CUDA framework is used to perform GPU acceleration. The model is trained on the high performance computing clusters, which have powerful GPUs like Nvidia GTX 980. The training data set consisted of 100 images of Monet's paintings, and some input samples are illustrated as Fig. 3. Most of them are in the style of impressionism. We first trained the LSTM network, and then we started to run the method iteratively. The different iterative outputs are shown as Figs. 4, 5, 6 and 7.

Fig. 3. Input samples.

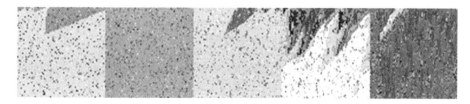

Fig. 4. 10 iterations.

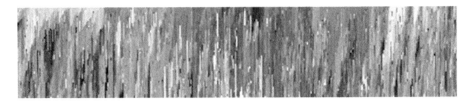

Fig. 5. 30 iterations.

Fig. 6. 60 iterations.

Fig. 7. 100 iterations.

5   Conclusion

This paper has demonstrated that algorithmic Monet-style images generation is possible with the use of recurrent neural networks, particularly the LSTM network. Interesting future directions include investigating the effect of adding layers of recurrent units and discovering the impact that additional layers have on performance. Similarly, it would be worthwhile to perform network training across different network architectures, and evaluate the time and memory consumption of the high performance computing clusters. We are eager to experiment with more complex architectures and larger data sizes to see how well our preliminary results generalize and evaluate the effect of network depth on other painting styles generation.

Acknowledgments. This research was funded by the grants (No. 61540062) from the Natural Science Foundation of China.

References

1. Hochreiter, S., Schmidhuber, J.: Long short-term memory. Neural Comput. **9**(8), 1735–1780 (1997)
2. Sutskever, I., Martens, J., Hinton, G.: Generating text with recurrent neural networks. In: Proceedings of ICML (2011)
3. Graves, A., Mohamed, A., Hinton, G.: Speech recognition with deep recurrent neural networks. In: Proceedings of ICASSP (2013)
4. Graves, A., Schmidhuber, J.: Offline handwriting recognition with multidimensional recurrent neural networks. In: Advances in Neural Information Processing Systems, vol. 21 (2008)
5. Kyprianidis, J.E., Collomosse, J., Wang, T., Isenberg, T.: State of the art: a taxonomy of artistic stylization techniques for images and video. IEEE Trans. Vis. Comput. Graph. **19**(5), 866–885 (2013)
6. Hertzmann, A., Jacobs, C.E., Oliver, N., Curless, B., Salesin, D.H.: Image analogies. In: Proceedings of the 28th Annual Conference on Computer Graphics and Interactive Techniques, pp. 327–340 (2001)
7. Ashikhmin, N.: Fast texture transfer. IEEE Comput. Graph. Appl. **23**, 38–43 (2003)
8. Mordvintsev, A., Olah, C., Tyka, M.: DeepDream - a code example for visualizing neural networks. Google Res. (2015)
9. Karpathy, A., Fei-Fei, L.: Deep visual-semantic alignments for generating image description. In: CVPR 2015 (2015)
10. Angeliki, L., Dat, T.N., Bernardi, R., Baroni, M.: Unveiling the dreams of word embeddings: towards language-driven image generation. arXiv:1506.03500
11. Gatys, L.A., Alexander, S.E., Matthias, B.: A neural algorithm of artistic style. arXiv:1508.06576
12. Bastien, F., Lamblin, P., Pascanu, R., Bergstra, J., Goodfellow, I., Bergeron, A., Bouchard, N., Bengio, Y.: Theano: new features and speed improvements. In: NIPS Workshop on Deep Learning and Unsupervised Feature Learning (2012)
13. Bergstra, J., Breuleux, O., Bastien, F., Lamblin, P., Pascanu, R., Desjardins, G., Turian, J., Warde-Farley, D., Bengio, Y.: Theano: a CPU and GPU math expression compiler. In: Proceedings of the Python for Scientific Computing Conference (SciPy), June 2010

Image Stylization for Yunnan Out-of-Print Woodcut Through Virtual Carving and Printing

Jie Li and Dan Xu[✉]

School of Information Science and Engineering,
Yunnan University, Kunming 650091, China
danxu@ynu.edu.cn

Abstract. Woodcut printing is a special art combining carving and printing skills. The difference of Yunnan Out-of-Print woodcut printing from ordinary printing is that carving alternates with printing in cycles to produce multi-color printings, and all colors are printed just out of one block which is recarved for each color. This is a complex process and requires high technical skills. We propose an image stylization method for Yunnan out-of-print woodcut through virtual carving and printing. First, image segmentation is applied to isolate areas for carving. In each segmented region, scores collected from real woodcut are placed to simulate the carving process. We introduce an algorithm to automate the placement according to the image feature. In the printing process, we mainly focus on the simulation of the mixture of oil paint and the special effect of random color blending in Yunnan out-of-print woodcut.

Keywords: Yunnan out-of-print woodcut · Virtual carving · Virtual printing · Stylization

1 Introduction

Woodcut is an important art form, which combines carving and printing. The common woodcut is monocolor. Multicolor woodcut needs multiple printings, which is usually done by several woodblocks, and each block prints only one color, this is called overprinting. Yunnan out-of-print woodcut is also multicolor, but it uses only one woodblock. For this purpose, carving alternates with the printing in cycles to gradually reduce the printable area of woodblock, so this technical is also known as reduction block printing woodcut. Figure 1 demonstrates the process of it.

Unfortunately, the creating of Yunnan out-of-print woodcut is a complex and time-consuming process. Artists will not know how the final result looks like until last printing, which means they should have a careful plan, including the segmentation of conceived images, the printing colors and the printing order. The

This work is supported by NSFC projects (No. 61163019, No. 61540062, No. 61271361), Key project of Yunnan applied basic research program (No. 2014FA021), and Digital Media Technology Key Laboratory of Universities in Yunnan.

A. El Rhalibi et al. (Eds.): Edutainment 2016, LNCS 9654, pp. 212–223, 2016.
DOI: 10.1007/978-3-319-40259-8_19

creating of Yunnan out-of-print woodcut goes with the destroying of woodblock, so this whole process is irreversible, and further copies beyond the first edition are impossible.

In this paper, we introduce a system devising 2D input image with Yunnan out-of-print woodcut characteristics. Following the process of real Yunnan out-of-print woodcut, there are mainly three key problems to be solved. Yunnan out-of-print woodcut needs multiple printings, each prints only one color. Artists should determine the region of each printing in advance, which we formulate as the image segmentation problem. The other two problems are the simulation of carving and printing. The sculpture is simulated by the placement of scores collected from real woodcuts, and the placement is guided by a highly smooth orientation field which adapted to the edge feature of the input image. In the virtual printing, we focus on the simulation of the special effects of the random mixture of oil paint during multiple printings.

Our main contribution is a complete solution for the simulation of Yunnan out-of-print woodcut from 2D images. We build a system visualizing the complex and abstract creating process of Yunnan out-of-print woodcut step by step. In each step, we provide user with enough controls to achieve their individual goals.

Fig. 1. The first four printing of Yunnan out-of-print woodcut

2   Characteristics of Yunnan Out-of-Print Woodcut

For woodcut printing, knife is used as pen, woodblock is used as paper sheet, and the final artwork can be seen as a combination of painting, carving and printing skills. Those special media and skills lead to several special effects which distinct woodcut from other art forms.

The first characteristic of woodcut lies in the score. Score is the language of woodcut, and woodcut is actually the permutation and combination of scores. Therefore, the final rendering result of our system largely depends on the quality of imitated scores. As Fig. 2(a) shows, two features could be finded:

- The shape of score is relatively rigid. In woodcut, image is engraved in the woodblock, which has a great resistance to the graver, so the track of graver won't be as flexible as that of pen on paper.
- Scores are commonly evenly distributed and similarly parallel to each other.

These features determine our virtual carving algorithms difference from other stroke-based methods. In oil painting, the interaction of strokes is allowed. While in ink painting, strokes are often reflected around the edge.

The second characteristic of Yunnan out-of-print woodcut lies in the printing process. Yunnan out-of-print woodcut uses oil paint to print multicolor paintings. In each printing, newly printed paint may mix with the previous printed paint, which may lead to new color. Therefore, the final result is still very colorful, despite the limited number of printed colors. Another feature is that some previous printing colors are randomly left in present printing (see Fig. 2(b)). Two reasons at different scales account for that. One is the low-frequency density variations of the pressure on the paper during printing. The other is the high-frequency density variations of woodblock grain texture.

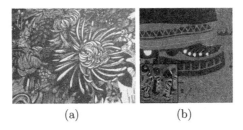

(a)   (b)

Fig. 2. Characteristics in Yunnan out-of-print woodcut: (a) Scores in common woodcut (b) Random color mixture

3   Related Work

Little research has been down on the stylization of woodcut. The first complete work was introduced by Shinji Mizuno's group from Japan [1–3]. They proposed an interactive modeling technique to form solid objects with curved surface. Users may interactivity carve the solid object with virtual chisels in real time. They also modeled the paper and ink to generate woodcut print from the carved block. Their work was eventually applied to Japanese prints Ukiyo-e, but the visual result isn't very impressive, maybe because they did not properly model the fine grain detail of the wood.

Mello et al. introduced an image-based rendering method without complex model [4]. It has four step, image segmentation, calculation of direction field, generation of woodcuts and rendering of woodcuts. To simulate the stroke of woodcuts, a function was used to control the width of the stroke along the trajectory. But the function is too simple. It only produces limited kinds of strokes which differ greatly from real strokes in woodcuts. Besides, this method only synthesizes monocolor woodcut.

4   Method

An overview of our approach is shown in Fig. 3. There are mainly 3 steps—image segmentation, carving and printing. First, input image is segmented basing on the Markov random field (MRF) [5]. Suppose that each region shares the same properties, so it will be printed in the same edition. The printing color of each region is simply computed by averaging colors of the input image's pixels under the region by default, or specified by user interactively. Let n denotes the number of image segments, all printing colors $\{c_1, c_2, \cdots, c_n\}$ are sorted by luminance to determine the printing order $\{k_1, k_2, \cdots, k_n\}$.

The carving process is simulated by the placement of score in each segmented region. This would be a tedious work, so we automate it using a stochastic algorithm guiding by a smooth orientation field computed from the input image. We also provide interfaces for user to improve the placement by adding, editing or removing scores. It should be noted that all gray images $(\{s_1, s_2, \cdots, s_n\})$ obtained in the virtual carving step actually means parts which shall be cut from virtual woodblock. The automatically placed scores may miss some details of image, so stylized edges using XDOG (eXtended Difference-of-Gaussians) [9] are applied to enhance the edge.

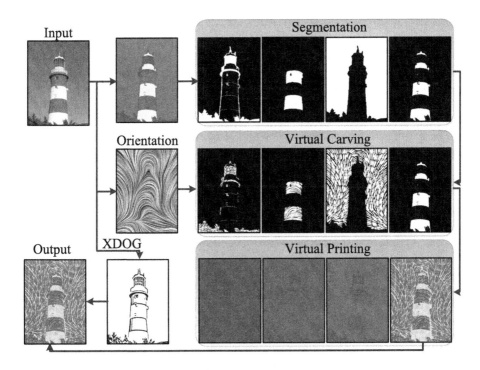

Fig. 3. Schematic overview of the proposed method

The printing process is simulated through the virtual over printing model described as below:

$$p_i = p_{i-1} * (1 - b_{i-1}) \oplus b_{i-1} * c_{k_i} \tag{1}$$

$$b_i = b_{i-1} - s_{k_i} \tag{2}$$

Where p_i is the result of the ith edition (p_0 is the original color of paper), b_i is the virtual woodblock ($b_0 = 1$), c_{k_i} is the printing color. Formula (2) denotes the carving process before each printing. Formula (1) denotes the printing process, which is based on the principle that smaller distance between woodblock and paper leads more paint transferred, where $\oplus$ means the mixture of oil paint basing on the Kubelka-Munk model [10]. To imitate the random color mixture effect, a random noise texture is added on the virtual woodblock to randomly disturb the mixture in each printing.

4.1   Image Segmentation

In Yunnan out-of-print woodcut, only a limited number (usually 5 to 8) of colors are printed, so artist should carefully design the printing colors and the region of them. We formulate this process as an image segmentation problem. Each segmented region will be printed with the same color, and the printing color may be computed by averaging region's original colors or be specified manually by users. In the computer vision, Markov random field (MRF) has become a popular tool for image segmentation because of the ability in modelling the spatial dependencies among pixels. Given the input image, feature vector containing color and texture information is extracted. Then, we substitute the feature vector into a Markov-based segmentation model.

The feature vector contains color and texture features. Three color components (r, g, b) of the image pixel compose the color feature. The texture feature is extracted from the smoothed structure tensor [6], which is defined by:

$$J_0 = \begin{pmatrix} I_x^2 * G & (I_x \cdot I_y) * G \\ (I_x \cdot I_y) * G & I_y^2 * G \end{pmatrix} = \begin{pmatrix} D & E \\ E & F \end{pmatrix}, \tag{3}$$

where I_x and I_y are the partial derivative of image I, G is the Gaussian kernel. Given the six dimensional vector (r, g, b, D, E, F), a PDE-based nonlinear diffusion filter is to apply to each channel of the vector for image denoising [7]. Then we calculate texture contrast $\sqrt{\lambda_1 + \lambda_2}$ and texture coherence $\sqrt{\lambda_1 - \lambda_2}$ as texture feature vector, where λ_1 and λ_2 are the major and minor eigenvalues of the filtered structure tensor. The texture feature vector combined with the diffused color vector makes up the final feature vector $(r, g, b, contrast, coherence)$. Finally, the feature vector is applied to the spatially variant finite mixture model (SVFMM) based on MRF to segment the input image [5]. Since both color and texture information are used, our approach performs well even when dealing images with textured regions shown in Fig. 4. Besides, the SVFMM model also enables user to specify the number of segmented regions.

Fig. 4. 2-class, 3-class and 4-class image segmentations using our method

4.2   Virtual Carving

The carving process is simulated by the placement of score in each segmented region. Instead of simulating score physically, different kinds of score textures collected from real woodcut are used. To guide the placement of score, an edge orientation is computed by using gradient information, and the computed orientation should be highly smooth to keep placed score rigid. Following this orientation, a stochastic algorithm is applied to automatically distribute the score evenly. In addition, stylized edges are extracted to enhance edges.

Score Texture. Instead of imitating score, we directly use score textures collected from real woodcut. In this way, the complex computation is avoided, while feature of real score is still preserved. Round graver, flat graver and triangle graver are most frequently used gravers. We first capture these 3 kinds of digital score images by scanning woodcut painting. Then, we extract single score interactively by using a closed form matting algorithm [8] to create the score library. To keep the diversity of scores, about total 200 different scores are collected as default options for users in the library, and users may also add new scores to it. Figure 6(a, b) shows scores of round graver and triangle graver.

Orientation Field. We use the mathematical interpolation method for the global smooth orientation. Some orientation around strong edges are chosen as control vectors for interpolation, and the number of control vectors directly determines the smoothness of interpolated orientation field. First, Canny edge detector is applied to the image for edge detection. To further reduce control vectors, image is divided into grids sized $n * n$ ($5 * 5$ by default). For each grid, an average orientation [4] is estimated:

$$\theta(i,j) = \frac{1}{2} * \tan^{-1}(\frac{V_x(i,j)}{V_y(i,j)}) \tag{4}$$

$$V_x(i,j) = \sum_{(u,v)\in W} 2G_x(u,v)G_y(u,v) \tag{5}$$

$$V_y(i,j) = \sum_{(u,v) \in W} (G_x(u,v)^2 - G_y(u,v)^2) \tag{6}$$

where $\theta(i,j)$ is the estimate of the local average orientation of the grid W centered at pixel (i,j), G_x and G_y are the partial derivative in x and y direction. To ensure the smoothness of final interpolated orientation, the estimated orientation should be consistent with its neighbor's orientation. The consistency level can be measured through:

$$C(i,j) = \frac{1}{N} \sqrt{\sum_{(i',j') \in D} d(\theta(i',j'), \theta(i,j))^2} \tag{7}$$

where $d(\theta, \theta') = min\{|\theta - \theta'|, \pi - |\theta - \theta'|\}$, D is a set of N neighboring grids. Orientation with small C is preserved as control vector. Given the control vectors, a global orientation field is interpolated. Spline and nearest neighbor interpolation methods are offered for users. Figure 5(a) shows the spline interpolated orientation, where lines are slightly curve. Figure 5(b) shows a piecewise constant orientation field obtained by the nearest neighbor interpolation, generated lines are much more rigid.

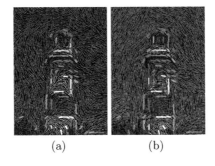

(a)   (b)

Fig. 5. Interpolated orientation field: (a) Spline interpolation; (b) Nearest neighbor interpolation. Large strokes are control vectors

Stroke Placement. Following the smooth orientation, streamlines are generated evenly. Each streamline, considered as the track of graver in woodcut, is with a score texture mapping to. So streamline actually determine the size and distribution of stroke. A random algorithm is used to generate a set of evenly-spaced streamlines. In the target region, a seed point is randomly selected. Then a streamline is integrated starting from the point and extending in both backward and forward direction until either it goes across other lines or it leaves the target domain. The algorithm ends when the target domain is distributed by streamlines fully. Two key points in the algorithm shall be further detailed:

- The density of streamline is an important global feature of the field. To control the density, each streamline is with a default width. Hence, by controlling the default width, we may control the density of the field. Points covered by the streamline are labeled, so that they won't be selected as seed points and other streamlines must not pass through them.

- The seed point is selected randomly in the target region, and it will be discarded if it has been labeled. When consecutive multiple selected points are discarded, we believe that the target region has been fully covered by lines with a high probability, so the algorithm stops.

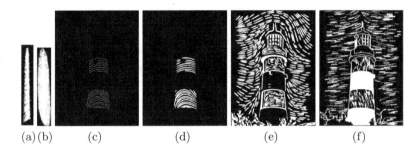

(a)(b)   (c)   (d)   (e)   (f)

Fig. 6. Virtual carving: (a) Score of triangle graver (b) Score of round graver (c) Streamlines; (d) Mapped scores; (e) Simulated black-and-white woodcut, (f) Mello's result

Edge Enhancement. As Fig. 6(c) shows, our method is effective to place evenly-spaced streamline with an accurate control on the density. By changing the streamline width, length and mapped scores, different styles of engraved virtual block would be obtained. The Fig. 6(d) illustrates generated virtual bock. It should be noted that each generated virtual block would be different since each seed point is determined randomly. The automatic stroke placement algorithm places stroke within each region, which may miss some details of image. To preserve these details, XDOG (eXtended Difference-of-Gaussians) is utilized to obtain stylized edges of image.

In this step, several gray images including XDOG edge will be obtained. Those gray images actually mean parts which should be carved away from virtual woodblock. However, by simply composting those images into one image, we get a white-and-black woodcut in Fig. 6(e). Compared to Mello's result in Fig. 6(f), scores in our result are much more real, and stylized edge gives rendering result more details.

4.3   Virtual Printing

Yunnan out-of-print woodcut uses oil paint to print multicolor paintings. To simulate the mixture of oil paint, the Kubelka-Munk (KM) model is used to perform color blending. In each printing, some previous printing colors are still randomly left in present printing. To simulate this random color mixing effect, a random noise texture using line integral convolution [11] is generated to randomly disturb each printing.

Kubelka-Munk Model. The mixture of oil paint is actually subtractive color mixtures. We use a simplified KM model [10] to perform the subtractive color blending of two colors with known ratio. First, colors specified in RGB are converted into absorption/scattering (K/S) ratios for each channel by:

$$A = \frac{k}{s} = \frac{(1-R)^2}{2R},$$ (8)

where R denotes the channel of RGB. Then, the mixed the absorption/scattering ratio A_{mix} is computed by

$$A_{mix} = r_1 * A_1 + r_2 * A_2,$$ (9)

where A_1 and A_2 are the absorption/scattering ratios of colors for mixture, r_1 and r_2 are their mixture ratios. Finally, this mixed ratio A_{mix} is converted back to RGB for rendering and display. The formula is shown below:

$$R_{mix} = 1 + A_{mix} - \sqrt{A_{mix}^2 + 2A_{mix}}$$ (10)

Fig. 7(b) illustrates the simulated result of subtractive color mixing using the simplified KM blending. Compared to the alpha color blending which is often used for additive color mixing shown in Fig. 7(a), our model captures straight forward paint mixing principles such as 'yellow and blue makes green'.

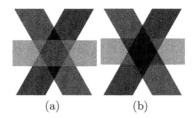

(a)   (b)

Fig. 7. (a) Additive color mixing; (b) Subtractive color mixing (Color figure online)

Random Color Mixture. We perform Line Integral Convolution (LIC) to generate a random noise texture to disturb the color mixture. An LIC image is usually obtained by low-pass filtering a white noise along the local streamlines of a vector field. By changing the vector field, the length or step of local streamline, different kinds of random texture could be obtained, shown in Fig. 8(a). Especially when the vector field is random, and the step of streamline is greater than 1, a gain noise texture which is similar to the random color mixture effect in woodcut could be obtained (see Fig. 8(b)).

The frequency of noise in real woodcut may not be constant, so we perform multi-frequency LIC [12] to generate multi-frequency noise texture. Given the generated noise texture I_{LIC}, we normalize it by using following formula to mapping the value to the range $[-1, 1]$.

$$I_{LIC} = 2 * (\frac{I_{LIC} - \min(I_{LIC})}{\max(I_{LIC}) - \min(I_{LIC})} - 0.5) \tag{11}$$

Considering the noise texture, the printing model in formula (1) will be:

$$p_i = p_{i-1} * (1 - (b_{i-1} + k * I_{LIC})) \oplus (b_{i-1} + k * I_{LIC}) * c_{k_i}, \tag{12}$$

where the weight k controls the magnitude of the turbulence. We empirically determine the $k = 0.05$ as a good default value. Figure 8(d, e) shows the rendering result with different k value.

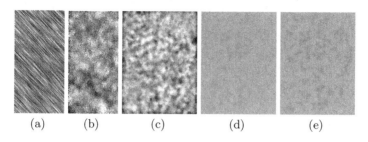

(a)   (b)   (c)   (d)   (e)

Fig. 8. (a) LIC texture, $direction = -45°$, $step = 1$; (b) LIC texture, random direction, $step = 2$; (c) multi-frequency LIC texture; (d) Random color mixing disturbed by (c), $k = 0.05$; (e) Random color mixing disturbed by (c), $k = 0.1$;

Virtual Over Printing. The whole over printing process is an iteration of printing and carving. Figure 9 illustrates the whole process. It starts with a virtual woodblock b_0 ($b_0 = 1$ means an uncarved woodblock), a paper sheet p_0, printing colors $\{c_1, c_2, \cdots, c_n\}$, printing order $\{k_1, k_2, \cdots, k_n\}$, a random noise texture I_{LIC}, and images to be carved $\{s_1, s_2, \cdots, s_n\}$. Following the printing order, select the printing color c_{k_i} and synthesize a virtual printing p_i using formula (12). Then, gray image s_{k_i}, which means regions of virtual woodblock

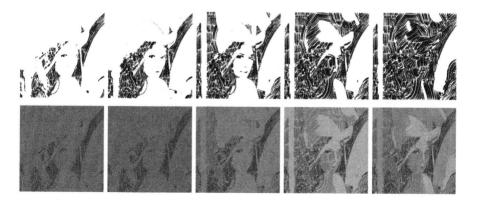

Fig. 9. Virtual over printing: the first row is the carved virtual block ($b_1 \sim b_5$); the second row is the result of each virtual printing ($p_1 \sim p_5$)

where last printing color c_{k_i} should be kept in the printing paper, is carved away using formula (2), so that the woodblock will become concave in those areas, and colors of printing paper in those areas will remain unchanged.

5   Result and Discussion

As mentioned before, some parameters are provided for users to control rendering result. Figure 10 shows several different results. In Fig. 10(a), the spline interpolation is utilized to compute the orientation. So the generated stroke is slightly curved. In contrast, Fig. 10(b) shows result using nearest neighbor interpolation, which leads to straight and rigid strokes. Users can also change the density, length or scores. Figure 10(c) is the rendering result with more short scores. Figure 10(d) is another rendering result.

There's also certainly room for further improvement. The quality of our rendering result largely depends on the semantically meaningful segment of input image, but image segmentation without user interaction can't always slice the image meaningfully. Our automatic score placement algorithm simulates the most frequently used way of score placement. There are some other ways of placing scores that will be simulated in the future work.

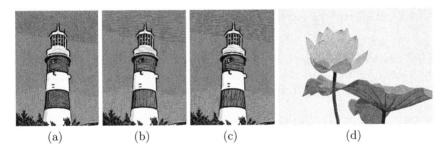

(a)   (b)   (c)   (d)

Fig. 10. Rendering results: (a) Curve Stroke; (b) Rigid Stroke; (c) Short Stroke; (d) Other rendering result

6   Conclusion

This paper presented a complete method for synthesizing Yunnan out-of-print woodcut from images through iteratively virtual carving and printing. To do that, we propose an over printing model combining the virtual printing and carving using only one piece of virtual woodblock. First, input image is sliced out through a MRF-based segmentation algorithm. Within segmented regions, scores collected from real woodcut are placed automatically following a global smooth orientation field to simulate the carving process. In the printing process, we use KM model to simulate the mixture of oil paint, and a random noise texture is used to disturb the mixture. Several impressive rendering results demonstrate the effectiveness of our approach.

References

1. Mizuno, S., Okada, M., Toriwaki, J.-i.: Virtual sculpting and virtual woodcut printing. Vis. Comput. **14**(2), 195–197 (1998)
2. Mizuno, S., Okada, M., Toriwaki, J.-I., Yamamoto, S.: Improvement of the virtual printing scheme for synthesizing ukiyo-e. In: Proceedings of the 16th International Conference on Pattern Recognition, pp. 1043–1046. IEEE (2002)
3. Mizuno, S., Kobayashi, D., Okada, M., Toriwaki, J.-I., Yamamoto, S.: Creating a virtual wooden sculpture and a woodblock print with a pressure sensitive pen and a tablet. Forma **21**(1), 49–65 (2006)
4. Mello, V., Jung, C.R., et al.: Virtual woodcuts from images. In: Proceedings of the 5th International Conference on Computer Graphics and Interactive Techniques, pp. 103–109. ACM (2007)
5. Blekas, K., Likas, A., Galatsanos, I., Lagaris, E.: A spatially constrained mixture model for image segmentation. IEEE Trans. Neural Netw. **16**(2), 494–498 (2005)
6. Brox, T., Boomgaard, R., Lauze, F., Weijer, J., et al.: Adaptive structure tensors and their applications. In: Visualization and Processing of Tensor Fields, pp. 17–47 (2006)
7. Catt, F., Lions, P.-L., Morel, J.-M., Coll, T.: Image selective smoothing and edge detection by nonlinear diffusion. SIAM J. Numer. anal. **29**(1), 182–193 (1992)
8. Levin, A., Lischinski, D., Weiss, Y.: A closed-form solution to natural image matting. IEEE Trans. Pattern Anal. Mach. Intell. **30**(2), 228–242 (2008)
9. Winnemöller, H.: Xdog: advanced image stylization with extended difference-of-gaussians. In: Eurographics Symposium on NPAR, pp. 147–156 (2011)
10. Blatner, A.M., Ferwerda, J.A., DarlingB.A., Bailey, R.J.: Tangi-paint: a tangible digital painting system. In: Color and Imaging Conference, Society for Imaging Science and Technology, pp. 102–107 (2011)
11. Cabral, B., Leedom, L.C.: Imaging vector Fields using line integral convolution. In: Proceedings of the ACM SIGGRAPH, pp. 263–270 (1993)
12. Kiu, M.H., Banks, D.C.: Multi-frequency noise for LIC. In: Proceedings of the 7th Conference on Visualization 1996, pp. 121–126. IEEE Computer Society Press (1996)

Cross-Platform Cloth Simulation API for Games

Wen Tang[1(✉)], Abhishek Sagi[2], Daniel Green[3], and Tao Ruan Wan[4]

[1] Bournemouth University, Poole, Dorset BH12 5BB, UK
wtang@bournemouth.ac.uk
[2] Auroch Digital, Bristol Games Hub, 77 Stokes Croft, Bristol, UK
gam3r@ymail.com
[3] School of Computing, University of Teesside, Middlesbrough TS1 3BA, UK
d@ngreen.org
[4] School of Computing and Engineering,
University of Bradford, Bradford BD7 1DP, UK
t.wan@bradford.ac.uk

Abstract. Physics simulation is an active research topic in games, because without realistic physics, even the most beautiful game feels static and lifeless. Although cloth simulation is not new in computer graphics, high level of details of cloth in video games is rare and mostly coarse due to complex and nonlinear physical properties of cloth, which requires substantial computing power necessary to simulate it in real-time. This paper presents a robust and scalable real-time cloth simulation framework by exploring a variety of modern simulation techniques to produce realistic cloth simulation for games. The framework integrates with OpenCL GPGPU library to leverage parallelism. The final result is an API for games development with enriched interactive environments.

Keywords: Game physics · Simulation algorithm · Cloth modelling

1   Introduction

Developing fundamental computational algorithms and software pipelines that can truly unleash the power of physics simulation in computer games has been a major research activity in computer graphics. Cloth simulation is important in creating believable virtual world, yet it is still an extremely difficult task due to complex and nonlinear physical properties of cloth, and real-time simulation of detailed cloth with realistic wrinkles and folds remains challenging in video games. In games, game play aspects (i.e. AI logic, player interactions, video and audio qualities) all demand computing resources, making cloth simulation secondary. As a consequence, cloth in most modern games is still coarse and primitive lacking fine details and realism. Modern games utilize popular open source physics engines to handle physically-based computation tasks such as collision detections and rigid-body physics. Physics engines such as Bullet Physics SDK [1] and Nvidia PhysX [2] support cloth dynamics, but their implementations have high platform specific dependencies with many undesirable drawbacks in terms of robustness and scalability of simulation algorithms.

© Springer International Publishing Switzerland 2016
A. El Rhalibi et al. (Eds.): Edutainment 2016, LNCS 9654, pp. 224–232, 2016.
DOI: 10.1007/978-3-319-40259-8_20

1.1   Non-linear Cloth Materials

Real-world cloth materials exhibit nonlinear behaviour due to their woven and fibrous structures. Nonlinear properties create distinctive appearances of cloth in folds and wrinkles. Unfortunately, most current cloth simulation techniques in games simply ignore these properties and use linear elastic models for simplicity. While using a linear model simplifies numerical simulation problem and generates visually plausible results, such simple simulations do not allow high fidelity to their real-world counterparts. While with standard methods, using traditional finite element methods often involves setting up complex constitutive models to determine material deformation behaviors, simple spring-and-mass systems demand using stiff material parameters to enforce the nonlinearity. Yet, even representing highly stiff springs with manually selected parameters, the process is in itself considered a difficult task. Previous work have considered various different approaches in order to realistically and/or accurately simulate biphasic nonlinear behaviors. For example, in cloth simulation, researchers have observed that one way to achieve fine scale details for winkles and folders in many fabrics is to model this nonlinear stress-to-strain relationship [3,4].

For cloth application in games, we explore the method of using an iterative Gauss-Seidel constraint procedure to obtain a good approximation to nonlinear cloth. The advantage of the algorithm is the simplicity of the algorithm in games applications.

1.2   Cross-Platform and Real-Time Cloth Simulation in Games

Real-time simulation performance is the key in games to ensure instant and rapid response times. Especially for networked games with a Model-View-Controller architecture, the simulation model is normally residing on the dedicated server to prevent cheating as well as desynchronization of the simulations, hence, simulation results need to be transmitted across the network.

We address the problem of developing highly parallel algorithms for high-resolution cloth simulation by utilizing OpenCL for parallel simulation. Tt provides additional benefits for OpenGL interoperability and allows cloth vertex buffers to be updated directly within the GPU avoiding data transfer between CPU and GPU memory. Our simulation framework API is cross-platform which is written in C/C++ and can be easily deployed onto multiple platforms such as PC, OSX, mobile devices (iOS and Android) and also video game consoles. In addition, our physically-based API for cloth has minimal external dependency, making it easy to integrate with other development tools.

Our cloth simulation framework alongside an appropriate rendering pipeline can efficiently simulate and render realistic cloth in real-time suitable for interactive game environments. The GPGPU implementation greatly accelerates the constraint based nonlinear computation and leverages the parallelism of the physics computation.

2   Simulation Algorithm

We represent cloth objects as triangular meshes. For the planar surface model the world space position of each vertex is denoted as $\boldsymbol{x}_i$ and its velocity being $\boldsymbol{v}_i$. We use the shorthand $\boldsymbol{x}_{ij}$ to represent the vector $\boldsymbol{x}_i - \boldsymbol{x}_j$ and the material space vector $\boldsymbol{u}_{ij}$ to express $\boldsymbol{u}_i - \boldsymbol{u}_j$. Lumped masses are used in our computation so that each node has a scalar mass m_i that is set to one third of the sum of material-space areas of its incident faces, multiplied by the material's area-density. Vertex normals $\boldsymbol{n}_i$ are computed using a weighted average of incident face normals.

For dynamic simulation, we take the approach of measuring in-plane membrane and out-plane bending separately. This is essentially computing the strain of triangular elements combined with a discrete bending metric described by Grinspun et al. and Bridson et al. [5,6]. This configuration is invariant to rigid-body transformations. Thus, the physically-based deformation can be modeled by the sum of in-plane membrane and out-plane bending energies, expressed by:

$$\mathbf{W}(\mathbf{x}) = \mathbf{W_M}(\mathbf{x}) + \mathbf{W_B}(\mathbf{x}) \tag{1}$$

where $\mathbf{W_M}(\mathbf{x})$ is the membrane energy as a summation over lengths of edges, and $\mathbf{W_B}(\mathbf{x})$ the discrete bending energy as a summation over mesh edges with the corresponding dihedral angle. These energies are calculated by:

$$\mathbf{W_M}(\mathbf{x}) = k_M \sum (1 - \|\boldsymbol{x}_{ij}\| / \|\boldsymbol{u}_{ij}\|)^2 \|\boldsymbol{u}_{ij}\|$$
$$\mathbf{W_B}(\mathbf{x}) \quad = k_B \sum (\theta_{ij} - \bar{\theta}_{ij})^2 \|\bar{\theta}_{ij}\|$$

where k_M and k_B are stretch and bending stiffness coefficients, respectively. Therefore, the dynamic system is governed by the ordinary differential equation of motion $\ddot{\mathbf{x}} = -\mathbf{M}^{-1}\nabla\mathbf{W}(\mathbf{x})$ where $\mathbf{x}$ is the vertices of the deformed geometry and $\mathbf{M}$ is the mass matrix. We use a semi-implicit integration scheme and nonlinear Gauss-Seidel iterative projections to constrain excessive deformations.

2.1   Strain Limiting Algorithm

The strain limiting method is applied as a filtering step between the velocity and the position update. Our constraint-based techniques are independent of the choice of dynamic models, and would also work with other triangular methods such as triangular finite element methods. The Gauss-Seidel iterative approach has fast convergency when operating on a small-scale. To avoid bias due to sequential iterations, we use random orderings.

The basic concept of strain limiting is to impose hard constraints within a dynamic system. In doing so, edge length constraints can be imposed during the update of node positions, while the bending angle between two triangle elements enforces restrictions on the flexural of the material. In our system, we enforce one-dimensional strain limits of length constraints. Given an edge connecting two nodes $\mathbf{x_a}$ and $\mathbf{x_b}$, the function of one-dimensional strain is defined as:

$$\varepsilon_{ab} = (|\mathbf{x_a} - \mathbf{x_b}| - l_0)/l_0 \tag{2}$$

where l_0 is the original edge length. Given the lower and upper bounds of the stretching/compression ratio $s = |\mathbf{x_a} - \mathbf{x_b}/l_0$ as $[s_{min}, s_{max}]$, the stain ε_{ab} is clamped to the range $[s_{min} - 1, \ s_{max} + 1]$ to enforce the constraint. For example, a material that is constrained to a compress/stretch ratio within range $[-10\%, \ 10\%]$ would have $s_{min} = 0.90$ and $s_{max} = 1.10$. Length constraints are enforced by moving both nodes along edges or just moving one node and letting the other be fixed if required by boundary conditions for a particular edge.

Dihedral angles across edges are used to enforce bending constraints [5,6]. Here, we adopt the same strategy used by Wang and his colleagues [4]. Bending constraints prevent the dihedral angle between two adjacent triangles from becoming too large or too small. Similarly, we enforce bending angle limiting coefficients $[\theta, \ \theta_{max}]$ i.e. degrees per unit length.

The strain limiting algorithm described above can yields the correct result in a single step for a single length constraint or bending constraint. However, each constraint enforcement affects positions of all nodes associated with it, resulting in a *highly undetermined* system. Therefore, enforcing constraints over an entire mesh requires either the Jacobi's method or the Gauss-Seidel method to solve the linear system.

We resolve to use the nonlinear Gauss-Seidel type solver that iteratively enforces each strain limit on triangular meshes. Boundary conditions are processed simultaneously with length and bending constraints so that enforcing one set of constraints would not violate others. The data structure designed in our system is flexible such that constraints required for boundary conditions can be enabled or disabled during run-time.

An impulse based collision response [6] is implemented. The vertex is projected to the surface of the incident object and its velocity is adjusted according to the penetration depth. Frictions are treated in a similar way using penetration depthes to generate dynamic friction forces on each penetrating vertex along the relative tangential velocity.

Figure 1 demonstrate the effects of strain limiting in producing much more realistic cloth with just a small number of iterations.

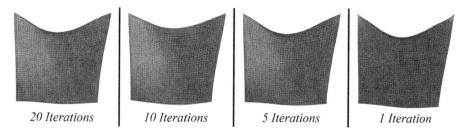

| *20 Iterations* | *10 Iterations* | *5 Iterations* | *1 Iteration* |

Fig. 1. Iterative strain limiting process pipeline to produce much more realistic cloth with only a small number of iterations (red representing over stretching of the cloth) (Color figure online).

Figure 2 shows the comparison of our simulation results with real cloth and the simulation results that were produced in [4] (with permission from authors).

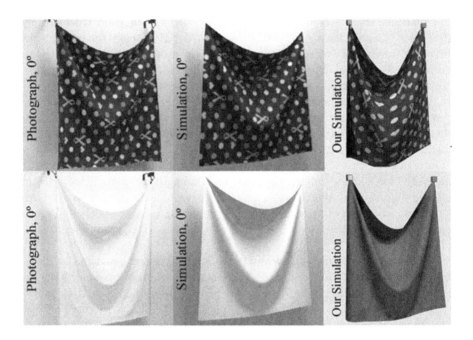

Fig. 2. Comparison of simulation results with real cloth.

3   Simulation Framework

The interconnectedness of cloth vertices means necessary changes to the original CPU calculation for basic GPU execution. Otherwise, attempting to update the same vertex from different threads at the same would cause a race condition. We employ a graph colouring algorithm to the cloth mesh to ensure that each cloth vertex is considered in isolation during each Gauss-Seidel iteration. We simultaneously compute multiple cloth objects to take the full advantages of parallelism by solving large single arrays indexed by values in the individual cloth objects.

3.1   Parallel Algorithm

In order to achieve efficient physics computation for cloth simulation, we explore a parallel computation paradigm using OpenCL GPU programming. With our simulation model and structure, it is a straight forward process to port the simulation into a parallel computation version on GPU. However, care must be taken when dealing with updating the simulation state of the cloth objects in a game environment.

Race Conditions: Race conditions can occur when solving cloth internal forces, nonlinear Gauss-Seidel strain limiting and triangle normals, where two vertices that share the same edge should not be updated by the same thread batch to avoid race conditions. Figure 3 illustrates the cases where race conditions can occur.

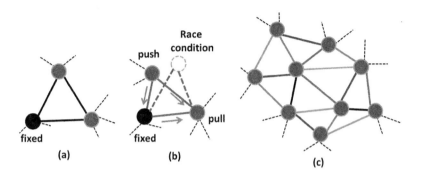

Fig. 3. A graph colouring scheme: race condition occurs when a node is operated by different physics conditions (push vs pull). In this example illustration, there are six groups of edges of the cloth structure that are represented by six different colours (Color figure online).

Graph Colouring Scheme: In order to avoid race conditions in parallel computation, a graph colouring scheme is used in solving an adaptive grid partial differential equation for dynamic irregular triangulated meshes in random surface simulations, so that the neighbouring vertices are not updated simultaneously [7]. Graph colouring was also used in iterative parallel algorithms for solving large irregular sparse matrix equations.

We implemented a graph colouring scheme for a constrained dynamic solver for cloth simulation in games. This scheme ensures that no two edges that share the same vertex in a mesh are in the same batch as shown in Fig. 3, where edges in the same colour are in the same batch. This scheme constructs the parallel computation into a graph. The *undirected graph* G is a set of vertices V and a set of edges E. The edges are of the form (i, j) where $i, j \in V$. A colouring of a graph G is a mapping $c : V \longrightarrow 1, 2, ..., s$ such that $c(i) \neq c(j)$ for all edges $(i, j) \in E$. $c(i)$ is referred to as the colour of the edge that are shared by vertices i and j. In comparison with Jacobi-style implementations such as in [9], which is based on the sum of forces applied by the surrounding links of each vertex, graph colouring is able to propagate updates through the cloth mesh efficiently.

We employ a sequential greedy algorithm for colouring the graph as following:

Data: Cloth Triangle Mesh
Result: Undirected graph with coloured edges
n = $|V|$;
Choose a random permutation $p(1), ..., p(n)$ of numbers $1, ..., n$ $U := V$
for $i = 1$ to n **do**
    $v := p(i)$ $S := colours of all coloured neighbors of v$
    $c(v) := smallest colour not in S$ $U := U - v$, U is the set of uncolored
    vertices.
end
    Algorithm 1: Sequential greedy algorithm for graph colouring

This batch operation is performed only once if the structure of the mesh remains unchanged and each batch is entirely parallel. In the case of remeshing, it can be dealt with by simply disabling links rather than re-batching. Although graph colouring requires a relatively large number of batches depending on the complexity of the interconnectedness of the mesh, it is possible to implement a batch-bound algorithm to reduce the overhead to execute not only in GPU time but also in CPU time to manage GPU execution. Figure 3 indicates there are six groups of edges of the cloth structure represented by six different colours, hence six batches operations.

4   Results and Discussion

Nonlinear cloth behaviour is achieved through a momentum conserving impulse based iterative strain limiting algorithm as described in the above section. Figure 4 compares simulation results with and without strain limiting, which shows that strain limiting models highly constrained inextensible cloth behaviour, thus producing more realistic simulation results.

We have evaluated our algorithm on a complex game environment-Atrium Sponza Palace [8], which has been the most popular 3D benchmark scene for testing global illumination and radiosity. We used the scene to test the real-time performance of the proposed system for real-time cloth simulation in games. The

Fig. 4. Strain limiting algorithm: left image shows a simulation without strain limiting, and right image is the result with strain limiting.

Fig. 5. Test scene: Atrium Sponza Palace with 10 curtains of simulated cloth in real-time plus 5 visible lights for interactive rendering, 25 fps archived on GPU.

first test is to use different cloth mesh resolutions. The test scene as shown in Fig. 5 contains high polygon counts of Sponza Atrium and 10 simulated curtains containing 208,800 edges, 35,990 vertices and 17,400 triangular faces, and the static Sponza Atrium has about 300,000 triangles and 5 light sources.

Our speed-ups over CPU-based algorithms are 3× faster compared to a single threaded CPU-based implementation on a mobile laptop. By performing 10 Gauss-Seidel iterations per curtain per frame, GPU implementation results in an average of 25 fps and an average of 8 fps on CPU simulation on Quad core i7 Processor with nVidia GT650M using OpenCL 1.2 on OSX. It is worth to note that performance may vary on different platforms due to OpenCL driver support and hardware capabilities.

5   Conclusion

We have presented a scalable framework to simulate realistic cloth in games on the GPU that is stable, fast and flexible enough to be used in interactive applications. For most of the strain limiting thresholds controlling the material stiffness, same values work well for different scenarios and different materials, which can be considered as an advantage of the algorithm being material independent. However, defining the exact relationship between the stretching and the bending stiffness remains an open challenge,especially for realistic nonlinear material models as in our simulation context. Finally, our system enables us to perform all the steps of cloth simulation on multiple high density meshes on GPU and avoid any data transfer between the CPU and GPU. Future work includes cloth self-collision and levels of detail.

References

1. Bullet Physics Engine: Real-time Physics Simulation (2014). http://bulletphysics. org/wordpress/
2. Cyril, Z.: Practical cloth simulation on modern GPU. Shader X4: Advanced Rendering with DirectX and OpenGL, Charles River Media, Newton Centre (2006)
3. Thomaszewski, B., Pabst, S., Strasser, W.: Continuum-based strain limiting. Proc. Eurograph. **28**, 569–576 (2009)
4. Wang, H., O'Brien, J.F., Ramamoorthi, R.: Multiresolution isotropic strain limiting. In: Proceedings of ACM SIGGRAPH Aisa, vol. 160, pp. 1–10 (2010)
5. Grinspun, E., Hirani, A. N., Desbrun, M., Schröder, P.: Discrete shells. In: Proceedings of SCA, pp. 62–67 (2003)
6. Bridson, R., Marino, S., Fedkiw, R.: Simulation of clothing with folds and wrinkles. In: Proceedings of SCA, pp. 28–36 (2003)
7. Allwright, J.R., Bordawekar, R., Coddington, P.D., Dincer, K., Martin, C.L.: A comparison of parallel graph coloring algorithms. Technical report, SCCS-666, Northeast Parallel Architectures Center at Syracuse University (1995)
8. CryENGINE 3: Sponza Model (2014). http://www.crytek.com/cryengine/ cryengine3/downloads
9. Tang, M., Tong, R., Narain, R., Meng, C., Manocha, D.: A GPU-based streaming algorithm for high-resolution cloth simulation. Comput. Graph. Forum **32**(7), 21–30 (2013)

Object Proposal Refinement Based on Contour Support for Augmented Reality

Xiao Huang$^{(\boxtimes)}$, Yuanqi Su, and Yuehu Liu

Xi'an Jiaotong University, Xi'an, Shaanxi 710049, People's Republic of China
huangxiao.xjtu@stu.xjtu.edu.cn

Abstract. Object detection and segmentation are indispensable for image scene understanding in augmented reality games. Object proposals delineate candidate objects in the image, and are widely used to speed up object searching in object detection and segmentation. This paper presents an approach for reducing the redundancy in object proposals. We compute contour support of object proposals, and construct contour support constraints using the characteristics of contour support distributions for foreground objects and image background. According to the constructed constraints, we propose the accepting and rejecting strategies to refine object proposals. Experiments demonstrate that our method reduces redundant object proposals and improves proposal accuracy for low proposal budgets.

Keywords: Contour support · Object proposal

1 Introduction

Image scene understanding is indispensable for augmented reality games. Recognized high-level scene descriptions are integrated with visible scene images, generating the scenes for augmented reality games. To understand image scenes, object detection and segmentation are necessary vision tasks.

To improve the computational efficiency of object detection and segmentation, object proposal generation [1,3] has become a promising technique during the recent years. Object proposal generator aims to approximately represent each object in the image by at least one generated region. Object proposals are used as a starting point for object detection [15,17] and semantic segmentation [2,8,9]. There are two representations of object proposals: bounding box [1,4,18] and pixel-wise segmentation region [3,11,12]. Region proposals contain detailed shape cues and support diverse image parsing tasks. Note that it is handy to convert region proposals to box proposals by constructing the minimal box enclosing a region.

Object proposals generated in an image usually contain image background and are redundant when compared with the amount of objects. To reduce the redundancy, [14] employs closed contour enclosed by box proposals. Box proposals without explicit closed contour are pruned for refining the proposal set.

© Springer International Publishing Switzerland 2016
A. El Rhalibi et al. (Eds.): Edutainment 2016, LNCS 9654, pp. 233–242, 2016.
DOI: 10.1007/978-3-319-40259-8_21

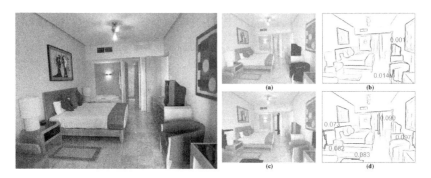

Fig. 1. Example object proposals generated in an image and their contour support. (a–b) Two object proposals corresponding to real objects and their contour support shown in an edge probability map. (c–d) Five object proposals corresponding to background regions and their contour support. The numbers in (b) and (d) denote the contour support of object proposals and lower values represent higher contour support.

Analogously, we refine the existing object proposals and yet we focus on region proposals instead of box proposals.

To refine region proposals, we compute the contour support [13] of each region proposal and prune proposals that do not satisfy constraints. Contour support describes the saliency of closed contour that is region proposal boundary. The saliency of closed contour is an important cue for separating foreground from background in the image [6,13,16]. Therefore, contour support can be used to represent the confidence of region proposals resembling objects, supporting the ranking of proposals. Figure 1 illustrates example object proposals generated in an image and their contour support. Clearly, object proposals with higher contour support are more likely to be real objects.

We employ the accepting and rejecting strategies to refine object proposals, respectively. The accepting strategy retains region proposals whose contour support is similar to that of image foreground (various objects). We compute the contour support distribution of various objects and extract its statistical characteristic as the constraint for accepting proposals. The rejecting strategy prunes region proposals whose contour support is similar to that of image background. We compute the contour support distribution of background regions and obtain its statistical characteristic as the constraint for rejecting proposals.

We conduct experiments on the PASCAL VOC2012 dataset and compare object proposal accuracy before and after the proposal refinement. Experiments demonstrate that our approach effectively reduces redundant object proposals and improves proposal accuracy under low proposal budgets, indicating the effectiveness of contour support.

2   Object Proposal Refinement

In this section, we compute the contour support of region proposals and construct the constraints to which region proposals should be subject. Region proposals

that do not satisfy the constraints are pruned in order to refine the existing
object proposal set.

2.1   Contour Support Computation

The contour support of a region proposal presents the coherence between the
region proposal boundary and image contour cues. To measure contour support,
we employ the evaluation scheme of [13] and thus compute contour gap formed
by region proposal boundary and contour cues. *Smaller contour gap indicates
stronger contour support.* We compute an edge probability map using structured
forests [5], representing image contour cues.

We first briefly introduce the contour gap used in [13]. Given a region R and
a set C of pixels on the region boundary, an edge indicator $E^p = [P(f^p) > T_e]$ is
used to show whether the coherence between a boundary pixel $p \in C$ and contour
cues satisfies the threshold requirement. $E^p = 1$ denotes that the coherence
requirement is satisfied, and the corresponding contour gap is 0. Through the
contour gap definition of individual pixels, the contour gap $G(R)$ of region R is
expressed as

$$G(R) = \frac{|C| - \sum_{p \in C} E^p}{|R|}, \tag{1}$$

where $|C|$ denotes the number of pixels on the region boundary and $|R|$ denotes
the region area. Because large regions usually lead to strong responses of $|C| -
\sum_{p \in C} E^p$, which is a bias, the region size $|R|$ is used as a normalization factor.

In the edge indicator E^p, $P(\cdot)$ is a logistic regression model; f^p is a feature
vector for pixel p; the threshold T_e denotes the degree that the coherence between
pixels and contour cues should achieve. Refer to [13] for the training of $P(\cdot)$, the
design of f^p, and the effect of T_e on contour gap computation. In experiments,
we use the same coefficients as [13] for $P(\cdot)$, and set T_e to a constant (0.05).

2.2   Contour Support Constraints

The contour support of a region proposal describes its boundary saliency. The
region proposal whose closed boundary has higher saliency is more likely to
be an object. Therefore, region proposals with strong contour support tend to
be regarded as object proposals, whereas region proposals with weak contour
support tend to be regarded as background regions.

On one hand, we retain region proposals if their contour support is higher
than a specific threshold. This is the constraint under which region proposals
are accepted as object proposals. On the other hand, we prune region proposals
if their contour support is lower than another specific threshold. This is the
constraint under which region proposals are rejected as object proposals.

To construct the above two constraints, we compute the contour support
distributions for real objects and background regions in images, respectively.
We employ the training and validation sets of PASCAL VOC2012 dataset and
generate region proposals using Selective Search [15]. In the chosen image set,

the human-annotated ground truth regions are regarded as real objects. We use the Jaccard coefficient, $\mathcal{J}(R, R^{'}) = \frac{|R \cap R^{'}|}{|R \cup R^{'}|}$, to compute the overlap of the ground truth region and the generated region proposal. If the overlap is less than 0.5, that region proposal is deemed as a background region.

Note that we utilize contour gap to describe contour support in a reverse manner. Therefore, accepting a region proposal with its contour support being higher than a contour support threshold is equivalent to accepting this region proposal with its contour gap being lower than a contour gap threshold. The rejecting case is similar.

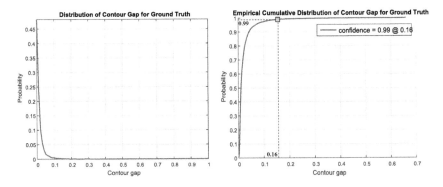

Fig. 2. Statistical analysis for the contour gap distribution of ground truth. **Left**: Probability distribution of contour gap for ground truth. **Right**: Empirical cumulative distribution of contour gap for ground truth; a confidence level (0.99) is set in order to select the corresponding contour gap value (0.16) as the acceptance threshold.

Figure 2 illustrates the statistical analysis for the contour gap distribution of ground truth. We consider the empirical cumulative distribution and set a confidence level (0.99), obtaining the corresponding contour gap value (0.16). We select this gap value as the *acceptance threshold*. Note that the contour gap of 99 % of ground truth is lower than the acceptance threshold.

Proposition 1. *The constraint under which a region proposal is accepted as an object proposal is that the contour gap of the region proposal is lower than the acceptance threshold.*

Figure 3 presents the statistical analysis for the contour gap distribution of background regions. In the left part of Fig. 3, we consider the probability distribution and empirical cumulative distribution of contour gap for background regions. It is clearly shown that the contour gap of background regions spreads in a wide range and overlaps with that of ground truth. Therefore, when the contour gap of a region proposal is lower than a threshold (0.47) computed in a confidence level (0.99), we cannot determine whether that region proposal is a background region. In this case, this paper adopts a strategy, which is similar

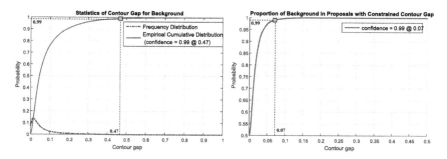

Fig. 3. Statistical analysis for the contour gap distribution of background regions. **Left**: Probability distribution and empirical cumulative distribution of contour gap for background regions; the contour gap of 99 % of background regions is lower than 0.47. **Right**: Contour gap values are incrementally selected, and region proposals with their contour gap being higher than the presently selected value are obtained; for these obtained proposals, the ratio of background regions is computed; under a confidence level (0.99), the corresponding gap value (0.07) is selected as the rejection threshold.

to [14], to consider all the region proposals generated in the chosen image set. As shown in the right part of Fig. 3, we incrementally select contour gap values and obtain region proposals whose contour gap is higher than the presently selected value. For these obtained proposals, the ratio of background regions is computed. When the ratio achieves a confidence level (0.99), the corresponding gap value (0.07) is selected as the *rejection threshold*. Therefore, if the contour gap of a region proposal is higher than the rejection threshold, the probability of the proposal being a background region is 99 %.

Proposition 2. *The constraint under which a region proposal is rejected as an object proposal is that the contour gap of the region proposal is higher than the rejection threshold.*

2.3   Accepting and Rejecting Strategies of Proposals

To refine object proposals, this paper employs the accepting strategy and the rejecting strategy, respectively. Let R and $G(R)$ be a region proposal and its contour gap.

For the accepting strategy, we retain region proposals whose contour support accords with that of objects. Specifically, we use the constraint of accepting region proposals and the corresponding acceptance threshold. If the contour gap of a region proposal is lower than the acceptance threshold, this region proposal is accepted as an object proposal:

$$G(R) < acceptance\ threshold \Rightarrow R\ is\ accepted. \qquad (2)$$

For the rejecting strategy, we prune region proposals whose contour support is similar to that of image background. Specifically, we use the constraint of rejecting region proposals and the corresponding rejection threshold. If the contour gap of a region proposal is higher than the rejection threshold, this region proposal is rejected as an object proposal:

$$G(R) > rejection\ threshold \Rightarrow R\ is\ rejected. \tag{3}$$

3 Experiments

Experiments are conducted on the validation set of PASCAL VOC2012 dataset [7]. This set contains 1449 images from 20 classes of objects. For each image, the ground truth objects are provided, including pixel-wise annotations and bounding box annotations. We focus on region proposals and evaluate both box proposal accuracy and region proposal accuracy.

To measure the accuracy of an object proposal, we consider the overlap (*i.e.* the Jaccard coefficient $\mathcal{J}$ in Sect. 2.2) between the ground truth and the object proposal. The overlap is the Intersection over Union (IoU) metric that is defined as the intersection of two regions divided by the area of their union. If the maximal overlap between a ground truth object and a set of generated object proposals is larger than a given threshold (on the interval $[0.5, 1]$), this ground truth is considered detected under the given threshold.

To evaluate the quality of region proposals, we use the Average Best Overlap (ABO), covering, and recall measures [12]. Given a set S of ground truth objects and a set P of generated object proposals, the ABO is computed using the overlap between each ground truth object $R \in S$ and the closest object proposal $R' \in P$: $ABO = \frac{1}{|S|} \sum_{R \in S} \max_{R' \in P} \mathcal{J}(R, R')$. Covering is an area-weighted measure and assigns higher importance to larger objects: $covering = \frac{1}{\sum_{R \in S} |R|} \sum_{R \in S} |R| \max_{R' \in P} \mathcal{J}(R, R')$. The recall is defined as the fraction of ground truth objects detected under a certain IoU overlap threshold α, and thus can be denoted by α-recall. The value of α is usually 0.5 or 0.7, and 0.7-recall focuses on a tighter fit between ground truth and object proposals.

For the evaluation of box proposals, we utilize the ABO, 0.5-recall, 0.7-recall, and Average Recall (AR) measures [11]. In addition, we employ the "recall versus number of boxes" curve to depict accuracy at different proposal budgets and the "recall versus IoU overlap threshold" curve to show the variation of recall over different localization precision. AR is computed using the area under the "recall versus IoU overlap threshold" curve in IoU range of 0.5 to 1.0. AR is known to be a particularly good predictor for detection performance [10].

3.1 Proposal Refinement Evaluation

We use Selective Search (SS) [15] to generate initial object proposals that are to be refined. For the implementation of SS, we utilize the default parameters (two segmentations and five color spaces) in the publicly available code. To refine proposals, the accepting and rejecting strategies apply to the initial object proposals, respectively. Let A-SS and R-SS be the accepting and rejecting strategies integrated with SS.

Table 1. Region proposal accuracy. Four proposal budgets are considered.

Method	# prop. = 100				# prop. = 500			
	ABO	Covering	0.5-recall	0.7-recall	ABO	Covering	0.5-recall	0.7-recall
SS [15]	0.376	0.429	0.268	0.095	0.552	0.628	0.587	0.262
A-SS	0.411	0.472	0.329	0.121	0.570	0.642	0.623	0.282
R-SS	0.449	0.513	0.387	0.160	0.594	0.679	0.675	0.338
	# prop. = 1000				# prop. = maximal amount			
	ABO	Covering	0.5-recall	0.7-recall	ABO	Covering	0.5-recall	0.7-recall
SS [15]	0.600	0.678	0.689	0.335	0.653	0.740	0.788	0.438
A-SS	0.613	0.694	0.715	0.368	0.654	0.740	0.792	0.443
R-SS	0.627	0.711	0.732	0.397	0.650	0.733	0.786	0.435

Table 2. Box proposal accuracy. Four proposal budgets are considered.

Method	# prop. = 100				# prop. = 500			
	AR	ABO	0.5-recall	0.7-recall	AR	ABO	0.5-recall	0.7-recall
SS [15]	0.220	0.531	0.538	0.241	0.457	0.708	0.850	0.560
A-SS	0.257	0.561	0.592	0.298	0.486	0.728	0.871	0.612
R-SS	0.306	0.597	0.659	0.359	0.518	0.746	0.886	0.653
	# prop. = 1000				# prop. = maximal amount			
	AR	ABO	0.5-recall	0.7-recall	AR	ABO	0.5-recall	0.7-recall
SS [15]	0.538	0.757	0.908	0.676	0.637	0.815	0.941	0.801
A-SS	0.562	0.772	0.914	0.706	0.636	0.815	0.940	0.801
R-SS	0.583	0.782	0.919	0.729	0.624	0.807	0.935	0.785

Table 1 illustrates the region proposal accuracy before and after the refinement under four proposal budgets. Similarly, Table 2 shows the box proposal accuracy. In the case of relatively low proposal budgets (100, 500, 1000), both our accepting strategy and our rejecting strategy improve the proposal accuracy. In addition, our rejecting strategy provides a more significant improvement.

Figure 4 presents the box proposal recall at different IoU overlap thresholds under four proposal budgets. For low proposal budgets (100, 500, and 1000), A-SS and R-SS improve the box proposal recall upon SS. Figure 5 illustrates the box proposal recall for a varying proposal budget under three IoU overlap thresholds (0.5, 0.7, and 0.9). For all three IoU thresholds, A-SS and R-SS improve the box proposal recall upon SS.

As shown in Tables 1 and 2 as well as in Fig. 4, when the maximal proposal amount is evaluated, SS and A-SS have almost identical proposal accuracy while R-SS is a little inferior. The maximal amount for the proposals generated by SS in an image is 2997 on average. In contrast, A-SS and R-SS obtain 2327 and 1472, respectively. Because R-SS and A-SS are the refinements of SS, SS provides the

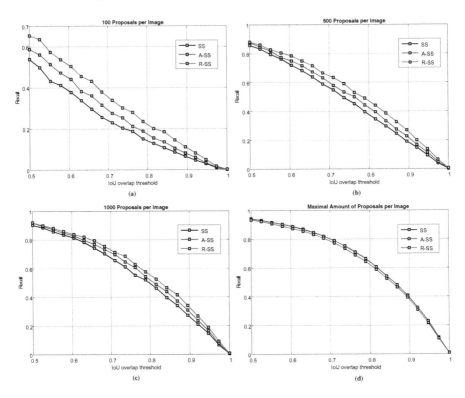

Fig. 4. Box proposal recall at different IoU overlap thresholds under four proposal budgets.

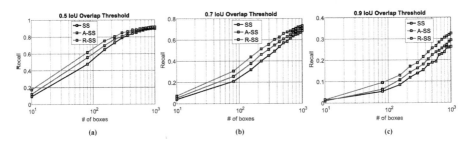

Fig. 5. Box proposal recall for a varying proposal budget under three IoU overlap thresholds.

limit performance for R-SS and A-SS when the maximal proposal amount is considered. However, for relatively low proposal budgets, R-SS and A-SS obtain better proposal accuracy than SS. Therefore, for the same proposal budget, A-SS and R-SS contain more objects than SS and reduce redundant background regions, indicating the effectiveness of contour support.

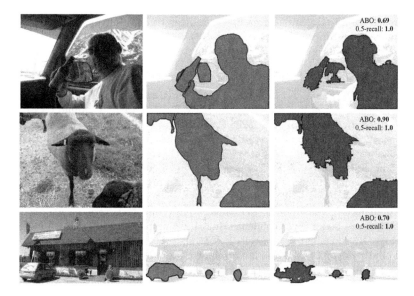

Fig. 6. Object proposals for three images from PASCAL VOC2012 dataset. From left to right: input images, ground-truth instance segmentations, region proposals refined by our approach with their accuracy measures (ABO and 0.5-recall).

Most of the execution time in our proposal refinement lies in the computation of contour support. On average, it takes about 4.7×10^{-2} s to compute the contour support of a region proposal in Matlab using a single thread. Figure 6 shows region proposals refined by our approach in three example images.

4   Conclusion

This paper presents a simple and effective approach for improving the quality of object proposals. The characteristics of contour support distributions provide the constraints to which object proposals should be subject. According to the constraints, we propose the accepting and rejecting strategies for refining object proposals. Experimental results demonstrate that our method reduces the redundancy of object proposals and improves proposal accuracy for low proposal budgets, indicating the effectiveness of contour support. In the future it would be interesting to explore alternative ways for computing contour support.

Acknowledgements. This work is supported by National Natural Science Foundation of China under Grant No. 91520301.

References

1. Alexe, B., Deselaers, T., Ferrari, V.: Measuring the objectness of image windows. IEEE Trans. Pattern Anal. Mach. Intell. **34**(11), 2189–2202 (2012)

2. Carreira, J., Li, F., Sminchisescu, C.: Object recognition by sequential figure-ground ranking. Int. J. Comput. Vis. **98**(3), 243–262 (2012)

3. Carreira, J., Sminchisescu, C.: CPMC: automatic object segmentation using constrained parametric min-cuts. IEEE Trans. Pattern Anal. Mach. Intell. **34**(7), 1312–1328 (2012)

4. Cheng, M.M., Zhang, Z., Lin, W.Y., Torr, P.: Bing: binarized normed gradients for objectness estimation at 300fps. In: IEEE Conference on Computer Vision and Pattern Recognition, pp. 3286–3293 (2014)

5. Dollár, P., Zitnick, C.L.: Structured forests for fast edge detection. In: IEEE International Conference on Computer Vision, pp. 1841–1848 (2013)

6. Estrada, F.J., Jepson, A.D.: Robust boundary detectionwith adaptive grouping. In: IEEE Conference on Computer Vision and Pattern Recognition Workshop, p. 184 (2006)

7. Everingham, M., Van Gool, L., Williams, C.K., Winn, J., Zisserman, A.: The Pascal visual object classes (voc) challenge. Int. J. Comput. Vis. **88**(2), 303–338 (2010)

8. Girshick, R., Donahue, J., Darrell, T., Malik, J.: Rich feature hierarchies for accurate object detection and semantic segmentation. In: IEEE Conference on Computer Vision and Pattern Recognition, pp. 580–587 (2014)

9. Hariharan, B., Arbeláez, P., Girshick, R., Malik, J.: Simultaneous detection and segmentation. In: European Conference on Computer Vision, pp. 297–312 (2014)

10. Hosang, J., Benenson, R., Schiele, B.: How good are detection proposals, really? In: British Machine Vision Conference, pp. 1–12 (2014)

11. Krahenbuhl, P., Koltun, V.: Learning to propose objects. In: IEEE Conference on Computer Vision and Pattern Recognition, pp. 1574–1582 (2015)

12. Krähenbühl, P., Koltun, V.: Geodesic object proposals. In: European Conference on Computer Vision, pp. 725–739 (2014)

13. Levinshtein, A., Sminchisescu, C., Dickinson, S.: Optimal image and video closure by superpixel grouping. Int. J. Comput. Vis. **100**(1), 99–119 (2012)

14. Lu, C., Liu, S., Jia, J., Tang, C.K.: Contour box: rejecting object proposals without explicit closed contours. In: IEEE International Conference on Computer Vision, pp. 2021–2029 (2015)

15. Van de Sande, K.E., Uijlings, J.R., Gevers, T., Smeulders, A.W.: Segmentation as selective search for object recognition. In: IEEE International Conference on Computer Vision, pp. 1879–1886 (2011)

16. Wang, S., Kubota, T., Siskind, J.M., Wang, J.: Salient closed boundary extraction with ratio contour. IEEE Trans. Pattern Anal. Mach. Intell. **27**(4), 546–561 (2005)

17. Wang, X., Yang, M., Zhu, S., Lin, Y.: Regionlets for generic object detection. In: IEEE International Conference on Computer Vision, pp. 17–24 (2013)

18. Zitnick, C.L., Dollár, P.: Edge boxes: locating object proposals from edges. In: European Conference on Computer Vision, pp. 391–405 (2014)

Sketch-Based Retrieval in Large-Scale Image Database via Position-Aware Silhouette Matching

Shijie Hu[1], Hongxin Zhang[2], Sanyuan Zhang[1],
Zishuo Fang[1], and Qi Huang[1,2(✉)]

[1] College of Computer Science and Technology, Zhejiang University,
Hangzhou 310027, China
segahu@126.com, syzhang@zju.edu.cn, kylehq@163.com
[2] State Key Lab of CAD&CG, Zhejiang University, Hangzhou 310027, China
zhx@cad.zju.edu.cn

Abstract. We propose an interactive sketching tool called SKIT to explore image database. The aim is to achieve fast result convergence according to the visual user query. Our main contribution is a new interactive image exploration approach which dynamically adapts to user sketches and provides feedback. The novel user interface is suitable for a range of interactive image-database access applications. In addition, we propose a position-aware matching approach for SKIT to support translation-free sketch searching. Experimental results demonstrate that our method outperforms state-of-the-art approaches with respect to the superior user interface and matching results.

Keywords: Sketching · Visual database · Interactive image search · Image synthesis

1 Introduction

There are massive images which are mainly stored in unstructured databases in the internet. These image databases, which are typically labeled with semantic information extracted from surrounding text, contain useful visual information for many applications. Services and tools for exploring such image repositories in education and entertainment purpose are provided commercially by mainstream internet companies. Users are drawn to these services for inspiration resulting in increased user acquisition and retention in accessing web services. Still, querying and exploring these large visual data sets remains a challenge owing to the unstructured organization involved.

The state-of-the-art approach to this problem is content-based image retrieval (CBIR), i.e., querying similar images that match an example image. The main drawback of CBIR is that it is not always appropriate to describe the user's dynamic thinking using a fixed starting image. The alternative method of sketch-based image retrieval (SBIR) has recently received increased research attention (Thomee and Lew 2012) because of its interactive nature (Yang et al. 2011; Bozas and Izquierdo 2012; Eitz et al. 2012a, b), sketch-based shape retrieval, and the booming mobile device

© Springer International Publishing Switzerland 2016
A. El Rhalibi et al. (Eds.): Edutainment 2016, LNCS 9654, pp. 243–256, 2016.
DOI: 10.1007/978-3-319-40259-8_22

market. SBIR provides a free-form drawing interface to perform searches from scratch. The main challenge with sketching is that not all users are able to draw sketches which precisely convey their ideas. This leads to a varying degree in the quality of the results.

In this paper, we propose an interactive tool called SKIT (stands for sketch-based image thinking) which is used to explore an image database (as shown in Fig. 1) with the aim of quickly converging to the desired results. Our main contribution is a new approach to interactive image searching that dynamically adapts to user sketches and provides real-time feedback. SKIT is novel with regard to a number of technical contributions. Although portions of SKIT follow the basic framework of CBIR, we propose a new technique involving position-aware matching which allows for multiple image matches according to different sub-regions of the image. In addition, the user interface for progressive image searching is unique to this work.

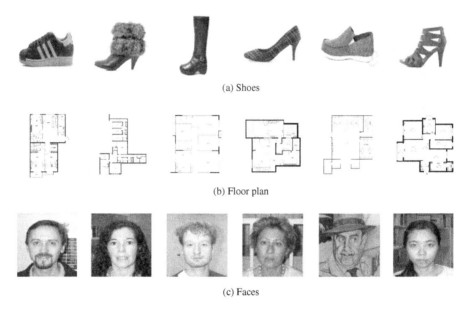

(a) Shoes

(b) Floor plan

(c) Faces

Fig. 1. Image samples in our database.

While some previous work has focused on pure SBIR (Yang et al. 2010; Eitz et al. 2012a, b) and some existing methods help users draw basic shapes (Igarashi et al. 1999; Arvo and Novins 2000; Igarashi and Hughes 2001; Lee et al. 2011; Hu and Collomosse 2013), to our knowledge, we are the first to develop an interactive user interface to assist image database exploration with guided sketching.

2 SKIT Approach

SKIT consists of three main components: (1) an index structure of edge pixels (edgel) for a given image database and the associated edge maps; (2) a contour image matching method that rapidly retrieves images matching the user sketch based on a position-aware matching score; and (3) an intuitive user interface which displays a shadow of weighted edge maps beneath the users' sketching to help guide the search process.

2.1 Database Construction

To demonstrate the main idea of SKIT, we collected approximately 20 thousand images from the internet. Each image is automatically labeled with a category recognized from the surrounding text. For verification purposes, we choose three categories of images for our experiments: "lamp", "shoes", and "human face". We sampled 274, 654, and 435 images from each of the three categories, respectively.

2.2 Edge Extraction

In contrast to general recognition computing tasks, our method requires thick, long, and connected edges to describe the rough contour shape of each give image. To extract such visually significant edges, we use the Line Segment Detector (LSD) edge extraction method (Gioi et al. 2010). Compared with traditional point-wise differential methods, LSD adopts a region-based strategy. Edgels are detected in regions using the gradient distribution within local areas. This helps to alleviate the negative effects of point-wise noise, suppress small deviations, and extract smoother edges. At the same time, trivial textures are filtered to some extent since they do not correspond to strongly oriented regions and are rendered visually inferior to long directed edges. Finally, this method works in linear time without parameter tuning, making it applicable to large images without dependencies on varying image conditions. A comparison among the Canny corner detector (Canny 1986), gradient based approach (Bhat et al. 2010), and the LSD method is demonstrated in Fig. 2.

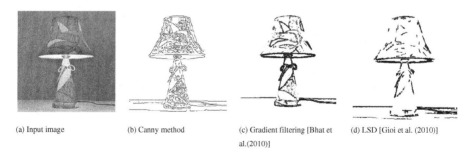

(a) Input image   (b) Canny method   (c) Gradient filtering [Bhat et   (d) LSD [Gioi et al. (2010)]
                                                    al.(2010)]

Fig. 2. Illustration of edge extraction methods.

2.3 Pre-Processing

We scale all images to a 256 × 256 pixel resolution and convert them into grayscale images. Next, we divide every processed image into a set of K overlapping sub-images which cover the original image with the same subdivided configuration. To balance between the computational complexity and the matching accuracy, we experimentally determined that four sub-images each with a 192×192 pixel resolution and 2/3 overlap between neighbors is sufficient for our application. We employ LSD to extract the edges from each sub-image with a scale factor s = 0.8. Finally, we create the inverted edgel index by placing each edgel into a bucket (x, y, θ), similar to (Yang et al. 2011).

2.4   Position-Aware Silhouette Matching

Once the edgel index is established, SKIT is ready to accept sketching queries and return matching feedback for the purpose of image database exploration. In this section, we discuss the image search process according to meet user expectations. Given a database image D and a query sketch image Q which is scaled to match the size of D, we define a hit counter

$$h(p; Q) := \{ matrix1listsq \in N_Q(p, r) \quad \text{and} \quad \theta_p = \theta_q, 0 \qquad \text{otherwise}, \quad (1)$$

to determine if pixel p in D maintains the same edgel in Q around the position v_p, where $N_Q(p, r)$ is a neighborhood edgel set of Q centered at position v_p with radius r. To ensure the adequate performance of Oriented Chamfer Matching (OCM) in comparing object contours, we use a basic matching score to measure the similarity between D and Q,

$$M(D; Q) := \frac{1}{|D|} \sum_{p \in D} h(p; Q). \qquad (2)$$

In our approach, instead of directly computing the similarity for the entire sketch image Q, we use K overlapped sub-images $I(j)$ $(j = 1, \ldots, K)$ which cover the entire image. We take advantage of the index structure to efficiently compute the sub-image similarity score $M(D(j); Q)$, as shown in Eq. 2.

$$\tilde{M}(D; Q) := \sum_{i=1, j=1, \ldots, K}^{K} \max \quad P(i, j) M(D^{(i)}; Q^{(j)}). \qquad (3)$$

We then calculate the overall similarity by integrating the different parts. A simple choice for the position-aware penalty function $P(i, j)$ is as follows:

$$P(i, j) = \frac{1 + \delta_{i,j}}{2} \qquad (4)$$

where $\delta_{i,j}$ is the Kronecker's delta function (i.e., $\delta_{i,j} = 1$ when $i = j$ and otherwise $\delta_{i,j} = 0$). The symmetric Oriented Chamfer Matching with position-aware penalty (OCM-P) is given by:

$$Sim(D, Q) := \sqrt{\tilde{M}(D; Q) * \tilde{M}(Q; D)} \tag{5}$$

2.5 Image Ranking and Structure Tensor

Same as in the original OCM method, OCM-P is still indexable. We use an efficient ranking algorithm which leverages the edgel index structure to achieve rapid execution of 'database to sketch' matching. As shown in Fig. 3, given a query sketch and its pre-generated hit map, we first generate K sub-images. For each non-zero element at position (x, y) in channel θ of the hit function, the algorithm accesses its corresponding entry and inverted list in the index structure, and then examines all of the sub-image IDs. Each ID contributes one hit to the similarity score of the corresponding sub-image. The algorithm then analyzes every non-zero element, and sums up the hit numbers for each image. After that, by dividing the number of total edgels $|D(\cdot)|$ for each sub-image as shown in Eq. 2, we obtain $K \times K$ similarity scores. Finally, we can rank database images according to these normalized similarity scores and select the top 10 images.

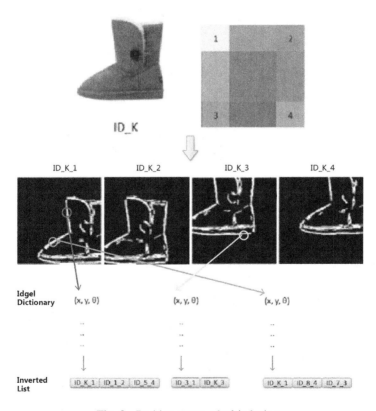

Fig. 3. Position-aware edgel indexing.

2.5.1 Two-Sided Filtering

Two-sided filtering is an efficient approach to ranking when working with a large database. For this method, we first perform a coarse ranking over all of the images to determine the top 30 images. We then perform a more involved calculation to obtain the accurate top-10 ranking on this LSD is a set of line segments (Gioi et al. 2010). We only accumulate hits corresponding to line segments where $hit(p) > 0$ is satisfied for at least 30 % of the segment length to form the precise $M(Q(i);D_k(j))$.

2.5.2 Structure Tensor

In practical applications, we determined that two-sided filtering produced only a limited improvement in the overall search results. We thus present an alternative filtering method using the structure tensor approach during the second round of sorting (Eitz et al. 2009; Hu and Collomosse 2013). The structure tensor method is based on the main unit direction such that an image block is represented by a vector approximating the gradient direction of the block thereby encoding the local structure. Images and sketches are decomposed a × b grids of blocks. The structure tensor $T(I)$ is densely computed over greyscale image I and averaged within each block to form a descriptor:

$$T(I) = \begin{pmatrix} \frac{\partial I}{\partial x}\frac{\partial I}{\partial x} & \frac{\partial I}{\partial x}\frac{\partial I}{\partial y} \\ \frac{\partial I}{\partial x}\frac{\partial I}{\partial y} & \frac{\partial I}{\partial y}\frac{\partial I}{\partial y} \end{pmatrix}. \tag{6}$$

2.6 Shadow Synthesis

Once the system returns the top 10 images D_i, a shadow image S is synthesized according to this image set to form the background of the sketch area to guide sketching. To do so, we first generate 10 corresponding edge maps E_i using the gradient-based descriptor (Bhat et al. 2010). The shadow image S is then calculated by blending the 10 E_i:

$$S(j,k) = \sum_{i=1}^{10} W_i(j,k)E_i(j,k)L_i(j,k) \tag{7}$$

where $W_i(j,k)$ is the shadow weight. We use a similar weighting scheme as ShadowDraw (Lee et al. 2011) to compute W. The edge descriptor in (Bhat et al. 2010) is not suitable for cases when the image contains many medium-scale textures because it generates superfluous shadows. Therefore, to allow the user to focus only on the major contour information, we filter the original edge map E with the LSD edge map $L_i(j,k)$ to remove these textures. Since our sketch-matching works in a patch-based manner, we perform the best displacement transform (from nine possible transforms) to each edge map D_i that matches the sketch prior to the blending step in Eq. 7. Thus, a suitable shadow map for guiding sketching is obtained. Figure 4 shows an example of shadow synthesis.

(a) Edge maps

(b) Sketch   (c) Shadow

Fig. 4. Shadow synthesis.

To display the shadow map without distracting from the user's actual drawing, we apply a Gaussian blur to the shadow image to remove noisy and faint edges. We also use a transparency factor α over the entire shadow to control the visibility. The opacity (visibility) of the shadow increases with the number of strokes drawn by the user. This helps reduce distractions at the beginning of the drawing process.

3   User Interface

Figure 5 illustrates the user interface prototype of SKIT. It is designed to be straightforward and intuitive but provides a full set of functional features for exploring large image databases including the following key components. To ensure that the paint brush (function 2 in Fig. 5) provides a realistic drawing process and allows for smooth lines, we employ several useful functions from the Processing.js API (Fry and Reas 2014). When the user completes a stroke, our system calculates the Bézier control point of this stroke and redraws this line using the Bézier curve. The eraser (function 3 in Fig. 5) as well as the redo/undo buttons (functions 7 and 9 in Fig. 5) are provided to allow for a natural sketching ability when using SKIT. The drawing area (function 12 in Fig. 5) covers 480 × 480 pixels and the user can draw in this area using a mouse or Wacom Pad. The interface is clear and concise, allowing any user to quickly understand how to use it and focus on drawing query ideas rather than troubleshooting. The shadow information synthesized from the search results is displayed as the background in the drawing area (see Sect. 2.6). This user interaction element is inspired by ShadowDraw (Lee et al. 2011), which has proven valuable for users with average levels of skill in sketching. Function 11 in Fig. 5 displays the top 8 ranked images. If the user stops the cursor over one of the ten pictures, this picture is enlarged to allow the user to see it more clearly. The user can then easily drag the picture to copy it to a local file system if desired or to the drawing area to begin the next cycle of searching. The additional feedback from the resulting images provides more shape hints, allowing the user to make improvements to the sketch. This can help the search results converge faster to the user's intention, especially for novice users. Even with the shadow information, users may still require additional help in starting the drawing. We provide a reference image function (function 1 in Fig. 5) which shows the reference image under the drawing area. The user can drag this image onto the drawing area and use it to trace out the sketch. As the number of strokes increases, the background (reference image) gradually fades. Otherwise, if the user no longer needs the reference image, clicking button 3 (Fig. 5) clears the reference image. This function allows the user to start with a focused concept and prevents noisy search feedback. Meanwhile, it provides an additional advantage in terms of system architecture. With this option, the

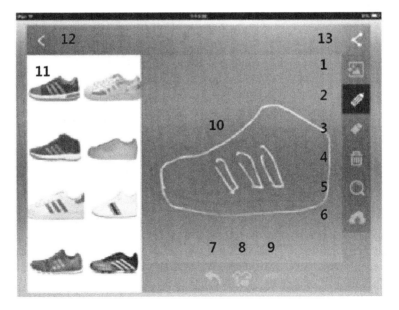

Fig. 5. The user interface of SKIT.

service provider can deploy the SKIT system in a distributed way. Matches for different categories are performed on different computing nodes, avoiding the memory bottleneck of the original IOCM described in Yang et al. (2011).

4   Results and Discussion

For the prototype of our system, we focused on the SKIT proof-of-concept and implemented the system in python and C++ with un-optimized code. The front-end web page is constructed in HTML5 and JavaScript to provide a comfortable UI and vivid rendering effects.

To verify the proposed method, we collected three image datasets from different sources. The RGB-0 dataset includes a wide variety of animation material and commercial images, the RGB-1 dataset is a collection of frontal face images, and the RGB-2 dataset is fetched from the housing intermediary website, where most images are housing plans.

4.1   Search Precision

To test the retrieval accuracy, we perform separate tests using the first sort alone and the first sort combined with the structure tensor. The results sorted using the input image only are largely appropriate but they do contain some irrelevant images. After applying the structure tensor, the image retrieval results are fully consistent with the user's intentions. Figures 6 and 7 are in effect a comparison of the results before and after the application of the retrieval structure tensor. For example, the "Coral" search yields significant differences between the two ranking methods since the first method relies more heavily on the contour lines resulting in unreasonably high scores during the matching process. The structure tensor method uses the main direction of each unit to perform a secondary sort, thereby optimizing the set of search results. Since the secondary ranking is based on the first sort, it is very efficient and has a minimal impact on the efficiency of the retrieval process.

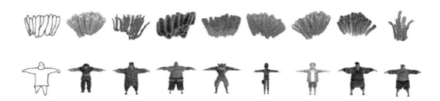

Fig. 6. Secondary sort using the straightforward comparison on RGB-0 dataset.

4.2   Pre-Classification

Several tests demonstrated the occurrence of unrelated results, as shown in Fig. 8. We tested a deep learning classification on the database which eliminated out-of-category

Fig. 7. Secondary sort using the structure tensor on RGB-0 dataset.

results. The original image input by the user leads to unrelated images included in the retrieved results. Thus, this temporary scheme provides an optional constraint layer in category retrieval based on manual user selection. Future research should further explore this topic.

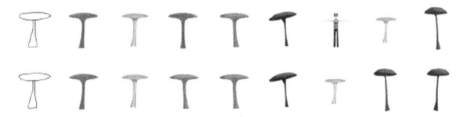

Fig. 8. Pre-classification.

4.3   Comparison

We implemented a revised version of MindFinder (Yang et al. 2010) to perform a fair performance comparison. In our implementation, we use the LSD edge descriptor for both methods. As demonstrated in Fig. 9, SKIT returns more reasonable results than MindFinder in the freeform sketch scenario in RGB-0. This is because SKIT uses a patch-based matching strategy to overcome the difficulty of displaced contour for free-form sketching. The shadow hints allow the user to intuitively express ideas through sketching and to explore relevant images.

Although we share similar UI elements with ShadowDraw (Lee et al. 2011), the underlying index mechanism and matching method are quite different. As illustrated in Fig. 10, SKIT can provide more accurate matching results corresponding to user sketches. Additionally, since we use a similar indexing scheme to MindFinder, both SKIT and MindFinder are capable of processing larger data sizes than ShadowDraw.

4.4   More Examples

Figure 11 shows an example of step-by-step exploration of the "face" category of the image database. Our database contains many images of the same person with different facial expressions. Most of users follow a fixed routine in their sketches. For example, suppose that a user wants to find a woman with long hair. In step 1, the user draws an

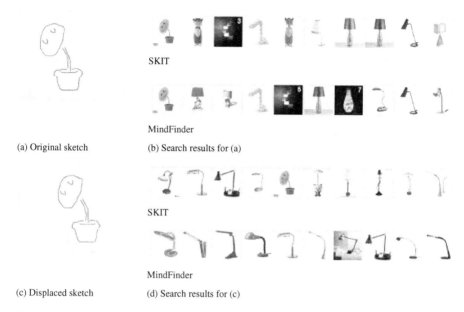

(a) Original sketch   (b) Search results for (a)

SKIT

MindFinder

(c) Displaced sketch   (d) Search results for (c)

SKIT

MindFinder

Fig. 9. Illustration of a "lamp" search comparing SKIT with MindFinder (Yang et al. 2010).

SKIT

ShadowDraw

(a) Sketch   (b) Search results

Fig. 10. Illustration of a "shoe" search comparing SKIT to ShadowDraw (Lee et al. 2011).

oval to form the outer contour of the face. The search results return different faces among the top 10 images. In step 2, referring to the shadow and the top 10 images, the user revises the contour and draws the most prominent features of the face according to the desired output. Here the user adds the long hair and the output includes eight out of ten images which correspond to the woman with long hair. In step 3, the user adds more strokes according to the shadow resulting from step 2. In this example, we notice that when the user adds more details to the sketch, the results deteriorate. Since there are many faces in the database the superfluous details can obtain high matching scores with otherwise irrelevant images.

Experiments on the RGB-2 data set provide a challenging scenario for sketch-based image retrieval. The floor plan images lead to a system recall rate of 57 %, a lower retrieval rate than for the other two image data sets. Still, the results fall in an

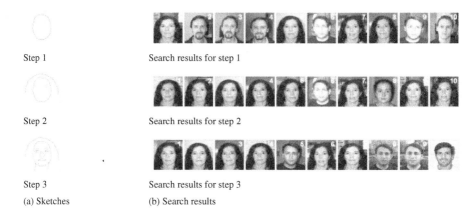

Step 1   Search results for step 1

Step 2   Search results for step 2

Step 3   Search results for step 3

(a) Sketches   (b) Search results

Fig. 11. Illustration human face sketch searches.

acceptable range. A potential reason for the low rate is that the edge segments in floor plan images are dense and similar, precluding suitable discrimination. This effect should be part of future improvements to this application (Fig. 12).

Fig. 12. Performance of the SKIT method on the RGB-2 dataset.

5   Applications

In commodity image retrieval, one feasible solution is to use an existing commercial image and perform the "look for the same model" operation. Alternatively, a "take-photo-and-buy" approach retrieves similar models based on a user-inputted photo. The largest shopping platform, Taobao, provides these functions to customers with good performance in terms of retrieval efficiency and satisfactory success rates. Still, the image retrieval methods are not yet mature. Thus, we consider that sketch-based retrieval can be applied to such commodity-retrieval applications.

To pursue this idea, we collaborate with a local company called "TaoTao search" to implement an image retrieval iPad App for garment sketches. The front-end of our system is an IOS application where the user provides the sketch. And the background system consists of our proposed method which provides the retrieval service in an image database containing more than 2 million images. After sketching, the user clicks "search" and the service returns the matching goods to the App terminal. The App terminal then allows the user to choose to browse or buy later. Figure 13 shows screen capture of our App.

Fig. 13. Illustration of a real application of our method for exploring image in a database with more than 2 million images. This is an iPad App called 'FuShiHui'.

6   Conclusion

We present an image search system that guides a user to sketch by dynamically synthesizing shadows derived from thousands of images. We demonstrate that our method can retrieve relevant images in real-time based on incomplete and evolving sketches by the user. Although our method can be viewed as a combination of MindFinder and ShadowDraw, our user interface provides a superior image data exploration experience. We will further explore the possibility of integrating other patch-based methods such as (Bozas and Izquierdo 2012). In the near future, we will explore possibilities to integrate more accurate feature descriptors into our processing pipeline to increase the quality of the image search results. And finally, as a challenging job in SBIR, we will try to integrate color sketches into the system so as to provide more flexibility for creative users.

Acknowledgement. This work was supported in part by the Key Natural Science Foundation of Zhejiang Province, China through grant LZ12F02002 and the Science and Technology Program of Zhejiang Province (2016C33139).

References

Arvo, J., Novins, K.: Fluid sketches: continuous recognition and morphing of simple hand-drawn shapes. In: UIST, pp. 73–80 (2000)

Canny, J.: A computational approach to edge detection. IEEE Trans. Pattern Anal. Mach. Intell. **8**(6), 679–698 (1986)

Eitz, M., Hildebrand, K., Boubekeur, T., Alexa, M.: A descriptor for large scale image retrieval based on sketched feature lines. In: ACM Sketch Based Modeling, pp. 29–36 (2009)

Eitz, M., Richter, R., Boubekeur, T., Hildebrand, K., Alexa, M.: Sketch-based shape retrieval. ACM Trans. Graph. **31**(4), 31 (2012a)

Fry, B., Reas, C.: A port of the processing visualization language (2014). http://processingjs.org/

von Gioi, R.G., Jakubowicz, J., Morel, J.M., Randall, G.: LSD: a fast line segment detector with a false detection control. IEEE Trans. Pattern Anal. Mach. Intell. **32**(4), 722–732 (2010)

Hu, R., Collomosse, J.P.: A performance evaluation of gradient field hog descriptor for sketch based image retrieval. Comput. Vis. Image Underst. **117**(7), 790–806 (2013)

Igarashi, T., Hughes, J.F.: A suggestive interface for 3D drawing. In: UIST, pp. 173–181 (2001)

Igarashi, T., Matsuoka, S., Tanaka, H.: Teddy: a sketching interface for 3D freeform design. In: SIGGRAPH, pp. 409–416 (1999)

Lee, Y.J., Zitnick, C.L., Cohen, M.F.: ShadowDraw: real-time user guidance for freehand drawing. ACM Trans. Graph. **30**(4), 27 (2011)

Eitz, M., Hays, J., Alexa, M.: How do humans sketch objects? ACM Trans. Graph. **31**(4), 44 (2012b)

Thomee, B., Lew, M.S.: A performance evaluation of gradient field hog descriptor for sketch based image retrieval: a survey. Indian J. Med. Res. **1**(2), 71–86 (2012)

Yang, C., Changhu, W., Liqing, Z., Lei, Z.: Edgel index for large-scale sketch-based image search. In: CVPR, pp. 761–768 (2011)

Yang, C., Hai, W., Changhu, W., Zhiwei, L., Liqing, Z., Lei, Z.: Mindfinder: interactive sketch-based image search on millions of images. ACM Multimedia, pp. 1605–1608 (2010)

Krizhevsky, A., Sutskever, I., Hinton, G.E.: Imagenet classification with deep convolutional neural networks. In: NIPS 2012, pp. 1106–1114 (2012)

ProcPlan: A Procedural Evaluation Strategy for Tourist Attractions Planning

Chanchan Xu, Guangzheng Fei[✉], and Honglei Han

School of Animation and Digital Arts,
Communication University of China, Beijing, China
gzfei@cuc.edu.cn

Abstract. Due to the relationship between design quality, tourist enjoyment, tourist satisfaction, tourist numbers, and tourist revenues, this paper intends to discover the influences which the tourist buildings' arrangement has on tourist behavior and enjoyment in a scenic spot, and present a procedural method to evaluate the tourist attractions' design quality in a quantified way. Through crowd simulation and several iterations, the evaluation system tries to lead the designers to a better configuration of the scenic buildings. The involved gamification stimulates the user to pursue a higher score. A case study illustrates the applicability and effectiveness of our strategy.

Keywords: Crowd simulation · Pedestrian tourist · Serious game · Agent-based model · Tourist satisfaction

1 Introduction

Tourism has become one of the biggest revenues for one district, and more places have inclined to explore the value of nature beauty. Evaluation for tourist attraction planning can help designers and administrators find a more efficient way to receive reputation, draw tourists' interests and gain profits. There exist many research works which assess a design scheme in the forms of theory or anaphase questionnaires. However, in this paper, we attempt to do the evaluation in a procedural way, which is through crowd simulation.

Crowd simulation plays an important role in adding realism to the virtual environment by bringing life to the virtual worlds, which makes it a popular issue in the production of entertainment content creation, security evaluation and urban planning. While most researches focusing on addressing problems in the simulation of emergency circumstances, such as battles or disaster scenes, this paper aims to apply crowd simulation to the evaluation of tourist attractions planning in a virtual tourism scenario, which is a typical non-emergency environment. We hope that the result of our research can be employed to provide spatial analysis of effects which tourist buildings have on tourists' impression, support planners, managers and administrators with their visually decision making processes and assist them in improving the spatial arrangement of public facilities to meet the tourists' needs. Gamification is also involved to stimulate the user to pursue a higher score, while obtaining a better arrangement of tourist buildings.

© Springer International Publishing Switzerland 2016
A. El Rhalibi et al. (Eds.): Edutainment 2016, LNCS 9654, pp. 257–266, 2016.
DOI: 10.1007/978-3-319-40259-8_23

The contributions of our work are as follows:

- Propose a procedural way, a crowd simulation method to evaluate the tourist attractions planning.
- Intend to provide an assist tool for the designers, managers and administers in their first planning stage, and help them with the improvement of their design schemes.
- Using an internal motivation mechanism–*gamification* to stimulate the user positively: a higher score corresponding to a better arrangement of the buildings and also a better design scheme.

The rest of our paper is organized as follows. Section 2 introduces some previous works relating to tourist attractions evaluation and crowd simulation. In Sect. 3, we outline the whole evaluation strategy. Section 4 presents a detailed illustration of the evaluation strategy, and in Sect. 5, a case study is performed to analyze the performance of our method. Conclusions and future works are discussed in the final section.

2 Related Work

There exist many research works on tourist sites evaluation, where most of them are based on consumer satisfaction. Consumer satisfaction is early proposed in paper [1, 2], and the definition of it has many various versions. Kozak [3] summarized four measurement approaches for consumer satisfaction: expectation-performance, importance-performance, disconfirmation and performance-only. Parasuraman et al. [4] proposed a famous measurement scale–SERVQUAL which is commonly used nowadays [5, 6]. Gronroos defined three dimensional facts to decide the tourist satisfaction [7]. Taylor proposed the SERVPERF [8] and made a comparison with SERVQUAL. NDSERQUL model proposed by Brown measured the disconfirmation between the pre-purchase expectations and the perceived performance after the purchase [9]. Hughes [10] believed the tourist satisfaction possess relativity, which meaned that the tourist can also be satisfied even though his or her expectation was not fulfilled. He also divided the tourist satisfaction into four levels: very satisfied, quite satisfied, satisfied and not very satisfied. Jonhyeong [11] developed a measurement scale to assist the understanding and effectiveness improving of memorable experience. For further information, please refer to paper [12].

While most works focus on exploring the relationship between tourist satisfaction, tourist expectation and tourist loyalty through questionnaires and website survey, we intend to use the performance-only approach, apply the tourist enjoyment as a replacement of the tourist satisfaction and employ a procedural way, which is crowd simulation, to evaluate the planning performance.

Researches of crowd simulation can be mainly divided into two categories: macroscopic methods and microscopic methods. The macroscopic methods [13, 14] concentrate upon the whole crowd's movement features while the microscopic methods mainly focus on the characteristics of individual behaviors involving both physiological and psychosocial factors [15]. Between them, the microscopic methods show great advantage in obtaining fine-grained results in the simulation of heterogeneous individuals, which makes them quite proper in most simulation applications. Among them, agent-based method is a typical and also a popular approach in large scale crowd simulation and is also used in our method. To develop our pedestrian tourist simulation model we take inspiration from the hierarchical behavior model proposed by Reynolds [16] and ViCrowd model proposed by Musse et al. [17] to take a fully consideration of the complex factors of tourist crowds. Motion planning is not the key issue in this paper. Here we only focus on the description of our procedural evaluation, not on the navigation and motion planning of the crowd.

3   An Overview of Evaluation Design

Here we present a brief look and a prelude introduction of our evaluation strategy, including the evaluation criterion, scenario description and evaluation process.

3.1   Evaluative Criterion

Our evaluation strategy is based on an interesting finding between tourist revenues and tourist enjoyment (Fig. 1).

Fig. 1. Relationship circle of design quality, tourist enjoyment, tourist satisfaction, tourist numbers, and tourist revenues

There exists a meaningful positive relationship between the design quality, tourist enjoyment, tourist satisfaction, tourist numbers, and tourist revenues. Each promotes the following one: A good design quality increases the tourist enjoyment, the addition in enjoyment reflects the addition of tourist satisfaction, higher satisfaction attracts more people to come to this place, more tourists bring more profits and the gains in income help improve the design quality. Accordingly, we employ the tourist enjoyment as the quality evaluation criterion and help analyze the influence which scenic buildings' arrangement has on tourist enjoyment.

3.2   Scenario Description

According to our observation, the tourism scenarios share some similarities. First, the scenic environment contains limited paths for the tourists to walk. Besides, except for those walking paths and the buildings for visiting, other places are forbidden to access especially in mountain areas, considering the tourists security. What's more, the movement of the tourists from one place to another happens along the walking paths.

Due to the traits above, we intend to use a two-dimensional raster image to describe the background of the environment and depict the walking path with waypoint graphs. By doing so, the environment can be easily constructed while maintaining the scene features. The background image can be a bird-eye view of the undeveloped attraction scene or a hand-drawn map of the scenic spot (shown in Fig. 2), and is mapped on a plane mesh. Besides, considering the map scale of the plane mesh to the real scene, we set the plane mesh as 100 units wide, and adjust the height according to the bird-eye view image.

Fig. 2. Scene representation (with waypoints)

3.3 Evaluation Process

The whole process of our evaluation is listed as follows (Fig. 3):

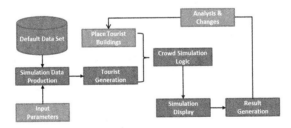

Fig. 3. Evaluation process (light blue ones represent for user's manipulations, purple ones for the program process) (Color figure online)

Firstly, the users need to input the parameters such as the tourist number, tourist speed, tour time limit and so on for simulation initialization (see in Table 1); then the program runs the crowd simulation process in a semi-automatic way, which means in this time, you can still change the tourist buildings' position; during the simulation, the tourist agents wander round the whole scene according to their own attributes and preferences, and gain enjoyment values about the tourist scene; when the simulation is over, a detailed analysis table is given for the user. On the basis of the presented results, the user can make changes of the tourist building arrangement and do the simulation again to see the differences. In the following section, we will introduce the evaluation strategy we designed for the tourist scenario.

Table 1. Main parameters for initialization

Parameters	Description
Arrival speed	Arrival speed of the tourists
Population ratio	Distribution ratio of man, woman, old and young
Full limit	Time limit for tourists to stay in the scenic spot
Sense range	Radius of the perception area
Building cost	The cost of scenic building

4 Design for Evaluation Strategy

4.1 Modeling of Tourist Attributions and Behaviors

In our paper, the tourist is described with agent-based model method. We intend to map a real human being's attributes to our agent model. These attributes include physiological and sociological aspects, such as classifications of the population, conceptions on the environment, awareness about the neighborhood agents, communications with other agents, emotions, appreciation for the scenic buildings and so on. Inspired by the ViCrowd and the two-layered model in paper [15], we design our agent model to contain the external and internal information. The external information relates to the knowledge which the agent perceived from the outside environment including the awareness of the neighborhood scenic buildings and agents, the location of itself and so on. Other external information also contains the perception of the team (group with a tour guide) and team members. Internal information means the intrinsic features of the agent such as moving speed, emotions, preference of the particular buildings and so on. Figure 4 is an illustration of the two kinds in our agent model.

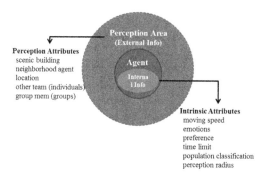

Fig. 4. External and internal attributes of the agent

While in the tourist scenarios, tourists tend to follow a nearly fixed and simple behavior pattern: keep proceeding along the path until encounter a tourist building; then deflect to appreciate the scenic buildings; after a period of viewing time, return back to the path and move forward again. The tourists' physical strength may decrease gradually by time. When their energy falls below a certain threshold, the tourists may become tired or exhausted. In this time, a resting spot can help the tourists recover energy. If the tourists lose interest for the rest scenery or feel too exhausted to move on or just exceed the time limit, they will tend to leave.

With social relationship such as kinship or leader-follower, individuals may travel in groups. Groups with kinship often consist of family members or friends while groups with leader-follower relate to tour teams with a tour guide. Different social relationship leads to different behavioral features. Take decision making for example, the groups with kinship such as family members or friends tend to balance their interests and find the proper way to go. Besides, one of the group members may play an essential role in the decision making process, which means his or her opinions weigh higher than others. In a leader-follower group (called "team" here), the leader makes the decision according to a pre-decided route and the followers simply follow the leader while keeping a distance.

4.2 Heuristic Procedural Modeling for Tourists' Enjoyment

Tourists are the ones who tend to enjoy the pleasure and to pursue larger pleasure unconsciously. This leads to the main theory basis of our evaluation strategy, which is pursuing pleasure is the intrinsic motivation of tourists. When wandering the scenic spot, tourists mainly appreciate the attractions to gain their enjoyment.

We define the tourist enjoyment as the pleasure tourists received from appreciating the scenic spot in limited time. It can be accumulated, for one feels more joyful in viewing two scenic buildings than viewing one. It can be related to viewing time, for one may receive much more pleasure from the very first beginning of appreciating the scenic building per minute than after a long staring at it. It can be affected by the tourist's current physical statement, for when the tourist is full of energy, he or she may involve a little bit more in enjoying the the scenic spot's beauty, and when the tourist is tired or even exhausted, he or she may eager to find a place for rest or just leave. It can also be affected by the total visiting time in the scenic spot. For when the visiting time exceeds a limitation, the tourist may give up the following viewing spots and choose the nearest exit to leave. Besides, the scenic spot may cause an overall impression to tourists and this impression may have slightly difference for different individuals. What's more, different people have their preferences for different scenic buildings, namely different types of buildings possess different attraction degrees to different people. Considering the age and gender, tourists can have four categories: man, woman, old and child, among which man and woman represent young, mid-young or mid-aged people with different gender; old and child represent the specific groups with two extreme ages.

So we summarize a generalized equation for tourist enjoyment as follows:

$$J_T = \sum_{i=1}^{n} J_{ibase} + \sum_{j=1}^{m_i} \sum_{i=1}^{n} w_{ij} * J_{ij} \tag{1}$$

Where, J_{ibase} is the basic impression agent$_i$ has on the current whole tourist scenario, w_{ij} represents the influence weight of tourist building$_j$ to agent$_i$, J_{ij} represents the perceived enjoyment of agent$_i$ by viewing building$_j$, n is the number of tourists, and m_i is the number of tourist buildings agent$_i$ has viewed.

We believe that the value w_{ij} is affected by the emotion of the tourist agent and also the viewed time of the agent. For when a tourist is in a bad mood, such as being tired or exhausted, he or she may less appreciate the scenic building, and a long-time wandering in the same site also brings less pleasure for the tourist. So the weight can be further written as:

$$w_{ij} = w_{emotion} + w_{viewedT} \tag{2}$$

As for the calculation of J_{ij}, it is based on the hypothesis that every building owns its own glamour, and this affection forces may be a bit higher for the tourists who especially fond of this building.

$$J_{ij} = p_{ij} * g_{jbase} \tag{3}$$

Where, g_{jbase} is for the basic glamour of building$_j$ and p_{ij} is the preference of the tourist agent$_i$ on building$_j$.

So, Eq. (1) can be:

$$J_T = \sum_{i=1}^{n} J_{ibase} + \sum_{j=1}^{m_i} \sum_{i=1}^{n} \left(w_{emotion} + w_{viewedT} \right) * p_{ij} * g_{ibase} \tag{4}$$

5   Case Study

5.1   Case Design and Specifications

We employ the evaluation method with a program in the form of the game developed with Unity 5.1. For more precise evaluation, we make some simplification and specifications in this case.

- As the value J_{ibase} blurs among different individuals and is hard to give the exact value. Here we just suppose that all the tourists have the same impression of the tourist site and remove it from the calculation equation.
- In this case, we set the viewed time of the tourist with a constant and regard the physical strength to be the biggest influence factor. According to the physical strength, the tourist emotions can be divided into normal, tired, exhausted, and depleted, using a piecewise function to calculate the $w_{emotion}$.

$$w_{emotion} = \begin{cases} 1 & 0.3 \leq r \leq 1.0 \\ r & 0.1 \leq r \leq 0.3 \\ 0 & 0 \leq r \leq 0.1 \end{cases} \tag{5}$$

Where, r is the ratio of current physical strength to the full physical strength of the tourist.

- All the buildings are divided into three levels: Level 1, Level 2 and Level 3. The buildings in the same level share the same glamour value which is specified through input.
- p_{ij} is an experimental value, in our case, it is 1.5 for favorable buildings and 1.0 for normal buildings.

Here, we classify the tourist buildings into five categories: scenic spots, shopping center, theatre, recreational facilities, and resting facilities which is correspondingly favored by man, woman, old, young and all.

5.2 Results and Analysis

We employ preset models to represent different kinds of tourist buildings (see in Fig. 5), and then design three arrangement plans (shown in Fig. 6) for comparison.

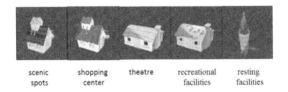

| scenic
spots | shopping
center | theatre | recreational
facilities | resting
facilities |

Fig. 5. Preset models for facilities

The results and tables shown above can reveal some interesting relationships between the tourist facilities' arrangement and the tourist enjoyment. The three scenes are same in facilities' numbers and kinds and also share the same initialized parameters sets. From Fig. 5(a), it can be figured out that the number of the ones whose satisfaction is below 60 % or being depleted when leaving the scenario is very high. In Fig. 5(b), the only change we've made is to move the resting facility to the middle of the scene, and we can see a clearly increase in the enjoyment value. This gives us the advice that putting the resting facilities in the middle and in the end of the tour journey can improve the tourists' enjoyment. As in Fig. 5(c), putting the facilities which favor by most of the tourists to the main road can greatly increase the incomes.

In our case study, we employ gamification, which is score-stimulation to arouse the tourists' aspiration in pursuing higher score, which is a positive promotion for the performance.

(a) scene 1

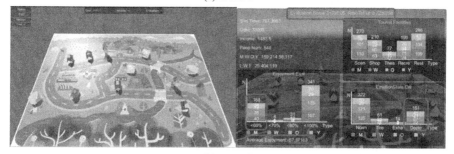

(b) scene 2

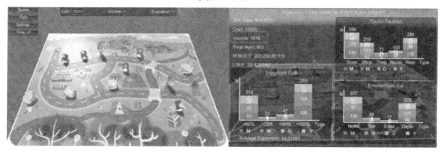

(c) scene 3

Fig. 6. Influences of different facilities arrangement on tourist satisfaction (Color figure online)

6 Conclusion and Future Work

This paper presents a procedural way for tourist scenario evaluation through crowd simulation iterations, which can be used to assist the designers for quick change and improvement with their design scheme. A case study illustrates the effectiveness and applicable of our strategy. The following research will focus on providing the user a more realistic crowd simulation performance and a more honest revivification of the scenic spots when keeping a high efficiency.

Acknowledgments. This work is supported by the National Key Technology R&D Program under Grant No. 2012BAH62F02.

References

1. Beard, J.G., Ragheb, M.G.: Measuring leisure satisfaction. J. Leisure Res. **12**, 20–33 (1979)
2. Oliver, R.L., Linda, G.: Effect of satisfaction and its antecedents on consumer preference and intention. Adv. Consum. Res. **8**, 88–93 (1981)
3. Kozak, M.: Comparative assessment of tourist satisfaction with destinations across two nationalities. Tour. Manag. **22**, 391–401 (2001)
4. Parasuraman, A., Zeithaml, V.A., Berry, L.L.: SERVQUAL: a multiple-item scale for measuring consumer perceptions of service quality. J. Retail. **64**, 12–40 (1988)
5. Van Dyke, T.P., Kappelman, L.A., Prybutok, V.R.: Measuring information systems service quality: concerns on the use of the SERVQUAL questionnaire. MIS Q. **21**, 195–208 (1997)
6. Jiang, J.J., Carr, C.L.: Measuring information system service quality: SERVQUAL from the other side. MIS Q. **26**, 145–166 (2002)
7. Grönroos, C.: A service quality model and its marketing implications. Eur. J. Mark. **18**, 36–44 (1993)
8. Taylor, S.A., Cronin, J.J.: SERVPERF versus SERVQUAL: reconciling performance-based and perceptions-minus-expectations. J. Mark. A Q. Publ. Am. Mark. Assoc. **58**, 125–131 (1994)
9. Brown, T.J., Churchill, G.A., Peter, J.P., Brown, T.J., Churchill, G.A., Peter, J.P.: Improving the measurement of service quality. J. Retail. **69**, 127–139 (1993)
10. Hughes, K.: Tourist satisfaction: a guided "cultural" tour in North Queensland. Aust. Psychol. **26**, 166–171 (1991)
11. Jonghyeong, K.: Development of a scale to measure memorable tourism experiences. Eur. J. Tourism Res. **51**, 12–25 (2012)
12. Lee, H.M., Smith, S.L.J.: A visitor experience scale: historic sites and museums. J. China Tourism Res. **11**, 255–277 (2015)
13. Hughes, R.L.: A continuum theory for the flow of pedestrians. Transp. Res. Part B Methodol. **36**, 507–535 (2002)
14. Chenney, S.: Flow tiles. In: Proceedings of the Acm Siggraph/Eurographics Symposium on Computer Animation, vol. 132, pp. 249–250 (2004)
15. Xiong, M., Lees, M., Cai, W., Zhou, S., Low, M.Y.H.: Hybrid modelling of crowd simulation. Procedia Comput. Sci. **1**, 57–65 (2010)
16. Reynolds, C.W.: Steering Behaviours for Autonomous Characters. Engine Population Generator Physical Geometry Individual Agents Crowd Simulation Engine Individual Behavior Model-1 Individual Behavior Model-4 Individual Behavior Model-2 Individual Behavior Model-3 Individual Behavior (1999)
17. Musse, S.R., Thalmann, D., Morphet, J.: Motion control of crowds. eRENA (1999)

A Survey on Processing of Large-Scale 3D Point Cloud

Xinying Liu, Weiliang Meng[✉], Jianwei Guo,
and Xiaopeng Zhang[✉]

NLPR-LIAMA, Institute of Automation, CAS, Beijing, China
{weiliang.meng,xiaopeng.zhang}@ia.ac.cn

Abstract. This paper provides a comprehensive overview of the state-of-the-art for processing large-scale 3D point cloud based on optical acquisition. We first summarize the general pipeline of point cloud processing, ranging from filtering to the final reconstruction, and give further detailed introduction. On this basis we give a general insight over the previous and latest methods applying LIDAR and remote sensing techniques as well as Kinect on analysis techniques, including urban environment and cluttered indoor scene. We also focus on the various approaches of 3D laser scenes scanning. The goal of the paper is to provide a comprehensive understanding on the point cloud reconstruction methods based on 3D laser scanning techniques, and make forecasts for future research issues.

Keywords: Lidar · Point cloud · Reconstruction · Urban environment · Indoor scene

1 Introduction

Large-scale 3D point cloud and LIDAR (Light Detection And Ranging) technique are hot topics that gradually emerges and become ubiquitous in recent years, mainly used for large-scale 3D point cloud generation. Currently acquisition of both indoor and outdoor environments is widely developed and used in many fields such as navigation, architecture and real estate, and is getting popularity thanks to the appearance of 3D laser scanning machines and range cameras.

Compared to other modeling techniques, the merits of point cloud data obtained by LIDAR and Kinect are irreplaceable. First, the data is real and truthful, like the saying "what you see is what you get". Second, big scale data indicates millions of points or even more, which contains rich information to be processed such as millimeter level accuracy. However, the existing noise makes it difficult to calculate interlaced objects like trees or other plants. Another shortage in current methods is the lack of combination of position, color and strength together to generate models. The existing algorithms usually deal with point cloud position but ignore true color of each point, which needs further improvement.

To achieve better results from the large-scale scanning point cloud data by LIDAR, many studies have attempted to establish or improve the point cloud processing algorithms. In these methods, the major challenge lies in how to identify the noise and

© Springer International Publishing Switzerland 2016
A. El Rhalibi et al. (Eds.): Edutainment 2016, LNCS 9654, pp. 267–279, 2016.
DOI: 10.1007/978-3-319-40259-8_24

classify the cluttered scene. Fortunately, there are some open source libraries emerged for dealing with point cloud, i.e., Point Cloud Library (PCL) of [1], which is a fully developed library for n-D Point Clouds and 3D geometry processing.

2 Point Cloud Processing

The processing of point cloud has already been developed and regulated as sophisticated mechanisms. We summarize the basic steps for the point cloud processing as shown in Fig. 1.

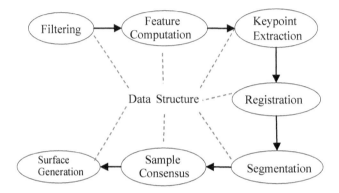

Fig. 1. Basic point cloud processing steps

2.1 Filtering

Filtering is usually the first step for point cloud treatment, which deals with noisy points, outliers, holes and data compression to obtain "clean" data.

Filtering methods have already been studied for a long time, [2, 3] similarly used some filtering methods in order to detect target like plane terrain surface, classify buildings as well as tiny elements such as electrical power lines. Act as an implement, [4] used first pulse data to improve the result. Instead of classifying points in a local neighborhood, [5] first segmented the point cloud into patches in which all points can be connected through a smooth path of nearby points and then these segments were classified based on their geometric relationships with the surrounding segments.

2.2 Feature Estimation

Feature as a key criterion plays important role in judging and estimating points. Local feature and global feature are two ways of estimating curvature and the normal of points. For feature estimation, [6] first developed a robust algorithm which can extract surfaces, feature lines and feature junctions from noisy point clouds. Later improvement involved [7] in whose work feature detection and reconstruction were recognized as problem during input occurs, described by a point cloud.

2.3   Key Point Extraction

Key point is also known as point of interest. Located on 3D point cloud or surface model, it can be detected and obtained by defining some certain standards and then extracting. Technically speaking, the number of such kind of points is far more less than the one of original one, thus making it possible for us to analyze what we really concern about. One thing to mention is that key point can be combined with local feature descriptors to be considered as key descriptors, moving forward to compactly represent the data we previously get from either Kinect or things like that. Some famous descriptors like SIFT and SURF are often used in this procedure.

2.4   Registration

In the area of reverse engineering, computer vision and ones like digital heritage, point clouds usually have defects such as incomplete data, translation and rotation dislocation. In order to obtain a complete data model, an appropriate coordinate transformation is needed, and sets of points obtained from different perspectives are merged into a unified coordinate system, and then operations like visualization can be carried out. When it comes to registration, [8] successfully handled a cluttered scene.

2.5   Segmentation

Segmentation is to assign a public label to similar region or surface. Methods in [9] mentioned smoothness constraint. According to the work of [9], the segmentation methods can be divided into 3 categories, where the target shape played as a judgment criterion.

1. Edge based segmentation. Typical variations on this were reported earlier in [10, 11]. Two stages were included here: edge detection and points grouping. One was to detect the outlines of the borders between different regions while the other mainly generated final segments
2. Surface-based segmentation. The similarity measure lies on local surface properties to conduct segmentation. Points with spatial distance and similar surface properties are merged together. One of the good performances is its noise-resistance. Similar to the previous one, surface-based segmentation also has two major categories: bottom-up which starts from seed-pixels and then grow and top-down which starts by putting the points together and fitting a single surface to it. [12, 13]
3. Scanline-based segmentation. Each row is considered as a scan-line and treated independently with each other in the first stage. So this method is especially suitable for range images. Typical application is [14] dealing with artificial construction.

2.6 Sample Consensus

Methods like random Sample Consensus (RANSAC) and primitives like planes and cylinders are commonly employed or combined freely in this procedure. Early work used Voronoi point insertion in local tangent spaces and Moving Least Squares (MLS) projection to realize the sampling. After that there was [15–17] in the same period developing different version of Locally Optimal Projector (LOP) to effectively overcome outliers and noise. While the latest work by [18] presented an edge-aware manner which has higher robustness.

2.7 Surface Generation

Surface reconstruction is widely used in broad scope, ranging from data visualization, machine vision to medical technology even aerospace. [2, 19, 20] are some latest research in this field. Far more work has been done before. More discussions about surface reconstruction will be included in the Sects. 3 and 4.

2.8 Data Structure

At the end of the pipeline of whole point cloud processing, we should pay much attention to the data structure which is a key problem for point data storage and processing, as high efficient structure has critical effects to the algorithm speed and storage. Quick search method based on the neighborhood is realized here. [21] for the kd-tree and [22] for the octree are all excellent research in this field.

3 Urban Environment Laser Scanning

One of our focuses is to analyze the commonly used methods on the point cloud of outdoor large scenes, and from this part, we will focus on the Lidar information acquisition and data processing of urban environment, which is used most as one kind of large-scale scenes.

3.1 Target of Laser Scanning and Remote Sensing for Urban Environment

Most research are engaged into the management of recovering single buildings or downtown area, while newly rising of researches are aiming at residential area. It is worth mentioning that [23] showed how to get detailed scanned data: two or more rotating laser scanners were taken on a moving car, even a helicopter to scan in full view.

Dense buildings: An earlier work [24] first worked out ways to rapidly and automatically reconstructing large-scale model base on remote sensor data. The next year saw an explosion of great work [25, 26]. Recently was [27] who proposed a 3D urban scene reconstruction method based on the exploration of properties of architectural scenes. A supplement was [28] that considered trees and topologically complex grounds almost at the same time.

Residential area reconstruction is a newly emerge interest topic. In contrast to multiple-floors or high-rise buildings mentioned in [29–31] gave a unique idea to decompose and reconstruct irregular low buildings. Another problem to address is the dense trees that frequently appear in company with residential buildings. Aiming at these areas, related research well defined the problem and found a comparatively clear way to detect the vegetation. Other previous work include [32, 33].

3.2   Scanning Methods and Solutions

Great efforts have been dedicated to the 3D reconstruction of urban environments from point data sets. But there are still challenges to be addressed when it comes to significantly complex.

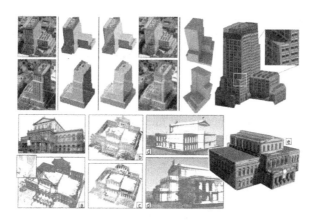

Fig. 2. Pipelines of Zheng et al. [26] (up) and Vanegas et al. [34] (down)

3.2.1   Manhattan-World (MW) Grammars

[26] combined the existing mapping and navigation databases with computer vision methods following Manhattan World assumption. What's more [34] developed the MW methods so that an independent complete model can be obtained to describe buildings with partial texture. Figure 2 shows the pipelines of the two methods for contrast. [25] took MW into consideration and created flat roof models. Tracing back to [36] we found an origin of this MW method. At that time researchers had observed that most indoor and outdoor (city) scenes were designed on a Manhattan three-dimensional grid.

3.2.2   Aerial LiDAR Method

Many research efforts have addressed the complex problem of modeling cities from aerial LiDAR data. Several automatic pipelines have been introduced by recent work (e.g., [32, 37, 38]). The work above all removed some kinds of trees and noise, while the remaining objects were divided into ground points and building patches which were gridded then.

There are still some problems to be solved so that objects other than planar can also be reconstructed. Therefore works aiming at primitive emerged. Based on a RJMCMC sampler, [39] established two steps to combine parametric models. Work [37, 40] also addressed this problem and detected planes via user interaction. Studies [24, 35, 41, 42] acted as implements to show this method.

3.2.3   Multi-view Stereo (MVS) Algorithm

Different from data captured by LiDAR methods, MVS combines various viewpoints together. [27] proposed a 3D urban scene reconstruction method based on exploration of properties of architectural scenes. Briefly, it utilized a given set of calibrated photographs to generate point clouds, and an MVS algorithm was used in the process, whose details were given in [43]. [44] presented MVS imagery that sometimes had spatially heterogeneous point distributions without induced adjacent relationships among each two points, including outliers.

As a supplement was a patch-based MVS (PMVS) algorithm presented in [43]. It used a sparse set of matched key points for matching, expanding and filtering. This process was repeated until a visibility constraint to filter away false matches can be applied.

3.3   Major Objects of Urban Remote Sensing

Several papers indicated that there were three representative elements in the urban scenes we would concern about, namely buildings, trees and ground.

Buildings are one of the most important elements when dealing with urban environment. Objects namely roof and wall are all focus of numerous studies. [19] well interpreted the reconstruction of such parts (see Fig. 3). As illustrated on Fig. 4, [28] simplified mesh-patches while keeping a high accuracy. **Trees** are always sort of troublesome when it comes to accurate reconstruction. Although [31] truly involved scenes as residential area, its treatment about trees was still a simplified template matching method. The other method such as using billboard for trees' representation would be a shortcut, but from the street view, a more realistic tree modeling was more necessary such as [45].

Fig. 3. Reconstruction of roof and wall

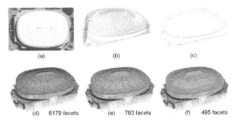

Fig. 4. Simplified mesh-patches

Ground independently can make up an important landscape no matter in which fields. Point cloud related things mainly concentrate in surface reconstruction. A continuous surface is often used to represent ground. Generally speaking plane is considered as an imitation of ground.

3.4   Advantages/Disadvantages of Existing Methods

Because of the diversity and complexity of our references, limitations and contributions cannot be completely included in this paper. Here we briefly give a summary as following:

1. For Manhattan-World methods, there are mainly three limitations. MW assumption results are the first one. Although the MW parts are efficiently reconstructed, there are still lots of architecture not belongs to the type.
2. Second, according to a classification-depending idea, bad results may appear owning to great amount of noise and missing data.
3. Third, all the work above cannot effectively handing data sets with tiny change or poly tropic surface.

4   Indoor Scenes

The other of our focuses is to analyze the commonly used methods on the point cloud of indoor scenes. In contrast to external surface of buildings which are relatively piecewise flat, inside scenes are more complicated when it comes to 3D structures [46]. Let alone the endless furniture with various shapes, rooms in and out are also a big problem (Fig. 5).

Fig. 5. Complex indoor scene

Fig. 6. Different results in same searching premise

4.1   Scene Understanding

The major problem lies in the recognition of hundreds of objects; here we call them same kind with different shapes. Even one same kind of objects can have several forms (Fig. 6), thus increasing the difficulties when handling scanned data.

4.1.1   Separation

As addressed in [46] (see Fig. 7), classification and separation were interdependent issues, and the realization triggered an algorithm which went through the whole room by a search-classify region-growing process. [47] presented a method according to texture and surroundings to identify objects. [48] presented an algorithm for indoor scene separation. In the research classification labeled of features are detected and separated via graph-cut to the whole scene. [49] combined color, depth and contextual information together to realize a semantic labeling progress.

Fig. 7. Separation and classification outcome of Lee *et al.* [46]

4.1.2   Classification

As mentioned above, the classification methods of 3D box around objects is adopted by [50] while [51] made a supplement with physical considerations. Rather than the image understanding background, [52] first pre-segmented the obtained points and then found good way to detect repeating areas. The latest is [49] who used a graphical model to learn features and contextual relations across objects.

Apart from the two sub-problems, Geometric priors for objects are also involved. Similar to [53, 54] used geometry to represent individual objects, which were commonly utilized in understanding surroundings. Similar works include [55–57]. They all engaged in understanding indoor objects and filling missing parts.

4.2   Scanning Techniques

Also thanks to the quick development of range camera, scanning becomes an easy task. Among the vast literature, the possibility of real-time lightweight 3D scanning has been early demonstrated by [59]. When it comes to the up-to-date techniques, [60] presented a guided real-time scanning setup, where the incoming 3D data stream was continuously analyzed, and the data quality was automatically assessed.

For further study, repetition [61], symmetry [62, 63] also got some notice. Primitives as well played a role in the completion of missing parts. Other geometric proxies and abstractions including curves, skeletons, planar abstractions, etc. have been used. In the context of image understanding, indoor scenes have been abstracted and modeled as a collection of simple cuboids [58] to capture a variety of man-made objects.

4.3   Scene Modeling

Several decades ago people have set about to use laser scanner on a mobile robot to obtain indoor circumstance. Literature introduced ICP (iterative closest point) or SLAM (simultaneous localization and mapping) techniques. However the limitation of expensive hardware took the two to an end. However, For instance, parts can act as entities for discovering repetitions [52], training classifiers, or facilitating shape synthesis. In [60], multiple objects of a single category could also be represented by a smaller set of part-based template. Expensive matching is usually a basement of these approaches, along with no low memory footprint real-time realizations.

5   Conclusions

Point cloud and large-scale scenes based on optical acquisition are topics that are gaining increasing attention by recent years, and new relative researches spring up constantly. So far, remarkable progress has been made in both basic processing of traditional point sets and newly developed approaches in scanning streets, parks and households. Meanwhile, algorithms continuously appear to improve the previous ones. What people have done not only solves the problems of understanding what a large environment we are staying in, but also helps better drawing blue print for the coming city construction as well as detailed decoration.

Challenges still exist and we need to do better jobs. Acquired models need to be more accurate and less noisy, data sets need to be greatly enlarged, and results of reconstruction also have much more to be revised.

With the development of technology, more accurate range cameras come into use which will largely promote the solution and accuracy of point cloud. Besides, improved algorithms can shorten the calculation time meanwhile enhance their robustness. The expected result is to clearly obtain point data and successfully reconstruct all kinds of architecture as much as possible. Trees, heritage buildings, and some irregular ones are the main problems that to be solved.

This survey mainly provides an overview of the previous works, and relative methods and ideas included should be further explored from the references in order to gain a more over-all understanding. Our goal is to lay the foundation for the novices in this field, and we hope we can give valuable insights into this important research and encourage new ones.

Acknowledgments. This work is supported in part by the National High-Tech Research and Development Program of China (863 Program) with No. 2015AA016402, and in part by National Natural Science Foundation of China with Nos. 61571439, 61561003,61372190, and 61271431.

References

1. Rusu, R.B., Cousins, S.: 3D is here: point cloud library (PCL). In: IEEE International Conference on Robotics and Automation, vol. 47, pp. 1–4 (2011)
2. Chen, J., Bautembach, D., Izadi, S.: Scalable real-time volumetric surface reconstruction. ACM Trans. Graph. (TOG) **32**(4), 113 (2013)
3. Sohn, G., Dowman, I.J.: Terrain surface reconstruction by the use of tetrahedron model with the MDL criterion. Int. Arch. Photogrammetry Remote Sens. Spat. Inf. Sci. **34**(3/A), 336–344 (2002)
4. Brovelli, M.A., Cannata, M., Longoni, U.M.: Managing and processing LIDAR data within GRASS. In: Proceedings of the GRASS Users Conference, vol. 29, September 2002
5. Sithole, G., Vosselman, G.: Filtering of airborne laser scanner data based on segmented point clouds. Int. Arch. Photogrammetry Remote Sens. Spat. Inf. Sci. **36**(Part 3), W19 (2005)
6. Kim, K., Kim, J.: Dynamic displacement measurement of a vibratory object using a terrestrial laser scanner. Measur. Sci. Technol. **26**(4), 45002–45012 (2015)
7. Gumhold, S., Wang, X., MacLeod, R.: Feature extraction from point clouds. In: Proceedings of 10th International Meshing Roundtable, vol. 2001, October 2001
8. Rusu, R.B., Blodow, N., Beetz, M.: Fast point feature histograms (FPFH) for 3D registration. In: IEEE International Conference on Robotics and Automation, ICRA 2009, pp. 3212–3217. IEEE, May 2009
9. Rabbani, T., van Den Heuvel, F., Vosselmann, G.: Segmentation of point clouds using smoothness constraint. Int. Arch. Photogrammetry Remote Sens. Spat. Inf. Sci. **36**(5), 248–253 (2006)
10. Sappa, A.D., Devy, M.: Fast range image segmentation by an edge detection strategy. In: Third International Conference on 3-D Digital Imaging and Modeling, Proceedings, pp. 292–299. IEEE (2001)
11. Byun, J., Na, K.I., Seo, B.S., et al.: Drivable road detection with 3D point clouds based on the MRF for intelligent vehicle. In: Mejias, L., Corke, P., Roberts, J. (eds.) Field and Service Robotics. STAR, vol. 105, pp. 49–60. Springer, Heidelberg (2015)
12. Volk, R., Stengel, J., Schultmann, F.: Building information modeling (BIM) for existing buildings — literature review and future needs. Autom. Constr. **38**(5), 109–127 (2014)
13. Xiang, R., Wang, R.: Range image segmentation based on split-merge clustering. In: Proceedings of the 17th International Conference on Pattern Recognition, ICPR 2004, vol. 3, pp. 614–617. IEEE, August 2004
14. Vosselman, G.: Advanced point cloud processing. In: Photogrammetric Week, vol. 9, pp. 137–146 (2009)
15. Huang, H., Li, D., Zhang, H., Ascher, U., Cohen-Or, D.: ACM Trans. Graph. **28**, 176 (2009)
16. Miao, Y., Diaz-Gutierrez, P., Pajarola, R., Gopi, M., Feng, J.: In: IEEE SMI, vol. 28 (2009)
17. Öztireli, A.C., Guennebaud, G., Gross, M.: Comput. Graph. Forum **28**, 493 (2009)
18. Huang, H., Wu, S., Gong, M., Cohen-Or, D., Ascher, U., Zhang, H.R.: Edge-aware point set resampling. ACM Trans. Graph. (TOG) **32**(1), 9 (2013)
19. Lafarge, F., Keriven, R., Brédif, M., Vu, H.: A hybrid multi-view stereo algorithm for modeling urban scenes. IEEE Trans. Pattern Anal. Mach. Intell. (PAMI) **35**(1) (2013)
20. Yu, J., Turk, G.: Reconstructing surfaces of particle-based fluids using anisotropic kernels. ACM Trans. Graph. (TOG) **32**(1), 5 (2013)
21. Saftly, W., Baes, M., Camps, P.: Hierarchical octree and kd tree grids for 3D radiative transfer simulations (2013). arXiv preprint arXiv:1311.0705

22. Díaz-Más, L., Madrid-Cuevas, F.J., Muñoz-Salinas, R., Carmona-Poyato, A., Medina-Carnicer, R.: An octree-based method for shape from inconsistent silhouettes. Pattern Recogn. **45**(9), 3245–3255 (2012)

23. Rutzinger, M., Elberink, S.O., Pu, S., Vosselman, G.: Automatic extraction of vertical walls from mobile and airborne laser scanning data. Int. Arch. Photogrammetry Remote Sens. Spat. Inf. Sci. **38**(Part 3), W8 (2009)

24. Poullis, C., You, S.: Automatic reconstruction of cities from remote sensor data. In: IEEE Conference on Computer Vision and Pattern Recognition, CVPR 2009, pp. 2775–2782. IEEE, June 2009

25. Zhou, Q.Y., Neumann, U.: 2.5D dual contouring: a robust approach to creating building models from aerial lidar point clouds. In: Daniilidis, K., Maragos, P., Paragios, N. (eds.) Computer Vision –ECCV 2010. LNCS, vol. 6313, pp. 115–128. Springer, Heidelberg (2010)

26. Zheng, Q., Sharf, A., Wan, G., Li, Y., Mitra, N.J., Cohen-Or, D., Chen, B.: Non-local scan consolidation for 3D urban scenes. ACM Trans. Graph.-TOG **29**(4), 94 (2010)

27. Fu, W., Zhang, L., Li, H., Zhang, X., Wu, D.: Efficient 3D Reconstruction for urban scenes. In: Huang, D.-S., Bevilacqua, V., Figueroa, J.C., Premaratne, P. (eds.) ICIC 2013. LNCS, vol. 7995, pp. 546–555. Springer, Heidelberg (2013)

28. Lafarge, F., Mallet, C.: Creating large-scale city models from 3D-point clouds: a robust approach with hybrid representation. Int. J. Comput. Vis. **99**(1), 69–85 (2012)

29. Müller, P., Zeng, G., Wonka, P., Van Gool, L.: Image-based procedural modeling of facades. ACM Trans. Graph. **26**(3), 85 (2007)

30. Nan, L., Sharf, A., Zhang, H., Cohen-Or, D., Chen, B.: SmartBoxes for interactive urban reconstruction. ACM Trans. Graph. (TOG) **29**(4), 93 (2010)

31. Lin, H., Gao, J., Zhou, Y., Lu, G., Ye, M., Zhang, C., Liu, L., Yang, R.: Semantic decomposition and reconstruction of residential scenes from LiDAR data. In: ACM Transactions on Graphics, Proceedings of SIGGRAPH 2013, vol. 32, no. 4 (2013)

32. Zhou, Q.Y., Neumann, U.: A streaming framework for seamless building reconstruction from large-scale aerial lidar data. In: IEEE Conference on Computer Vision and Pattern Recognition, CVPR 2009, pp. 2759–2766. IEEE, June 2009

33. Secord, J., Zakhor, A.: Tree detection in urban regions using aerial lidar and image data. Geosci. Remote Sens. Lett. IEEE **4**(2), 196–200 (2007)

34. Vanegas, C.A., Aliaga, D.G., Benes, B.: Automatic extraction of manhattan-world building masses from 3D laser range scans. IEEE Trans. Vis. Comput. Graph. **18**(10), 1627–1637 (2012)

35. Matei, B.C., Sawhney, H.S., Samarasekera, S., Kim, J., Kumar, R.: Building segmentation for densely built urban regions using aerial lidar data. In: IEEE Conference on Computer Vision and Pattern Recognition, CVPR 2008, pp. 1–8. IEEE, June 2008

36. Coughlan, J.M., Yuille, A.L.: The Manhattan world assumption: regularities in scene statistics which enable Bayesian inference. In: NIPS, pp. 845–851, December 2000

37. Verma, V., Kumar, R., Hsu, S.: 3D building detection and modeling from aerial lidar data. In: 2006 IEEE Computer Society Conference on Computer Vision and Pattern Recognition, vol. 2, pp. 2213–2220. IEEE (2006)

38. Lafarge, F., Descombes, X., Zerubia, J., Pierrot-Deseilligny, M.: Building reconstruction from a single DEM. In: IEEE Conference on Computer Vision and Pattern Recognition, CVPR 2008, pp. 1–8. IEEE, June 2008. (You, S., Hu, J., Neumann, U., Fox, P.: ICCSA, p. 579 (2003))

39. Zebedin, L., Bauer, J., Karner, K., Bischof, H.: Fusion of feature- and area-based information for urban buildings modeling from aerial imagery. In: Forsyth, D., Torr, P., Zisserman, A. (eds.) ECCV 2008, Part IV. LNCS, vol. 5305, pp. 873–886. Springer, Heidelberg (2008)

40. Tse, R., Gold, C., Kidner, D.: Using the delaunay triangulation/voronoi diagram to extract building information from raw lidar data. In: 4th International Symposium on Voronoi Diagrams in Science and Engineering, ISVD 2007, pp. 222–229. IEEE, July 2007. (Toshev, A., Mordohai, P., Taskar, B.: IEEE CVPR, p. 398 (2010))

41. Xu, H., Gossett, N., Chen, B.: Knowledge and heuristic-based modeling of laser-scanned trees. ACM Trans. Graph. (TOG) **26**(4), 19 (2007)

42. Li, H., Zhang, X., Jaeger, M., Constant, T.: Segmentation of forest terrain laser scan data. In: Proceedings of the 9th ACM SIGGRAPH Conference on Virtual-Reality Continuum and its Applications in Industry, pp. 47–54. ACM, December 2010

43. Nan, L., Xie, K., Sharf, A.: A search-classify approach for cluttered indoor scene understanding. ACM Trans. Graph. (TOG) **31**(6), 137 (2012)

44. Hedau, V., Hoiem, D., Forsyth, D.: Thinking inside the box: using appearance models and context based on room geometry. In: Daniilidis, K., Maragos, P., Paragios, N. (eds.) ECCV 2010, Part VI. LNCS, vol. 6316, pp. 224–237. Springer, Heidelberg (2010)

45. Silberman, N., Fergus, R.: Indoor scene segmentation using a structured light sensor. In: 2011 IEEE International Conference on Computer Vision Workshops (ICCV Workshops), pp. 601–608. IEEE, November 2011

46. Lee, D.C., Gupta, A., Hebert, M., Kanade, T.: Estimating spatial layout of rooms using volumetric reasoning about objects and surfaces. In: NIPS, vol. 1, no. 2, p. 3, November 2010

47. Gupta, A., Efros, A.A., Hebert, M.: Blocks world revisited: image understanding using qualitative geometry and mechanics. In: Daniilidis, K., Maragos, P., Paragios, N. (eds.) ECCV 2010, Part IV. LNCS, vol. 6314, pp. 482–496. Springer, Heidelberg (2010)

48. Xu, K., Li, H., Zhang, H., Cohen-Or, D., Xiong, Y., Cheng, Z.Q.: Style-content separation by anisotropic part scales. ACM Trans. Graph. (TOG) **29**(6), 184 (2010)

49. Mitra, N.J., Flöry, S., Ovsjanikov, M., Gelfand, N., Guibas, L.J., Pottmann, H.: Dynamic geometry registration. In: Symposium on Geometry Processing, pp. 173–182, July 2007

50. Xu, K., Zheng, H., Zhang, H., Cohen-Or, D., Liu, L., Xiong, Y.: Photo-inspired model-driven 3D object modeling. In: ACM Transactions on Graphics (TOG), vol. 30, no. 4, p. 80. ACM, August 2011

51. Xiang, Y., Savarese, S.: Estimating the aspect layout of object categories. In: 2012 IEEE Conference on Computer Vision and Pattern Recognition (CVPR), pp. 3410–3417. IEEE, June 2012

52. Zheng, Y., Chen, X., Cheng, M.M., Zhou, K., Hu, S.M., Mitra, N.J.: Interactive images: cuboid proxies for smart image manipulation. ACM Trans. Graph. (TOG) **31**(4), 99 (2012)

53. Rusinkiewicz, S., Hall-Holt, O., Levoy, M.: Real-time 3D model acquisition. In: ACM Transactions on Graphics (TOG), vol. 21, no. 3, pp. 438–446. ACM, July 2002

54. Kim, Y. M., Mitra, N.J., Huang, Q., Guibas, L.: Guided real - time scanning of indoor objects. In: Computer Graphics Forum, vol. 32, no. 7, pp. 177–186, October 2013

55. Thrun, S., Wegbreit, B.: Shape from symmetry. In: Tenth IEEE International Conference on Computer Vision, ICCV 2005, vol. 2, pp. 1824–1831. IEEE, October 2005

56. Mitra, N.J., Pauly, M., Wand, M., Ceylan, D.: Symmetry in 3D geometry: extraction and applications. In: Computer Graphics Forum. Blackwell Publishing Ltd., Hoboken, February 2013

57. Schnabel, R., Wahl, R., Klein, R.: Efficient RANSAC for point - cloud shape detection. In: Computer Graphics Forum, vol. 26, no. 2, pp. 214–226. Blackwell Publishing Ltd., Hoboken, June 2007

58. Jain, A., Thormählen, T., Ritschel, T., Seidel, H.P.: Exploring shape variations by 3D - model decomposition and part - based recombination. In: Computer Graphics Forum, vol. 31, no. 2pt3, pp. 631–640. Blackwell Publishing Ltd., Hoboken, May 2012

59. Sinha, S.N., Steedly, D., Szeliski, R., Agrawala, M., Pollefeys, M.: Interactive 3D architectural modeling from unordered photo collections. In: ACM Transactions on Graphics (TOG), vol. 27, no. 5, p. 159. ACM, December 2008
60. Schnabel, R., Degener, P., Klein, R.: Completion and reconstruction with primitive shapes. In: Computer Graphics Forum, vol. 28, no. 2, pp. 503–512. Blackwell Publishing Ltd., Hoboken, April 2009
61. Demisse, G.G., Borrmann, D., Nüchter, A.: Interpreting thermal 3D models of indoor environments for energy efficiency. J. Intell. Robot. Syst. 77(1), 55–72 (2015)
62. Anguelov, D., Taskarf, B., Chatalbashev, V., Koller, D., Gupta, D., Heitz, G., Ng, A.: Discriminative learning of markov random fields for segmentation of 3D scan data. In: IEEE Computer Society Conference on Computer Vision and Pattern Recognition, CVPR 2005, vol. 2, pp. 169–176. IEEE, June 2005
63. Recognition of 3D point clouds in urban environments. In: Computer Vision. IEEE (2009)

A Method of Real-Time Image Correction for Multi-aircrafts Cooperative Detection

Ge Fu$^{(\boxtimes)}$, Xiao-gang Yang, Xiao-pei Tang, Ai-gang Zhao,
and Nai-xin Qi

Rocket Force University of Engineering, Xi'an 710025, Shanxi, China
15662989997@163.com

Abstract. Aiming at the problem of the geometric distortion of the real-time image under the condition of multi- aircrafts cooperative detection, an effective method for the geometric correction is proposed. First multi-aircrafts cooperative terminal guidance model is established, especially the relationship between terminal detection angle and the initial position. Second the detecting angle model combined with the actual parameters, is analyzed, then put forward a real-time image geometric correction method; Simulation of the detection angle geometric distortion is applied to real-time image. Last using normalized product correlation algorithm for a large number of matching simulation, then get matching threshold, a real-time image geometric correction experiment is carried out. The simulation results show that the proposed method is effective,which provides theoretical basis for the reformation of reference image and the further improvement of the algorithm.

Keywords: Multi-aircraft · Cooperative detection · Real-time image · Geometric correction

1 Introduction

Modern battlefield environment is becoming increasingly complex and the new concept of weapons is an endless stream. It is urgent to stand in the system of high level to enhance the operational capability of weapon systems and combat efficiency. Multi-aircrafts formation can be more efficient than a single aircraft to complete the task. Advantages of multi-aircraft formation include: enhance the feasibility, accuracy, robustness and flexibility of the mission; improve the efficiency of the weapons and the completion of the task etc. For example, f aced with the threat of the modern defense system, multi-aircrafts learn from each other through mutual communication and information sharing, which make the enemy's air defense and missile system face greater pressure. It can not only greatly enhances the aircraft penetration ability, electronic warfare, and as a kind of new operational strategy, has a unique advantage in the realization of "reconnaissance-attack" operational integration and saturation attack tactical application, but also can improve the effect aicraft integrated combat effectiveness [1, 2].

The aircraft can use a variety of sensors, which provide the information base for aircraft navigation and guidance. Multi-aircrafts cooperative work further through cooperative detection to complete cooperative reconnaissance and collaborative surveillance, collaborative search, collaborative tasks such as object recognition based on abundant

A. El Rhalibi et al. (Eds.): Edutainment 2016, LNCS 9654, pp. 280–290, 2016.
DOI: 10.1007/978-3-319-40259-8_25

and multidimensional battlefield sensitive information and to achieve the full range grasp of flight environment accurately [3–5].Scene matching guidance technology is one of the most important ways to realize the aerocraft precise guided and positioned, and is also a more advanced and effective guidance strategy after repeatedly battle tested [6, 7]. For years, researchers at home and abroad made unremitting efforts in this area, many superior scene matching algorithms [8, 9] were provided, and have made some research results in the algorithm performance evaluation, index system establishment and evaluation method [10, 11], but for multi-aircrafts cooperative detection, real-time image geometric correction problem is rarely discussed. In fact, when attack the targets from different direction, multi-aircrafts will have corresponding geometric distortion in real-time image detection. Although with there is a certain degree of adaptability for reference image, when real-time image geometric distortion exceeds a threshold value, the matching accuracy will be reduced, and even cause false matching. If master the real-time image geometric distortion mechanism, and carry out geometric correction for real-time image, we can not only reduce the workload of repreparation of reference image,but also improve the accuracy of task, which is significance to improve the rate of success. In this paper, we mainly study the multi-aircrafts detection model in the terminal. Through analysing the model, areal-time image geometric correction method was proposed, combining with the normalized product correlation algorithm simulation, the validity of the method is verified in this paper.

2 Description for the Geometric Correction of Real-Time Image

Multi-aircrafts system was required to attack the target from different directions in cooperative detection conditions, which enhance the effectiveness. The preparation of reference image is a complex process. Prepare the corresponding reference image for each aircraft system would reduce the operational efficiency and time. In order to achieve the goal that attack successfully using planned reference image, it is necessary to correct the distortion of real-time image. The study of the geometric correction method for real-time image is divided into two problems.

(1) The establishment of the detection model. Taking the collaborative detection of two aircrafts as an example, the schematic diagram of the detection model is shown in the Fig. 1.

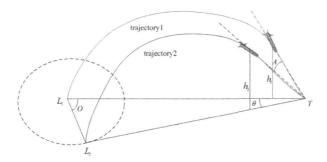

Fig. 1. Detection angle schematic

L_1 is the initial position of the reference aircraft1 and L_2 is the initial position of the aircraft2. Take aircraft1 as the reference aircraft, due to the different positions, there will be a angle θ between the trajectories surface of aircraft1 and aircraft2, when they arrive the height h_1 and h_2 at the terminal respectively, the detection angle A between two trajectories tangent occur. L_1L_2 is the distance between the two aircrafts, the angle O is the deviation angle, TL_1 and TL_2 are the distance of flight of aircraft1 and aircraft2 respectively, so the angle θ between two trajectories surface can be calculated, to obtain the value of the angle A, the problem is transformed to establish the model of the relationship between the angle θ and the angle A.

(2) The correction of real-time image. After making clear the detection model, it is necessary to carry out the geometric correction for real-time image, and verify the matching performance of the real-time image and the reference image.

3   Establish Model and Design the Method

The detection model is converted into mathematical problems and the relationship between the angle of the trajectories surface and the angle of the detection is also the relationship between the space angle and the projection angle. For a more intuitive analysis of the model, an example analysis was given combined with the parameters.

3.1   Detection Model

As shown in the Fig. 2, F_1' and F_2' are the projection points of F_1 and F_2 on the ground respectively, the attack angle of aircraft1 and aircraft2 at the point F_1 is α and β respectively. By using trigonometric function and cosine theorem, we can describe the model like this:

$$\begin{cases} \cos\theta = (TL_1^2 + TL_2^2 - L_1L_2^2)/2TL_1gTL_2 \\ \cos A = (TF_1^2 + TF_2^2 - F_1F_2^2)/2TF_1gTF_2 \\ \cos O = (L_1L_2^2 + TL_1^2 - TL_2^2)/2TL_1gL_1L_2 \\ TF_1 = TF_1'/\cos\alpha \\ TF_1 = TF_2'/\cos\beta \end{cases} \quad (1)$$

By using the formula above, the relation between the angle θ and positions and the relationship between the angle A and the angle θ are obtained:

$$\begin{cases} \cos\theta = (TL_1 - L_1L_2\cos O)\Big/ TL_1\sqrt{TL_1^2 + L_1L_2^2 - 2TL_1 \bullet L_1L_2\cos O} \\ \cos A = \sin\alpha\ \sin\beta + \cos\theta\ \cos\alpha\ \cos\beta \end{cases} \quad (2)$$

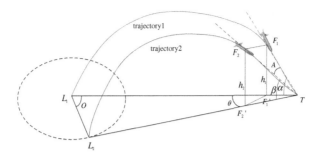

Fig. 2. The mathematical model schematic of detection angle

3.2   Example Analysis

According to the actual operation of the aircraft, the range and the actual value of each parameter is simulated and shown in Table 1.

Table 1. Related parameters

NO.	Parameter	Range	Actual value
1	L_1L_2	0~50 km	Deviation distance
2	O	0~360°	Deviation angle
3	θ	0~45°	Trajectories surface angle
4	TL_1	600~1200 km	Flight distance
5	α	70~85°	Attack angle
6	β	70~85°	Attack angle
7	A	0~45°	Detect angle

Based on the data above, we drawn curves of trajectories surface angle θ and detection angle A to reflect the relationship between the parameters more clearly.

As shown in the Fig. 3a and b, we get the curves of trajectories surface angle by the range of 600 km and 1000 km, and the two aircrafts distance range from 0 to 50 km.

The trajectories surface angle has increased when the distance of two aircrafts increased and deviation angle vary in 0 ~ 90 degrees in the condition of certain distance. That is, the farther away of the two aircrafts, the greater the angle of the trajectories surface, and the relationship between trajectories angle and deviation angle shows periodic variation within 0 to 360 degrees; There shows a descending relationship between trajectories surface angle and flight distance under the condition of fixed position.

We believe that the attack angle of aircraft1 and aircraft2 is approximately equal at the end of the flight. As shown in the Fig. 4, we got the curve that described the relationship between detection angle and the trajectories surface angle according to the detection model.

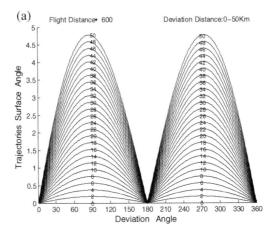

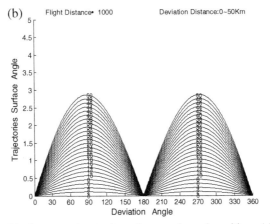

Fig. 3. The relationship between the track surface angle and position. (a) The relationship between positions and trajectories surface angle in 600 km distance. (b) The relationship between positions and trajectories surface angle in 1000 km distance

As shown in the Fig. 4, the greater the angle of attack, the greater the angle of detection in the condition of certain angle of trajectories surface; The greater the angle of trajectories surface, the greater the angle of detection under the condition of certain angle of attack.

3.3   Real-Time Image Geometric Correction Method

Combined with the establishment of the model above and the example analysis process, this paper proposed a method of real-time image geometric correction:

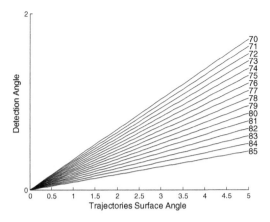

Fig. 4. The relationship between detection angle and trajectories surface angle

(a) Based on the relative position between the starting points of the multi-aircrafts and the reference point, the deviated angle and deviated distance of the multi-aircrafts from the reference aircraft are determined;

(b) Combined with the deviated angle and the deviated distance, according to the relationship between the angle of the trajectories surface and the initial position of the multi-aircrafts, the angle of the trajectories surface between multi-aircrafts and the reference aircraft is calculated;

(c) According to the relationship between the detection angle and the angle of the trajectories surface, calculate the detection angle between multi-aircrafts and the reference aircraft;

(d) Detect whether the detection angle is in the reference image adaptive threshold, if the angle is in the range of the threshold, it indicates that the reference image can adapt to the detection angle change and match successfully; if it is not in the range of the threshold, indicating that the starting position deviation leads to an over large angle, reference image is not able to match successfully, we need to get the real-time image correction.

To sum up, the flow chart of multi-aircrafts real-time image geometric correction method is shown in the Fig. 5.

4   Simulation Experiment and Analysis

In order to get the threshold of the reference image, 1000 scene matching area real-time images that sizes of 256×256 were taken for the simulation of reference image adaptability [12], and the normalized product correlation algorithm was used to match the experiment. Normalized product correlation algorithm is defined as follows.

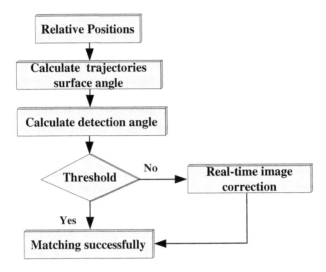

Fig. 5. Flow chart diagram of real-time geometric correction

$$M(i,j) = \cos\theta = \frac{\sum\limits_{s=1}^{m}\sum\limits_{t=1}^{n} S(i+s-1, j+t-1) * T(s,t)}{\sqrt{\sum\limits_{s=1}^{m}\sum\limits_{t=1}^{n} S(i+s-1, j+t-1)^2}\sqrt{\sum\limits_{s=1}^{m}\sum\limits_{t=1}^{n} T(s,t)^2}} \qquad (1-3)$$

The closer the value of $M(i,j)$ (Nprod coefficient) to the "1", the better of the matching effect, when it is greater than a threshold value, we think that the match is successful.

As the projective transformation of the detection image can be ignored in high altitude, respectively, the real-time images are processed with $0 \sim 20$ degree of geometric distortion, matching with the original reference images. As shown in the Fig. 6, the distortion threshold angle curve of the 1000 real-time images matching with the reference images is shown in the figure.

Due to the difference of gray value in image, different reference image has different angle adaptive threshold. Take the data shown in Fig. 6 in order, 92 % (not the part of the red) of the pictures' thresholds are above 9°, so we can take 9° as the adaptive threshold angle for real-time image.

Take a scene matching area as an example of real-time image geometric correction simulation experiment, and take a 64 × 64 size of the matching reference image at the coordinates (38, 75), the matching experiments process of original image, real-time image that distortion of 10 degrees and geometric corrected real-time image are shown in the Fig. 7a–c.

The original matching coordinate is (39, 74), whose matching error was within 1 pixel, and the matching peak was significantly; When generated 10 degrees of geometric distortion, the matching results became (50, 65), whose error is more than

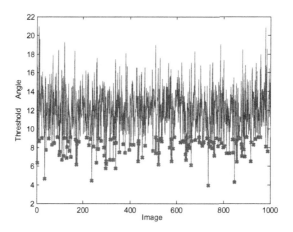

Fig. 6. Threshold angle of one thousand real-time images

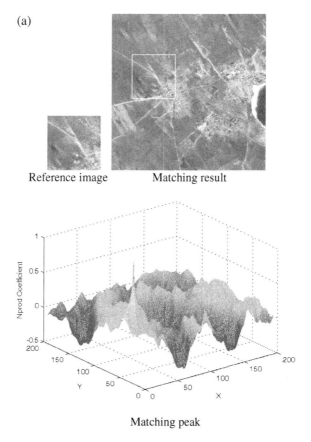

Fig. 7. The procedure of scene match experiment. (a) The matching procedure of original image. (b) The matching procedure of 10 degrees of geometric distortion image. (c) The matching procedure of geometric distortion correction image

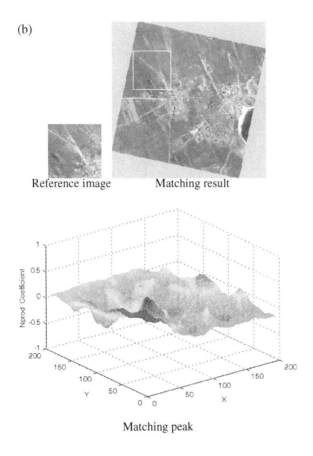

(b)

Reference image   Matching result

Matching peak

Fig. 7. (continued)

10 pixels, and the matching peak was decreasing with the increasing of detection angle, that is, the match effect was decreasing gradually; After corresponding geometric distortion correction, the matching result became (41, 72), the matching error is less than 3 pixels, and the matching peak is obvious, accurate matching is realized effectively.

5 Conclusions

This paper established multi-aircrafts cooperative detection model, focused on the model of terminal angle detection, and got the relationship between multi-aircrafts positions and detection angle. Example analysis is given combined with the actual parameters. A geometric correction method for multi-aircrafts real-time image is proposed. On the basis of the model, using the normalized product correlation matching algorithm, a lot of simulation experiments were carried out to obtain the threshold angle of the scene matching under the condition of geometric distortion. The simulation

(c)

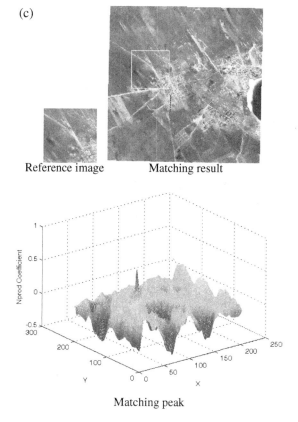

Reference image   Matching result

Matching peak

Fig. 7. (continued)

results verify the effectiveness of the method proposed, which provides a theoretical basis for reference image reformation and the further improvement of the adaptive algorithm. In this paper, we ignored the influence caused by the affine transformation of the real-time image, and adopt the homologous image. The adaptability of the reference image in the case of multi factors fusion requires further study.

References

1. Feinerman, O., Korman, A., Lotker, Z., Sereni, J.S.: Collaborative search on the plane without communication. In: ACM Symposium on Principles of Distributed Computing, pp. 77–86 (2012)
2. Li, Z., Rui, Z., Shiyu, Z.: Missile formation salvo attack decentralized cooperative guidance method. J. Aviat. **32**(2), 281–290 (2011)
3. Liu, Z.: Development of unmanned aerial vehicle technology abroad. Ship Electron. Eng.
4. York, G., Pack, D.J.: Ground target detection using cooperative unmanned aerial systems. J. Intell. Rob. Syst. **65**(1–4), 473–478 (2012)

5. Cheng, X.M., Dong, C., Chun, T.L.: Survey of cooperative path planning for multiple unmanned aerial vehicles. Appl. Mech. Mater. **668**(1), 388–393 (2014)
6. Yang, X., Cao, F., Huang, X., Meng, F.: Scene matching simulation of reference map preparation method. J. Syst. Simul. **22**(4), 850–853 (2010)
7. Yang, X., Dong, M., Cao, F., et al.: A practical scene matching simulation method. J. Syst. Simul. **16**(3), 363–365. 369 (2004)
8. Zhao, F.: The scene matching algorithm, performance evaluation and application of national defense science and technology, University Master's degree thesis (2002)
9. Chaoyang, C., Guilin, Z., Zheng, Y.H.: Scene matching algorithm performance evaluation. Infrared Laser Eng. **27**(3), 38–41 (1998)
10. Yang, L., Fengwei, Z., Jin, S.: Research on the selection method of Red IME Scene Matching Area
11. Xiao, L., Wu, H., Tang, S., Liu, Y.: Modeling and simulation of digital scene image synthesis using image intensified CCD under different weathers in scene matching simulation system. In: Baik, D.-K. (ed.) AsiaSim 2004. LNCS (LNAI), vol. 3398, pp. 607–616. Springer, Heidelberg (2005)
12. Goedeme, T., Tuytelaars, T., Van Gool, L.: Fast wide baseline matching for visual navigation. In: Proceedings of the 2010 IEEE Computer Society Conference on Computer Vision and Pattern Recognition vol. 7, pp. 24–29 (2010)

A Flexible and Easy-to-Use Platform to Create Advanced Edutainment Applications

Nagore Barrena, Andrés Navarro, and David Oyarzun[(✉)]

Vicomtech-IK4 Research Centre,
Paseo Mikeletegi 57, 20009 San Sebastián, Spain
{nbarrena,anavarro,doyarzun}@vicomtech.org

Abstract. This paper describes the results of a R&D project focused on the creation of a flexible and easy-to-use platform for creating advanced multimedia applications, with strong focus on education and leisure contexts. Most of the similar existing platforms lack of enough flexibility to create different kind of content, or they require a strong technical background for authoring applications. In this project, a balance between flexibility and easiness has been fulfilled. Several use cases, whose authors have different levels of technical background, have been defined to validate it.

Keywords: Authoring tools · Virtual reality · Augmented reality · Multimedia applications

1 Introduction

The design and deployment of advanced multimedia applications for education and/or leisure usually presents two kind of problems. Existing platforms present a lack of flexibility, or in other case, they require a moderated-high expertise on computer programming.

The platform presented in this paper is the result of a R&D project looking for creating complex multimedia applications in an easy way, and with its focus on edutainment use cases.

The main novelty of the platform is the adequate balance between the flexibility of the system and the easiness of use. This feature has been validated by using the platform on several use cases with different requisites, and being used by designers with different levels of technical knowledge and background.

The platform, as defined by the project, should fulfill these requirements:

- It should be flexible for creating complex multimedia content. The platform should provide tools for creating complex content easily. Moreover, it should be able to load pre-created multimedia content.
- It should be flexible for applying several pedagogical methodologies. The platform is expected to be valid for education sector, therefore, each application case could require different pedagogical methodologies that optimizes the learning process. The platform should give support to this.

A. El Rhalibi et al. (Eds.): Edutainment 2016, LNCS 9654, pp. 291–300, 2016.
DOI: 10.1007/978-3-319-40259-8_26

- It should be an integral solution for edutainment use cases. The goal of the platform is not only to create advanced applications but also to use them in educational environments, therefore, monitoring, evaluation and feedback tools would be also implemented.
- It should be easy to use. The platform should include an easy-to-use set of tools that can be used by users with non-expert profiles.

To obtain this, three complementary concepts have been defined and the platform allows the configuration of them: the process, the content and the context. Authors with expertise in some of these concepts have the flexibility to use tools to create complex results following their expertise, and they can apply easy-to-use tools to create those concepts where they are no experts.

The paper is structured in this way: the next section explains the related work on this area, Sect. 3 presents the main concepts and platform architecture and Sect. 4 describes two use cases that are considered meaningful for the validation. Finally conclusions and ideas for future work are presented.

2 Related Work

The use of new technologies is rising, spreading also to more traditional areas, such as education. It is very important to improve the educational process taking advantage of science, new technologies and resources that can enhance learning. Nowadays, the use of IT tools to support education is a reality which is optimizing the teaching and learning processes. In this way, edutainment concept is borne, and several works [1, 2, 3] explore and approve the benefits of IT and games in education.

Digital Game-Based Learning (from now on GBL) methodology [3] describes an approach to teaching, where students explore relevant aspect of games in a learning context designed by teachers. Teachers and students collaborate in order to add depth and perspective to the experience of playing the game.

In the work of Tanaka et al. [4], a game to learn to improve movement habits to solve the problem of obesity is presented. However, in the work of Georgiev et al. [6], a gem for English language learning is introduced.

The interest and use of mobile devices in all areas of society is growing. For this reason, it was necessary to extend the use of these kinds of devices in learning processes; M-Learning concept appearing [6]. The learning process is increased with these devices, as well as the communication and shared knowledge is powered. Chen et al. [7] presents an effective and flexible learning environment for English learning using M-Learning methods. In the same way, Wang et al. [8] presents a study to find a suitable M-Learning models for Chinese college students.

However, develop a full game or IT application for a determined purpose has a expensive cost and only can be done by programing experts. The teachers need to configure and generate new games and IT applications easily.

Hence, authoring-tool platforms born to allows non-expert user to generate a whole application easily. U-CREATE [9], INSCAPE [10] and STORYTEC [11] are an example: storytelling systems and authoring tools for creation and representation of story based scenarios for a different domains such as edutainment for a non-expert user.

Web technologies allows using online applications via laptop, tablet and mobile outweigh the common problems of installed offline desktop software. In addition, these kind applications support the easy diffusion and user collaboration and centralized the data. In this way, the edutainment applications and authoring tools that are developed as web applications are risings, as can be proved in different works [12, 13].

3 Platform Overview

3.1 Design Principles

The platform represents a learning object (or activity, task, experience) as a combination of three components (or elements): the process, which specifies the execution flow, the content, which defines the elements presented to the user, and the context, which contains the information related to the current execution instance.

The user interacts with the content, which presents the specific information of the instance from the data contained in the context. Such interaction generates events that are notified to the process. The process handles those events altering the context or the content based on its defined execution flow.

Process. The process is modeled as a finite state machine (FSM). A FSM is an abstract machine that contains a set of states and it can only be in one of them at a time, transitioning from one to another based on events or conditions. In the platform, the states of the process determine the learning procedure of the [activity] and the machine changes its current state based on the triggered events resulted from the interaction and the evaluation of conditions of the context information.

Content. In order to represent different forms of multimedia information (i.e. text, audio, video, 3D models) that can be located in the three-dimensional space, contain certain behaviour or allow a specific interaction, the content is modeled as an entity-component system (ECS). In an ECS the objects that form the content are entities composed of different components that provide the functionality or behaviour. Using composition over inheritance avoids the implementation of deep inheritance hierarchies and allows a greater flexibility and reusability of the code [14].

Context. Each instance of the activity contains specific information of the current execution. The nature of the information depends on the specific activity, including text, lists, images or the composition of several of those types. Therefore, the context is modeled as semi-structured data, allowing the required flexibility that should contain the needed information to establish relationships and to self-describe its own structure [15].

3.2 System Architecture

The system is divided into modules that contain everything related to a certain functionality, including 3D rendering, Augmented Reality or Graphical User Interfaces. Each module provides different elements to the platform's three main components, process, content and context.

The FSM that models the process component is implemented as a set of states that contain actions. Once the FSM transitions to a certain state, it executes the actions on that state. Transitions between states are triggered by identified events. Modules can register specific actions related to their functionality (Fig. 1).

For example, AR module can register an action that configures the marker used on the tracking process.

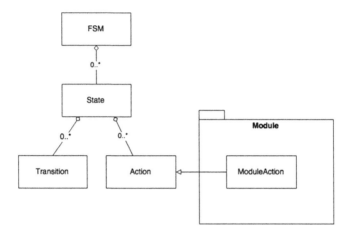

Fig. 1. Conceptual structure of the FSM architecture

The ECS that models the content component is implemented on the principle of isolating data from logic. In this way, the components determine the behaviour of the entity and contain the data and the logic that processes entities is contained in the systems. Therefore, interaction with the ECS is simplified to the modification of components attributes and serialization of the ECS is reduced to the serialization of simple data container components. Modules can register components that determine a behaviour related to their functionality and systems that process that entities (Fig. 2).

For example, 3D module can register a 3D model component that contain the information of geometry and texture of a visualization, and it can register a rendering system that process entities with that component resulting in a 3D visualization.

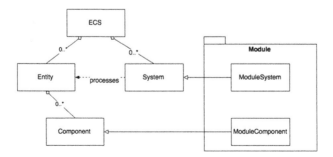

Fig. 2. Conceptual structure of the ECS architecture

The semi-structured data that model the context component is implemented as a document-oriented database, using JSON as data transmit format. Each module can define its own data structures allowing to establish connections between actions, components and data, or in other words, relationships between process, content and context. The straightforward implementation of a synchronization client and server of the data allows to develop a collaborative solution.

The presented modular architecture allows to create different configurations of applications or services that can interpret an activity. The same activity composed by its process, content and context can be executed in platforms capable of running different sets of modules, which might depend on the capabilities of such platforms (Fig. 3).

For example, having an activity with content that combines 3D models and AR, a web browser application, not capable of executing the AR module, only processes the 3D component while a mobile application processes both components.

Following the similar principle, a service can be created that only contains a module that processes certain components, such as a synchronization server for the context. For instance, the AR module includes the functionality needed to process images as visual markers, which can be deployed as a service on the cloud.

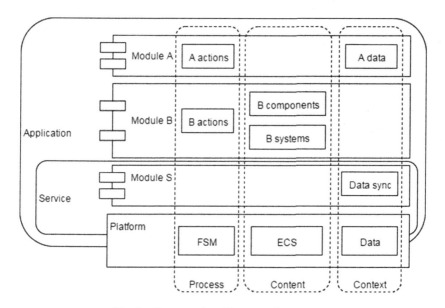

Fig. 3. Conceptual architecture of the system

3.3   Tools

Several tools have been developed on top of the platform to ease creation, supervision and examination tasks (Fig. 4). Consistent with the modular architecture of the platform, the structure of the tools is divided in modules that can be enabled per activity.

Authoring Tool. The authoring tool allows creators to generate activities, covering the definition of theirs three main components. To that end, the architecture of the authoring tool allows to specify in each module custom edition interfaces for the specific elements that they provide to the platform. For example, the 3D module that provides a 3D model entity component can export an interface to handle the selection of the material properties.

Monitoring Tool. The monitoring tool allows tutors to supervise the realization of the activity. Thanks to the isolation of the execution information into the activity's context component, synchronization of that context is only required to implement real-time monitoring.

Analysis Tool. The analysis tool allows educators to evaluate the results of the activities. From the learners organization structure and their profiles information, relationships and comparisons can be established between the results, obtaining insight knowledge of learning performance.

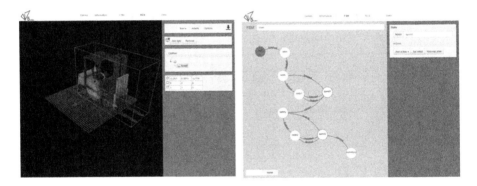

Fig. 4. Some screenshots of the creation process

4   Use Cases

Two use cases have been defined to validate the flexibility of the platform. First of them emphasizes the creation of applications with complex content. Therefore, an augmented reality environment is created. Second one is more focused on processes, and context, and to do so, a virtual reality and collaborative environment for learning purposes is created.

Sections 4.1 and 4.2 explains both use cases and go in depth their creation processes.

4.1   Use Case I: Augmented Reality Application for Welcome and Safety Protocol for New Workers

The augmented reality (from now on AR) technology enriches real environment adding to it virtual useful information. In order to educate new workers in the prevention of occupational risks, some companies consider AR technology very useful.

In this way, the editor presented in this work is a very useful tool, to non-expert user can configure an AR applications ad-hoc to the needs of each prevention of occupational risks courses.

This section describes how the editor presented in this work was used for a specific company in order to use AR technology in theirs occupational risk educational process for the new workers.

Using the flowchart method, the non-expert users can configure a sequence of AR scenes connected through specific conditions, generating an entire AR application. This flowchart has in consideration all the aspects of the company and the safety that the new worker has to be known.

For each scene, a marker is defined. This marker is used to recognize the scene or step of the application where the user (new worker) is located and to added configured virtual and multimedia elements correctly and accurately.

As can be seen in the configured flowchart (Fig. 1), different scenes are defined to represent different risk situations and rules that the worker has to be carrying out. In the first two scenes the first steps of the course are defined, which are bound to the company introduction and basic information like working hours, etc. In order to presents this information to the worker, a marker is defined (company brand poster) and virtual 3D Model with some text is going to renderer when the device recognize it, in order to present the company main activity. Defined timeout is used as condition to move from the first step to the second.

Then, the rest of the flowchart and scenes sequences are destined to the basic prevention of the occupational risk and safety knowledge that the worker has to be taking into account to work in the company. A bottom is defined in this case to move for the second step to the third in order to know when the user has the basic information of the company clear and want to start with this second part of the course.

In this second part of the course, different steps are defined, where using different markers and different virtual and multimedia material the different risks and rules are explained.

Once the course is defined using the web editor, and then it is launched in the mobile device by the final user (new worker). The configuration is saved in the cloud service. To execute correctly an AR application, it is necessary to localize the device in the current environment in real-time (recognize the markers). For this purpose a AR SDK is developed, which execute a computer vision algorithms to do this recognition using the camera of the device. In order to localize the marker in the real environment, the system needs to know which marker is founded. For this reason, a marker is linked with a scene and must be trained previously by the AR SDK.

As mentioned previously, the configuration of the application done in by the web editor is saved in the cloud. At the same time, the needed AR SDK follows a client-server architecture, where the training process is done in the cloud and tracking process locally and in real-time.

To sum up, the defined AR application is configured using the web editor as can be seen in the Fig. 4. This configuration is saved in the cloud, where an AR SDK is launched in order to train all the markers defined and linked with the scenes. Then, a mobile device downloads the course configured, and using the AR SDK to recognize

Fig. 5. Configured mobile AR application running in the device

defined markers, and defined application logic the application is running correctly. The Fig. 5 shows configured application running in the mobile device.

4.2 Use Case II: Virtual Reality Application for Collaborative Learning

This use case is no so focused on content but on context and processes. The goal is to create a purely virtual reality environment for collaborative learning purposes. The end-users are able to connect together inside the virtual world and they can use

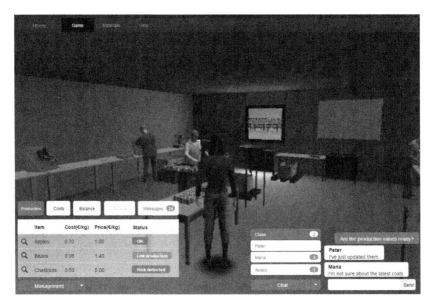

Fig. 6. Screenshots of the collaborative use case

collaboration tools like chat or dashboards and play a role inside the learning environment. The environment includes also agents with autonomous behaviors personalized by 3D avatars embedded in the environment.

Content is configured follows the same drag-and-drop philosophy that in the previous use case. Then, different collaborative elements and the autonomous behavior of agents are created following a graph-based chart. Their reactions when users interact with them can be also configured.

Moreover, several tools such as collaborative forms, excels, etc. are also included to enrich the learning process and their result is automatically sent to the teacher or the expert who is evaluating the learners' progress.

Figure 6 shows a screenshot of the resulting application where several end-users are interacting in real time.

5 Conclusions

This paper presents the platform resulting from a R&D project focused on the development of a set of tools that allow the easy creation of complex multimedia applications for edutainment purposes.

The resulting platform fulfils these requirements

- It allows the creation of complex multimedia content.
- It makes easier the application several pedagogical methodologies.
- It is an integral solution for the edutainment use cases.
- It is easy to use.

Three complementary concepts have been defined and their creation tools have been implemented: the content, the process and the context, to facilitate the authoring of applications by users with different kinds of expertise.

Two use cases have been designed and deployed to validate the flexibility of the authoring tools. One more focused on creation of applications with complex content and the other one focused on the creation of processes and context.

Future work is related with the addition of more communication tools and the easy creation of more ubiquitous collaborative applications; and the development of some edition tools for pre-created contents that make easier the adaption of multimedia contents to several kind of applications.

References

1. Egenfeldt-Nielsen, S.: Beyond Edutainment: Exploring the Educational Potential of Computer Games. Lulu. com (2005)
2. Blunt, R.: Does game-based learning work? Results from three recent studies. In: The Interservice/Industry Training, Simulation & Education Conference (I/ITSEC), NTSA, Orlando, Florida, USA, pp. 945–954 (2007)
3. Prensky, M.: Computer games and learning: digital game-based learning. In: Handbook of Computer Game Studies, vol. 18, pp. 97–122 (2005)

4. Tanaka, K., Kataoka, T., Hasegawa, M.: Virtual sport system for optimum exercising based on a user model. In: Chang, M., Kuo, R., Kinshuk, Chen, G.-D., Hirose, M. (eds.) Learning by Playing. LNCS, vol. 5670, pp. 283–290. Springer, Heidelberg (2009)

5. Meyer, B.: Learning English through serious games – reflections on teacher and learner performance. In: Chang, M., Kuo, R., Kinshuk, Chen, G.-D., Hirose, M. (eds.) Learning by Playing. LNCS, vol. 5670, p. 293. Springer, Heidelberg (2009)

6. Georgiev, T., Georgieva, E., Smrikarov, A.: M-learning-a new stage of E-learning. Int. Conf. Comput. Syst. Technol.-CompSysTech 4(28), 1–4 (2004)

7. Chen, C.M., Hsu, S.H., Li, Y.L., Peng, C.J.: Personalized intelligent m-learning system for supporting effective English learning. In: 2006 IEEE International Conference on Systems, Man and Cybernetics, SMC 2006, vol. 6, pp. 4898–4903. IEEE, October 2006

8. Wang, Wei, Zhong, Shaochun, Zhang, Zhuo, Lv, Senlin, Wang, Lina: Empirical research and design of M-learning system for college English. In: Chang, Maiga, Kuo, Rita, Kinshuk, Chen, Gwo-Dong, Hirose, Michitaka (eds.) Learning by Playing. LNCS, vol. 5670, pp. 524–535. Springer, Heidelberg (2009)

9. Sauer, S., Osswald, K., Wielemans, X., Stifter, M.: U-create: creative authoring tools for edutainment applications. In: Göbel, S., Malkewitz, R., Iurgel, I. (eds.) TIDSE 2006. LNCS, vol. 4326, pp. 163–168. Springer, Heidelberg (2006)

10. Göbel, S., Becker, F., Feix, A.: INSCAPE: storymodels for interactive storytelling and edutainment applications. In: Subsol, G. (ed.) ICVS-VirtStory 2005. LNCS, vol. 3805, pp. 168–171. Springer, Heidelberg (2005)

11. Gobel, S., Salvatore, L., Konrad, R.: StoryTec: a digital storytelling platform for the authoring and experiencing of interactive and non-linear stories. In: International Conference on Automated solutions for Cross Media Content and Multi-channel Distribution AXMEDIS 2008, pp. 103–110. IEEE, November 2008

12. Pranantha, D., Bellotti, F., Berta, R., De Gloria, A.: A format of serious games for higher technology education topics: a case study in a digital electronic system course. In: 2012 IEEE 12th International Conference on Advanced Learning Technologies (ICALT), pp. 13–17. IEEE, July 2012

13. Pranantha, D., Bellotti, F., Berta, R., De Gloria, A.: Puzzle-it: An HTML5 serious games platform for education. In: Göbel, S., Müller, W., Urban, B., Wiemeyer, J. (eds.) GameDays 2012 and Edutainment 2012. LNCS, vol. 7516, pp. 134–143. Springer, Heidelberg (2012)

14. West, M.: Evolve your hiearchy. Game Dev. 13(3), 51–54 (2006)

15. Buneman, P.: Semistructured data. In: Proceedings of the Sixteenth ACM SIGACT-SIGMOD-SIGART Symposium on Principles of Database Systems. ACM (1997)

Bike-Sharing Prediction System

Qiang Cai[1,2], Ziyu Xue[1,2(✉)], Dianhui Mao[1,2], Haisheng Li[1,2], and Jian Cao[1,2]

[1] School of Computer and Information Engineering,
Beijing Technology and Business University, Beijing 100048, China
{caiq,maodh,caojian}@th.btbu.edu.cn, xzy_88@126.com,
li_haisheng@163.com
[2] Beijing Key Laboratory of Big Data Technology for Food Safety,
Beijing Technology and Business University, Beijing 100048, China

Abstract. Bike Sharing System is a dynamic network. This paper proposes a method to balance the network and allocate the bikes in each station to avoid the imbalance happening. Real-time monitoring takes too much time to reallocate the bikes if an imbalance has occurred so it cannot tackle this problem well. And most of sharing systems cannot focus on the influenced factors and overlook assuring the creditability of the prediction. In this paper, we propose **a hierarchical prediction model** to predict the number of bikes. It mainly contains the following parts. First, we propose a clustering algorithm to cluster bike stations into groups using Gaussian Mixture Model (GMM). Second, gradient Boosting Regression Tree(GBRT) is adapted to predict the entire triffic. Third, we predict the proportion across clusters and the inter-cluster transition using a multi-factor-based inference model. Finally, we adapte **Geo-Space Contrary Prediction Model** to compare with the same period prediction datasets to improve the results. Based on Citi Bike system data in NYC, from Apr. 1st, 2014 to Sept. 30th, 2014 and the influenced factors, our model outperforms baseline approaches and can be applied to various geograph scene.

Keywords: Bike-sharing prediction · Urban computing · Geo-Space contrary prediction model

1 Introduction

With the development of civic facilities in large cities, it is important to provide a convenient transportation mode for people's commutes. With the increasing acceptability of cycling trips, Bike-Sharing System is more and more important. Users can check-out a bike at a station near their initial location, and check-in close to their destination. Using a card when checking out/in a bike will give some information in a record, like bike ID, station ID and duration time. But the system is challenging because it needs rebalance at each station. Many factors affect the system, such as meteorology, correlation between stations, workday or rest day and so on. It would be too late to reallocate bikes if an imbalance has occurred.

Bike-sharing systems are currently spreading across the globe: Wang et al. [1] analyze the operation of several different systems in 2010. It focuses on the strategic

© Springer International Publishing Switzerland 2016
A. El Rhalibi et al. (Eds.): Edutainment 2016, LNCS 9654, pp. 301–317, 2016.
DOI: 10.1007/978-3-319-40259-8_27

planning of the network design. Shaheen et al. [2] estimate about 100 bike-sharing programs planned in 22 countries in 2009. With the popular support in 2011, more than 5000 bikes are available to users across 405 stations. But this programs could not adapt to the growing data. Liu et al. [3] address the problem by finding optimal stations using mathematical programming techniques. They formulate the problem as a nonlinear mixed-integer problem and use a commercial solver to solve it. Vogel and Mattfeld [4] present a methodology for strategic and operational planning by data mining. Vogel and Mattfeld [5] use serval mathematic formulations for the balancing problem. In the static case, users' demand is assumed to be negligible. But the methods we mentioned above, they ignore the relationship about the stations.

In 2012, Contardo et al. [6] introduce a dynamic public bike-sharing balancing problem arising from the daily operations during peak hours and they provide lower and upper bounds in short computing times. Hamon et al. [7] discuss an adaptation to this case, the method relies on the notion of communities to build a complex networks in 2013 and the bicycle trips connecting the stations to get more accurate results. But metrology has a great impact on the accuracy about the predictions.

Yexin et al. [8] propose a hierarchical prediction model to predict the number of bikes that will be rent from/returned to each station cluster in a future period so that reallocation can be executed in advance. They considered more factors and use k-means to cluster the station to greater stations. But their method may have some error points. The prediction will be better after treatment the error. The cluster algorithm is not the best way to cluster on map.

We use a model to predict the proportion and distribute the bikes dynamically before the imbalance occurring and consider more factors. We propose a Geo-Space contrary prediction model to check and influence the prediction results. The following section is an illustration about the factors:

(1) **Working-day:** More people may check-out/in a bike on a working day than a rest day. There is more dissimilarity about them. During peak commuting hours, the line chart shows a rise rate. During a rest day or holiday, the peak rate will rise at about 9 o'clock, people may go out for fun at that time.

(2) **Meteorology:** More people may check-out/in a bike on a sunny day than a rainy day. It also exists between cool day and a warm day. The wind speed also influences it. Meteorology has common experience every year for every city. Although predicting traffic under rare conditions is as important as that under ordinary conditions, traditional machine learning models are only trained to fit the majority of observations.

Our method uses hierarchical prediction model and Geo-Space contrary prediction model to tackle these challenges, which is comprised of the major components: Station clustering algorithm to cluster individual stations based GMM algorithm according to their geographical locations and historical transition patterns; building a prediction model to predict the total check-out of the whole city based on time and meteorology features; using a check-out proportion prediction model to predict the check-out proportion with the meteorology and others; an inter-cluster transition prediction model to predict the dynamic bike transition; a check-out/in inference algorithm to calculate the check-out/in of each station cluster based on the outputs of the former components; a

Geo-Space contrary prediction model to describe the relationship between the space and time, meanwhile, check the prediction model with the history conditions.

2 Overview

2.1 Nouns Definition

We simply introduce these nouns.

Working day: $W_t = \{0, 1, 2\}$ is a variable representing the attribution of the day. If working day: $W_t = 0$; if weekends: $W_t = 1$; if holiday: $W_t = 2$. Holiday has a little bit different than weekends, so we distinguish them in this paper.

Meteorology: $M_t = (w_t, p_t, v_t)$ is a vector. In period t, w_t means weather, p_t means temperature, v_t means wind speed, all of them influence on M_t.

Check-out/in: $O_{ci,t}$ and $I_{ci,t}$ mean the number of bikes which checked-out/in in the cluster C_i in period t.

2.2 Model Introduction

2.2.1 Prediction Model

We use this process when dealing it, the process consists of following parts:

We leverage GBRT to learn an entire traffic model by using the historical check-out/in data, meteorology data and work-day data.

There are many stations in our study, so we propose a bike clustering algorithm based Gaussian Mixture Model (GMM) to cluster stations into groups. It can get a better input for the later steps. Comparing to the method of minimizing the TSD, like K-means, maximizing the log-likelihood has better clustering results.

We use the inter-cluster transition learning to predict the bike's transition for check-in prediction after a bike is checked out, use inter-cluster transition matrix to describe where a bike will be checked in. We need to predict the check-out proportion across clusters through its similarities.

Finally, the paper proposes a method to calculate the duration time. Each pair of clusters is described by a lognormal distribution, whose parameters are calculated by maximum likelihood estimation.

2.2.2 Geo-Space Contrary Prediction Model

We propose a model to predict the proportion and the result, as a comparison of today's history. Figure 1 is a Geo-Space. The bottom of cuboid is used as a cluster for each station. Z-axis as time-axis, means 17 h (from 6:00 am to 11:00 pm), from bottom to top. We divide the city into a rectangle, and each square represents a cluster of stations. If the check-out proportion is higher than the check-in proportion, the cube is marked as red color, or marked as blue if check-in proportion higher.

Figure 1 shows the general appearance of a day. This model shows the general situation: more cubes show as blue color when people go to work on 7 o'clock, and more cubes show as red color on 9 o'clock. It means more people ride bike to work in the morning, return their bike when they arrive at the company about 9 o'clock.

The same thing that happened in off hours. We get the general direction in the movement, there are more bike transition from cluster form cluster 1 to 10 in Fig. 1. The statistics time about 1 h.

We also get the general direction in the movement, there are more bike transitions from cluster 1 to 10 from 7:00 am to 9:00 am on 26th Aug. 2014, shown in Fig. 1. That may mean more people move from station 1 to station 10 on their way to companies. The duration is about 2 h. We can allocate bikes dynamically after 9 o'clock to prevent unbalancing.

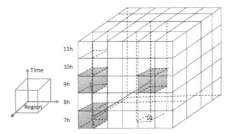

Fig. 1. Contrary prediction model (Color figure online)

We use Geo-space contrary prediction model to predict the general direction. Finally, we use the contrary prediction model compare with the prediction result, save the same result, and delete the results that's far from the standards.

3 Methods

3.1 Bike Station Clustering

To deal with all the bike stations are more complicated before our prediction. It was a relief that we found the stations had behavioral affinities with its neighbors, we tried to cluster them firstly.

In order to find the common rules between the neighbor stations. We choose the stations in NYC bike System like Fig. 2(a), and looking for the relationship between the neighboring stations. We choose Station 72, which in the W 52 St & 11 Ave, latitude 40.76727 and longitude −73.9939; Station 457, which in Broadway & W 58 St, latitude 40.76695 and longitude −73.9817; Station 327, which in W 56 St & 10 Ave, latitude 40.76825 and longitude −73.9886, and Station 11; Station 513 and Station 335 in NYC.

Figure 2(b) and (c) show the check-out/in proportion in the six stations. It is easy to group because neighbor stations have the similar performance, like Station 72, Station 457, Station 327 (Fig. 2(b)) and Station 513, Station 335, Station 11 (Fig. 2(c)). We mark the same performance using the blue and red box that they have the same trend. In this paper, we cluster the stations using GMM algorithm.

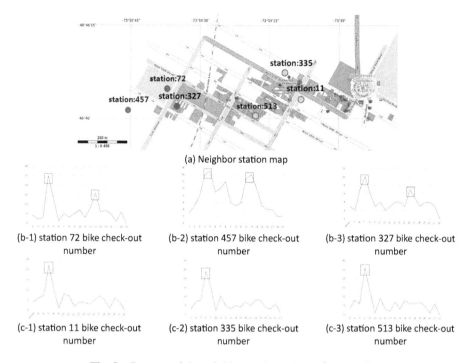

(a) Neighbor station map

(b-1) station 72 bike check-out number

(b-2) station 457 bike check-out number

(b-3) station 327 bike check-out number

(c-1) station 11 bike check-out number

(c-2) station 335 bike check-out number

(c-3) station 513 bike check-out number

Fig. 2. Contrast of the neighbor stations (Color figure online)

3.1.1 Gaussian Mixture Mode Cluster Model

Gaussian Mixture Mode can be mixed the Gaussian model. The probability of each appeared point is the result of several Gauss mixing. Figure 3 shows the result of cluster. The dots are the stations, the big points are clusters of the station. There are three clusters in Fig. 3.

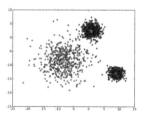

Fig. 3. Cluster the neighbor stations

In this method, we provide the number of region in NYC as K Gaussian distribution. Every Gaussian distribution can influence the bike station, and the predominant factor is πk. x is the number of the bike station, and θ is parameters of the Gauss model [4, 9].

$$\begin{cases} p(x;\theta) = \sum_{k=1}^{K} \pi_k p_k(x;\theta_k) \\ \theta = \{\pi_1,\ldots,\pi_k,\theta_1,\ldots,\theta_k\}, \sum_{k=1}^{K} \pi_k = 1, \pi_k \in [0,1] \\ p_k(x;\theta_k) = N(x;\mu_k,\sum k) \end{cases} \qquad (1)$$

Here, we estimate the model parameters π_k for each class of impact factors which can calculate in Eq. 2. μ_k calculates in Eq. 3. $\sum k$ is the covariance matrix shown in Eq. 4.

$$\pi_k = \frac{\sum_{i=1}^{M} Q^i\left(z_k^{(i)}\right)}{M}. \qquad (2)$$

$$\mu_k = \frac{\sum_{i=1}^{M} x^{(i)} Q^i(z_k^{(i)})}{\sum_{i=1}^{M} Q^i(z_k^{(i)})}. \qquad (3)$$

$$\sum k = \frac{\sum_{i=1}^{M}(x^{(i)} - \mu_k)(x^{(i)} - \mu_k)^T Q^i(z_k^{(i)})}{\sum_{i=1}^{M} Q^i(z_k^{(i)})}. \qquad (4)$$

After that, we use expectation maximization (EM) algorithm to calculate the cluster's results shown in Eq. 5.

$$l(\theta) = \sum_{i=1}^{M} \sum_{Z^{(i)}} Q^i(z^{(i)}) \log \frac{p(x^{(i)}, z^{(i)}; \theta)}{Q^{(i)}(z^{(i)})} \equiv \sum_{i=1}^{M} \sum_{k=1}^{K} Q^i(z_k^{(i)}) \log \pi_k N(x^{(i)}; \mu_k, \sum k). \qquad (5)$$

There are two steps to use when GMM using EM algorithm, the first one is E-step, the second one is M-step. E-step uses observed data and existing model to predict the missing station and prepares for the M-step.

$$Q^i\left(z_k^{(i)}\right) = p\left(z_k^{(i)} | x^{(i)}; \theta\right) = \frac{\pi_k N(x^{(i)}; \mu_k, \sum k)}{\sum_{k=1}^{K} \pi_k N(x^{(i)}; \mu_k, \sum k)}. \qquad (6)$$

Here, M-step will take the derivative of the log-likelihood to obtain estimates directly.

Using this method, we get the iterations until convergence, then the $Q^i\left(z_k^{(i)}\right)$ can be used for clustering. We group individual stations into clusters according to its geo-graphical locations and transition patterns. In Fig. 4, the points with the same color mean the stations in the same cluster. Figure 4(a) is the original drawing before clustering, Fig. 4(b) is the clustering result using GMM model.

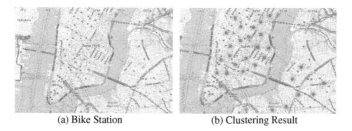

(a) Bike Station   (b) Clustering Result

Fig. 4. Use GMM method to cluster (Color figure online)

3.1.2   Time Vector

Our paper builds a t-matrix for each cluster. It uses the column to represent the time period. Each entry is the probability that a bike will be checked in to cluster. Figure 5 is the example of all time vector, we get a Transit-Matrix after that. After getting the time vector, we cluster the stations again, using the GMM algorithm.

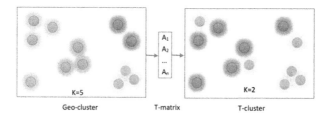

Fig. 5. Time vector

3.2   Influenced Factor for the Model

Our model can be affected by many factors, like meteorology, working day and other events. We download the meteorology (http://mesowest.utah.edu/) and add the working day data on it [10, 11].

3.2.1   GBRT

GBRT [12] is the abbreviation of the Gradient Boosting Decision Tree. We predicted the hierarchical prediction model firstly. The entire traffic is predicted by GBRT model, which is a non-parametric statistical learning technique for regression, is one of the most effective machine learning models for prediction.

Fig. 6. GBRT model

We first compute a sequence of simple regression trees: $\{t_1(x), t_2(x), \cdots, t_r(x)\}$. The process is shown in Fig. 6.

Here, each tree is built to predict the residual of the preceding trees and calculate in Eqs. 7 and 8.

$$t_i = argmin_g \sum_{t=1}^{N} L(y_t - T_{i-1}, t(x_t)). \tag{7}$$

$$T_{i-1} = \sum_{l=1}^{i-1} t_l(x). \tag{8}$$

Here, L is a loss function in Eq. 7, $\{x_t, y_t\}_{t=1}^{N}$ s the training dataset.

GBRT model should accumulate all the results of the regression tree as the final one. Each tree learns the residual error from the last tree.

Predictions are made of the combining decision of $\{t_1(x), t_2(x), \cdots, t_r(x)\}$ shown in Eq. 9.

$$T(x) = t_1(x) + t_2(x) + \ldots + t_r(x). \tag{9}$$

Here, x is the features corresponding and it has the significant influenced on the entire traffic; y is the ground truth. T(x) is the prediction results.

3.2.2 Meteorology

Unlike the other traffic, meteorology would affect the bike trip. This paper considers the influence factors of the meteorology. The most important factors are the weather, wind speed and temperature. We use them to train GBRT model.

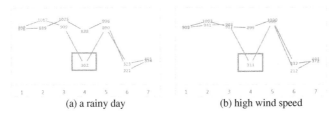

(a) a rainy day   (b) high wind speed

Fig. 7. Meteorology factor (Color figure online)

When the weather gets warmer, the curves have an upward trend. There are some abnormal points when we observe the charts. We use green box in Fig. 7 around it.

Comparing with the same period of last week (blue one), the orange line has the abnormal point The green boxes in Fig. 7(a) is in a rainy day and Fig. 7(b) is in a day with high wind speed [13]. They were significantly lower than the corresponding values for the same period.

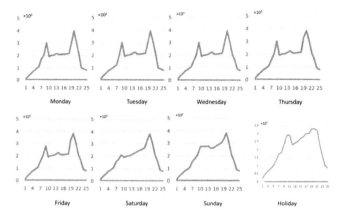

Fig. 8. A week entire traffic in NYC

3.2.3 Work Day and Holiday

This paper calculates the check-out number from a week, and draw in Fig. 8. We can discover the rule: it has the similar trend among weekdays and the similar trend on weekends. The last picture in Fig. 8 is the entire traffic in the Chrisms day in 2014, is similar with weekends.

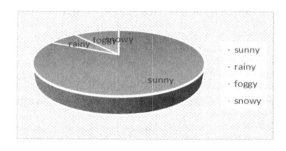

Fig. 9. Weather influenced to the model (Color figure online)

3.3 Prediction Model of the Check-Out Cluster and Check-In Cluster

We use multi-factor to construct the prediction model. The model can guarantee the sum of the check-out proportion. Similarly, we use the unbalanced meteorology dataset, Fig. 9 shows the weather distribution in NYC from 1st Apr. to 30th Sep. in 2014.

This model includes many functions, like time, temperature, wind-speed, weather and working day. We divide the periods into $1, 2\ldots T$; check-out proportion as CO_1, $CO_2\ldots CO_T$; check-in proportion as $CI_1, CI_2\ldots CI_T$; features as $f_1, f_2\ldots f_T$. We define the multi-similarity function in periods f_i to f_{i+1} as $W(f_i, f_{i+1})$. We can calculate in Eq. 10.

$$\min \sum_{t=T+1}^{time} L(E_t \times CO_t, E_t \times \widehat{CO}_t). \tag{10}$$

Here, T means the number of the historical data. The ground truth is $E_t \times CO_t$ nd the prediction value is $E_t \times \widehat{CO}_t$ L means the prediction error. $W(f_i, f_{i+1})$ can calculate in Eq. 11.

$$W(f_i, f_{i+1}) = \lambda_1(i, i+1) \times \lambda_2(w_i, w_{i+1}) \times K((p_i, v_i), (p_{i+1}, v_{i+1})). \tag{11}$$

Here, P_i shown in Eq. 12.

$$\widehat{p_{i+1}} = \frac{\sum_{i=1}^{T} W(f_i, f_{i+1}) \times CO_i}{\sum_{i=1}^{T} W(f_i, f_{i+1})}. \tag{12}$$

This paper has clarified some certain rules and properties. We define the similarity in Eq. 13.

$$\lambda(time_1, time_2) = x_{t1,t2} \in \{0, 1, 2\} \times \rho_1^{\Delta hourdist(t1,t2)} \times \rho_2^{\Delta dist(t1,t2)}. \tag{13}$$

Here, x can equal 0, 1 or 2. When x equal to 0 means week day; equal to 1 means weekends; equal to 2 means holiday. $\Delta hourdist$ and $\Delta dist$ mean the distance between in the hours and the distance between in the time period shown in Eqs. 14 and 15.

$$\Delta h(t_1, t_2) = \min\{r(t_1, t_2), 24 - r(t_1, t_2)\}. \tag{14}$$

$$\Delta d(t_1, t_2) = [\frac{|t_1 - t_2|}{24}]. \tag{15}$$

Here, Δh denotes the distance of two time periods. Δd is the distance of two time periods from the perspective of the day and week. $r(t_1, t_2)$ shown in Eq. 16.

$$r(t_1, t_2) = \mod(|t_1 - t_2|, 24). \tag{16}$$

Meteorology is the most important factor in our paper. We add an error correction item in the model. The error correction is influenced by the temperature and wind speed in Eq. 17.

$$\widehat{p_{i+1}} = \frac{\sum_{i=1}^{T} W(f_i, f_{i+1}) \times CO_i}{\sum_{i=1}^{T} W(f_i, f_{i+1})} + \sum_{j=1}^{J} \varphi_j e_{t-j}. \tag{17}$$

The factors $\{e_{t-j}\}$ are the prediction errors in period t-j. where $j = 1, 2\ldots J$, and J is a threshold of the time lag [14, 15].

3.4 Geo-Space Contrary Prediction Model

After clustering, we use clustering results construct the cube. Each block represents the clustering results of several stations. According to the deviations, the model draws the regional color (red means check-in proportion is higher, blue means check-out proportion is higher). We also calculate the error from the data D_{now} and the nearby data D_{last}. For example, if today is Friday (e.g. 18, Feb., 2014), we will compare the check-out/in number with the last Friday (e.g. 11, Feb., 2014) shown in Eq. 18 and got the result δ_i which shown in Eq. 19.

$$\text{error} = \sqrt{\left(D_{now} - D_{last}\right)^2}. \tag{18}$$

$$\delta_i = compare(error, T). \tag{19}$$

If δ_i s higher than the threshold. We will check the meteorology. If today is a rainy day either has a high wind speed or has a lower temperature, we mark the data in normal range. If not, we mark it as an error data and replace it.

We cut the cube into levels for each hour shown in Fig. 10. We find some interesting law on it:

When people go to work between 7:00–8:00, check-out proportion is higher, the model shows in blue color (Fig. 10(a) and (b)). After that, when people reach their destination between 9:00–10:00, the model shows in red color (Fig. 10(c) and (d)).

According to the historical data, we can rebalance the bikes before the confusion happened and use the contrary method to predict the results [13, 16].

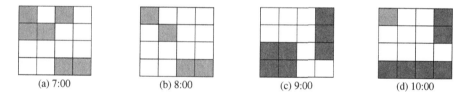

(a) 7:00   (b) 8:00   (c) 9:00   (d) 10:00

Fig. 10. Contrary prediction model from 7:00 to 10:00 (Color figure online)

4 Experiments

4.1 Instruction

(1) **Dataset**

This paper uses the data of Citi Bike system, which is in NYC, from 1st Apr. to 30th Sep. in 2014. Data format is *(trip duration, start station ID, end station ID, start time, end time)*, it also has the longitude and the latitude.

The meteorology data format is *(date, weather, temperature, wind speed)*. The work day data format is *(date, property)*.

We set training data from 1st Apr. to 10th Sep. The others is used in testing data.

(2) **Metric**

We use the values of Root Mean Logarithmic Squared Error (RMLSE) and Error Rate (ER) to measure the results shown in Eqs. 20 and 21.

$$RMLSE = \frac{1}{T}\sum_{t=1}^{T} \sqrt{\frac{1}{m}\sum_{i=1}^{m} \left(\log\left(\widehat{X_{Ci,t}}+1\right) - \log(X_{Ci,t}+1)\right)^2}. \qquad (20)$$

$$ER = \frac{1}{T}\sum_{t=1}^{T} \frac{\sum_{i=1}^{m} |\widehat{X_{Ci,t}} - X_{Ci,t}|}{\sum_{i=1}^{m} X_{Ci,t}}. \qquad (21)$$

(3) **Baseline**

We compare our method with nine baselines.

HA: It is a method to choose the average value of the historical results.
ARMA: It is a method to understand and predict the future values in a time series.
GBRT: It is a method to predict directly, similar to entire traffic prediction.
HP-KNN: It is a method to predict the entire traffic, and allocate each cluster based the proportion across clusters.

(4) **Other methods**

We use grid clustering and k-means clustering compared with our method which using GMM clustering.

Grid clustering cluster algorithm (GC): It is a method which divides the city into uniform grids clustering. We divide the city into uniform grids. The stations fall into the same grid means in the same cluster.

K-means cluster algorithm: It is a cluster algorithm, given group classification number k ($k \leq n$). The method should cluster the data into k groups and considers the distance only [16]. Bipartite clustering (BC) method use K-means to cluster.

4.2 Result

(1) **Clustering results**

The number of clusters should be chosen by knowledge and experiences. We cluster all the stations into 23 clusters [7], and compared the three methods, named GC, BC and Gaussian Mixture Model cluster (GMC). Figure 11 shows the results. Figure 11(a) is the map of NYC, the red boxes are the important areas when we clustering. Figure 11 (b), (c) and (d) are cluster results when using GC, BC and GMC algorithm.

(2) **Check-out/in results**

We compare the results with the different methods using HA, ARMA, GERT, HP-KNN and HP-MSI. We calculate the value of RMLSE and ER in the Table 1.

When use HP-KNN and HP-MSI, the results shown that BC are better than GC, because both of them are hierarchical prediction methods and BC can improve the accuracy of proportion prediction. GMC has the best performance, because this algorithm builds a distribution model for each category, and trying to find the best model for each category. And GMM algorithm is suitable for regional clustering.

We show the value of RMLSE and ER in check-out proportion in Table 1 and check-in proportion in Table 2.

GMC averages fell 1.94 % in RMLSE by comparing with GC. The value of ER has a small decrease, about 0.26 %. GMC also decreased when compared with BC in RMLSE and ER, about 0.14 % and 0.26 %.

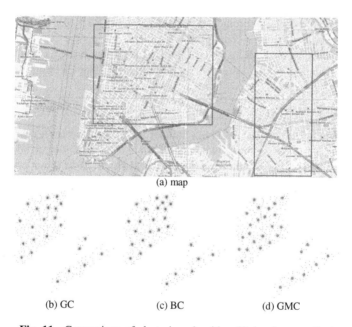

(a) map

(b) GC   (c) BC   (d) GMC

Fig. 11. Comparison of clustering algorithm (Color figure online)

Table 1. Check-out prediction error

Methods	Baseline	HA	AEMA	GBRT	HP-KNN	HP-MSI
RMLSE	GC	38.7%	37.1%	38.6%	37.7%	37.1%
	BC	37.2%	35.4%	36.9%	35.8%	34.9%
	GMC	37.1%	35.3%	36.8%	35.6%	34.7%
ER	GC	35.3%	34.6%	31.1%	29.8%	28.8%
	BC	35.5%	34.6%	31.4%	29.9%	28.2%
	GMC	35.1%	34.4%	31.0%	29.7%	28.1%

Table 2. Check-in prediction error

Methods	Baseline	HA	AEMA	GBRT	HP-KNN	HP-MSI
	GC	37.7%	36.3%	38.2%	37.5%	36.5%
RMLSE	BC	36.5%	35.2%	36.5%	36.0%	35.0%
	GMC	36.4%	35.2%	36.3%	36.0%	34.9%
	GC	34.7%	34.0%	30.9%	30.2%	29.7%
ER	BC	35.2%	34.4%	30.9%	29.5%	29.0%
	GMC	35.1%	34.2%	30.8%	29.3%	28.8%

We calculate the check-in prediction and the values of RMLSE and ER in Table 2. It also has a good result when compared with others.

Comparison between GMC and GC, the RMLSE has been reduced 1.48 % in average, and decrease a little when compared with BC. The ER value is similar to Table 1.

(3) **Contrary prediction result**

We use the contrary prediction results to compare with the prediction data. We delete the data which is far. For example, when comparing with the same period, the rent-in number of the bicycles has a significant decline on March 5, 2014 (Float criterion is up and down in 50 %), shown in Fig. 12(a). The contrary detection model judges the point is abnormal. Then the model checks the weather conditions with the history. The condition shows that day is a rainy day. The point is reserved since it is caused by the weather.

We change the rent-in rates a 60 per cent cut on March 10, 2014 which is a sunny day. The contrary detection model judges the point is abnormal. Comparing with the weather conditions, the point is judged as abnormal. The model uses the average value of the history data to adjust the point, shown in Fig. 12(b).

In order to obtain the effect of the contrary model, we calculate the prediction error and show the results in Table 3. (G.A.C means using the contrary prediction in GMM).

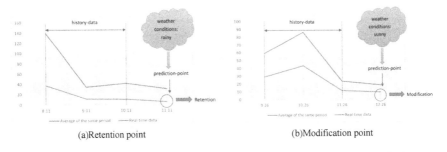

(a)Retention point   (b)Modification point

Fig. 12. Contrary prediction model processing procedure (Color figure online)

Table 3. Prediction error after contrary prediction

Method	Baseline	HA	AEMA	GBRT	HP-KNN	HP-MSI
	Prediction error of check-out					
RMLSE	GMC	37.1%	35.3%	36.8%	35.6%	34.7%
	G. A.C	36.4%	35.0%	36.6%	35.5%	34.5%
ER	GMC	35.1%	34.4%	31.0%	29.7%	28.1%
	G. A.C	34.8%	34.0%	30.8%	29.2%	27.3%
	Prediction error of check-in					
RMLSE	GMC	36.4%	35.2%	36.3%	36.0%	34.9%
	G. A.C	36.0%	34.9%	36.1%	35.8%	34.7%
ER	GMC	35.1%	34.2%	30.8%	29.3%	28.8%
	G. A.C	34.7%	34.0%	30.5%	29.2%	28.3%

When we use the contrary model in the check-in/out results, our methods have an improvement again.

After that, average results decrease 2.24 % in RMLSE by comparison with GC, 0.44 % by comparison with BC in check-out process. Compared the value of GC and BC using ER, G.A.C decreased 0.7 % in average. Check-in process had a similar good performance. It decreases 1.74 % and 0.34 % when compared with GC and BC in RMLSE value, and decreases 0.56 % and 0.46 % in ER value.

Figure 13 shows line charts when comparing with the four methods in the baselines. We aim to decrease the prediction error. Our method is in the lower position in all pictures that means the method has a good performance.

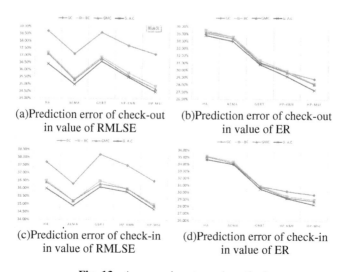

(a)Prediction error of check-out in value of RMLSE

(b)Prediction error of check-out in value of ER

(c)Prediction error of check-in in value of RMLSE

(d)Prediction error of check-in in value of ER

Fig. 13. A comparison to each method

In the future, we will strengthen the effect of the contrary prediction model and use more factors to influence the prediction model.

5   Conclusion

Bike Sharing System is a dynamical network, predict the situation before the unbalance occurring is important in the system. This paper proposes a prediction model and a contrary prediction model to solve this problem. The prediction model contains a bike clustering algorithm using GMM method to cluster the bike stations, and a multi-factor-based algorithm to predict the check-out/in proportion of each station clusters. This paper also proposes a contrary prediction model to predict the accuracy of the results, which is calculated in the last step. It bases on the historical, meteorology and calendar data, which can mark the degree of deviation in prediction results, and decide to keep or replace it.

We evaluate our model on NYC datasets, the results are beyond those baseline methods. Our model is better than others and suitable various geography scenes. The next phase, we will consider more factors to influence the prediction model and strengthen the effect of the contrary prediction model.

Acknowledgement. This work was partially supported by Beijing Natural Science Foundation (NO. 4162019), General Project of Beijing Municipal Education Commission science and technology development plans (NO. SQKM201610011010) and National Natural Science Foundation of China (NO. 61402023).

References

1. Wang, S., Zhang, J., Liu, L., Duan, Z.Y.: Bike-sharing-a new public transportation mode: state of the practice & prospects. In: IEEE International Conference on Emergency Management & Management Sciences, pp. 222–225 (2010)
2. Shaheen, S.A., Guzman, S., Zhang, H.: Bikesharing in Europe, the Americas, and Asia: past, present, and future. Transp. Res. Rec. J Transp. Res. Board **2143**(1316350), 159–167 (2010)
3. Liu, L., Li, Y., Xu, G.H.: Empirical study of bike sharing service satisfactions in Wuhan City. Logistics Eng. Manag. (05), 31–32 (2011)
4. Vogel, P., Mattfeld, D.C.: Strategic and operational planning of bike-sharing systems by data mining – a case study. In: Böse, J.W., Hu, H., Jahn, C., Shi, X., Stahlbock, R., Voß, S. (eds.) ICCL 2011. LNCS, vol. 6971, pp. 127–141. Springer, Heidelberg (2011)
5. Vogel, P, Mattfeld, D.C.: Optimal inventory management of a bike-sharing station. In: Second International Conference on Computational Logistics, vol. 45, issue 10, pp. 1077–1093 (2013)
6. Contaro, C., Morency, C., Rousseaud, L.M.: Balancing a dynamic public bike-sharing system[J/OL]. www.cirrelt.ca/DocumentsTravail/CIRRELT-2012-09.pdf
7. Hamon, R., Borgnat, P., Flandrin, P., et al.: Networks as signals, with an application to bike sharing system. In: 2013 IEEE Global Conference on Signal and Information Processing (GlobalSIP), pp. 611–614 (2013)

8. Yexin, L., Yu, Z., Huichu, Z., Lei, C.: Traffic prediction in a bike sharing system. In: USA: Proceedings of the 23rd ACM International Conference on Advances in Geographical Information Systems (2015)
9. Windmeijer, F.: A finite sample correction for the variance of linear efficient two-step GMM estimators. J. Econometrics **126**(1), 25–51 (2005)
10. Yoon, J.W., Pinelli, F., Calabrese, F., Calabrese, F.: Cityride: a predictive bike sharing journey advisor. In: Proceedings of the 13th IEEE ICMDM (2012)
11. Yu, Z.: Methodologies for cross-domain data fusion: an overview. ACM Trans. Big Data **1** (1) (2015)
12. Friedman, J.H.: Greedy function approximation: a gradient boosting machine. Ann. Stat. **29** (5), 1189–1232 (2001)
13. Bargar, A., Gupta, A., Gupta, S., Ma, D.: Interactive visual analytics for multi-city bike-share data analysis. In: Proceedings of the 3rd Urbcomp (2014)
14. Borgnat, P., Robardet, C., Abry, P., Flandrin, P., Rouquier, J., Tremblay, N.: A dynamical network view of Lyon's Vélo'v shared bicycle system. In: Mukherjee, A., Choudhury, M., Peruani, F., Ganguly, N., Mitra, B. (eds.) Dynamics On and Of Complex Networks, vol. 2, pp. 267–284. Springer, Heidelberg (2013)
15. Vogel, P., Greiser, T., Mattefeld, D.C.: Understanding bikesharing systems using data mining: exploring activity patterns. Procedia-Soc. Behav. Sci. **20**(1), 514–523 (2011)
16. Kaltenbrunner, A., Meza, R., Grivolla, J., Codina, J., Banches, R.: Urban cycles and mobility patterns: exploring and predicting trends in a bicycle-based public transport system. Pervasive Mob. Comput. **6**(4), 455–466 (2010)
17. Kanungo, T., Mount, D.M., Netanyahu, N.S., Piatko, C.D., Silverman, R.: An efficient k-means clustering algorithm: analysis and implementation. IEEE Trans. Pattern Anal. Mach. Intell. **24**(7), 881–892 (2002)

A Support Network for Distributed Systems

Sahar Badri, Paul Fergus$^{(\boxtimes)}$, and William Hurst$^{(\boxtimes)}$

School of Computing and Mathematical Sciences,
Liverpool John Moores University, Byrom Street, Liverpool L3 3AF, UK
S.K.Badri@2010.ljmu.ac.uk,
{p.fergus,w.hurst}@ljmu.ac.uk

Abstract. Critical infrastructures are the backbone of everyday life and their protection from cyber-threats is an increasingly pressing issue for governments and private industries. Not only is effective security costly, the requirements individual critical infrastructures have been often unique, meaning their security systems have to be tailored to match their specific needs. As a result of these factors, simulation can play a key role in the advancement of security measures in a cheap, safe and effective way. In this paper, the development of a distributed support system is presented. The system employs behaviour analysis techniques to support interconnected infrastructures and distribute security advice throughout an interdependent system of systems. The approach is tested through the simulation, which is used to build realistic data from 8 critical infrastructures. The research is inspired by the human immune characteristics.

Keywords: Critical infrastructure · Simulation · Distributed system · System of systems · Data analysis

1 Introduction

Interdependency is considered the main challenge for critical infrastructures. Operating as a mutually interdependent network, treated as a system of systems, failures and successful cyber-attacks have the potential to cause a cascading effect. Understanding the interconnectivity behaviour between the critical infrastructures, and how it changes depending on the complexity, can reduce the effect before cascading occurs. Moreover, this would control the damage and limit the impact [1].

Simulation has a key role in the advancement of critical infrastructure protection. Its use is becoming a common technique for the testing of cyber-attack prevention measures and for improving the level of the security techniques [2]. A simple system can be created to represent a larger infrastructure and allow for realistic testing to take place [3].

It is clear that there are many benefits of using simulation. It helps in conducting experimentation on a realistic representation of a system, without the worry that any damage done would have a real impact [3]. In particular, when testing against cyber-attack resilience and developing new approaches to security, critical infrastructure simulation is of great benefit.

In our past work, the focus was on creating a support network against cyber-attacks using the human immune system mechanism as inspiration for the design [4]. In order

© Springer International Publishing Switzerland 2016
A. El Rhalibi et al. (Eds.): Edutainment 2016, LNCS 9654, pp. 318–330, 2016.
DOI: 10.1007/978-3-319-40259-8_28

to demonstrate the approach, a simulation framework of 8 critical infrastructures is presented in this paper. Furthermore, the big data analysis techniques used to identify patterns of abnormal behaviour and share threats between infrastructures is discussed.

Specifically, in this paper, the simulation of 8 interdepend critical infrastructures is presented. The simulation is established using a professional plant simulator: Siemens Tecnomatix. Using this simulation, realistic data is constructed through its operation. The data is subsequently used to further our investigation into a support framework for distributed and interconnected systems.

The remainder of the paper is planned as follows: Sect. 2, presents a background on critical infrastructures, interdependency, CI modelling and highlights the important of the simulation. Section 3 introduces the simulation design and development. Section 4 provides an overview of the system implementation. Subsequently, Sect. 5 contains the evaluation of the system. The paper is concluded in Sect. 6.

2 Background

In this section, a discussion on critical infrastructure growth and interdependency characteristics is put forward. The focus is on the interdependency connection between the critical infrastructures and a number of modelling examples are discussed.

2.1 Critical Infrastructures and Interdependency

Infrastructure is the main source of development and economic construction process of any country, and different types of urban development depend on the size and the provision of infrastructure elements, which help guide the development of new areas. Infrastructure constitutes a raw head of the development process and economic construction, different types of urban development depends on the size and the provision of infrastructure elements of style, which contributes to guiding the development of new areas. Critical infrastructures have an important influence in an urban environment. However, many infrastructures, such as power plants, are considerably outdated and are difficult to repair [5].

The National Institute of Standards and Technology define critical infrastructures in the Executive Order EO as any physical or virtual systems and assets that would affect the nation security, public economy and health service by their failure or damage occurred to them [5].

Critical infrastructure assets are also explained by Command and Leavenworth [6] and can be divided into three categories. First, the physical assets, which could be tangible or intangible. Secondly, human assets, that can represent vulnerabilities by having privileged access to important information or systems. Third, cyber assets, which include hardware, software, data, and which all, serve the network functionality.

Critical infrastructure security attracts the attention of various research fields. Yusufovna *et al.*, indicate this area, such as energy resources, finance, food, health, government services, manufacturing, law and legislation, transportation [7]. In addition,

Baud and Bellot, include additional areas such as water, information and telecoms, chemical, industry, agriculture, postal and shipping, and the defence industry [8].

Many infrastructure systems facilitate in Europe operate as local networks [8], similarly to isolated islands due to their age. Due to this, there has been an imaginary barrier isolates each infrastructure than other.

However, in the result of the global expansion and with the Internet revolution, infrastructures have become highly complex and have increased the interdependency at the physical and network layers. Therefore, the interdependency is considered to be one characteristic that can raise several concerns; in particular the analysis and modelling of interdependencies due to the complicated interactions [9, 10].

A number of factors contribute to make the interdependency more complex. For example, time scales, geographic scales, cascading and higher order effects, social/psychological elements, operational procedures business policies, restoration and recovery procedures, government regulatory, legal, policy regimes and finally stakeholder concerns [9]. These aspects can have a very negative impact on the system so services need to be secured against any type of attack and mitigation plans should be in place to counter the effects of other disasters. In order to achieve this, security planning must anticipate on a large-scale.

2.2   Critical Infrastructure Modelling

The role of one infrastructure influences the functioning of others, which can be referred to as interdependency.

Currently, there are some simulation programs which contain smart, built-in models for many common real systems. These programs help to analyse the inputs and outputs and do all the 'hard' work required and give good and comprehensive results. In addition, carries out simulations of complex models in record times compared to programs developed.

Research in this area ordinarily would require the purchase of critical infrastructure hardware, which is extremely expensive and impractical. This has led to the development of specific software-based simulators such as Tecnomatix [11], and the adaptation of existing software-based simulators such as OMNET++, Simulink and Matlab [12]. These software simulators allow for affordable representations of critical infrastructure systems, by modelling their behaviour, interactions and the integration of their specific protocols (e.g. MODBUS).

The interest in simulation has increased as an appropriate and effective education process in a recent year. Simulation has become a process of concepts, activities, experiments done through the computer, and have become an important and prominent role in the educational process [13]. Al-essa defines simulation as a method for teaching students that bring elements from the real world, overriding difficulties such as material cost or human resources [14].

Simulation influences other areas of science, such as computer science. Smith, discuss a number of simulation advantages [15], which can be highlighted as followed:

1. Simulation has an important role in the study and implementation of experiments to complex and different dilemmas
2. Simulation method helps to observe changes in the formulation of the dilemma
3. Their use helps with the study of the system and identify clear results
4. Simulation can help in the training of specialists and students on the foundations required in the scientific analyses
5. Individuals are able to gain experience for those working in the field of simulation of any system
6. Information and conclusions for future positions can be ascertained
7. Simulation can be used to pre-test systems before applying them into the real-world
8. Save money by manufacturing test and predicted the quality of the product.
9. To predict the behaviour of the product in rare circumstances.

2.3   Simulation Types

Simulation can be divided into four types as Al-esaa *et al.*, present [15]:

- Simulation Physical - This type of simulation uses the physical material, such as leadership of the aircraft.
- Procedural Simulation - This type of simulation designed to learn a series of acts or steps, such as training on the steps to run a machine or device, or diagnosis of certain diseases in medicine.
- Situational Simulation - This type differs from a procedural simulation where the learner a key role in the scenario that presents not just learns the rules and strategies as in the previous species. The role of the learner to discover the positions of appropriate responses by repeating the simulation
- Process Simulation - This type of simulation learner it does not result in any role in the simulation it is an external observer and experimenter, at a time when the learner cannot watch the movement of electrons or the speed of light, it can watch it in the simulation process by making it easier to grasp such concepts. For example [16] as an example of a system that observes the behaviour of Critical Infra-structures.

In order to simplify the simulation system types, Smith divided the simulation types into two main categories [15]; either an educational simulation through a hands-on experience or through a visual demonstration by watching someone else. In the following section, the development of our simulation environment is presented. The critical infrastructure models can be used for collecting realistic data. In turn, the data can be used to develop new approaches to security.

Depending on the previous simulation type's the number of research that has used one of the simulation type to simplify their models, can be found in [17].

3   Simulation and Approach

In our research to date, a system framework, which is able to identify threats to a network and communicate the potential impact, has been forward [2].

The system monitors the operations of an infrastructure and identifies any abnormalities which occur in its operation. This will be done through the development of an inference model of correct behaviour. The system assists and guides critical infrastructures on how to behave when abnormal behaviour is detected. This information is then shared to other infrastructures; drawing from the concept of the human immune system characteristic. Information related to abnormal behaviours is sent throughout the distributed systems in order to prevent cyber-attacks from having a cascading impact.

In order to test this approach; a significant amount of data is required from multiple critical infrastructures. For that reason, a simulated system of systems is essential to provide the data needed for testing.

3.1 Purpose

In order to develop the simulation environment, the first stage involves designing the purpose of the emulation and planning out its aim. The goal is to develop a simulation which can be used to provide realistic data about the behaviour of 8 interconnected critical infrastructures.

Using this approach enables the collection of data from individual infrastructures, as individual systems, as well as from the system as a whole which is a system of systems. Within the simulation, failures can be introduced which disrupt the service provision but there is no single point of failure which can crash the simulation as a whole.

3.2 Design and Process

Figure 1 present the 8 critical infrastructures, which can be presented as follows:

1. Electricity Grid
2. Water Distribution
3. Factory
4. Nuclear Power Station
5. Coal Power System
6. Hydroelectricity System
7. Sewage System
8. The compound of Houses.

Each of the critical infrastructure systems was given a graphical icon to represent its function more clearly. They can be opened up to show the different objects which allow the system to function and be interconnected.

The process flow of the simulation is displayed in Fig. 2, which displays a high-level view of the various simulation processes involved. The process flow identifies the steps which the simulation goes through to generate data.

In the following section, the implementation stage is presented along with a detailed account of the various components which form part of the simulation.

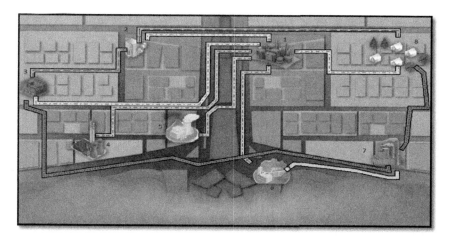

Fig. 1. Simulation overview

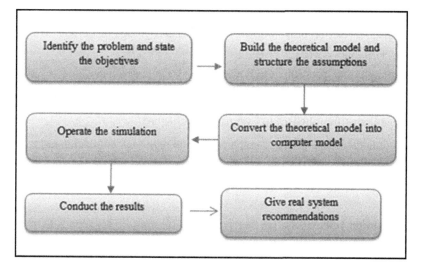

Fig. 2. Process flow

4 Implementation

The simulation is based on object-oriented modelling, where each component inserted is an individual object. Each can be adjusted and used to construct data. In order to simulate the design, objects are created and inserted for each of the components, which together form the simulation environment. Figure 3 displays the expanded view of the housing, one of the 8 infrastructures, also seen at high level in Fig. 1. The housing compound is an end-user of the services provided by the other infrastructure in the system.

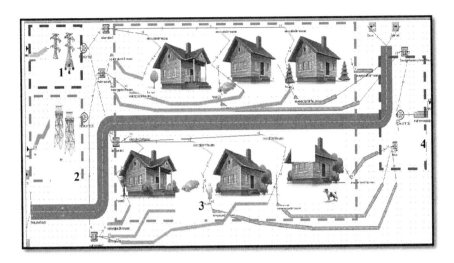

Fig. 3. Simulated compound infrastructure

The diagram can be broken down into four main groups of objects. The groups include supply lines from other infrastructures, for example:

1. Electricity power plant input to houses
2. Water Distribution System inputs to houses
3. Housing compound
4. Sewage drains from houses to external infrastructure.

Each of the mechanisms has a graphical icon to represent its function more clearly. The simulated plant consisted of 147 components in total, including connections and interfaces.

4.1   Individual Infrastructures

The following, Figs. 4 and 5, display the Water Distribution System and the Electricity Power Plant (which form part of the individual groupings in Fig. 1). The Water Distribution System (referred to as grouping 2 in Figs. 1 and 3) is displayed in Fig. 4. It consists of a main water resource, the sea, a main electricity cable from the power plant and a transport system to send the water through pipes and feed both the houses in the compound and a factory. The Water Distribution System is controlled by a FlowControl to pump the water for both the Houses and the Factory, divided equally.

Figure 5 displays the inside of the Electricity Power Plant (group 1 in both Figs. 1 and 3), which combines three different critical electricity sources from the hydro-electricity system, the nuclear power and coal power system. It also feeds three critical infrastructures through a FlowControl object, including houses, factory and water distribution system.

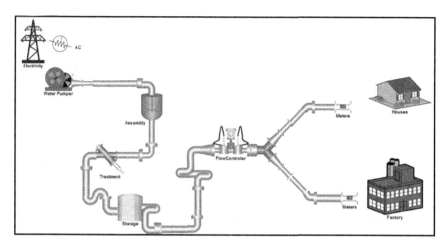

Fig. 4. Water Distribution System

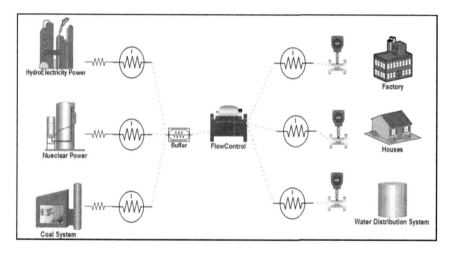

Fig. 5. Electricity Grid

4.2   Data Construction

Within the simulation, each of the components has a random failure implemented. This was done to make the system behave differently each time it runs and to account for faults, which occur in real-life critical infrastructures. Random failures are implementing an Availability Percentage. The Availability Percentage refers to the chances of a machine or components being ready to use at any given time taking into account failures and blockages, which is calculated using the formula:

$$Availability = MTBF/(MTBF + MTTR) \qquad (1)$$

Where MTTR is the Mean Time To Repair and MTBF is the Mean Time Between Failures. In the following subsection, an example of abnormal behaviour, which could occur in the Water Distribution System and the Electricity Power Plant, is highlighted. The behaviour changes should affect the houses compound.

4.3 Data Collection

In order to achieve the aim of this research, two critical infrastructures were selected from the simulation and had a fault introduced into their mechanisms. The fault is a representation of a cyber-attack taking place. The aim is to identify how the attack changes the service of the houses for electricity and water.

Specifically, a fault in both the water Pipe 1 and the water pipe connected to the houses compound inside the water distributed critical infrastructure are selected to perform a cyber-attack on. While a fault in the electricity hydroelectricity cable and the electricity cable to houses inside the electricity system are selected as targets. Both were selected as they are key components within each infrastructure and would represent realistic targets for attackers.

The Water Distribution Infrastructure and the Electricity Grid are comprised of 10 and 7 components consequently. Both normal operational data and abnormal data are collected from the simulation. Normal data refers to the system when not under attack. Data collection is conducted with a sampling rate of 4 Hz (which is every 0.25 of a second) for two days. This resulted in 619200 rows of both normal and abnormal raw data. From the datasets, records of data were constructed by selecting features from the datasets at 5-min intervals. This resulted in 572 records of data.

In the following section, we demonstrate a data classification technique for identifying behaviour changes and discuss how the results can be used to construct behavioural models for threat communication in a system of systems.

5 Evaluation and Data Analysis

The process involves in detecting abnormal behaviour for sharing with other infrastructures. 1,144 records of data are used for the classification process consisting of 572 normal and 572 abnormal behaviour records. The records of data are comprised of 4 features that have form 80 features for the electricity system and 94 features for the water system. The feature vectors in this paper are generated using four features, which are: Mean, peak frequency, Lower frequency, Standard Divisions and the Mode. The literature reports that Mean frequency and sample provides an ideal representation of the system behaviour. Since the standard deviation is a valid measure that indicates the distance value from the mean. Both the mean and the standard division have been selected as features in order to give an accurate comparison in generating the classifiers.

Table 1. Classification results for the Electricity Grid

Classifiers	AUC%	Sensitivity	Specificity
LDC	76.57	0.68	0.99
UDC	79.37	0.70	0.99
QDC	61.18	0.56	0.98
SVC	64.51	0.58	1.00
ParzenC	64.51	0.58	1.00
NaivebC	81.11	0.72	0.99
PolyC	76.57	0.68	0.99

Table 2. Classification results for the Water Distribution System

Classifiers	AUC%	Sensitivity	Specificity
LDC	77.62	0.77	0.78
UDC	57.51	0.54	1.00
QDC	57.51	0.54	1.00
SVC	61.36	0.68	0.58
ParzenC	61.36	0.68	0.58
NaivebC	61.36	0.68	0.58
PolyC	77.79	0.77	0.78

5.1   Results

Using the following techniques to detect behaviour changes, patterns of behaviour can be developed and communicated to other infrastructures for mitigation and remediation planning. For this approach machine learning classifiers are used to detect normal and abnormal behaviour in both water and electricity systems. The results are presented in Tables 1 and 2. The tables present the result of the classification process, which involved using 7 well-known machine learning algorithms, which will be illustrated in the next subsection.

5.2   Classifiers

The paper involve number of classification techniques, Fergus *et al.* have defined it and clarify their usage as follow [18]: the linear discriminant classifier (LDC), quadratic discriminant classifier (QDC), uncorrelated normal density based classifier (UDC), polynomial classifier (POLYC), parzen classifier (PARZENC) and the support vector classifier (SVC). LDC, QDC and UDC are density based classifiers. LDC will generate discriminant functions for not normally distributed. While QDC assumed that the dataset following a normal distribution function. UDC work parallel as QDC but computation of a quadratic classifier, between the classes in the dataset, is done by assuming normal densities with uncorrelated features.

The POLYC used untrained classifier with the dataset and adds polynomial features. PARZENC is considered a non-linear classifier that use training dataset and their parameters when building the classifier. The SVC support vector networks. It is highly used in industry with a non-label dataset or few label in order to point decide which class a new data point will be in. NaivebC is a simple constructing classifier. It considers each of the contributed features independently to the probability [19].

Behaviour changes as a result of a fault in the Water Distribution System, are best observed by the Naivebc classifier which achieves 81 % AUC classification. Whereas the behavioural changes in the Electricity Grid were best observed using the PolyC classifier. In addition, the Sensitivity and Specificity detection rates are also higher than other classifiers in both Naivebc and PolyC. This refers to the detection of normal and abnormal behaviours respectively.

Using the above techniques to detect behaviour changes, it is clear that the selected classifiers can be used to identify abnormal behaviours in multiple critical infrastructure types. Moreover, the sensitivity and specificity results were successful in detecting the normal behaviour. The next section considers the implications of the findings and highlights how, in our future work, we will use this approach to set up a support network to mitigate critical infrastructure cascading failure.

5.3   Discussion

The results support that we could take advantage of assessing system behaviour to create a critical infrastructure support network. The aim is to alert other associated infrastructure of impending or detected attacks which could cause.

Initially, LDC, QDC and UDC performed less effectively than Naivebc and PolyC. The evaluation presented in this chapter demonstrates how normal behaviour can be identified in a system using data classification techniques. That was presented by the two cases: the abnormal behaviour in the Water Distribution System and the Electricity Grid and how it affects the houses compound.

Our simulator and classifiers seem to be the best fit to simulate the AIS in the CI. However, different experimental procedures would be required in order to verify the research main idea and support it. That could be made by including the rest of the Critical Infrastructures components in our main simulation plant. Moreover, the abnormal behaviours might be studied in depth toward the rest of the other Critical Infrastructures to compare the accuracy between the different CI's, which help to understand the CI interdependency.

Basing on the immune system characteristic, developing a distributed database, which can be a used as a backup for each CI, would help in building a pattern of the abnormal signal be treated as a pool of abnormal signals that will increase the level of security. Moreover, depending on the network connectivity between the CIs, the system would then start to share the new abnormal behaviour with interconnected partners. This would help other CI plan for an emerging attack of cascading impact. At all times, an administrator overviews the system functions.

6 Conclusion

Critical infrastructure interconnectivity is one the main challenges when countering the growing cyber-threat. As such, the development of a critical infrastructure simulation is presented in this paper. The simulation can be used to create substantial datasets. Using the data constructed through simulation, an approach for sharing cyber-attack information with other infrastructures, is offered. Using NaivebC and PolyC, two data classification techniques, we achieved high accuracy in the detection of abnormal behaviours for the case study. The abnormal behaviours represent cyber-attacks on a critical infrastructure. This information is then shared to other infrastructures to act as a warning for the prevention of the attack on interconnected infrastructures.

References

1. Laugé, A., Hernantes, J., Sarriegi, J.M.: The role of critical infrastructures' interdependencies on the impacts caused by natural disasters. In: Luiijf, E., Hartel, P. (eds.) CRITIS 2013. LNCS, vol. 8328, pp. 50–61. Springer, Heidelberg (2013)
2. E. Commission: Digital agenda: cyber-security experts test defences in first pan-European simulation. European Commission Press Release, November 2010
3. Davis, C.M., Tate, J.E., Okhravi, H., Grier, C., Overbye, T.J., Nicol, D.: SCADA cyber security testbed development. In: 2006 38th Annual North American Power Symposium, NAPS-2006 Proceedings, pp. 483–488 (2006)
4. Badri, S., Fergus, P., Hurst, W., Street, B.: Critical infrastructure automated immuno-response system (CIAIRS). In: 3rd International Conference, Malta (2016)
5. National Institute of Standards and Technology: Framework for improving critical infrastructure cybersecurity. Natl. Inst. Stand. Technol. 1, 1–41 (2014)
6. Command, D., Leavenworth, F.: Critical infrastructure threats and terrorism. In: DCSINT Handbook No. 1.02, 1st edn., no. 1, Distribution Unlimited (2006)
7. Yusufovna, F.S., Alisherovich, F.A., Choi, M., Cho, E., Abdurashidovich, F.T., Kim, T.: Research on critical infrastructures and critical information infrastructures. In: 2009 Symposium on Bio-inspired Learning and Intelligent Systems for Security, pp. 97–101 (2009)
8. Baud, L., Bellot, P.: Securing a critical infrastructure. In 2010 IEEE RIVF International Conference on Computing and Communication Technologies, Research, Innovation, and Vision for the Future (RIVF), pp. 1–4 (2010)
9. Rinaldi, S.M.: Modeling and simulating critical infrastructures and their interdependencies. In: Proceedings of the 37th Annual Hawaii International Conference on System Sciences, 2004, vol. 00, no. C, pp. 1–8 (2004)
10. Rinaldi, B.S.M., Peerenboom, J.P., Kelly, T.K.: Identifying, understanding, and analyzing: critical infrastructure interdependecies. IEEE Control Syst. 21(6), 11–25 (2001)
11. Siemens (2011). www.siemens.com/tecnomatix
12. Lewandowski, C.M., Co-investigator, N., Lewandowski, C.M.: Manufacturing Simulation with Plant Simulation and SimTalk, vol. 1. Springer, Heidelberg (2015)
13. Asteteh, D., Sarhan, O.: Education and e-Learning Technology. Darwael, Jorden (2007)
14. Al-esaa, A.: The effect of using simulation implementing strategy through computer teaching assistant in the immediate and delayed achievement, Jorden (1993)

15. Smith, R.: Simulation: the engine behind the virtual world. Smulation 2000 Ser., vol. 1, pp. 1–24 (1999)
16. Hurst, W., Merabti, M., Fergus, P.: Behavioural observation for critical infra-structure support. In: 13th Annual Postgraduate Symposium on the Convergence of Tele-communications, Networking and Broadcasting (2012)
17. Idowu, I.O., Fergus, P., Hussain, A., Dobbins, C., Al-Askar, H.: Advance artificial neural network classification techniques using EHG for detecting preterm births. In: 2014 Eighth International Conference on Complex, Intelligent and Software Intensive Systems, pp. 95–100 (2014)
18. Fergus, P., Cheung, P., Hussain, A., Al-Jumeily, D., Dobbins, C., Iram, S.: Prediction of preterm deliveries from EHG signals using machine learning. PLoS ONE **8**(10), e77154 (2013)
19. Lotte, F.: Study of electroencephalographic signal processing and classification techniques towards the use of brain-computer interfaces in virtual reality applications (2008)

Workshop on Intelligent Data Analytics and Visualization

Visually Exploring Differences of DTI Fiber Models

Honghui Mei[1], Haidong Chen[1], Fangzhou Guo[1], Fan Zhang[2], Wei Chen[1(✉)], Zhang Song[3], and Guizhen Wang[1]

[1] State Key Lab of CAD&CG, Zhejiang University, Hangzhou, China
meihonghui.zju@gmail.com, chenhd925@gmail.com, guofz1234@gmail.com,
wguizhen@gmail.com, chenwei@cad.zju.edu.cn
[2] Zhejiang University of Technology, Hangzhou, China
fanzhang@cad.zju.edu.cn
[3] Computer Science and Engineering, Mississippi State University, Starkville, USA
szhang@cse.msstate.edu

Abstract. Fiber tracking of Diffusion Tensor Imaging (DTI) datasets is a non-invasive tool to study the underlying fibrous structures in living tissues. However, DTI fibers may vary from subject to subject due to variations in anatomy, motions in scanning, and signal noise. In addition, fiber tracking parameters have a great influence on tracking results. Subtle changes of parameters can produce significantly different DTI fibers. Interactive exploration and analysis of differences among DTI fiber models are critical for the purposes of group comparison, atlas construction, and uncertainty analysis. Conventional approaches illustrate differences in the 3D space with either voxel-wise or fiber-based comparisons. Unfortunately, these approaches require an accurate alignment process and might give rise to visual clutter. This paper introduces a two-phase projection technique to reformulate a complex 3D fiber model as a unique 2D map for feature characterization and comparative analysis. To facilitate investigation, regions of significant differences among the 2D maps are further identified. Using these maps, differences that are difficult to be distinguished in the 3D space due to depth occlusion can be easily discovered. We design a visual exploration interface to study differences from multiple perspectives. We evaluate the effectiveness of our approach by examining two datasets.

Keywords: Diffusion tensor imaging · Fiber tracking · Difference visualization · Visual exploration

1 Introduction

Diffusion Tensor Imaging (DTI) [2] is a non-invasive *in vivo* magnetic resonance imaging technique that measures the diffusion of water in biological tissues. In tissues containing fibrous structures, the diffusion is faster along the fibers [14]. By fitting the distribution with a Gaussian model, a DTI tensor volume can

© Springer International Publishing Switzerland 2016
A. El Rhalibi et al. (Eds.): Edutainment 2016, LNCS 9654, pp. 333–344, 2016.
DOI: 10.1007/978-3-319-40259-8_29

be reconstructed from the raw Diffusion Weighted Imaging (DWI) volumes [24]. Tracing paths through the entire tensor volume produces a collection of DTI fibers. This process is known as fiber tractography or fiber tracking [1], which has been proven to be a useful technique for analyzing anatomical connectivity.

In spite of its potential, DTI remains limited in applications. Uncertainty is a major reason. DTI fibers vary from subject to subject due to variations in anatomy, and from scan to scan because of different subject positions, scanning motions and noises [14]. They are also sensitive to various parameters in tractography such as the integration step size and stopping criteria [3].

To comparatively visualizing and analyzing different DTI datasets, one of the major task is to represent and visualize differences within a collection of DTI datasets. Direct comparison of 3D DWI or DTI volumes [18,28] demands an accurate alignment process and misses the anatomical connectivity within each volume. Explicit depiction of the geometrical differences among DTI fiber models in the 3D space [3,7] is hindered by the spatial complexity of dense fibers. Comparison by using statistical tractography metrics [6] lacks the ability to locate regions of differences.

Projection techniques have been widely used to provide a holistic view of the overall structures and distributional patterns. Recent work extends this scheme into the exploration of DTI fiber models [4,25]. However, these solutions are well designed to explore the content of only a single fiber model. The main reason is that different fiber models do not share a common space for projection and comparison.

In this paper, we present a comparative visualization approach that supports quick identification and intuitive exploration of differences among DTI fiber models. After all datasets are registered into a common coordinate space, fiber models are embedded on a 2D visual plane by means of a two-phase projection technique. The embedding of a fiber model constructs a 2D scatterplot which are further represented as a continuous density map and a contoured density map. To provide an overview of the major differences among these maps, regions of differences (RoDs) are computed with a simple flood fill algorithm. Both *Juxtaposition* and *Explicit Encoding* are utilized within the visual exploration interface. We have verified the effectiveness of our approach on several DTI datasets.

In summary, the contributions of this paper are:

- A novel low-dimensional representation of complex fiber models for visual comparison and further regions of differences identification;
- An integrated visualization interface that provides users an intuitive way to explore differences in multiple perspectives.

The remaining parts are organized as follows. Related work are summarized in Sect. 2. Our approach is elaborated in Sect. 3. The visual exploration interface is described in Sect. 4. The results of our approach are discussed in Sect. 5. Finally, we conclude this paper in Sect. 6.

2   Related Work

Our work is related to several topics of visualization research including comparative visualization, uncertainty visualization, and DTI fiber model exploration.

2.1   Comparative Visualization

Recently, a wide variety of approaches have been developed in the field of comparative visualization. Gleicher et al. [12] summarized visual designs for comparisons into three categories: *Juxtaposition, Superposition,* and *Explicit Encoding.* Verma and Pang [29] proposed several solutions for comparative flow visualization at image level, data level, and feature level. Malik et al. [20] introduced a novel multi-view design for comparing and visualizing gray values and edges of several 3D CT datasets simultaneously. Schmidt et al. [26] proposed an approach for comparative visualization of multiple images. Their technique overcomes the scalability issues pertaining to the number of objects for comparison, and allows users to perform detailed cluster analysis in the regions of significant differences. Oelke et al. [22] designed a glyph representation called topic coins to encode information necessary for comparative document analysis.

In the field of DTI study, comparison is an important means to locate changes related to development, degeneration, and disease. One pioneering work [7] compares the generated fibers in the 3D space and uses saturation to indicate the magnitude of differences between corresponding points. This method is simple and intuitive, but only focuses on fiber structures and may result in visual clutter. In order to investigate the diffusion properties along fibers, group statistical analysis [5,13] is performed after aligning datasets and representing fibers with continuous functions. The key idea behind this method is that fibers are represented with a simplified form (like B-spline) to facilitate statistical comparison.

To study the diffusion property volumes such as the Fractional Anisotropy (FA) for multiple subjects, Smith et al. [28] presented Tract-Based Spatical Statistics (TBSS), which is a voxel wise analysis framework via a nonlinear registration followed by projection onto a skeleton. In addition to the study on DTI volumes, there has been some work on general-purpose group analysis of geometrical or volumetric datasets. For instance, Elvins and Jain [10] proposed to use a density histogram to describe a volume dataset. Though simple, it provides very low discrimination power. Other different feature descriptors have been proposed to accomplish similarity assessment, including transformational [11], topological [15], and statistical [23] signatures. Different from these methods, our approach generates a unique 2D signature map of a 3D fiber model for further comparison and exploration.

2.2   DTI Fiber Model Exploration

Exploring and manipulating a DTI fiber model in the 3D space pose many challenges, especially on providing intuitive interaction. Embedding the fibers into a 2D space with projection techniques has been demonstrated to be an effective means to study fiber models. Chen et al. [4] designed a novel interface by utilizing the multidimensional scaling (MDS) technique to facilitate quick and accurate 3D fiber selection on a 2D plane. Similarly, Jianu et al. [17] introduced a visual exploration paradigm by embedding 3D fibers on a 2D plane to reduce navigation efforts. Poco et al. [25] exploited the *Local Affine Multidimensional Projection (LAMP)* [19] technique to support fast visual exploration of large collection of DTI fibers. Demiralp et al. [9] presented a 2D path representations with a planar projection technique for studying fiber dataset. A web interface was also designed to support exploration. In general, the 2D visual representation captures the structures and patterns of the source dataset and is free of occlusion during interaction and exploration. However, most of these approaches focus on single fiber model exploration. This paper advances a computation-efficient two-phase projection technique to compare multiple fiber models.

3   Our Approach

Fig. 1 shows a schematic overview of our approach. In general, our approach consists of three main components. The preprocessing component registers all DTI volumes into a common space and reconstructs a 2nd order tensor in each voxel based on the Gaussian diffusion model. Fibers are then extracted according to the user-defined tracking parameters. Instead of direct comparing fiber models in the 3D space, we employ a two-phase projection technique followed by the density estimation to reformulate each fiber model as a 2D signature map. As a key benefit, these maps allow for intuitive recognition and quick comparison. A number of views and interactions are provided to discover and study differences among fiber models.

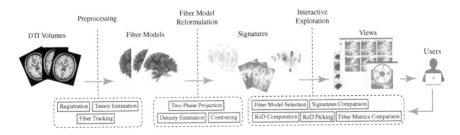

Fig. 1. An overview of our difference computation, visualization, and exploration pipeline for DTI fiber models.

3.1   Preprocessing

For accurate comparison, the alignment of all DTI volume datasets to a target is required. In our approach, FLIRT [16] is employed to perform a rigid registration.

After registration, a diffusion tensor field can be reconstructed of a DTI dataset. By tracing paths with numerical integration methods such as the second-order Runge-Kutta (RK2), a fiber model that captures the connectivity information of a DTI dataset is produced.

3.2   Fiber Model Reformulation

Let $\Gamma = F_1 \cup F_2 \cup ... \cup F_N$ be a fiber corpus consisting of N fiber models, and fiber model $F_i = \{f_i^j, j = 1, 2, ..., N_i\}$ has N_i fibers, where f_i^j denotes a fiber. To represent the variations among different fiber models, our approach generates a unique signature map S_i for each fiber model F_i.

Directly representing each fiber model F_i in the 3D space may cause visual clutter. Projection techniques [4,25] that focus on building a 2D visual representation for a fiber model can alleviate this issue. Before projection, all fibers must be reparameterized to make sure that they have the same number of vertices and orientations in order to calculate similarity measure used in LAMP technique [19,25].

To embed fibers on the visual plane, our approach employs the *Landmark MDS (LMDS)* technique [8] which performs a two-phase projection. A subset of fibers $\Gamma_{landmark} \subset \Gamma$ are selected from the fiber corpus as *landmark fibers*. Using these fibers as landmarks, LMDS can project each fibers $r \in \Gamma$ to its 2D location l_r on the visual plane. Throughout this paper, the longer mean of thresholded closest distance [30] is used to measure the dissimilarity between fibers:

$$d(p, q, t) = max(d_t(p, q, t), d_t(q, p, t)), \tag{1}$$

where $d_t(p, q, t) = mean_{u \in p, (min_{v \in q}\|u-v\|>t)} min_{v \in q} \parallel u-v \parallel$, u and v are vertices of fiber p and q respectively. The minimum threshold t is set to $0.5\,mm$ as suggested by [30].

Compared with other methods, this projection scheme reduces the computational complexity of dissimilarity estimation from $O(n^2)$ to $O(m^2 + m \times n)$. $m = |\Gamma_{landmark}|$ is the number of landmark fibers. $n = |\Gamma|$ is the number of fibers in the fiber corpus. Empirically, m is set to $\sqrt{n}$ in our implementation. One additional benefit of this scheme is its intrinsic parallelizability, because each fiber is embedded independently from each other using a fixed linear transformation.

In our implementation, we randomly selected 100 landmark fibers as random selection produces similar results to those use optimized selection methods provided in [8].

Density Estimation. The embedding of each fiber model F_i yields a 2D scatterplot (see Fig. 5 second row). Similar fibers are positioned close to each other in this scatterplot. To facilitate recognition and visualization, we further apply the kernel density estimation (KDE) to the scatterplot to produce a continuous 2D density map D_i (see Fig. 5 third row). A Gaussian kernel is used in our approach with the bandwidth h determined by the Silverman's rule of thumb [27] and can be modified by the user.

By dividing the range of the computed density into multiple intervals and coloring the elements within each interval, another contour-like map (see Fig. 5 fourth row) is generated. The contoured density map suppresses many undesired details for a quick comparison.

Consequently, each fiber model uniquely determines a signature map S_i: a discrete scatterplot associated with a continuous density map and a contoured density map.

3.3   Region of Difference Estimation

The *Juxtaposition* design that displays visualizations side by side in multiple views is a common way to explore differences and similarities among multiple datasets. However, it requires a large amount of mental workload to identify the differences. Inspired by [26], we employ an explicit difference encoding to assist users in identifying regions of differences (RoDs).

Specifically, the density variance $V(x)$ at each location x is computed as:

$$V(x) = \frac{1}{N} \sum_{i=1}^{N} (D_i(x) - \mu(x))^2, \tag{2}$$

where $\mu(x)$ is the average density at location x. In our implementation, we compute the density variance for each pixel of the densities generated by KDE. Then, a user-adjustable threshold is used to filter out pixels of low density variations. At last, the region growing algorithm [26] is employed to group disjoint pixels into regions. The resultant RoDs provide an overview of differences residing in the shown signatures. Users can flexibly pick a RoD to further explore the statistical differences of fibers embedded into this region.

As RoDs are generated from the results of density estimation, they are affected by the bandwidth h of the kernel function. When bandwidth increased, number of RoDs will be reduced and adjacent RoDs tend to merge together.

4   Visual Exploration Interface

The fiber models, the generated signatures, and the computed RoDs can be interactively explored in our integrated interface composed of a set of linked views. Figure 2 illustrates an overview of this interface.

Fiber Model List View. Each fiber model is represented as a rectangular glyph. Basic information and a snapshot are embedded (see Fig. 2(a)). The fiber models of interest can be dragged to the signature view for further exploration and comparison.

Signature View. Users can compare the signatures in the signature view to discover differences and similarities among fiber models. The signature view employs a juxtapositional design which shows the selected fiber models' signatures in a side-by-side fashion. Users can remove a signature from this view. In addition, following interactions are supported:

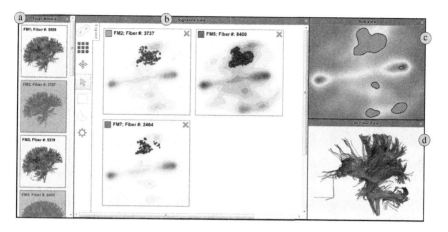

Fig. 2. The main views of our visual exploration interface. (a) The fiber model list view. (b) The signature view. (c) The RoD view. (d) The 3D fiber view.

Switching. Users can choose different forms of signatures (including the discrete scatterplot, the continuous density map, and the contoured density map) to be displayed.

Dragging. To facilitate comparison, signatures of interest can be dragged close to each other.

Selection. The *box* selection and *lasso* selection are provided to specify a region of interest. Linked selection simultaneously specify identical regions on different signatures. The selected fibers are shown in the 3D fiber view.

RoD View. As described above, the signature view shows the details of the selected fiber models' signatures. The identified RoDs are rendered as polygons overlaid on the average density map (see Fig. 2(c)). The Focus+Context interaction is implemented to inspect each individual RoD. Once users pick a RoD, a *DiffRadar* diagram will be displayed around. The *DiffRadar* diagram shows the detailed statistical variations of the selected fibers.

Figure 3 illustrates the design of our *DiffRadar* diagram. The radial layout is leveraged where each quantitative fiber metric corresponds to one of the equiangular axes. Five widely used fiber metrics are computed for those fibers embedded into the selected RoD: number of fibers (NF), total length (TL), average total length (ATL), total FA weighted length (TWL), and average FA weighted length (ATWL). Please refer to [5] for the computation details. The picked RoD is shown in the center of this diagram. The metrics of a fiber model are connected with polylines. To differentiate fiber models, a categorical color set is used.

3D Fiber View. As the axes in signatures do not have intrinsic meanings, linked views and interactions are demanded. Fibers selected from either the signature view or the RoD view are visualized as illuminated lines [21] in the 3D space. Users can easily understand and verify the findings in this view.

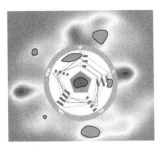

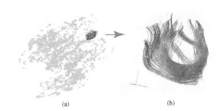

Fig. 3. An example *DiffRadar* diagram. The average density map is displayed at background as a context. RoDs are shown as polygons.

Fig. 4. Linked exploration: selected fibers in the signature view (a) are immediately rendered as illuminated lines in the 3D fiber view (b).

5   Results and Discussions

We implemented our approach based on a set of toolkits and libraries. The pre-processing is accomplished using a free software library FSL. Typically several minutes are needed to pre-compute a fiber model on our experimental platform. The algorithms (Sect. 3.2) are implemented with the standard C++. Computing dissimilarities between fibers are further accelerated with CUDA 5.5. The visualization interface is developed based on Qt 5.1. The rendering of DTI fibers utilized a GPU-accelerated illuminated line algorithm [21].

5.1   Fiber Model Characterization

We tested our approach on a set of 78 DTI data. Some of the subjects were scanned multiple times in the data.

The signatures generated with our approach characterize the overall structures and distributional patterns of each fiber model. The scatterplot reveals the similarities among fibers. Similar fibers are positioned close to each other. It is thus natural to perform feature exploration by studying the shape, layout, and distribution in this map. Users can select a region of interest and inspect the selected fibers in the 3D space (see Fig. 4).

Figure 5 shows the signatures of three healthy subjects **FM1**, **FM2**, and **FM3**. Generally, all of them present similar low-dimensional patterns. We can further inspect the detailed differences among them in the RoD view as shown in Fig. 6. From the *DiffRadar* diagram for RoD **R1** in Fig. 6(a), we find that subject **FM1** has much lower values in terms of quantitative metrics NF, TL, and TWL. However, as shown in Fig. 6(b) for RoD **R2**, subject **FM1** has slightly higher values in terms of these quantitative metrics compared to subject **FM2** and **FM3**. Anatomical variations mainly contribute to these differences.

5.2   DTI Tracking Parameter Study

This experiment intends to investigate whether the integration step size has a great influence on the tracking results. For this purpose, we generate several

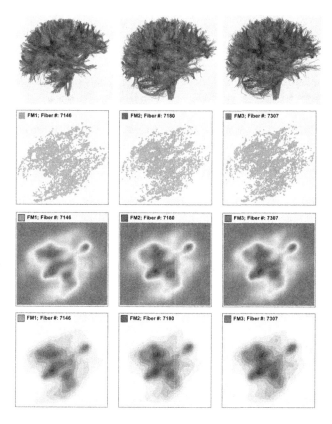

Fig. 5. Results for three fiber models selected from the atlas dataset. From top to bottom: the 3D fiber models, the 2D embedding, the continuous density maps, and the contoured density maps.

fiber models from a single DWI image with varied integration step size. Some of them have same integration step but few differences are caused by jittering of seeding locations. We selected six signatures which corresponding integration steps are 0.75, 0.75, 0.58, 0.58, 0.58 and 0.58.

The computed RoDs in Fig. 7(a) explicitly show the major differences among them. This indicate that the integration step size has a strong effect on the tracking results. That is because the step size determines how long a fiber can move forward and backward in the path tracing process. We also compute the RoDs for the last four signatures (see Fig. 7(b)). It can be easily verified that fewer RoDs are identified compared with Fig. 7(a), because there are smaller variations among the last four signatures.

5.3   Discussions and Future Work

Our approach shows promising effectiveness in displaying differences among fiber models. It can be regarded as an adaption of the low-dimensional projection

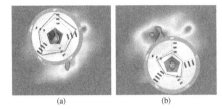

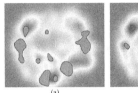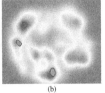

Fig. 6. The *DiffRadar* diagrams for two RoDs: **R1** and **R2**. The variation of **R1** is higher than that of **R2**.

Fig. 7. (a) The RoDs for six signatures. (b) The RoDs for the last four signatures. The same threshold is used.

scheme proposed in [4,17,25] to multiple datasets comparisons. Our projection scheme uses the same set of *landmark fibers* to build low-dimensional representations for fiber models. The low-dimensional embedding of the *landmark fibers* can be regarded as the backbone of these low-dimensional representations.

The axes of the low-dimensional projection layout do not have physical meanings. Understanding the projection depends on the user's ability to link locations in the 2D plane to the fibers in the 3D space. Our approach exploits the linked interaction to provide a fast and intuitive correspondence between points in the 2D embedding space and 3D fibers. However, it requires training and exploration time. We plan to enhance the correspondence between the 2D embedding space and the 3D space. One possibility is to label some representative fibers in the 2D embedding space.

Due to the limited human perception capability and screen space, it is challenging to simultaneously compare a large number of signatures in the signature view. The RoD view shows an overview to locate differences among them. However, when diving into the details, visual clutter might be produced in the *DiffRadar* diagram caused by too many overlapped polylines. Clustering and hierarchical exploration are a feasible solution as proven by [26]. This is an avenue for our future work. In addition, effective comparison models will be further studied as well.

6   Conclusion

This paper presents a novel comparative visualization approach for discovering and exploring differences among DTI fiber models. While previous methods compare DTI datasets in either a 3D physical space or a statistical metric space, our approach compares the datasets in a common embedding space. The core is a computation-efficient two-phase projection technique followed by a density estimation process to build the low-dimensional representations of fiber models. Using these low-dimensional representations, regions of significant differences are further explicitly computed. An integrated interface is designed to explore the differences. Experiments on different DTI datasets demonstrate the effectiveness of this approach. Some experts gave positive comments that being able to quickly compare and explore different fibers models with each other is definitely useful.

Acknowledgment. This work is supported by NSFC (61232012, 61422211, 61303141), Zhejiang NSFC (Y12F020172), and the Fundamental Research Funds for the Central Universities.

References

1. Basser, P.J., Pajevic, S., Pierpaoli, C., Duda, J., Aldroubi, A.: In vivo fiber tractography using DT-MRI data. Magn. Resonance Med. **44**, 625–632 (2000)
2. Basser, P.J., Pierpaoli, C.: A simplified method to measure the diffusion tensor from seven MR images. Magn. Resonance Med. **39**, 928–934 (1998)
3. Brecheisen, R., Vilanova, A., Platel, B., ter Haar Romeny, B.: Parameter sensitivity visualization for DTI fiber tracking. IEEE Trans. Vis. Comput. Graph. **15**(6), 1441–1448 (2009)
4. Chen, W., Ding, Z., Zhang, S., MacKay-Brandt, A., Correia, S., Qu, H., Crow, J.A., Tate, D.F., Yan, Z., Peng, Q.: A novel interface for interactive exploration of DTI fibers. IEEE Trans. Vis. Comput. Graph. **15**(6), 1433–1440 (2009)
5. Corouge, I., Fletcher, P.T., Joshi, S., Gouttard, S., Gerig, G.: Fiber tract-oriented statistics for quantitative diffusion tensor MRI analysis. Med. Image Anal. **10**(5), 786–798 (2006)
6. Correia, S., Lee, S.Y., Voorn, T., Tate, D.F., Paul, R.H., Zhang, S., Salloway, S.P., Malloy, P.F., Laidlaw, D.H.: Quantitative tractography metrics of white matter integrity in diffusion-tensor MRI. Neuroimage **42**(2), 568–581 (2008)
7. DaSilva, M.J., Zhang, S., Demiralp, C., Laidlaw, D.H.: Visualizing the differences between diffusion tensor volume images. In: Proceedings of the International Society for Magnetic Resonance in Medicine Diffusion MRI Workshop (2000)
8. De Silva, V., Tenenbaum, J.B.: Sparse multidimensional scaling using landmark points. Technical report, Stanford University (2004)
9. Demiralp, C., Jianu, R., Laidlaw, D.H.: Exploring brain connectivity with two-dimensional maps. In: Laidlaw, D.H., Vilanova, A. (eds.) New Developments in the Visualization and Processing of Tensor Fields. Mathematics and Visualization, pp. 187–207. Springer, Heidelberg (2012)
10. Elvins, T.T., Jain, R.: Web-based volumetric data retrieval. In: Proceedings of the First Symposium on Virtual Reality Modeling Language, pp. 7–12. ACM (1995)
11. Funkhouser, T., Min, P., Kazhdan, M., Chen, J., Halderman, A., Dobkin, D., Jacobs, D.: A search engine for 3D models. ACM Trans. Graph. **22**(1), 83–105 (2003)
12. Gleicher, M., Albers, D., Walker, R., Jusufi, I., Hansen, C.D., Roberts, J.C.: Visual comparison for information visualization. Inf. Vis. **10**(4), 289–309 (2011)
13. Goodlett, C.B., Fletcher, P.T., Gilmore, J.H., Gerig, G.: Group statistics of DTI fiber bundles using spatial functions of tensor measures. In: Metaxas, D., Axel, L., Fichtinger, G., Székely, G. (eds.) MICCAI 2008, Part I. LNCS, vol. 5241, pp. 1068–1075. Springer, Heidelberg (2008)
14. Hagmann, P., Jonasson, L., Maeder, P., Thiran, J.P., Wedeen, V.J., Meuli, R.: Understanding diffusion MR imaging techniques: from scalar diffusion-weighted imaging to diffusion tensor imaging and beyond 1. Radiographics **26**(suppl 1), S205–S223 (2006)
15. Hilaga, M., Shinagawa, Y., Kohmura, T., Kunii, T.L.: Topology matching for fully automatic similarity estimation of 3D shapes. In: Proceedings of the 28th Annual Conference on Computer Graphics and Interactive Techniques, pp. 203–212. ACM (2001)

16. Jenkinson, M., Bannister, P., Brady, M., Smith, S.: Improved optimization for the robust and accurate linear registration and motion correction of brain images. Neuroimage **17**(2), 825–841 (2002)
17. Jianu, R., Demiralp, C., Laidlaw, D.H.: Exploring 3d DTI fiber tracts with linked 2d representations. IEEE Trans. Vis. Comput. Graph. **15**(6), 1449–1456 (2009)
18. Jiao, F., Phillips, J.M., Gur, Y., Johnson, C.R.: Uncertainty visualization in hardi based on ensembles of ODFs. In: IEEE Pacific Visualization Symposium (PacificVis), pp. 193–200. IEEE (2012)
19. Joia, P., Paulovich, F.V., Coimbra, D., Cuminato, J.A., Nonato, L.G.: Local affine multidimensional projection. IEEE Trans. Vis. Comput. Graph. **17**(12), 2563–2571 (2011)
20. Malik, M.M., Heinzl, C., Groeller, M.E.: Comparative visualization for parameter studies of dataset series. IEEE Trans. Vis. Comput. Graph. **16**(5), 829–840 (2010)
21. Mallo, O., Peikert, R., Sigg, C., Sadlo, F.: Illuminated lines revisited. In: Proceedings of IEEE Visualization, pp. 19–26. IEEE (2005)
22. Oelke, D., Strobelt, H., Rohrdantz, C., Gurevych, I., Deussen, O.: Comparative exploration of document collections: a visual analytics approach. Comput. Graph. Forum **33**, 201–210 (2014). Wiley Online Library
23. Osada, R., Funkhouser, T., Chazelle, B.: Shape distributions. ACM Trans. Graph. **21**(4), 93–101 (2002)
24. Pajevic, S., Basser, P.J.: Parametric and non-parametric statistical analysis of DT-MRI data. J. Magn. Resonance **163**(1), 1–14 (2003)
25. Poco, J., Eler, D.M., Paulovich, F.V., Minghim, R.: Employing 2d projections for fast visual exploration of large fiber tracking data. Comput. Graph. Forum **31**, 1075–1084 (2012). Wiley Online Library
26. Schmidt, J., Groller, M.E., Bruckner, S.: Vaico: visual analysis for image comparison. IEEE Trans. Vis. Comput. Graph. **19**(12), 2090–2099 (2013)
27. Silverman, B.: Density estimation for statistics and data analysis. Chapman & Hall/CRC, Boca Raton (1986)
28. Smith, S.M., Jenkinson, M., Johansen-Berg, H., Rueckert, D., Nichols, T.E., Mackay, C.E., Watkins, K.E., Ciccarelli, O., Cader, M.Z., Matthews, P.M., et al.: Tract-based spatial statistics: voxelwise analysis of multi-subject diffusion data. Neuroimage **31**(4), 1487–1505 (2006)
29. Verma, V., Pang, A.: Comparative flow visualization. IEEE Trans. Vis. Comput. Graph. **10**(6), 609–624 (2004)
30. Zhang, S., Correia, S., Laidlaw, D.H.: Identifying white-matter fiber bundles in DTI data using an automated proximity-based fiber-clustering method. IEEE Trans. Vis. Comput. Graph. **14**(5), 1044–1053 (2008)

MyHealthAvatar: A Lifetime Visual Analytics Companion for Citizen Well-being

Zhikun Deng$^{(\boxtimes)}$, Youbing Zhao, Farzad Parvinzamir, Xia Zhao, Hui Wei,
Mu Liu, Xu Zhang, Feng Dong, Enjie Liu, and Gordon Clapworthy

University of Bedfordshire, Luton LU1 3JU, UK
{zhikun.deng,youbing.zhao,farzad.parvinzamir,xia.zhao,hui.wei,mu.liu,
xu.zhang,feng.dong,enjie.liu,gordon.clapworthy}@beds.ac.uk

Abstract. MyHealthAvatar is a European Commission funded project aimed to design a lifetime companion for citizens to collect, track and store lifestyle and health data to promote citizen well-being. MyHealthAvatar collects and aggregates life-logging data from wearable devices and mobile apps by integrating a variety of life-logging resources, such as Fitbit, Moves, Withings, etc. As a lifelong companion, the data collected will be too large for citizens, patients and doctors to understand and utilise without proper visual presentation and user interaction. This paper presents the key interactive visual analytics components in MyHealthAvatar to facilitate health and lifestyle data presentation and analysis, including 3D avatar, dashboard, diary, timeline, clockview and map to achieve flexible spatio-temporal lifestyle visual analysis to promote citizen well-being.

Keywords: MyHealthAvatar · Interactive visual analytics · Wearable computing · Lifestyle analysis

1 Introduction

The widespread use of wearable monitoring devices and mobile apps makes effective capture of life-logging personal health data come true. Effective collection of these long-term health-status data is valuable for clinical decisions and leads to strengthened interdisciplinary healthcare research and collaboration in supporting innovative medical care. However, the design of a mature and reliable healthcare platform for aggregating these heterogeneous life-logging data is extremely challenging due to heterogeneity of wearable devices connected, multi-dimensionality and high volume of the data set. To our knowledge, the literature survey suggests that no platform is reported to successfully aggregate heterogeneous data from different resources for effective data analysis in a proper and continuous manner. The MyHealthAvatar project [13,14] is a research project that aims to provide a unique interface that allows data access, collection, sharing and analysis by utilising modern ICT technology, overcoming the shortcomings

© Springer International Publishing Switzerland 2016
A. El Rhalibi et al. (Eds.): Edutainment 2016, LNCS 9654, pp. 345–356, 2016.
DOI: 10.1007/978-3-319-40259-8_30

of the existing resources which are highly fragmented. It is designed to be the citizen's lifelong companion, providing long-term and consistent health status information of the individual citizen along a timeline representing the citizen's life. Data sharing potentially provides an extensive collection of population data and offers extremely valuable support to clinical research. MyHealthAvatar believes that healthcare should not only care for patients but also look after the health and well-being of all citizens. It needs to be available to healthy people through maintenance of a healthy lifestyle and the notification of early symptoms. Hence, MyHealthAvatar targets both healthy citizens and patients. MyHealthAvatar offers significant assistance to users by:

- displaying related information in a body-centric view around the avatar.
- allowing simulation via access to the model repositories, supported by the computing resource that is provided by the architecture.
- performing visually assisted data analysis (i.e. visual analytics) to extract clinically meaningful information from the heterogeneous data of the individual and shared avatars, such as the patterns of symptoms, experience of treatments, medicines, self-care guidelines, risk factors etc.

In this paper, we investigate MyHealthAvatar as a life-logging data aggregator of wearable devices and mobile apps for general healthcare visual analysis. We give a comprehensive review of existing life-logging health data collection techniques. Then, the visual analytics components are introduced to effectively analyse health data collected from Fitbit [4], Moves [11] and Withings [17] by MyHealthAvatar. The experimental visual anlytics components demonstrates that MyHealthAvatar successfully records, stores and reuses the unified and structured personal health information in the long term, including activities, location, exercise etc. The data repository provided by MyHealthAvatar has also been successfully applied to several other projects for effective disease diagnosis, such as in CARRE [2] and MyLifeHub [15].

2   Related Work

This section reviews existing life-logging health data collection tools and technologies, including wearable sensors and devices based health data collection tools, mobile apps based health data collection tools and health information sharing platform.

2.1   Wearable Devices for Health Data Collection

Wearable device based health data collection tools traditionally refers to use of medical devices to monitor medical data, such as heart rate, blood pressure, glucose, etc. Recently, the use of wearable devices in life-logging data collection mainly indicates the record of some personal physical activity data. In particular, prior work has shown that wearable sensors can benefit individual patient's health and individual personal fitness. The most popular products are listed below:

- Fitbit [4] provides wearable devices which record steps, distance, and calories, etc. These devices communicate with a host computer using Bluetooth that sends their data directly to a user's account on the Fitbit website.

- Withings [17] is also a high-profile consumer-level activity device providing steps, distance, calories, heart rate, etc. Devices include wristband, watch, scales, blood pressure monitor, etc.

- iHealth Labs [9] offers a range of connected health products: blood pressure monitors, scales, activity trackers, glucometers, body analysis scale. Devices include blood pressure monitor, scales and body analysers, fitness tracker, glucometer, etc.

- Nike+ Fuelband [7] is worn on the wrist and records calories, steps, distance, and Nike's own unit of activity, termed "Nike Fuel". The device connects via USB to a host machine which synchronises the health data to a user's account on the Nike+ website.

- Jawbone Up [10] is also a activity device providing steps, distance, calories. Currently, Jawbone up can only be used with a mobile device, not supporting laptop and desktop PCs.

- The Apple Watch [1] is a smartwatch developed by Apple Inc. It incorporates fitness tracking and health-oriented capabilities as well as integration with iOS and other Apple products and services. The three rings of the Activity app provide a simple visual snapshot of the individual's daily activity, and can help motivate them to sit less, move more, and get some exercise.

- Samsung Gear [16] is a line of wearable computing devices produced by Samsung. The line includes the Android smartwatch Samsung Gear S and the successor S2, and the Gear Fit wristband. They monitor fitness activities including heart rate, steps, activity mode and sleep quality.

- Huawei wearables include Huawei Watch and Huawei Talkband. They monitor fitness activities including heart rate, steps, activity mode and sleep quality. The Huawei Watch tracks movement, activities, heart rate, exercise pattern and visualises the health information. Huawei TalkBand also monitors sleep quality.

2.2 Mobile App-Based Health Data Collection

Mobile applications are recently turning out to be a great source of user empowerment in healthcare fields. The most well-known mobile apps are based on observing GPS signal information for tracking user movement activities outdoor, including location, speed and distance. Some mobile apps explore the further use of mobile phone sensors for improving accuracy of tracking physical activities and observing other types of health information. Currently, the type of health data collected by mobile applications includes location, distance, speed, calories, heart rate, emotion and other manually recorded health data.

- Moves [11] is a very popular app for fitness and activity recording. Moves automatically records the step number and location of the user and calculates calories burned and distance of movement. It automatically recognises the activity type, such as walking, running, cycling, transport, etc. The user can either view the distance, duration, steps, and calories data on the mobile phone or export the data from the Moves server. The daily activities are visualised in a storyline in the app. The daily route can be visualised on the map.

- Google Maps Timeline [7] provides similar functionality to the Moves app. It is also based on the use of GPS to record users' path, speed, distance and elevation while they are walk, run, and bike or do any activities outside. The daily tracks can be shown on the map.
- Endomondo [3] is a GPS-based mobile application for tracking route, distance, duration, split times and calorie consumption. It can record a full history with previous workouts, statistics and a localized route map for each work out. Another important feature of Endomondo is to incorporate community and allow users to challenge friends and share results.

The main drawback of GPS-based mobile apps is a short battery longevity and only available for outdoor tracking. This might limit accuracy and continuities of life-logging captured personal activity data. Cardiio and Emotionsense are both research based mobile apps, which support only particular mobile system and have no API documentations for further development.

2.3 Health Information Sharing Platforms

Lastly, health information sharing platforms have come with the emergence of web-enabled healthcare services. Due to the great evolution of Internet technology, this is emerging as a new healthcare delivery trend. These web-based healthcare platforms provide a multi-functional server for users to store, manage and make basic visualisation of health data from various third party devices.

- Microsoft HealthVault [8] is intended to enable users to gather, store, and use and share personal health information through many medical devices. It enables a connected ecosystem with privacy and security-enhanced foundation including more than 300 applications and more than 80 connected health and fitness devices.
- Fluxtream [5] is an open-source non-profit personal data visualisation framework to help the users make sense of their life and compare hypotheses about what affects the well-being.
- MyFitnessCompanion [12] is another healthcare platform for users to manage their personal health data, including metrics like weight, heart rate & heart rate variability (HRV), blood pressure, food intake, blood glucose, insulin, asthma, etc. The functionalities are highly similar to Microsoft HealthVault. It has a real-time visualisation mode, which keeps track of and visualise all user measurement with simple time graph and can share these graphs with others.

Most of the health data collection devices, apps and health data repository platforms only provide very basic visualisation of the data they collected or imported. They lack a visualisation and data analysis strategy on a systematic level, especially for analysis of wide time range data from heterogeneous sources. In addition, the employment of user interactions have not seen being widely studied in data visualisation and analysis in those applications. In contrast, MyHealthAvatar provides standalone components as well as integrated views for interactive visual analysis of personal health and lifestyle data from multiple heterogeneous data sources.

Healthcare has been an important research and application field of data analysis and visualisation for several decades [19]. Behind healthcare visual analytics, much of the focus is on the visualisation of electronic health records (EHRs). [18] gives a detailed review of the related work, categorising by individual patients or group of patients. [25] also presents a recent review of innovative visual analytics approaches that have been proposed to illustrate EHR data, including [20–22, 24, 26, 27], etc.

Personal health information has been increasingly collectible and accessible in the information era. With the trend of "predictive, preemptive, personalized and participative" healthcare [23], more personalised data is desired for predictive analysis of medical care. Valuable lifestyle patterns can be discovered by analysing the personal data collected by sensors and apps. Together with the clinical information that has long played the major role in health and medical decision making, this information can introduce more added value for health monitoring and medical decision making.

MyHealthAvatar can not only directly access personal health and lifestyle data from devices such as Fibit, Withings, but also analyse the data to extract high level lifestyle data. Together with appropriate models, MyHealthAvatar aims to provide personalised health monitoring, analysis and risk management based on multiple heterogeneous data sources, which is a key difference from the existing health data sharing platforms or healthcare visual analytics systems.

3   Interactive Visual Analytics Components

MyHealthAvatar provides several web-based components for interactive visualisation and analysis of personal health and lifestyle data, including 3D avatar, dashboard, timeline, diary, clock view and map. Lifestyle, health, fitness and medical data are inherently time dependent. To visualise time-varying data, linear and radial layouts can used and user interaction is highly desired. A timeline is a linear visualisation of data spanning a long period while the clock view uses the common clock metaphor to interactively visualise daily events. A calendar is another common layout to visualise human-related events. To visualise spatiotemporal data, MyHealthAvatar uses the map and integrates the clock view with the map. A calendar-like diary is also provided for activity data input, edit and planning.

3.1   Dashboard

There are many components and data that can be accessed by the user from the web-based MyHealthAvatar portal. However, as there is a variety of data sources and data types, it is very difficult for a user to grasp an overview with important notifications from the scattered health status information. To present the user a quick overview of their health status, MyHealthAvatar provides a dashboard as the front page. The dashboard provides a summary of the user's latest health status and may present important notifications. It may include several simple visualisation components to depict data for a relatively recent period. Figure 1 shows the example dashboard with data tiles, map and a timeline. The user can interact with the map and the timeline to obtain more detailed information.

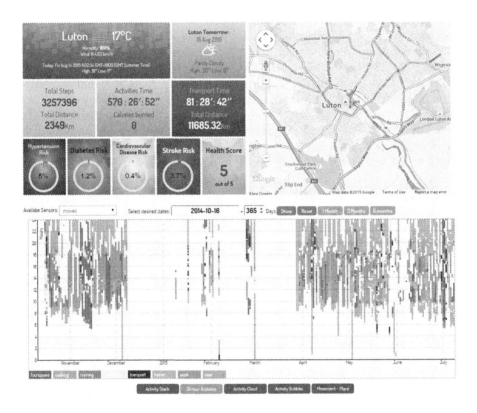

Fig. 1. An example screenshot of MyHealthAvatar dashboard

3.2   Diary

MyHealthAvatar provides health data collection, storage and access to end users. The data can either be automatically collected or manually input. For lifestyle and health tracking, the data are often time-dependant, especially date-dependant. A natural form of date-based data organisation, display and editing is a calendar, which is a traditional way to visualise daily events. In MyHealthAvatar, a calendar-based diary is used for daily data display as well as daily event input, editing and planning. Figure 2 shows an example view of the calendar with the event editor. The calendar displays a brief summary of the fitness data such as daily steps, walking and transportation distance, as well as calories burned. With the event editor the user can add events, providing the start and end time, location, and detailed descriptions. The user can add tags for events to facilitate event categorisation. The user can plan by adding events. The events and planning will be shown in the calendar.

3.3   Timeline

A timeline is a traditional method to visualise time-varying data and events in a linear layout. Compared to a calendar, a timeline is more suitable for visualising continuous variables which cover a relatively long period, such as health indicators and medical measurements. Activity events which are time dependent can also be shown in a timeline if a longer time scale is desired to view daily activity events and activities. In the current implementation, the timeline supports interactive visualisation of Fitbit/Withings sensor data as well as Moves data. There are five different visualisation styles including activity stack, 24-h activity, activity cloud, activity bubbles and movement-place. Activity stack shows activities directly on the timeline in a form similar to stack bar charts. A 24-h activity organises the activities on a daily basis for easier comparison of daily activity changes. The activity cloud uses concentric disks of different radius to represent the activities; activity bubbles use bubbles of different colour and radius. Movement-place shows the movement and place in the user's Moves data.

In addition to interactive time period selections and zooming, the timeline supports interactive filtering and automatic clustering of events as the number of events may be too large for web-based applications. Figure 3 shows an example of daily activity events visualised in a timeline.

3.4   Clock View

For daily activities, timeline provides visualisation over a relatively long period. Interactive timelines can provide zooming to smaller scales. However, the linear layout may make it difficult for the user to understand and compare daily events. A fine-grained view of activities within one day is better visualised in a radial layout. A natural, real-life way of radial daily time representation is the clock. MyHealthAvatar uses a similar radial layout called ClockView to visualise daily events. Movements and places from Moves data are visualised in the radial layout. Activity types are marked by icons and colours. When the user hovers the mouse over the icons more detailed information will be displayed, as shown in Fig. 4.

3.5   Map

While dairy, timeline and clock view are largely designed for visual analysis of temporal data, they can hardly be used to visualise spatial locations. A map is a

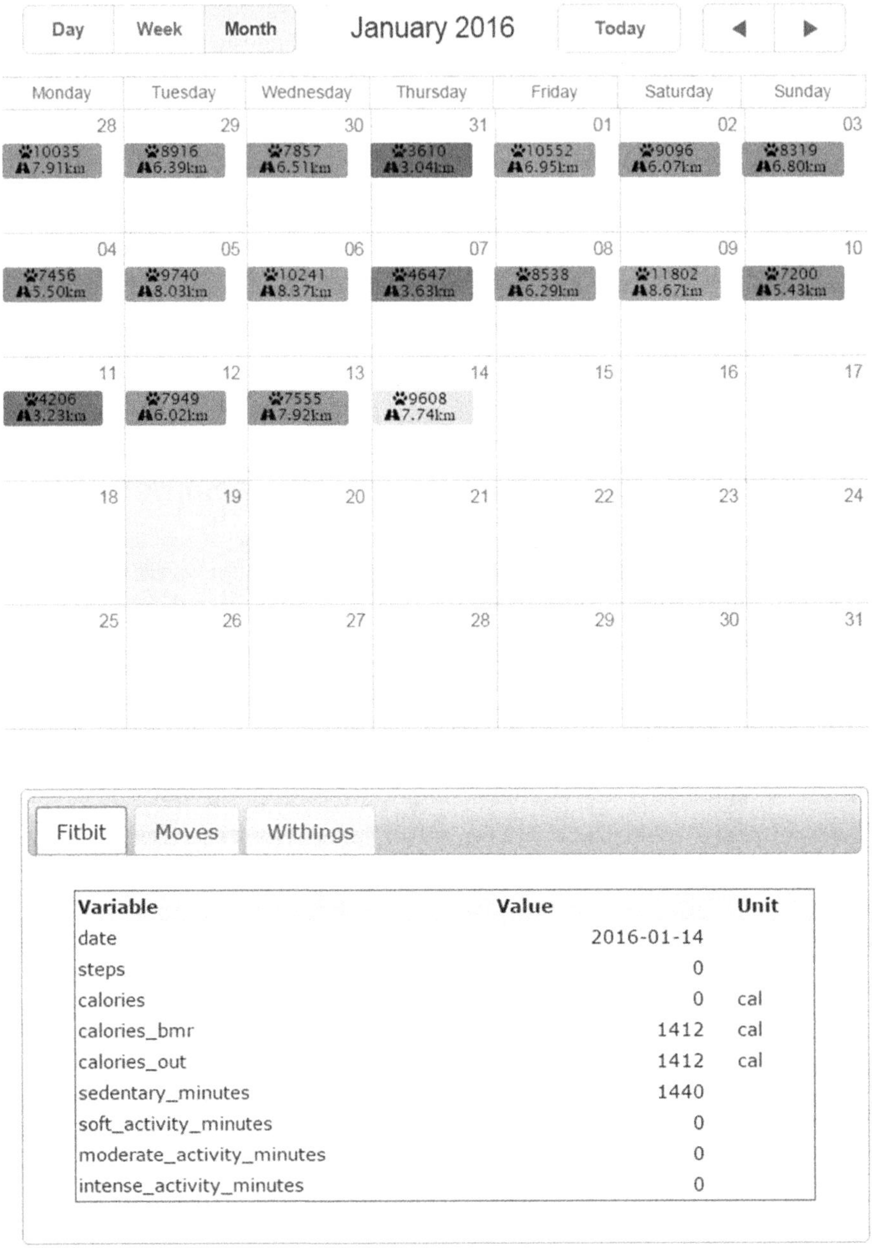

Fig. 2. An example view of the diary and information panel

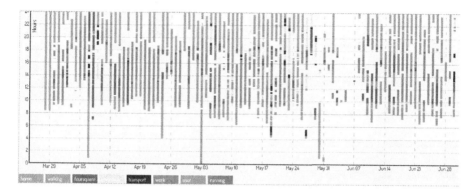

Fig. 3. A timeline view of daily events in a 24-h style

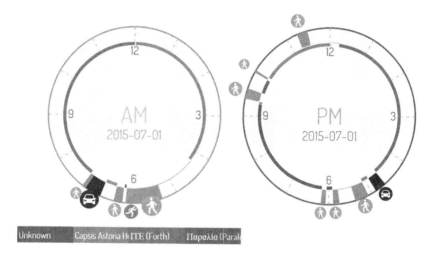

Fig. 4. A clockview example

natural choice to provide intuitive spatio-temporal visualisation and analysis of the user's locations and routes for better understanding and knowledge discovery of the lifestyle. The map implementation is based on Google Maps [6]. Currently, in MyHealthAvatar the map is used for visualisation and analysis of the Moves data only but it is capable of supporting other location-sensor-based apps.

In addition, MyHealthAvatar uses an integrated view which is called Life-Tracker to visualise and analyse events and activities, including diary, map and clock view, as shown in Fig. 5. The advantage of this compound view is that it provides integrated spatio-temporal visualisation and analysis. The page itself provides the user an extensive view of data collected from different sources and the user does not need to refer to multiple pages to view and analyse related spatio-temporal data collected and stored on the MyHealthAvatar platform.

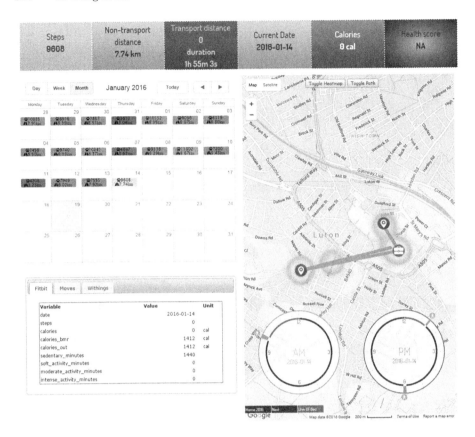

Fig. 5. An integrated view of diary, map and clockview

4   Conclusion and Future Work

MyHealthAvatar aggregates lifestyle and health data from a variety of hetero-geneous data sources to promote a citizen's lifetime well-being. It is extremely challenging for citizens, patients and doctors to view, utilise and understand these data without proper visual presentation and user interaction. To meet this challenge, MyHealthAvatar provides interactive visual analytics components to facilitate health and lifestyle data presentation and analysis, including 3D avatar, dashboard, diary, timeline, clock view and map. These components can be inte-grated to achieve flexible visual analysis of spatio-temporal lifestyle data. The current visual analytics work in MyHealthAvatar is only designed for a single user. In the next stage, MyHealthAvatar will focus more on data sharing among multiple users. How to effectively visualise data sharing and shared data will be more of interest. Consequently, interactive shared data visualisation and analysis will be the next-step work.

Acknowledgments. MyHealthAvatar project is funded by 7th Framework Programme of European Commission - ICT under agreement of FP7-ICT-2011-9. MyLifeHub project is funded by EPSRC under grant EP/L023830/1. CARRE project is funded by 7th Framework Programme of European Commission - ICT under agreement of FP7-ICT-611140. We would like to thank the European Commission and EPSRC for the funding and thank the project officers and reviewers for their indispensable support for both of the projects.

References

1. Apple Watch. http://www.apple.com/watch/. Accessed 19 Jan 2016
2. CARRE Project. http://www.carre-project.eu/. Accessed 06 Jan 2016
3. Endomondo. https://www.endomondo.com/. Accessed 20 Jan 2016
4. Fitbit. http://www.fitbit.com/. Accessed 06 Jan 2016
5. Fluxtream. https://fluxtream.org/. Accessed 06 Jan 2016
6. Google Maps. https://zygotebody.com/. Accessed 06 Jan 2016
7. Google Maps Timeline. https://www.google.com/maps/timeline. Accessed 10 Mar 2016
8. HealthVault. https://www.healthvault.com/. Accessed 06 Jan 2016
9. iHealth. http://www.ihealthlabs.com/. Accessed 06 Jan 2016
10. JawboneUp. https://jawbone.com/up/. Accessed 20 Jan 2016
11. Moves. https://www.moves-app.com/. Accessed 06 Jan 2016
12. myFitnessCompanion. http://myfitnesscompanion.com/. Accessed 20 Jan 2016
13. MyHealthAvartar Platform. http://www.myhealthavatar.org/. Accessed 06 Jan 2016
14. MyHealthAvartar Project. http://www.myhealthavatar.eu/. Accessed 06 Jan 2016
15. MyLifeHub project introduction. http://gow.epsrc.ac.uk/NGBOViewGrant.aspx?GrantRef=EP/L023830/1/. Accessed 18 Jan 2016
16. Samsung wearables. http://www.samsung.com/us/mobile/wearable-tech. Accessed 18 Jan 2016
17. Withings. http://www.withings.com/. Accessed 06 Jan 2016
18. Rind, A., Wang, T.D., Aigner, W., Silva, M., Wongsuphasawat, K., Plaisant, C., Shneiderman, B.: Interactive information visualization to explore and query electronic health records. Found. Trends HCI **5**((3), 207–298 (2011)
19. Reddy, C.K., Aggarwal, C.C.: Healthcare Data Analytics. Chapman & Hall, CRC, Boca Raton (2015)
20. Gotz, D., Stavropoulos, H.: Decisionflow: visual analytics for high-dimensional temporal event sequence data. IEEE Trans. Vis. Comput. Graph. **20**(12), 1783–1792 (2014)
21. Monroe, M., Lan, R., Lee, H., Plaisant, C., Shneiderman, B.: Temporal event sequence simplification. IEEE Trans. Vis. Comput. Graph. **19**(12), 2227–2236 (2013)
22. Plaisant, C., Mushlin, R., Snyder, A., Li, J., Heller, D., Shneiderman, B., Colorado, K.P.: Lifelines: using visualization to enhance navigation and analysis of patient records. In: Proceedings of the 1998 American Medical Informatic Association Annual Fall Symposium, pp. 76–80 (1998)
23. Shneiderman, B., Plaisant, C., Hesse, B.W.: Improving health and healthcare with interactive visualization methods. IEEE Comput. **46**(1), 58–66 (2013)

24. Wang, T.D., Plaisant, C., Shneiderman, B., Spring, N., Roseman, D., Marchand, G., Mukherjee, V., Smith, M.: Temporal summaries: supporting temporal categorical searching, aggregation and comparison. IEEE Trans. Vis. Comput. Graph. **15**(6), 1049–1056 (2009)
25. West, V.L., Borland, D., Hammond, W.: Innovative information visualization of electronic health record data: a systematic review. J. Am. Med. Inform. Assoc. **22**(2), 330–339 (2015)
26. Wongsuphasawat, K., Gotz, D.: Exploring flow, factors, and outcomes of temporal event sequences with the outflow visualization. IEEE Trans. Vis. Comput. Graph. **18**(12), 2659–2668 (2012). doi:10.1109/TVCG.2012.225
27. Wongsuphasawat, K., Guerra Gómez, J.A., Plaisant, C., Wang, T.D., Taieb-Maimon, M., Shneiderman, B.: Lifeflow: visualizing an overview of event sequences. In: Proceedings of the SIGCHI Conference on Human Factors in Computing Systems CHI 2011, NY, USA, pp. 1747–1756. ACM, New York (2011)

UIA: A Uniform Integrated Advection Algorithm for Steady and Unsteady Piecewise Linear Flow Field on Structured and Unstructured Grids

Fang Wang[1,2(✉)], Yang Liu[2], Dan Zhao[2], Liang Deng[2], and Sikun Li[1]

[1] College of Computer Science, National University of Defense Technology,
Changsha, Hunan, China
wwangfang@sina.com
[2] Computational Aerodynamics Research Institute,
China Aerodynamics Research and Development Center,
Mianyang, Sichuan, China

Abstract. Integration-Based geometric method is widely used in vector field visualization. In order to improve visualization efficiency based on integration advection, we propose a unified advection algorithm on steady and unsteady vector field according to common piecewise linear field data set analysis. The algorithm interpolates along spatial and temporal direction using cell gradient based method combined with advection process of 4th-order Runge-Kutta algorithm, which transforms multi-step advection into single-step advection. The algorithm can dramatically reduce computational load, and is applicable on any grid type and cell-centered/cell-vertexed data structure. The experiments are per- formed on steady/unsteady vector fields on 2-dimensional cell-centered unstructured grids and 3-dimensional cell-vertexed format grids. The result shows that the proposed algorithm can significantly improve advection efficiency and reduce visualization computational time compared with 4th-order Runge-Kutta.

Keywords: Scientific visualization · Integration-Based geometric method · Unsteady vector field · Piecewise linear

1 Introduction

Vector field visualization has always been a hot topic in scientific visualization [1]. Common vector visualization methods, such as integrated line/surface [2, 3], LIC [4], feature extraction [5], topology-based methods [6], etc., need to employ integration advection to calculate flow map data in order to directly generate geometry or calculate derived variables for rendering.

The vector field data, especially on unsteady field, are often labeled by large volume and high complexity. It is computationally intensive to carry out advection on these data sets which involve spatiotemporal interpolation as well as multi-step advection along temporal direction. The advection inefficiency has become the bottleneck of various vector visualization algorithms. There are two kinds of approaches to

© Springer International Publishing Switzerland 2016
A. El Rhalibi et al. (Eds.): Edutainment 2016, LNCS 9654, pp. 357–370, 2016.
DOI: 10.1007/978-3-319-40259-8_31

accelerate advection. On one hand, emerging device [7, 8] or large-scale parallelization [9–11], is employed. On the other hand, the algorithm itself is improved or reformed. Ueng, etc. [12, 13] propose an efficient integration algorithm for steady field on tetrahedral grid. Wang, etc. [14] propose a batch advection algorithm for curve integral on steady/unsteady vector field. However, the applicable scope of these algorithms limit to simplex grid and its process manner of unsteady vector field is complex.

In this paper, we follow the latter approach to analyze the characteristics of mostly common piecewise linear flow field such as velocity field from 2nd-orderformat in CFD. Based on RK4 with fixed temporal step approach and multi-step advection with spatiotemporal interpolation, we propose a Uniform Integrated Advection algorithm that has consistent form on steady and unsteady field, and can be used on both structured and unstructured grid with cell-centered and cell-vertexed format.

The contributions are summarized as follows.

1. We use cell-based vector gradient interpolation to unify linear interpolation of cell-centered and cell-vertexed format, which simplifies vector interpolation on non-spatiotemporal points.
2. Through combining spatiotemporal interpolation with multi-step advection of RK, we pre-calculate the transformation matrix of spatiotemporal grid cell, and propose an efficient advection algorithm that can obtain spatiotemporal locations of next time step by only one matrix-vector multiplication.
3. We extend the computation space and vector of unsteady field, and unify the process along spatial and temporal dimensions to design a Uniform Integrated Advection algorithm that has consistent form on steady and unsteady field.
4. We apply UIA to flow map computation on 2 analytical flow field. Then we verify the correctness and precision by calculating and rendering FTLE [15–17] field. The efficiency is also verified by comparing the execution time with RK4.

2   Uniform Integrated Computation Formula

In this paper, we separately use lowercase letters in bold italics to represent column vector of a vector, lowercase letters in italics to represent scalar, conventional letters in bold capital to represent matrix and uppercase letters in bold italics to represent the sets.

2.1   Piecewise Linear Field

While referring to grid based data representation, piecewise linear means that the variable is linearly distributed in a cell or small neighboring area of a vertex. For example, variable p is a function of 3-dimensional location. The value p_0 of a point in a cell or a vertex (x_0, y_0, z_0) is already known, then the value p of the point (x, y, z) in the same cell or close enough to (x_0, y_0, z_0) is represented by

$$p = p_0 + \frac{\partial p_0}{\partial x}(x - x_0) + \frac{\partial p_0}{\partial y}(y - y_0) + \frac{\partial p_0}{\partial z}(z - z_0) \qquad (1)$$

2.2 Gradient Computation of Arbitrary Cell-Centered Cell

When using RK approach advection in grid-based piecewise linear vector field, linear interpolation, which is on basis of 1-dimensional interpolation, on spatial and temporal dimension on non-vertex are required.

The grids are classified into two categories, i.e., structured and unstructured grids. The cell geometry of structured grid is unified and the connection relation- ship is simple. Hence it is comparatively easy to determine interpolation form. However, the cell geometry of unstructured grid is diverse and the connection relationship is complicated. Even various types of cell can co-exist in the same grid. Therefore, interpolation form can only be confirmed after the cell type is determined, which results in complex operations.

Linear interpolation also has relationship with the way how data is defined on grid. There are two formats called cell-centered, e.g., finite volume method [18, 19] in CFD and cell-vertexed, e.g., the result of finite difference method [20] in CFD. Cell-centered format refers that the data value associated with each cell is the value located at the center of the cell. However, cell-vertexed format defines value at each cell vertex. The linear interpolation algorithm can conveniently process cell-vertexed data. Thus the cell-centered data are often converted to cell-vertexed data for linear interpolation, which would cause precision loss due to field reconstruction [21].

In order to unify linear interpolation on different cells and data formats, we take advantage of gradient-based interpolation method to solve the physical variables on arbitrary spatiotemporal points using piecewise linear property.

We firstly take cell-centered data into consideration. Under piecewise linear premise, the variable gradient is a constant in each cell. If the value p and its gradient of a point inside the cell is known in advance, the value of arbitrary point of the cell can be derived by formula 1.

As cell is a closed graph, there exists Gauss theorem on the enclosed space:

$$\int_{\Omega} \nabla p \, da = \oint_{\partial\Omega} p \, ds \tag{2}$$

where ds is a directed line (2-dimensional) or facet (3-dimensional), and can be represented as the product of the line length or facet area and its unit outward normal vector, i.e., $ds = \mathbf{n} \cdot ds$. Then the numerical calculation formula of formula 2 is

$$\nabla p = \frac{1}{V} \sum_s p_s \cdot \mathbf{n}_s \cdot s \tag{3}$$

where V represents unit cell area or volume, s represents corresponding boundary line length or facet area, p_s and $\mathbf{n}_s$ represent the variable value at the boundary and its unit outward normal vector. p_s can be interpolated according to cell-centered value of two cells with shared line or facet. If the field data are calculated by CFD, then higher precision can be acquired by using Roe average computation [21, 22].

Vector gradient is a 2nd-order tensor, which can be viewed as a matrix composed by the gradient of each vector component. For instance, the gradient of 3-dimensional velocity field can be represented as

$$\nabla \mathbf{v} = \begin{bmatrix} \frac{\partial u}{\partial x} & \frac{\partial u}{\partial y} & \frac{\partial u}{\partial z} \\ \frac{\partial v}{\partial x} & \frac{\partial v}{\partial y} & \frac{\partial v}{\partial z} \\ \frac{\partial w}{\partial x} & \frac{\partial w}{\partial y} & \frac{\partial w}{\partial z} \end{bmatrix}. \tag{4}$$

2.3 Unified Interpolation of Cell-Centered and Cell-Vertexed Format

The data of cell-vertexed format are generally obtained by numerical simulation and measurement based on structured grid. There are two kinds of cell gradient computation method based on cell-centered format over cell-vertexed data set. The first one is to obtain the cell center location, and then use linear interpolation to calculate its value according to the variable value on vertex. The second one is to view the center as the vertex of the cell generated by connecting neighboring cell centers, which is shown by the dashed line in Fig. 1.

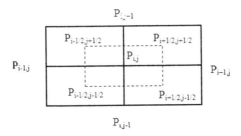

Fig. 1. Grid reconstruction.

The computation is still carried out on original vertex. However, the computation of corresponding outward normal vector, boundary variable value, and line length/facet area are based on the cell with dashed lines in formula 3. This method avoids linear interpolation for cell-centered value so as to reduce computation. Therefore, we use this method to calculate cell-vertexed data.

2.4 Integrated Computation of Steady Field

After cell gradient computation, the advection formula with linear system feature is derived by combining RK's advection method. In a cell, the velocity value $\mathbf{v}$ of arbitrary point can be represented by velocity $\mathbf{v}(\mathbf{x}_r)$ at cell center, velocity gradient $\nabla \mathbf{v}$ and the distance vector $\mathbf{x} - \mathbf{x}_r$ between cell center and vertex.

$$\mathbf{v} = \mathbf{v}(\mathbf{x}_r) + \nabla \mathbf{v}(\mathbf{x} - \mathbf{x}_r) \tag{5}$$

By applying formula 5 to RK4 iteration formula on steady field, there is

$$k_1 = v(x_n) = v(x_r) + \nabla v \cdot (x_n - x_r)$$
$$k_2 = v(x_n + hk_1/2) = k_1 + h\nabla v \cdot k_1/2$$
$$k_3 = v(x_n + hk_2/2) = k_1 + h\nabla v \cdot k_2/2 \qquad (6)$$
$$k_4 = v(x_n + hk_3) = k_1 + h\nabla v \cdot k_3$$
$$x_{n+1} = x_n + h/6 * (k_1 + 2k_2 + 2k_3 + k_4) = (\mathbf{I} + \mathbf{C}\nabla v)x_n + (\mathbf{C}v(x_r) - \mathbf{C}\nabla v x_r)$$

where $\mathbf{C} = h/6 * (6\mathbf{I} + 3h\nabla v + h^2 (\nabla v)^2 + h^3/4 * (\nabla v)^3)$.

In formula 6, the matrix $(\mathbf{I} + \mathbf{C}\nabla v)$ and vector $(\mathbf{C}v(x_r) - \mathbf{C}\nabla v x_r)$ are both constant such that they are calculated only once for integration advection at all points in each cell. Let $\mathbf{R} = \mathbf{I} + \mathbf{C}\nabla v, v_s = \mathbf{C}v(x_r) - \mathbf{C}\nabla v x_r$, then formula 6 is transformed into the following form:

$$x_{n+1} = \mathbf{R}x_n + v_s. \qquad (7)$$

Formula 7 has the same form with basic spatial geometric transformation in computer graphics [23]. By using homogeneous coordinate of x_n, $x'_n = (x_n^T, 1)^T$, formula 7 can be transformed into simpler form.

$$x_{n+1} = \mathbf{T}x'_n, where \ \mathbf{T} = (\mathbf{R}, v_s) \qquad (8)$$

As for n-dimensional flow field, $\mathbf{T}$ is a matrix with n rows and n + 1 columns.

2.5   Integrated Computation of Unsteady Field

The formula of applying RK4 on unsteady field is

$$k_1 = v(x_n, t_n)$$
$$k_2 = v(x_n + hk_1/2, t_n + h/2)$$
$$k_3 = v(x_n + hk_2/2, t_n + h/2) \qquad (9)$$
$$k_4 = v(x_n + hk_3, t_n + h)$$
$$x_{n+1} = x_n + h/6 * (k_1 + 2k_2 + 2k_3 + k_4)$$

As demonstrated by formula 9, both spatial and temporal interpolation are required while using RK approach on unsteady flow field. Hence it is impossible to deduce such a simple and efficient formula as formula 8. In piecewise linear field, the distribution along temporal direction is also piecewise linear. If there exists variable $p(x, t)$, according to Taylor expansion we have

$$p_{x+\delta x, t+\delta t} = p_{x,t} + \nabla p_{x,t}(\delta x, \delta t)^T, where \ \nabla p_{x,t} = (\frac{\partial p_{x,t}}{\partial x}, \frac{\partial p_{x,t}}{\partial t}). \qquad (10)$$

Based on this formula, we perform phase space extension to vector function. Let $\tilde{x} = (x^T, t)^T$ then $\tilde{v} = (v^T, 1)^T : \mathbb{R}^{n+1} \to \mathbb{R}^{n+1}$, which means spatial and temporal dimension can be treated equally. Thus, the original n-dimensional unsteady flow field is extended to (n + 1)-dimensional steady flow field. Therefore, we can bring the extended coordinate and velocity into steady RK4 formula, and deduce uniform computation formula like formula 6. Besides, we have

$$\tilde{x}_{n+1} = (\mathbf{I} + \tilde{\mathbf{C}}\nabla\tilde{v})\tilde{x}_n + (\tilde{\mathbf{C}}\tilde{v}(\tilde{x}_r) - \tilde{\mathbf{C}}\nabla\tilde{v}\tilde{x}_r), \, where$$
$$\tilde{\mathbf{C}} = \frac{h}{6}(6\mathbf{I} + 3h\nabla\tilde{v} + h^2(\nabla\tilde{v})^2 + \frac{h^3}{4}(\nabla\tilde{v})^3) \tag{11}$$

After using homogeneous coordinate $(\tilde{x}^{\mathrm{T}}, 1)^{\mathrm{T}}$, the uniform form of formula 8 is derived as follows.

$$\tilde{x}_{n+1} = \tilde{\mathbf{T}}\tilde{x}'_n. \tag{12}$$

As for n-dimensional unsteady flow field, $\tilde{\mathbf{T}}$ is a matrix with n + 1 rows and n + 2 columns. After solving, the vector consisted of first n elements of $\tilde{x}'$ is the integration advection location in space.

According to formula 8 and 12, we can conclude that integration advection inside a cell is a linear transformation operation in piecewise linear field. Once the transformation matrix is determined, integration advection can be implemented by limited number of multiplication and addition operations. Compared with RK, this approach can save a large amount of spatiotemporal integration operations to achieve higher efficiency.

3   Uniform Integrated Advection Algorithm

Based on the analysis from Sect. 2.1 to Sect. 2.4, UIA can be divided into pretreatment and advection computation.

Pretreatment process calculates transformation matrix for each cell, which consists of three parts. The first part is responsible for cell geometric computation, including area/volume, line length/facet area, and outward normal vector and so on. The second part calculates the boundary vector gradient and partial differential components solving. The transformation matrix computation is carried out in the third part. The main steps of the algorithm are illustrated as follows.

1. For cell-vertexed data, spatial grid is reconstructed and converted into cell- centered data using the method in Sect. 2.2. For cell-centered data this step is skipped.
2. Calculate spatial grid geometry data.
3. Spatial and vector extension on unsteady field using the method in Sect. 2.4.
4. Calculate transformation matrix for each cell according to advection step size.

Unsteady flow field from measurement or numerical simulation is generally a set of many transient fields. During pretreatment, the extended vector gradient needs to be calculated in transformation matrix computation, where the element contains spatial partial derivative and temporal partial derivative of each vector component. The spatial partial derivative is firstly derived using Gauss theorem, i.e., $\frac{\partial v_i}{\partial x}$, in transient field at time t_i. Then the temporal partial differential component is derived by central difference approach $\frac{\partial v_i}{\partial t} = \frac{v_{i+1} - v_i}{2\Delta t}$ according to corresponding vectors in transient fields at time t_i and t_{i+1}. The eventually vector gradient is finally used in integration in $[t_i, t_{i+1}]$.

The pretreatment algorithm only uses information of grid and vector field. Therefore pretreatment algorithm is independent of advection algorithm such that the pretreated transformation matrix can be stored in external memory for later visualization.

Advection algorithm employs seed-wised and step-wised strategy, and the main steps are illustrated as follows.

1. Start advection from initial time to end time at each seed as the starting point:
   (a) Find the cell of current point.
   (b) Solve the next point, set this point to current point and repeat the previous step until the advection termination condition is satisfied.

The termination condition of integration advection that is similar to RK approach, which is triggered when integration advection exceeds the field space boundary.

4   Algorithm Precision Analysis

While the field itself is piecewise linear, e.g., the velocity field from 2nd-order CFD, UIA's implicit piecewise linear hypothesis is consistent with raw field. The errors come from the advection algorithm. From the derivation we know that UIA is based on RK4 iteration. Therefore, the precision is as the same as RK4, i.e., $O(h^4)$.

UIA's implicit piecewise linear hypothesis would cause some precision loss, which stems from two aspects. Firstly, the derivative component higher than two order in Taylor expansion is neglected in vector (k_i) computation at non-vertex points using gradient, i.e.,

$$v(x + \delta x, t + \delta t) = v(x, t) + \left(\frac{\partial}{\partial x} \delta x + \frac{\partial}{\partial t} \delta t \right)^1 v(x, t) + O(\delta x^2 + \delta t^2). \quad (13)$$

Thus UIA has 2-order precision in time and space during vector (k_i) computation. From formulas 4 and 5 we know that x_{n+1} has the same precision of $O(\delta x^2 + \delta t^2)$ as k_i. Secondly, the inherent precision of RK4 advection is $O(h^4)$. Generally speaking, h and t are different in the order of magnitude. Hence the error from RK4 is negligible, and the ultimate precision of the proposed algorithm is $O(\delta x^2 + \delta t^2)$.

5   Experiments and Analysis

There are two analytical fields in our experiments as shown in Fig. 2. The first field is a Double-Gyre(DG) field [24, 25] in geophysical flows. DG field is 2-dimensional and present unsteady features by tuning the parameters. The velocity of DG field is defined as

$$v(x,t) = \begin{pmatrix} -\pi A \sin(\pi f(x,t)) \cos(\pi y) \\ \pi A \cos(\pi f(x,t)) \sin(\pi y) df(x,t)/dx \end{pmatrix}, where \begin{cases} f(x,t) = a(t)x^2 + b(t)x \\ a(t) = \varepsilon \sin(\omega t) \\ b(t) = 1 - 2\varepsilon \sin(\omega t) \end{cases}.$$

$$(14)$$

Another field is an ABC field [26], the expression of which is the resolution of Euler equations. This 3-dimensional field is inviscid and incompressible. The velocity of ABC field is defined by

$$v(x,t) = \begin{pmatrix} A \sin z + B \cos y \\ B \sin x + C \cos z \\ C \sin y + A \cos x \end{pmatrix} \qquad (15)$$

In the experiments, the region of DG field is set to $[0,2] \times [0,1]$. We use cell-centered data of triangle unstructured cell where the distance between vertex is uniform. The region of ABC field is set to $[0, 2\pi]^3$, and uses cell-vertexed data of hexahedral structured cell. All algorithms are run on a platform with 3.9 GHz Intel Xeon X5760 CPU. Only single thread is performed for efficiency comparison.

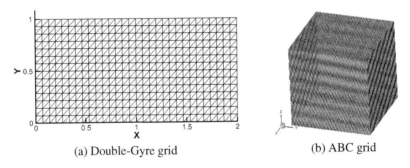

(a) Double-Gyre grid   (b) ABC grid

Fig. 2. Computational grid.

In order to investigate the grid scale and advection step size impaction on the result, the number of vertex of DG field is set to 129*65 and 1001*501, and the number is set to 64^3 and 128^3 in ABC field. Meanwhile, the advection step size is set to 0.01 and 0.001. The center of each cell is selected as seed.

5.1   Cell-Centered DG Field of 2-Dimensional Unstructured Grid

We set $A = 0.1$, $\omega = \pi/5$ in formula 14. The velocity field is generated by solving the velocity at the center of each cell. The generated field is steady with $\varepsilon = 0$, and unsteady with $\varepsilon = 0.1$. The transient fields are generated from time $t = 0.0$ to $t = 10.0$ with step size 0.1, i.e., 101 fields in all. The results of execution time and speedup ratio are shown in Table 1.

Table 1. CPU time (in seconds) and speedup ratio comparison between RK4 and UIA on DG field

Grid scale and type	Advection step size	RK4	UIA	Speedup ration	UIA (Without pretreatment time)	Speedup ratio
129*65	0.01	20.15	2.57	7.84	2.57	7.84
(steady)	0.001	187.34	19.85	9.44	19.85	9.44
1001*501	0.01	15186.2	3111.08	4.88	3111.08	4.88
(steady)	0.001	183.62	36.87	4.98	36.87	4.98
129*65	0.01	37.49	4.86	7.71	4.46	8.40
(unsteady)	0.001	368.73	34.24	10.77	34.24	10.77
1001*501	0.01	266.47	69.10	3.86	40.44	6.59
(unsteady)	0.001	29297.7	3970.12	7.38	3970.12	7.38

While using RK4 to calculate the velocity of every spatial point by formula 14, the computational error of advection is $O(h^4)$. As h is set to 0.01 and 0.001, the error of this approach is 10^{-8} and 10^{12} order of magnitude, which is negligible compared with $\delta x^2 + \delta t^2$. Thus the result approximates to exact solution, and the absolute value of difference between this result and UIA is viewed as UIA error.

The average errors at all seeds which $x = 0.002$ on unsteady DG velocity field solved by UIA are shown in Table 2.

Table 2. Average errors of UIA at all seeds which $x = 0.002$

Grid scale	Advection step size	Average error	$\delta x^2 + \delta t^2$
129*65	0.01	0.0012	0.0321
	0.001	0.0012	0.0321
1001*501	0.01	0.0002	0.0128
	0.001	0.0002	0.0128

Thereafter, the results are used in FTLE [15, 27] computation. The visualization outcome is shown in Fig. 3.

5.2 Cell-Vertexed ABC Field of 3-Dimensional Structured Grid

We set $A = \sqrt{3}, B = \sqrt{2}, C = 1$ in formula 14, the velocity field is a steady field. If we set $A = \sqrt{3} + 0.5t\sin(\pi t), B = \sqrt{2}, C = 1$ ABC field is unsteady. The transient fields are generated from time t = 0.0 to t = 8.0 with step size 0.1, i.e., 81 fields in all. Table 3 shows the results of execution time and speedup ratio.

The average errors at all seeds where $z = 2.773$ on unsteady ABC velocity field solved by UIA are shown in Table 4.

Thereafter, the results are used in FTLE [16, 28] computation. The visualization result is shown in Fig. 4.

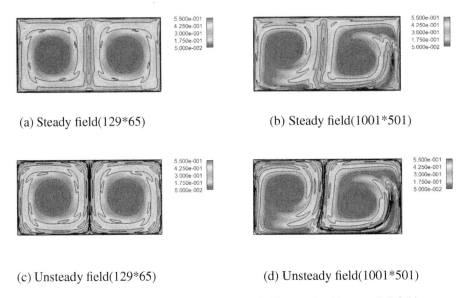

(a) Steady field(129*65)   (b) Steady field(1001*501)

(c) Unsteady field(129*65)   (d) Unsteady field(1001*501)

Fig. 3. FTLE color mapping and contour of different algorithms on DG field.

Table 3. CPU time (in seconds) and speedup ratio comparison between RK4 and UIA on steady ABC field

Grid scale and type	Advection step size	RK4	UIA	Speedup ration	UIA (Without pretreatment time)	Speedup ratio
64^3	0.01	21.21	1.91	11.10	1.86	11.40
(steady)	0.001	211.41	18.03	11.73	18.00	11.75
128^3	0.01	177.58	29.68	5.98	29.39	6.04
(steady)	0.001	1755.02	179.73	9.76	179.41	9.78
64^3	0.01	187.91	12.71	14.78	7.01	26.81
(unsteady)	0.001	385.21	37.81	10.19	32.32	11.92
128^3	0.01	1558.92	206.90	7.53	155.65	10.02
(unsteady)	0.001	3263.71	485.51	6.72	435.72	7.49

Table 4. Average errors of advection at all seeds which $z = 2.773$

Grid scale	Advection step size	Average error	$\delta x^2 + \delta t^2$
64^3	0.01	0.0280	0.0389
	0.001	0.0312	0.0389
128^3	0.01	0.0065	0.0218
	0.001	0.0075	0.0218

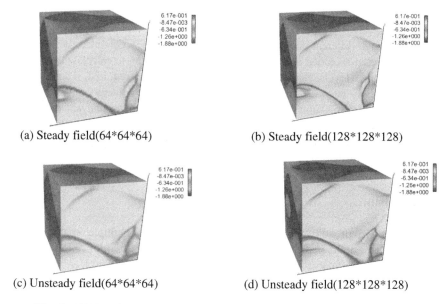

(a) Steady field(64*64*64)

(b) Steady field(128*128*128)

(c) Unsteady field(64*64*64)

(d) Unsteady field(128*128*128)

Fig. 4. FTLE color mapping and contour of different algorithms on ABC field.

5.3   Result Analysis

The experiment shows that the UIA error is in line with the analysis in Sect. 4, where the upper limit doesn't exceed $\delta x^2 + \delta t^2$. As shown in Tables 3 and 4, the error improvement brought by integration step size reduction is comparatively limited. According to Sect. 4, if there is difference in order of magnitude between $\delta x^2 + \delta t^2$ and h^4, UIA error mainly comes from the 2nd-order derivative truncation error of Taylor expansion based on piecewise linear hypothesis in vector field which has derivatives higher than 2nd-order. Therefore, a bigger step size could be used to improve the algorithm efficiency. On the contrary, the grid scale has a greater impact on precision. As shown in Tables 3 and 4, the error is significantly reduced with grid scale reduction. In practice, vector field is often fixed and related to grid scale in measuring and computation. Hence, considerable advection step size can be determined based on grid and time scale analysis in order to achieve the balance between precision and efficiency.

The UIA speedup ratio is often in the range [3, 12]. With the increase of advection steps, the speedup ratio with pretreatment is gradually approaching to the ratio without pretreatment. Once pretreatment is calculated, it can be repeatedly used in consecutive advection computation. Thus the pretreatment overhead doesn't increase with the advection step number, and its proportion in overall overhead is decreased. If the time of advection computation and pretreatment is different in order of magnitude, the pretreatment time is negligible.

UIA requires matrix multiplication and spatial location computation of advection point in advection computation regardless of steady and unsteady field. For each vector component of steady field, traditional RK4 interpolation requires three 1-dimensional linear interpolations regardless of the 2-dimensional triangle or quadrilateral geometry.

As for 3-dimensional grid, tetrahedral and hexahedral need 6 and 7 linear interpolation operations respectively. Thus it is hard to derive consistent computation measurement formula because of different interpolations on various cell types. On unsteady field, RK4 spatial interpolation is carried out on two transient fields in order to calculate the location vector in two time levels, then a linear interpolation is also required. Therefore, the number of unsteady interpolation is more than twice of steady interpolation. However, unsteady location computation is in line with UIA. According to the analysis, the amount of UIA computation is easy to estimate in the case of determined number of grid dimensions, scale and transient fields. Due to the dependence on grid geometry, the computational overhead of RK4 varies on different grid types, which is hard to estimate.

6 Conclusion

In this paper we propose UIA algorithm, which coverts multiple spatiotemporal interpolations and multi-step time advection into single matrix multiplication such that the computation is dramatically reduced. After theoretically analyzing UIA's precision, we verify the correctness through data sets with cell- centered and cell-vertexed format on structured and unstructured grids using2-dimensional DG field and 3-dimensional ABC field. The experimental precision conforms to theoretical analysis. Moreover, the experiments also show that UIA has obvious advantage in computation involving large number of seeds (e.g., FTLE) compared with RK4.

Advection algorithm is considerably fundamental, so that UIA can be applied to various visualization techniques such as stream line/surface, path line/surface, time line/surface, streak line/surface, LIC and so on. Besides, UIA is highly parallelizable so that it is suitable for implementation on parallel devices like GPGPU and MIC, which can further reduce advection time.

The limitation of UIA is that the transformation matrix needs to be recalculated while the step is not fixed, which could cause some inefficiency. Our future work includes researches on parallel UIA based on data partition, efficient advection algorithm with changing step size, and high precision advection on data set that is not piecewise linear distributed, such as CFD field from high order discrete Galerkin numerical simulation.

Acknowledgments. This work is supported by Chinese 973 Program (2015CB755604) and the National Science Foundation of China (61202335).

References

1. Chen, W., Shen, Z., Tao, Y.: Data Visualization. Publishing House of Electronics Industry, Beijing (2013)
2. Mcloughlin, T., Laramee, R.S., Peikert, R., et al.: Over two decades of integration- based, geometric flow visualization. Comput. Graph. Forum **29**(6), 1807–1829 (2010)
3. Edmunds, M., Laramee, R.S., Chen, G., et al.: Surface-based flow visualization. Comput. Graph. **36**(8), 974–990 (2012)

4. Laramee, R.S., Hauser, H., Doleisch, H., et al.: The state of the art in flow visualization dense and texture-based techniques. Comput. Graph. Forum **23**(2), 203–221 (2004)
5. Post, F.H., Vrolijk, B., Hauser, H., et al.: The state of the art in flow visualisation: feature extraction and tracking. Comput. Graph. Forum **22**(4), 775–792 (2003)
6. Pobitzer, A., Peikert, R., Fuchs, R., et al.: The state of the art in topology-based visualization of unsteady flow. Comput. Graph. Forum **30**(6), 1789–1811 (2011)
7. Murray, L.: GPU acceleration of Runge-Kutta integrators. IEEE Trans. Parallel Distrib. Syst. **23**(1), 94–101 (2012)
8. Camp, D., Krishnan, H., Pugmire, D., et al.: GPU acceleration of particle advection workloads in a parallel, distributed memory setting. In: Eurographics Symposium on Parallel Graphics and Visualization, pp. 1–8. The Eurographics Association (2013)
9. Nouanesengsy, B., Lee, T.-Y., Shen, H.-W.: Load-balanced parallel streamline generation on large scale vector fields. IEEE Trans. Vis. Comput. Graph. **17**(12), 1785–1794 (2011)
10. David, C., Christoph, G., Hank, C., et al.: Streamline integration using MPI- hybrid parallelism on a large multicore architecture. IEEE Trans. Vis. Comput. Graph. **17**(11), 1702–1713 (2011)
11. Peterka, T., Ross, R., Nounesengsy, B., et al.: A study of parallel particle tracing for steady-state and time-varying flow fields. In: Proceedings of the 2011 IEEE International Parallel and Distributed Processing Symposium (2011)
12. Ueng, S.K., Sikorski, K., Ma, K.L.: Fast algorithms for visualizing fluid motion in steady flow on unstructured grids. In: IEEE Visualization Conference, pp. 313–320. IEEE Computer Society (1999)
13. Ueng, S.K., Sikorski, K., Ma, K.L.: E client streamline, streamribbon, and stream- tube constructions on unstructured grids. IEEE Trans. Vis. Comput. Graph. **2**(2), 100–110 (1996)
14. Wang, W., Wang, W., Li, S.: Batch advection for the piecewise linear vector field on implicial grids. Comput. Graph. **54**, 75–83 (2016)
15. Shadden, S.C., Lekienb, F., Marsdena, J.E.: Definition and properties of Lagrangian coherent structures from finite-time Lyapunov exponents in two- dimensional aperiodic flows. Phys. D **212**(34), 271–304 (2005)
16. Shi, K., Seidel, H.-P., Theisel, H., et al.: Visualizing transport structures of time- dependent flow fields. IEEE Comput. Graph. Appl. **28**(5), 24–36 (2008)
17. Haller, G.: Langrangian coherent structures. Annual Rev. Fluid Mech. **47**(1), 137–162 (2015)
18. Barth, T.J., Jespersen, D.C.: The design and application of upwind schemes on unstructured meshes. Aiaa J. **0366**(13), 1–13 (1989)
19. Jameson, A., Schmidt, W., Turkel, E.: Numerical solution of the Euler equations by finite volume methods using Runge-Kutta time stepping schemes. Aiaa **1259**(11), 20040–24325 (1981)
20. Anderson, J.D.: Computational Fluid Dynamics. China Machine Press, China (2007)
21. Ma, Q., Xu, H., Zeng, L., et al.: Direct raycasting of unstructured cell-centered data by discontinuity Roe-average computation. Vis. Comput. **26**(6), 1049–1059 (2010)
22. AIAA: Improved reconstruction schemes for the Navier-Stokes equations on un- structured meshes. In: Proceedings of the AIAA Paper (1994)
23. Hearn, D., Baker, M.: Computer Graphics. Publishing House of Electronics Industry, Beijing (1998)
24. Coulliette, C., Wiggins, S.: Intergyre transport in a wind-driven, quasigeostrophic double gyre: an application of lobe dynamics. Nonlinear Process. Geophys. **7**(1/2), 59–85 (1999)
25. Chad, C., Francois, L., Paduan, J.D., et al.: Optimal pollution mitigation in Monterey Bay based on coastal radar data and nonlinear dynamics. Environ. Sci. Technol. **41**(18), 6562–6572 (2007)

26. Kundu, P.K., Cohen, I.M.: Fluid Mechanics. Academic Press, New York (2004)
27. Leung, S.Y.: An Eulerian approach for computing the finite time Lyapunov exponent. J. Comput. Phys. **230**(9), 3500–3524 (2011)
28. Haller, G.: Distinguished material surfaces and coherent structures in three- dimensional fluid flows. Phys. D **149**(4), 248–277 (2001)

Data Mining, Management and Visualization in Large Scientific Corpuses

Hui Wei$^{(\boxtimes)}$, Shaopeng Wu, Youbing Zhao, Zhikun Deng,
Nikolaos Ersotelos, Farzad Parvinzamir, Baoquan Liu,
Enjie Liu, and Feng Dong

Department of Computer Science and Technology,
University of Bedfordshire, Luton, UK
{hui.wei,shaopeng.wu,youbing.zhao,zhikun.deng,
nikolaos.ersotelos,farzad.parvinzamir,baoquan.liu,
enjie.liu,feng.dong}@beds.ac.uk

Abstract. Organizing scientific papers helps efficiently derive meaningful insights of the published scientific resources, enables researchers grasp rapid technological change and hence assists new scientific discovery. In this paper, we experiment text mining and data management of scientific publications for collecting and presenting useful information to support research. For efficient data management and fast information retrieval, four data storages are employed: a semantic repository, an index and search repository, a document repository and a graph repository, taking full advantage of their features and strength. The results show that the combination of these four repositories can effectively store and index the publication data with reliability and efficiency and hence supply meaningful information to support scientific research.

Keywords: Data management · Distributed storage · NoSql · Text mining · Visualization · Document repository · Elasticsearch · Graph database

1 Introduction

Digital libraries of scientific published papers are the main channel for acquiring cutting edge knowledge for scientific workers. This system presented is designed to help researchers overcome the limitations in pursuing scientific discovery through the analysis of published research papers. A large number of papers in computer graphics have been collected to study the trends of topic changes with the time. Most digital libraries concentrate on single document analysis. Our project DrInventor [1] tries to help the user overcome the difficulties in pursuing scientific discovery. The initiative is to discover scientific creativity and technological change to facilitate scientific research. Researchers normally search citations from public digital libraries. They use keywords to find relevant publications from their titles, abstracts, mesh terms or full text. Due to the size of the libraries, finding the right papers is not easy and our system is designed to help them.

The remainder of the paper is organized as follows. In Sect. 2 we describe how we collect, analyse and extract information from raw resources. In Sect. 3 we discuss

© Springer International Publishing Switzerland 2016
A. El Rhalibi et al. (Eds.): Edutainment 2016, LNCS 9654, pp. 371–379, 2016.
DOI: 10.1007/978-3-319-40259-8_32

managing these data in suitable data repositories to help efficient querying related data. And in Sect. 4, we present two visualization demos to display our processing results in two cases.

2 Data Collection

As these citations are semi-structured, they follow a certain template (e.g. ACM). The basic information we need has to be extracted from the original documents in pdf format. With the aid of further text analysis, we convert the original pdf files into plain text files by using Apache PDFBox [2], an open source Java tool for working with PDF documents. These original pdf files are kept since they are still useful to users. We separate these papers according to their publication data (e.g. year, volume). A corpus is defined with properties such as organization, conference, year. In each phrase we process one corpus. If there is a failure in one corpus, it will not affect the other corpuses.

The data collection phrase has three targets:

- extraction of basic information of a paper such as authors, title, abstract sentences, doi, which can be used to provide brief information about a paper and to provide a unique ID for each paper, hence avoiding duplicated processing.
- extraction of references, citation information, and hence from each paper to build up relation chains among the publications.
- extraction of standard keywords and their frequency from each paper. With these results, we could further calculate the topics from the information.

The data collection work is also used in EC project CARRE [3].

2.1 Metadata Extraction

We implement Metadata extraction by using a text processing pipeline supported by the GATE Text Engineering Framework [4]. A text file is broken down into sentences, then tokenized and POS tagged with the ANNIE system [5], followed by recognizing person names and numbers with gazetteers. With all this information, we then use a series of grammar rules (JAPE: Java Annotation Pattern Engine [6] rules) for the extraction of meaningful information:

1. Define "Macro"s from ACM format to find important markers, such as "ACM Reference Format" at the start of a converted txt file; "Abstract" tag, "Keywords" tag, "Introduction" tag, "DOI" tag, "year" tag, "Author" tag, "CR Categories" tag and so on. Make JAPE rules to output "author", "year", "title" tags.
2. Search for two consecutive sentences with first sentence containing {authorTag} {yearTag} or {authorsTag}{yearTag}. From these two sentences, reference title, year, authors are extracted.
3. Search for abstract sentences, located between the "Abstract" tag and the "CR Categories" tag.
4. Search for keywords list sentences starting from "the Keywords" tag, ending at the "Introduction" tag.

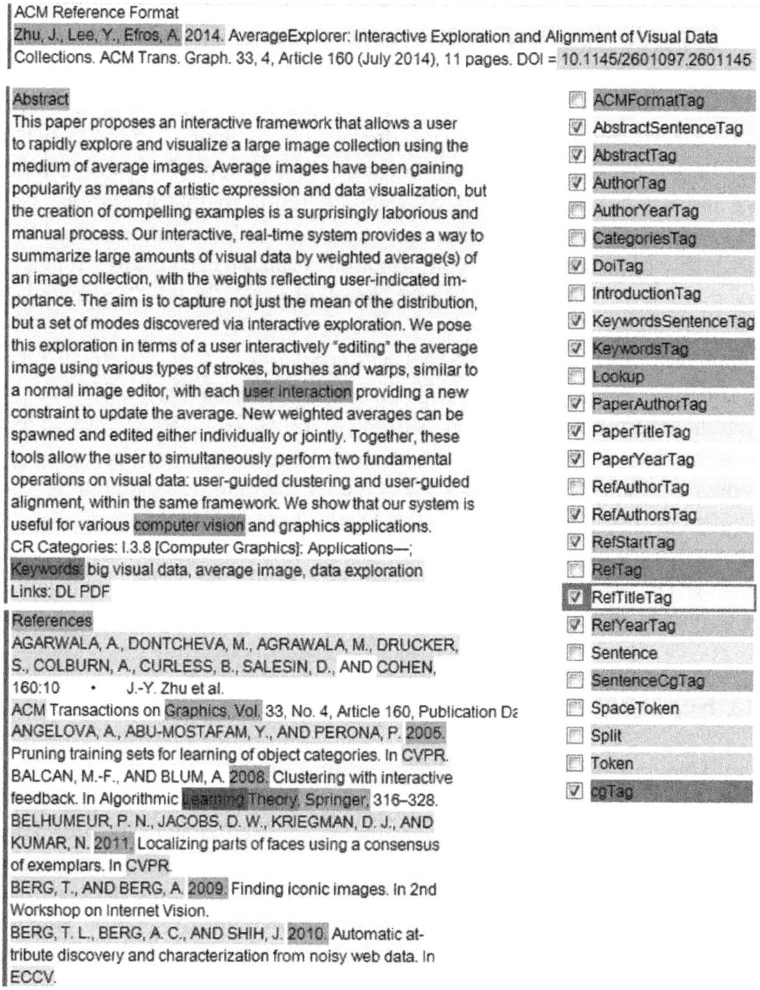

ACM Reference Format
Zhu, J., Lee, Y., Efros, A. 2014. AverageExplorer: Interactive Exploration and Alignment of Visual Data
Collections. ACM Trans. Graph. 33, 4, Article 160 (July 2014), 11 pages. DOI = 10.1145/2601097.2601145

Abstract
This paper proposes an interactive framework that allows a user
to rapidly explore and visualize a large image collection using the
medium of average images. Average images have been gaining
popularity as means of artistic expression and data visualization, but
the creation of compelling examples is a surprisingly laborious and
manual process. Our interactive, real-time system provides a way to
summarize large amounts of visual data by weighted average(s) of
an image collection, with the weights reflecting user-indicated importance. The aim is to capture not just the mean of the distribution,
but a set of modes discovered via interactive exploration. We pose
this exploration in terms of a user interactively "editing" the average
image using various types of strokes, brushes and warps, similar to
a normal image editor, with each user interaction providing a new
constraint to update the average. New weighted averages can be
spawned and edited either individually or jointly. Together, these
tools allow the user to simultaneously perform two fundamental
operations on visual data: user-guided clustering and user-guided
alignment, within the same framework. We show that our system is
useful for various computer vision and graphics applications.
CR Categories: I.3.8 [Computer Graphics]: Applications—;
Keywords: big visual data, average image, data exploration
Links: DL PDF

References
AGARWALA, A., DONTCHEVA, M., AGRAWALA, M., DRUCKER,
S., COLBURN, A., CURLESS, B., SALESIN, D., AND COHEN,
160:10   •   J.-Y. Zhu et al.
ACM Transactions on Graphics, Vol. 33, No. 4, Article 160, Publication Da
ANGELOVA, A., ABU-MOSTAFAM, Y., AND PERONA, P. 2005.
Pruning training sets for learning of object categories. In CVPR.
BALCAN, M.-F., AND BLUM, A. 2008. Clustering with interactive
feedback. In Algorithmic Learning Theory. Springer, 316–328.
BELHUMEUR, P. N., JACOBS, D. W., KRIEGMAN, D. J., AND
KUMAR, N. 2011. Localizing parts of faces using a consensus
of exemplars. In CVPR.
BERG, T., AND BERG, A. 2009. Finding iconic images. In 2nd
Workshop on Internet Vision.
BERG, T. L., BERG, A. C., AND SHIH, J. 2010. Automatic at-
tribute discovery and characterization from noisy web data. In
ECCV.

ACMFormatTag
AbstractSentenceTag
AbstractTag
AuthorTag
AuthorYearTag
CategoriesTag
DoiTag
IntroductionTag
KeywordsSentenceTag
KeywordsTag
Lookup
PaperAuthorTag
PaperTitleTag
PaperYearTag
RefAuthorTag
RefAuthorsTag
RefStartTag
RefTag
RefTitleTag
RefYearTag
Sentence
SentenceCgTag
SpaceToken
Split
Token
cgTag

Fig. 1. Metadata extraction.

The above rules apply to ACM publications, with some modifications needed over different time periods. By applying these rules, each paper is mapped to one metadata and is stored in the document repository.

Figure 1 shows the basic metadata information, including titleTag, authorTag, yearTag doiTag etc., extracted with multi tags. The citing list of one citation is extracted with citing title, author and year tags. Keywords information in cgTag is also extracted in context to help calculating keywords frequency.

2.2   Keywords Extraction

The Microsoft Academic Search (MAS) API [7] allows developers to build applications by leveraging the data and functions of MAS. They supply a keyword function that represents keyword objects in many fields such as "Biology, Chemistry, Engineering Mathematics, Physics, Computer Science" and so on. In the computer science category, domains like "Algorithms & Theory, Artificial Intelligence, Computer Vision, Data Mining, Databases, Graphics" are described separately. We target our research in the "Computer > Graphics" domain, from which we collected 13,670 keywords. In a scientific publication, the usage of a group of keywords reflects its topic. We use these 13K keywords as standard terms to match phrases used in a computer graphics paper. These 13K computer graphics keywords are used for every citation to collect keyword frequency information. Then we need to store it in a suitable repository that can be easily mapped with standard words in the Computer Graphics (CG) citation context.

The keywords we fetched from MAS API contain a variety of terms for the same meaning, such as "three dimensional", "3D" and "three-dimensional". For machine processing, these terms will be treated as different terms. To understand these terms, an ontology is introduced into the system to share this conceptualization [8, 9]. These "3D" synonyms should be treated as same "type" in the ontology with multi "same As" links. We defined predicate "rdf:type" and "owl:sameAs" for this purpose in Sesame [10] RDF repository and convert all these standard terms into Resource Description Framework (RDF) triples. By building up this "OWLIM-LITE" repository with "Owl-max" ruleset, this repository is connected as the ontology from GATE Gazetteer.

3 Data Repository

Apart from keywords stored in the RDF repository, a document repository CouchDB [11] is employed for metadata and a raw data repository. In order to enhance full text search ability, the search engine Elasticsearch [12] is used to store the abstract part of the metadata in JSON format. Graph databases are very efficient in traversing relationships [13], which are suitable for dealing with citing relations between citations. We benefit from these four repositories in terms of flexibility, efficiency, convenience, and intuition.

We use Sesame RDF to store computer graphics (CG) terms or keywords as ontologies (Fig. 2); the benefit of RDF storage is that we can update it when new terms are created or synonyms of an existing term are found. With inferencing and querying

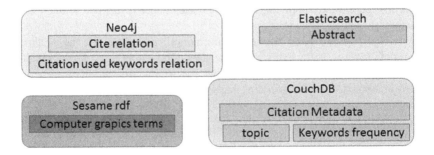

Fig. 2. Data is managed in four NoSql repositories.

support, our ontology is connected with GATE as language resources. Then this language resource is used to create an ontology Gazetteer in GATE. To recognize these CG terms, a Jape Transducer with JAPE rule file is defined to pick out these terms and give them a unified tag (cgTag in Fig. 1).

The metadata that describes the basic information of a citation is managed in the Document repository, CouchDB. Keyword frequency of a document reveals what a citation talks about with standard domain terms. This information is stored in CouchDB at the data collection stage. Abstract information from a citation is an important summary. This data extracted from the raw PDF file is stored as an attachment at the data collection stage.

CouchDB is designed for web application, a raw PDF citation file can be stored as an attachment to its metadata. The attachment presented by a URL can be easily passed to another file consumer, since a URL mapped to this file can be identified by its document ID. As a schema-free database, one document's data is allowed to have any number of properties. From that character, inheritance classes could be mapped into the same data document. That means it gives the user the freedom of mapping data with more properties or fewer. Views in CouchDB is a kind of design document which supplies output of a group of related data. As these view design documents are written by the user through JavaScript, the calculation ability is more flexible than SQL. Validation function is a special property of a design document. From both old and new document content as input, this function gives the user the ability to verify relation of properties or relation of new and old documents. The Map/Reduce function supplied by CouchDB is useful for aggregation data to create a summary of a group of data.

Although views are the tool for querying data on CouchDB documents, full text search cannot be achieved even through Elasticsearch Rivers [14]. Elasticsearch is introduced for this propose. At the data processing stage, citation data (abstract information, a few basic metadata properties and document ID) read from CouchDB is loaded into the search engine. As a shared entity, the citation object is stored in the Document repository with the full set of properties, while in search engine the citation object with basic properties is loaded. The link between these two cross-repository objects of the same citation is the same ID. So the citations found by the search engine can be tracked with full information in the Document repository.

Graph databases are very efficient in traversing relationships. We select Neo4j as the Graph database storing relationships of citations and relationships between citation and keywords. Relationships between citations can be defined in many cases. The citing relationship describes the reference list of a citation. This information can be gathered from the citation itself. The cited relationship describes other citations which use this given citation as a reference. This information also can be gathered from the Document repository by using a query. But detecting similar citing or cited papers between two given papers needs massive deep querying that is not efficient. So the Graph database is used in our system. It loads data from the Document repository to create relationships of reference (citation) and usage (keywords) at the data processing stage. In the graph repository, a relation can be described by a path; it is more efficient and convenient to find a path in the graph repository.

4   Citation Data Visualization

4.1   Cited Relationship

As mentioned before, reference information is extracted from the raw PDF file. Due to formatting problems, some references are extracted without exactly matching a paper title even though they exist in the Document repository. But we still have a large number of relations in the Graph repository. At this stage we treat citations within "SIGGRAPH" as internal papers, citations from other digital libraries like IEEE as external reference papers. As we have processed metadata from raw SIGGRAPH for 13 years of citations, one SIGGRAPH paper citing other SIGGRAPH papers can be tracked, otherwise these cited papers can only be treated as references.

In order to extract meaningful data, we present our "be cited" relationships in a D3 [15] chord diagram.

The data structure in the Graph repository can be treated as many trees if we treat starting nodes as the root of its reference tree. In our Chord diagram, only root nodes and leaf nodes of the required length path are presented.

Figure 3(F) presents 13-year paper citing relations. The data are papers that have relationships between them more than length 6 in 13 years. Short arc papers have normally been published in recent years and the longer arc papers normally in earlier years. Querying these inheritance relations from the Graph database is much more efficient than in other types of database. The longer the arc, the more length 6 citing papers are related to the paper. These longer arc papers are more likely to be root nodes of depth 7 tree structures. Figure 3(G) presents the relation between the given single citation and its indirect citing papers with mouse hover on a paper title. The diagram shows only citing papers of this input paper and hides other papers. Due to image space limitations, all paper titles are reduced to 20 characters. Figure 3(H) presents citations as cited citations in the year 2013 corpus and their citing citations. As we have 13 year corpuses from 2002 to 2014, those citing papers are published papers from the year 2014 corpus. From H we can easily recognize a paper in brown named "Globally optimal dir" is cited more times than others.

Topic Distribution. Figure 4 uses keywords data linked with the paper year property to calculate topic modelling. The probabilities of topics are shown according to their proportion. The topics were retrieved by the Latent Dirichlet Allocation (LDA) algorithm. The algorithm assumes the documents were produced in a probabilistic generative model, which discovers the topics in every document or a corpus. The figure shows six selected topic variations from year 2005 to 2014. The proportion of the topic is represented by height at each time along the horizontal axis. The topic colours correspond to the legend colours and texts. The interactive functions would offer more information, e.g. mouse hover on a topic of certain year. Then the topic name, year and value of the topic are shown with the pointer. Comparing to [16], which uses a matrix-like style to present topics, ours has more explicit and simple visibility and operations.

The project only concentrates on the computer graphic documents from proceedings of ACM SIGGRAPH. For example, a decreasing publication number can be seen in the topic of "image compression" while a chopping pattern shows in the topic of

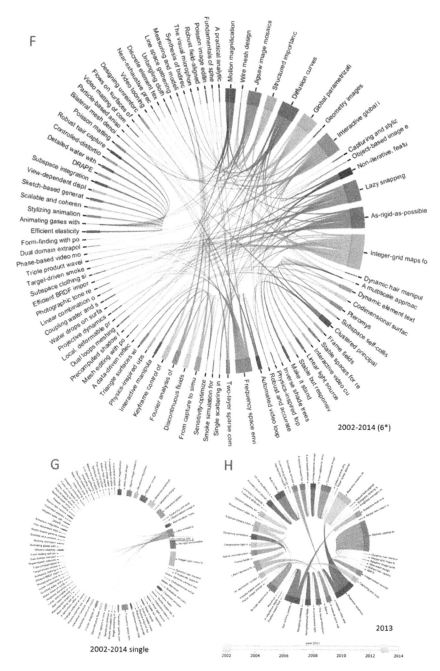

Fig. 3. Chord diagram. F: 13-year corpuses of length 6 cited relations. G: singlecited relations. H: one year cited relations.

topics

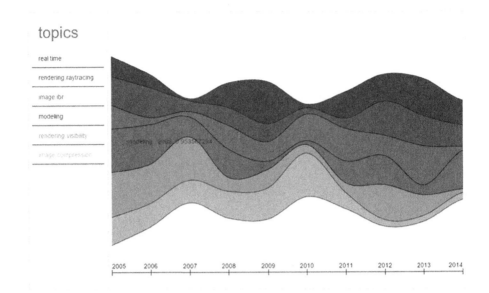

Fig. 4. Topic river visualisation

"real time". From these trends, the users can judge research topic trends by years. More information, such as topic contents, topic-related documents and their publication details, will be added in the next stage.

5   Conclusion

In this paper, we present our work on text mining and data management on a large number of scientific publications for collecting and presenting citation information and topic trends to facilitate research work. Four data storages including a semantic repository, an index and search repository, a document repository and a graph repository are employed for efficient data management and fast information retrieval. The experiment results show that the combination of these four repositories can efficiently store and index the publication data reliably to supply valuable information to support scientific research, which further helps researchers to derive meaningful insights of the published scientific resources more conveniently, enabling them to grasp technological change more quickly and hence assists new scientific discovery.

Acknowledgments. The research is supported by Dr Inventor project {the European Union Seventh Framework Programme ([FP7/2007-2013]) Dr Inventor under grant agreement no. 611383} and CARRE project {the Seventh Framework Programme of European Commission – ICT under agreement of FP7-ICT-611140}.

References

1. DrInventor. http://drinventor.eu/
2. pdfbox. https://pdfbox.apache.org/
3. CARRE. https://www.carre-project.eu/
4. Cunningham, H., Maynard, D., Bontcheva, K., Tablan, V.: GATE: a framework and graphical development environment for robust NLP tools and applications. In: Proceedings of 40th Anniversary Meeting of the Association for Computational Linguistics (ACL 2002), Philadelphia, July 2002
5. ANNIE. https://gate.ac.uk/sale/tao/splitch6.html#chap:annie
6. Thakker, D., Sman, T., Lakin, P.: GATE Jape Grammar Tutorial, Version 1.0, A, Pictures, UK (2009)
7. Microsoft Academic Search (MAS) API. http://academic.research.microsoft.com/
8. Gruber, T.R.: A translation approach to portable ontology specifications. Knowl. Acquis. **5** (2), 199–220
9. Jin, L., Liu, L.: An ontology definition metamodel based ripple-effect analysis method for ontology evolution. In: Proceedings of 10th International Conference on Computer Supported Cooperative Work in Design, pp. 1–6. doi:10.1109/CSCWD.2006.253032
10. Fensel, D., Hendler, J., Lieberman, H., Wahlster, W., Berners-Lee, T.: Sesame: an architecture for storing and querying RDF data and schema information. In: MIT Press eBook Chapters: Spinning the Semantic Web: Bringing the World Wide Web to Its Full Potential, pp. 197–222 (2005)
11. CouchDB. http://couchdb.apache.org/
12. Elasticsearch. https://www.elastic.co/products/elasticsearch
13. Grolinger, K., Higashino, W.A., Tiwari, A., Capretz, M.A.M.: Data management in cloud environments: NoSQL and NewSQL data stores. J. Cloud Comput.: Adv. Syst. Appl. **2**(22), 2–22 (2013). doi:10.1186/2192-113X-2-22
14. Elasticsearch Rivers. https://www.elastic.co/guide/en/elasticsearch/rivers/1.4/index.html
15. D3. http://d3js.org/
16. Alexander, E., Kohlmann, J., Valenza, R., Witmore, M., Gleicher Serendip, M.: Topic model-driven visual exploration of text corpora. In: IEEE Conference on Visual Analytics Science and Technology (VAST), pp. 173–182 (2014)

Visual Analytics for Health Monitoring and Risk Management in CARRE

Youbing Zhao[1]([✉]), Farzad Parvinzamir[1], Hui Wei[1], Enjie Liu[1], Zhikun Deng[1], Feng Dong[1], Allan Third[2], Arūnas Lukoševičius[3], Vaidotas Marozas[3], Eleni Kaldoudi[4], and Gordon Clapworthy[1]

[1] University of Bedfordshire, Luton LU1 3JU, UK
{youbing.zhao,farzad.parvinzamir,hui.wei,enjie.liu,zhikun.deng,feng.dong,
gordon.clapworthy}@beds.ac.uk
[2] Knowledge Media Institute, The Open University, Milton Keynes, UK
allan.third@open.ac.uk
[3] Biomedical Engineering Institute, Kaunas University of Technology,
Kaunas, Lithuania
{arunas.lukosevicius,vaimaro}@ktu.lt
[4] Physics of Medical Imaging and Telemedicine, School of Medicine,
Democritus University of Thrace Dragana, Alexandroupoli, Greece
kaldoudi@med.duth.gr

Abstract. With the rise of wearable sensor technologies, an increasing number of wearable health and medical sensors are available on the market, which enables not only people but also doctors to utilise them to monitor people's health in such a consistent way that the sensors may become people's lifetime companion. The consistent measurements from a variety of wearable sensors implies that a huge amount of data needs to be processed, which cannot be achieved by traditional processing methods. Visual analytics is designed to promote knowledge discovery and utilisation of big data via mature visual paradigms with well-designed user interactions and has become indispensable in big data analysis. In this paper we introduce the role of visual analytics for health monitoring and risk management in the European Commission funded project CARRE which aims to provide innovative means for the management of cardiorenal diseases with the assistance of wearable sensors. The visual analytics components of timeline and parallel coordinates for health monitoring and of node-link diagrams, chord diagrams and sankey diagrams for risk analysis are presented to achieve ubiquitous and lifelong health and risk monitoring to promote people's health.

Keywords: CARRE · Visual analytics · Wearable sensor · Health monitoring · Risk management

1 Introduction

The widespread use of wearable monitoring devices and mobile apps makes ubiquitous capture of life-logging personal health data a reality. Effective collection

© Springer International Publishing Switzerland 2016
A. El Rhalibi et al. (Eds.): Edutainment 2016, LNCS 9654, pp. 380–391, 2016.
DOI: 10.1007/978-3-319-40259-8_33

of long-term health-status data is valuable for clinical decisions and leads to strengthened interdisciplinary healthcare research and collaboration in supporting innovative medical care. With different types of wearable sensor the healthcare platform can aggregate heterogeneous health and medical data for health monitoring, disease prediction and risk management in a ubiquitous, personalised and continuous manner.

In this paper we present the ongoing work of visual analytics in the CARRE project [1] – Personalized Patient Empowerment and Shared Decision Support for Cardiorenal Disease and Comorbidities – funded by the 7th Framework Programme of the European Commission, which aims to provide innovative means for the management of cardiorenal diseases with the assistance of wearable sensors.

Wearable device based health data collection tools traditionally refers to use of medical devices to monitor medical data, such as heart rate, blood pressure, glucose, etc. Recently, the use of wearable devices in life-logging data collection mainly indicates the record of some personal physical activity data. CARRE uses Fitbit [2], Withings [6] and iHealth citeiHealth devices to record steps, distance, calories, heart rate, sleep quality, blood pressure, weight, etc.

The target of CARRE is to provide personalised empowerment and shared decision support for cardiorenal disease, which is the condition characterised by simultaneous kidney and heart disease while the primarily failing organ may be either the heart or the kidney. In CARRE, sources of medical and other knowledge will be semantically linked with sensor outputs to provide clinical information personalised to the individual patient, so as to be able to track the progression and interactions of comorbid conditions. The ultimate goal is to provide the means for patients with comorbidities to take an active role in care processes, including self-care and shared decision-making, and also to support medical professionals in understanding and treating comorbidities via an integrative approach.

The CARRE repository acts as the central point of information storage for all CARRE applications. It conforms to the principles of the Semantic Web and the guidelines of Linked Data. The Linked Data guidelines can be summarized as follows:

Information stored in the CARRE repository consists of 'RDF triples'. RDF is a standard format for representing semantic data on the Web; an item of RDF data is a triple, which corresponds to a statement of the form 'subject predicate object'. Each term is a URI, often drawn from a standard vocabulary or ontology, making it easy to link triples from different sources – to allow Linked Data. RDF can be accessed through a SPARQL endpoint: SPARQL is a query language, much like SQL in syntax. The triples stored in the CARRE repository are either public or private. For private data, data privacy and security mechanisms have been deployed.

The CARRE repository [21] stores general medical knowledge relating to risk associations, evidence and observables, and is available for public querying without authentication, as it contains no personally identifying data for any patient and serves as a general-purpose resource for medical knowledge in a semantic format.

In CARRE the risk model is a large semantic graph structure data consisting of interlinked entities, such as risk elements and risk evidence, that are either related to ground knowledge in cardio-renal disease and comorbidities (symptoms, diseases, risk factors, treatments, medical evidence source data, educational content, etc.) or personalised to each patient (patient demographics, medical history, sensor data, lifestyle data, etc.) [13]. The data structure of the risk factor repository is shown in Fig. 1.

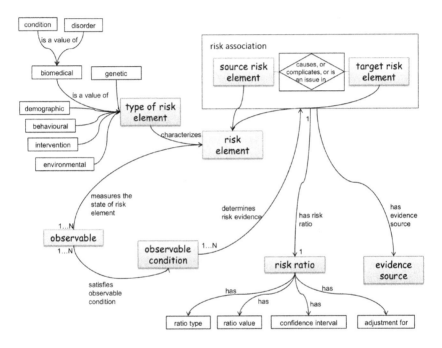

Fig. 1. The risk model structure in the CARRE risk repository

The key concepts in the CARRE risk factor network are defined as follows:

- Risk Element: Risk elements include all the disorders/diseases involved in the comorbidity under discussion as well as any other risk causing agent, e.g. demographic (e.g. age, sex, race), genetic (gene polymorphisms), behavioural (e.g. smoking, physical exercise), environmental (e.g. air pollution, allergens) or even an intervention (e.g. pharmaceutical substances, contrast agents).
- Risk Association: The association of one risk element as the risk source with another risk element, which is the negative outcome under certain conditions, is a 'risk association'. A source risk element can be associated to a target risk element with more than one risk association.

- Risk Ratio: The association is always accompanied by the likelihood of the negative outcome occurring. This likelihood is expressed as a 'risk ratio', which is the ratio of the probability of the negative outcome when the person is exposed to the risk agent over the probability of the negative outcome when the person is not exposed to the risk agent.
- Risk Observable: In a risk association the prerequisite circumstances relate directly to the existence of the risk agent (source risk target) and/or its severity, and/or any other specific conditions. These are reported via certain 'observables', that is, physical variables that can be measured or otherwise ascertained (e.g. biomarkers, biometric variables, biological signals and other non-biological factors, e.g. environmental).

Currently there are 98 risk factors, 53 risk elements, 253 risk evidences, 63 observables and 60 evidence sources in the CARRE risk data repository.

The risk model provided by CARRE can also been applied to other platforms for effective health monitoring and disease diagnosis. For example, the bridging of the CARRE risk model and the life-logging platform MyHealthAvatar [4,5] is under investigation.

To view and understand both the health status data and the risk data, visual analytics is indispensable in CARRE to provide patients and clinicians the ability to visualise, understand and interact with this linked knowledge and also take advantage of personalised empowerment services. The aim is to help medical professionals to better understand the individual patient's disease development and help patients to understand their own disease development, which in turn assists them to adhere to the self-management plan.

This paper presents the first stage of the CARRE Visual Analytics implementation: timeline and parallel coordinates are employed for health monitoring and correlation analysis, node-link diagrams, chord diagrams etc. are chosen for risk factor visualisation and risk analysis. A preliminary version of personalised risk visualisation and disease propagation simulation is demonstrated.

The paper is organised as follows: Sect. 2 introduces related work in health data visual analytics; Sect. 3 discusses major visual analytics components of CARRE for health monitoring and risk management and Sect. 4 concludes with the summary and future work.

2   Related Work

Healthcare has been an important research and application field of data analysis and visualisation for several decades [8]. Behind healthcare visual analytics, much of the focus is on the visualisation of electronic health records (EHRs). [7] gives a detailed review of the related work, categorising by individual patients or group of patients. In each category, the work is further divided by visual analytics of time series data or status at a certain time point. [23] also presents a systematic review of innovative visual analytics approaches that have been proposed to illustrate EHR data.

Lifelines [18] is a pioneer work in visualisation of individual patient records, which provides a general visualisation environment for problems, diagnoses, test results or medications using timelines.

Lifelines2 [22] provides visualisation of temporal categorical data across multiple records, which is better for a doctor to view to discover and explore patterns across these records to support hypothesis generation, and find cause-and-effect relationships in a population.

LifeFlow [25] and EventFlow [16] are tools for event sequence analytics for a group of patients. They extract and highlight the common event sequence from patient records.

Outflow [24] and DecisionFlow [10] uses Sankey diagrams [19] to help to visualise and analyse the causal relationships of events in complex event sequences.

The existing work has made a detailed visual analytics research mostly on EHRs and event analysis. While the work on predictive visual analytics of healthcare data is highly valuable [17], it is still rare due to its complexity.

Personal health information has been increasingly collectible and accessible in the information era. With the trend of "predictive, preemptive, personalized and participative" healthcare [20], more personalised data is desired for predictive analysis of medical care. In addition, with the development of wearable sensor technologies, there is a vision of the merging of health sensors and medical sensors, which will bring the fusion of personal health information and the medical sensor data in the future. Together with the clinical information that has long played the major role in health and medical decision making, personal health information can introduce more added value for health monitoring and medical decision making.

CARRE can not only directly access personal health and lifestyle data from devices such as Fibit, Withings and iHealth, but also access data from multiple heterogeneous data sources via Microsoft HealthVault [3]. Together with proven risk models [13] extracted from medical literatures, CARRE aims to provide personalised risk management and analysis, which is a key difference from the existing healthcare visual analytics systems.

3   CARRE Visual Analytics

Visual analytics combines automated analysis techniques with interactive visualisations for an effective understanding, reasoning and decision-making on the basis of very large and complex datasets [14]. It is designed to promote knowledge discovery and utilisation of big data via effective visual paradigms and well-designed user interactions. In visual analytics, visualisation becomes the medium of an interactive analytical process, where humans and computers cooperate using their respective distinct capabilities for data processing and visual recognition for the most effective results. Thus, in visual analytics, user interaction constitutes the key for a user-centred data exploration. Visual analytics is an indispensable technology for information processing in the big data era.

In CARRE the data can be generally categorised into fitness data collected from sensors/apps, biomarker data from personal electronic health records

(PHR) and risk factor data extracted from medical literatures. The role of visual analytics is to visualise health data, risk factor data and the integrated visual analysis of health data and risk factor data. In the current first stage implementation, CARRE provides web-based components for interactive health data visualisation and risk analysis, including healthline and parallel coordinates for fitness and biomarker data, node-link diagram, chord diagram and sankey diagram for risk factor data visual analysis and a preliminary experiment on personalised risk visualisation and disease progression simulation.

3.1   Fitness and Biomarker Data Visualisation

Healthline. Lifestyle, health, fitness and medical data are inherently time dependent. To visualise time-varying data, a linear form timeline is a natural choice. A healthline is a special form of timeline to visualise multiple variables of continuous fitness statistics and biomedical markers which may cover a long period. Data trends can be observed from the variable curves and data correlations may be discovered by comparison of the data curves of the multi-variables. As the data records may cover a long time range, interactive techniques such as zooming and overview+details [9] are employed in the healthline visualisation. The users can also select the variables they are interested in the variable legend list to perform a user defined variable filtering. Figure 2 shows multiple biomarkers visualised in the interactive healthline in CARRE.

Parallel Coordinates. The technique of parallel coordinates is an approach for visualising multiple quantitative variables using multiple axes which are placed parallel to each other in the most common case [12]. The advantage of parallel coordinates is that it supports visualisation of multiple variables and correlation

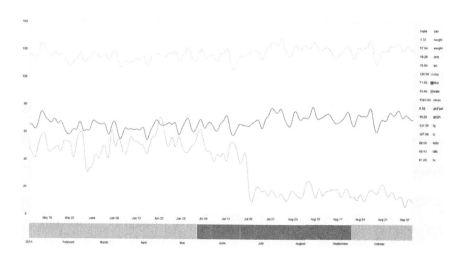

Fig. 2. The healthline visualises personal fitness and biomarker data

between attributes can be discovered by certain visualisation patterns. It is a common technique of visualising high-dimensional data and analyzing multivariate data. In CARRE there are a number of fitness and biomarker variables and both patients and medical practitioners like to view or study correlations among different variables. Consequently, parallel coordinates is chosen for multi-variable correlation visualisation analysis of fitness and biomarker data. An example view of the parallel coordinate view is shown in Fig. 3 where negative correlations can be found between walking minutes and blood pressure as well as BMI (Body Mass Index).

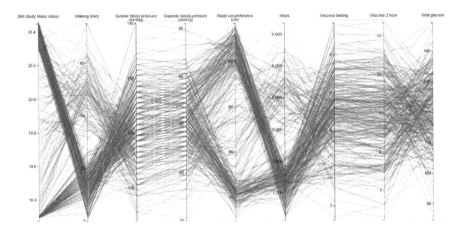

Fig. 3. Fitness and biomarker visualisation and correlation analysis based on Parallel Coordinates

3.2 Risk Factor Visualisation

As introduced in Sect. 1, the risk factor data in the CARRE repository is essentially a graph whose nodes are risk elements with multiple attributes attached, such as risk observables. Each directed edge represents a risk factor directed from the source to the target risk element. In CARRE node-link diagrams as well as other graph visualisation techniques, such as chord diagrams [11], sankey diagrams [19], etc., are used to visualise the risk factor graph. In this paper we focus on the node-link diagram and chord diagram which can be used by professionals and patients to view the risks.

Node-Link Diagram. Node-link diagram [15] is one traditional technique to visualise graph data structure visually. Figure 4 is a force-directed node-link diagram visualisation of all 53 risk elements and 98 risk factors in the current CARRE repository. The node-link diagram clearly visualises risk associations and promotes studying and understanding of the risk factor data base. Through the visual analytic interface, users are able to explore different diseases by dragging them to the centre to clearly see the relationships. By interactively viewing the graph, a patient also understands their risks in a more intuitive manner.

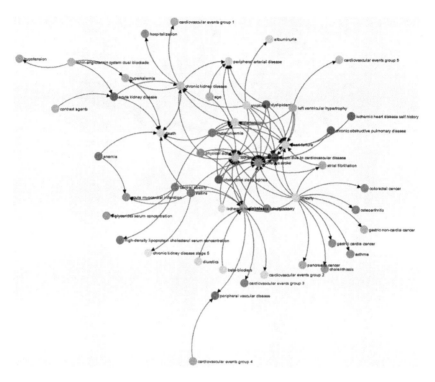

Fig. 4. Force-directed layout based node-link diagram of risk elements and risk factors in CARRE: the whole risk factor database

Chord Diagram. The disadvantage of the node-link diagram is that without proper handling, when the number of nodes and links increase, the visualisation will become increasingly messy for effective recognition by human beings, as obvious in Fig. 4. Though filtering may be applied based on the conditions of a particular patient, it does not help for the visual analysis of the whole risk factor database. Fortunately there are some network visualisation techniques to alleviate the problem, such as the chord diagram [11], as shown in Fig. 5.

The benefits of the chord diagram are that all the nodes are arranged on a circle and the edges from one node are grouped and bundled, which reduces the hairball problems which occur in the node-link diagram. With proper mouse hover interactions all the edges from or to one node can be highlighted, thus making the observation of the connections from or to one node much easier.

Fig. 5. Chord diagram of risk elements and risk factors in CARRE

The chord diagram clearly visualises the relationships of all risk elements in the repository and is particularly useful when professionals check and insert new risks.

3.3   Visual Analytics of Personalised Risks and Disease Progressions

The ultimate goal of CARRE is to integrate the sensor data and the risk factor database to promote risk discovery, prediction and management, and individual health monitoring. In the first stage of CARRE visual analytics, we also made a prototype of interactive risk visualisation based on individual conditions and inputs. As shown in Fig. 6, the node-link diagram only shows the related risk elements and risk factors based on the patient's profile, thus greatly reducing the complexity the original diagram. Moreover, the risk associations update dynamically based on changes in the patient's conditions. Currently, this is achieved by the interactive adjustment of some of the fitness and biomarker data. For

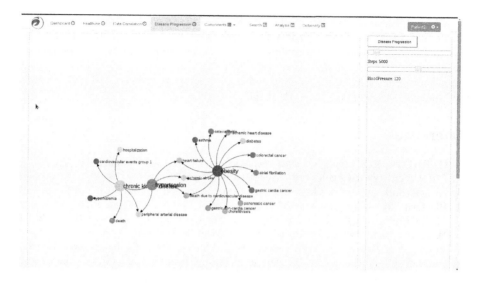

Fig. 6. Interactive risk visual analysis: risks filtered and changed according to the conditions of a particular patient

example, if the blood pressure drops to the normal range, the hypertension risk element will disappear. In another example if the user walks more, the obesity risk element and all risk factors related to obesity will disappear.

4   Conclusions and Future Work

With the increasing popularity of wearable sensors, people are more interested in studying the applications of the sensors for lifestyle tracking and decision support for professional clinicians. While the amount of data collected by wearable sensors is huge, without visual analytics it is almost impossible to carry out any effective data analysis. This paper introduces in particular the role of visual analytics for exploiting sensor data for health monitoring and risk management in CARRE. Multiple variable time-dependant data visualised in a linear healthline helps to study and analyse fitness and biomarker data in CARRE, especially when proper user interaction techniques are incorporated. Parallel coordinates are very useful for correlation analysis of the fitness and biomarker samples. The network of risk elements and risk factors can be visualised with node-link diagrams and chord diagrams, with the latter preferable when the number of nodes becomes large. Moreover, a prototype of individual patient based interactive risk visualisation, prediction and management is presented to show the future directions of our work. In conclusion, interactive visual analytics is critical and effective in sensor-assisted health risk management and analysis; the future work will focus on integrating the risk model more closely with the process of the individualised and dynamic risk management, prediction and visualisation.

Acknowledgments. CARRE project is funded by the European Commission's 7th Framework Programme – ICT under agreement FP7–ICT–611140. The related MyHealthAvatar project is funded by the European Commission's 7th Framework Programme – ICT under agreement FP7–ICT–2011–9. We would like to thank the European Commission for the funding and thank the project officers and reviewers for their indispensable support for both of the projects.

References

1. CARRE Project. http://www.carre-project.eu/. Accessed 06 Jan 2016
2. Fitbit. http://www.fitbit.com/. Accessed 06 Jan 2016
3. HealthVault. https://www.healthvault.com/. Accessed 06 Jan 2016
4. Platform, M.: http://www.myhealthavatar.org/. Accessed 06 Jan 2016
5. MyHealthAvartar Project: http://www.myhealthavatar.eu/. Accessed 06 Jan 2016
6. Withings. http://www.withings.com/. Accessed 06 Jan 2016
7. Rind, A., Wang, T.D., Aigner, W., Miksch, S., Wongsuphasawat, K., Plaisant, C., Shneiderman, B.: Interactiveinformation visualization to explore and query electronic health records. Found. Trends HCI **5**(3), 207–298 (2011)
8. Reddy, C.K., Aggarwal, C.C.: Healthcare Data Analytics. Chapman & Hall, CRC, Boca Raton (2015)
9. Cockburn, A., Karlson, A., Bederson, B.B.: A review of overview+detail zooming and focus+context interfaces. ACM Comput. Surv. (CSUR) Surv. **41**(1), 1–31 (2009)
10. Gotz, D., Stavropoulos, H.: Decisionflow: visual analytics for high-dimensional temporal event sequence data. IEEE Trans. Vis. Comput. Graph. **20**(12), 1783–1792 (2014)
11. Holten, D.: Hierarchical edge bundles: visualization of adjacency relations in hierarchical data. IEEE Trans. Vis. Comput. **12**(5), 741–748 (2006)
12. Inselberg, A., Dimsdale, B.: Parallel coordinates: a tool for visualizing multidimensional geometry. In: Proceedings of the 1st IEEE Symposium on Visualization, pp. 361–378. IEEE (1990)
13. Kaldoudi, E., Third, A., Gotsis, G., Roumeliotis, S., Karvelyte, N.,Rimseviciu, L., Pafili, K., Papazoglou, D., Juozalenaite, G., Semertzidou, E., Visockiene, Z., Zigerido, K.: CARRE Deliverable D.2.2: Functional Requirements and CARRE Information Model. https://www.carre-project.eu/project-info/deliverables/ (July 2015). CARRE: Personalized Patient Empowerment and Shared Decision Support forCardiorenal Disease and Comorbidities, FP7-ICT-61140
14. Keim, D., Kohlhammer, J., Ellis, G., et al.: Mastering the Information Age - Solving Problems with Visual Analytics. Eurographics Association, Goslar (2010)
15. Liu, S., Cui, W., Wu, Y., Liu, M.: A survey on information visualization: recent advances and challenges. Vis. Comput. **30**(12), 1373–1393 (2014)
16. Monroe, M., Lan, R., Lee, H., Plaisant, C., Shneiderman, B.: Temporal event sequence simplification. IEEE Trans. Vis. Comput. Graph. **19**(12), 2227–2236 (2013)
17. Groves, P., Basel Kayylai, D.: The big-data revolution in US health care: Accelerating value and innovation (2013)
18. Plaisant, C., Mushlin, R., Snyder, A., Li, J., Heller, D., Shneiderman, B., Colorado, K.P.: Lifelines: using visualization to enhance navigation and analysis of patient records. In: Proceedings of the 1998 American Medical Informatic Association Annual Fall Symposium, pp. 76–80 (1998)

19. Riehmann, P., Hanfler, M., Froehlich, B.: Interactive sankey diagrams. In: Proceedings of IEEE Symposium on Infomation Visualization InfoVis 2005, pp. 233–240. IEEE (2005)
20. Shneiderman, B., Plaisant, C., Hesse, B.W.: Improving health and healthcare with interactive visualization methods. IEEE Comput. **46**(1), 58–66 (2013)
21. Third, A., Kaldoudi, E., Gotsis, G., Roumeliotis, S., Pafili, K., Domingue, J.: Capturing scientific knowledge on medical risk factors. In: K-CAP2015: 8th International Conference on Knowledge Capture. ACM (2015)
22. Wang, T.D., Plaisant, C., Shneiderman, B., Spring, N., Roseman, D., Marchand, G., Mukherjee, V., Smith, M.: Temporal summaries: Supporting temporal categorical searching, aggregation and comparison. IEEE Trans. Vis. Comput. Graph. **15**(6), 1049–1056 (2009)
23. West, V.L., Borland, D., Hammond, W.: Innovative information visualization of electronic health record data: a systematic review. J. Am. Med. Inform. Assoc. **22**(2), 330–339 (2015)
24. Wongsuphasawat, K., Gotz, D.: Exploring flow, factors, and outcomes of temporal event sequences with the outflow visualization. IEEE Trans. Vis. Comput. Graph. **18**(12), 2659–2668 (2012). doi:10.1109/TVCG.2012.225
25. Wongsuphasawat, K., Guerra Gómez, J.A., Plaisant, C., Wang, T.D., Taieb-Maimon, M., Shneiderman, B.: Lifeflow: visualizing an overview of event sequences. In: Proceedings of the SIGCHI Conference on Human Factors in Computing Systems CHI 2011, NY, USA, pp. 1747–1756. ACM, New York (2011)

Robust Color Gradient Estimation for Photographic Volumes

Bin Zhang, Yubo Tao, and Hai Lin[✉]

State Key Laboratory of CAD and CG, Zhejiang University,
Hangzhou, People's Republic of China
lin@cad.zju.edu.cn

Abstract. Photographic volumes keep the original color in each voxel, and play an important role in medical and biological researches. The gradient is one of the most widely used attributes in volume visualization. However, it is more difficult to accurately estimate gradients for photographic volumes than scalar volumes. Current gradient estimators for photographic volumes do not work well for all cases, especially when the data is noisy. In this paper, we propose a new method to estimate gradients accurately and robustly for photographic volumes. Colors are directly used for gradient estimation instead of being converted to grayscale values, to ensure the accuracy of the gradient direction. For each of three gradient components in x, y and z directions, different filters are combined to reduce the negative effect of noises and generate an accurate result. Experiment results show that the proposed method can estimate gradients robustly in the presence of noise and outperforms other gradient estimators in photographic volume visualization.

Keywords: Photographic volume · Color gradient · Volume rendering

1 Introduction

Photographic volumes have proven its importance in medical and biological researches, as the original color (a RGB vector) is recorded in each voxel. With the help of modern cryo-imaging systems, scientists have acquired a large amount of photographic volume data sets, such as the whole mouse data set [15] and the human data sets from the Visible Human Project (VHP) at the National Library of Medicine [18]. Volume visualization is an effective technique to present these data sets to researchers. By making use of different transfer functions, researchers can explore these data sets intuitively and efficiently. The gradient plays an important role in both rendering and transfer function design. In direct volume rendering, gradient directions are commonly used as surface normals for the calculation of different lighting effects [7,9]. Gradients and gradient magnitudes are also widely used to detect material boundaries in transfer function design [6,12,14,17].

© Springer International Publishing Switzerland 2016
A. El Rhalibi et al. (Eds.): Edutainment 2016, LNCS 9654, pp. 392–402, 2016.
DOI: 10.1007/978-3-319-40259-8_34

In scalar volume data sets, the gradient can be simply derived by the method of finite difference, which is easily understandable and can be computed efficiently. In contrast, it becomes a difficult problem to derive the accurate gradient direction and magnitude from colors in photographic volumes. One feasible solution is to convert the color into a grayscale value before gradient calculation. Through an RGB-to-grayscale conversion, the mature gradient estimation algorithms in the scalar field can be utilized without any modification. However, it relies too much on the decolorization and there has not yet been a perfect decolorization method. As a result, the gradient estimation is not always accurate, especially when the data is noisy. A better option is to estimate gradients from colors directly, such as the color distance gradient [2], which replaces the finite differential calculation with the color distance measure. Although the color distance gradient has found its place in photographic volume rendering, it does not take into account the influence of noise and the unsigned distance based color difference metric can provide the magnitude but not direction of the gradient accurately.

In this paper, we propose a new method to generate an accurate and robust estimation of both the gradient direction and magnitude by directly making use of colors in photographic volumes. In our method, the robust color morphological gradient (RCMG) operator [4] is used as a gradient estimator, while lowpass filters are applied in the other two orthogonal directions to reduce the affection of noise. By applying the RCMG operator and the lowpass filter in different orders, we can get a group of different estimations of the same gradient component. Then an aggregation operator is used to generate the final gradient. The gradient direction and gradient magnitude generated from our method are compared with results from other gradient estimation methods. We also make a comparison of their impacts on volume rendering and transfer function design. The experiment results show the superiority in accuracy and robustness of the proposed method, especially for noisy data sets.

2 Related Work

The gradient is quite useful in volume visualization. It can be used to help to specify opacities and colors for voxels. Levoy et al. [8] first introduced to volume rendering the gradient vector as surface normals for rendering surfaces in the volume and the gradient magnitude for opacity mapping. This work inspired the design of a lot of 2D transfer functions. For example, Kindlmann et al. proposed semi-automatic generation of both 1D and 2D transfer functions [6,12]. Roettger et al. [14] integrated spatial information into 2D transfer function and proposed spatialized transfer function. With the help of the gradient magnitude, one can easily extract material boundaries from the massive data set. Sereda et al. [17] proposed LH transfer functions based on a histogram generated by following the change of gradient directions. Recently, Zhang et al. [19] proposed an intuitive color based transfer function for photographic volumes and extended it to 2D with the gradient magnitude.

The gradient can also be used to enhance the shading effect with the gradient based Blinn-Phong shading model. Shading is an essential cue for shape and depth perception. Correa et al. [1] studied gradient estimation methods for rendering unstructured-mesh volume data and provided a detailed description on different gradient estimation methods. For scalar volumes, finite difference is often used to calculate the gradient. However, gradient estimation for photographic volumes is not as easy as for scalar volumes. Different gradient estimation methods have been proposed to solve the problem. The most simple solution is to convert the color to a grayscale value and use a finite difference operator to obtain an estimation of a grayscale gradient. Other methods directly estimate gradients from colors. Since colors can be represented in different color spaces, such as RGB, CIELUV, CIELAB, and HSV [13], and different color spaces can generate different gradient estimations. The CIELUV color space and the CIELAB color spaces are more perceptually uniform and the color gradient is related to the human perception of colors, so they are preferable rather than the commonly used RGB space. David S. Ebert et al. [2,10] computed color distance gradient in the CIELUV color space and used the gradient in their opacity transfer functions. Gargesha et al. [5] extended this method to define their own opacity transfer functions and presented some meaningful results of feature detection. Due to current data acquisition methods, noises are possibly introduced to photographic volumes. However, these methods much more easily suffer from noises in the gradient estimation.

A large number of work has been done on color gradient estimation in image processing. Some of them have competitive performance in the presence of noise, such as minimum vector dispersion (MVD) edge detector [16], robust color morphological gradient (RCMG) operator [4], and robust gradient vector estimation scheme. The effectiveness of these methods have been proven in the gradient estimation for color images. Inspired by these methods, this paper proposes a new gradient estimation method to calculate both the gradient direction and magnitude for photographic volumes accurately and robustly, even for the noisy data sets.

3   Robust Color Gradient Estimation

Gradient estimation for the color data is not as easy as that for the scalar data or the general vector data. The gradient represents the trend of the data. It points in the direction of the maximum rate of increase of data values. Its magnitude remains small within the same material and becomes larger as it comes to the boundaries of different materials. As for the color data, the gradient should points in the direction of the maximum rate of change of the colors, and its magnitude should reflect the degree of variance of the colors in its direction. This involves much of the human perception and it is difficult to measure. In image processing, researchers have studied a lot on how to get accurate and robust gradients for color images for the purposes of image segmentation, edge detection and so on. Designing transfer function based on the gradient can be seemed as a similar purpose in photographic volume rendering. An accurate gradient can result in an accurate data classification. The RCMG estimator [4] can obtain a better estimation of the gradient of color images in the presence of noise. The method proposed by Nezhadarya et al. [11] produces a better gradient direction and make the estimation of the color gradient much more robust. A more accurate result can be obtained if we follow its model to develop a gradient estimator for photographic volume.

In image processing, the highpass filter is often used to estimate the gradient for edge detection, and the lowpass filter is often used for smoothing purpose. Individual points are reduced in smoothing so that noise in data can be reduced. Since data sets acquired from the nature are often noised in some degree, conventional gradient estimators often combine highpass filters and lowpass filters to reduce the effect of noises [3]. Following this idea, to make the color gradient estimation more accurate and more robust, we use the RCMG estimator in one direction and lowpass filters in the orthogonal directions when calculating gradient components.

To calculate the gradient of a color vector at position $p(x_p, y_p, z_p)$, we sample a cubic window W of size $3 \times 3 \times 3$ which is centered at (x_p, y_p, z_p) and then the three components of the gradient $g = (g_x, g_y, g_z)$ are calculated separately. Figure 1 presents an illustration of the process of calculating the gradient component g_x. Let $f_{i,j,k}$, where i, j and k are natural numbers in the range of $[1, 3]$, denote a color vector in the sample window W. The gradient estimation process is accomplished by three kinds of operations, highpass filtering, lowpass filtering and an aggregation operation. The process will be described in detail in the following.

Highpass Filtering. For each row (j, k) along the x axis, we apply the RCMG operator to perform the highpass filtering operation. Assuming that v_1, v_2 and v_3 are the input vectors of the RCMG estimator, with vector differences between each pair of these color vectors we can define a 3×3 matrix of differential vectors, denoted by

$$D = \{d_{i,j} | d_{i,j} = v_i - v_j, \ \forall i, j = 1, 2, 3\}. \tag{1}$$

As the pairwise pixel rejection scheme [4] does, the pairs of vectors with the maximum Euclidean norm are removed from the matrix D during the gradient calculation. Let D' be the set of differential vectors after values removed, a row of input vectors v_1, v_2, v_3 can be highpass filtered by

$$H(v_1, v_2, v_3) = d_{\hat{i},\hat{j}}, \ \forall d_{i,j} \in D', \|d_{\hat{i},\hat{j}}\| > \|d_{i,j}\|, \tag{2}$$

The output of Eq. 2 is a differential vector selected from D'. Each row of the colors in the sample window W can be filtered as

$$h_{j,k} = H1(f_{1,j,k}, f_{2,j,k}, f_{3,j,k}). \tag{3}$$

A matrix of differential vectors of size 3×3 is produced by this highpass operation, as shown in the top left picture of Fig. 1.

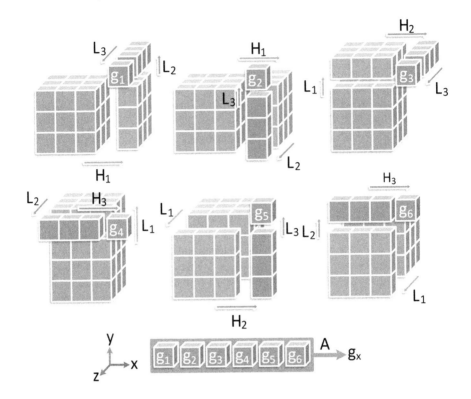

Fig. 1. The process of calculation of the gradient component g_x with the proposed method applied in a window of size $3 \times 3 \times 3$

Lowpass Filtering. To reduce the effect of possible noise in the original data, the lowpass filter L is applied in both y and z directions.

$$L(v_1, v_2, v_3) == median(v_1, v_2, v_3), \qquad (4)$$

which takes three vectors as input. Function $median$ here stands for element-wise-median operation. As shown in the top left picture of Fig. 1, the 3×3 matrix is lowpass filtered in vertical direction by the median filter L and produce a 1×3 vector v^L,

$$v_k^L = L(h_{1,k}, h_{2,k}, h_{3,k}). \qquad (5)$$

Then the lowpass filter is applied to the vector v^L and the estimation of the gradient component is calculated as its norm,

$$g_1 = \|L(v_1^L, v_2^L, v_3^L)\| \qquad (6)$$

Aggregation Oparation. As the RCMG operator is nonlinear, by changing the order in which we apply these filters, we can get another five different gradient component estimation results. For example, by applying the lowpass filter in z direction first, then the highpass filter in x direction and then the lowpass filter in y direction, we can obtain the result g_5 as shown in Fig. 1. Noted that the operators $H1$, $H2$ and $H3$ in Fig. 1 are all RCMG operators but they differ in inputs and outputs, so different symbols are used to distinguish them. $H1$ accepts a three-dimensional window as input and outputs a two-dimensional matrix. $H2$ accepts a two-dimensional matrix and produces a vector. $H3$ accepts a vector and results in a single value, which is the norm of Eq. 2. So do the operators $L1$, $L2$ and $L3$. After all the possible orders are traversed, we get six results $g_1, g_2, ..., g_6$. Then, an aggregation operator is proposed to aggregate the six results from different order combinations of the filters to produce the final gradient component, instead of choosing one from them. The aggregation operator we used here is *signed mean* function,

$$g = A(g_1, g_2, ..., g_6, v^*)$$

$$= \sum_{i=1}^{6} \frac{g_i}{6} \times sign(\|\frac{v_2^* + v_3^*}{2}\| - \|\frac{v_1^* + v_2^*}{2}\|). \tag{7}$$

The sign is computed from the vector of the outputs of the second filter operation. The vector, which is denoted by v^* in Eq. 7, could be v^L from a low filter or v^H from a highpass filter. With this aggregation operation, we can finally get the gradient component g_x,

$$g_x = A(g_1, g_2, ..., g_6, v). \tag{8}$$

The processes for estimating gradient components g_y and g_z follow the same way. The only difference lies on the direction in which the highpass and lowpass operators are used.

4 Result

In order to demonstrate the validity of the proposed gradient estimator, we compared it with the color distance gradient method and the Sobel operator. The Sobel operator is performed on grayscale volumes generated from the corresponding photographic volumes with the *rgb2gray* conversion in MATLAB. The color distance gradient is calculated by measuring the distance between two colors. The unsigned distance metric proposed by Ebert et al. [2] can give the magnitude but not the direction of the gradient. To make our experiment a fair comparison, the sign of each gradient component in the color distance gradient is given by the difference of corresponding voxels in the grayscale volume.

We first evaluate the robustness of our method. Noised data sets used in the experiment are generated by adding the pepper and salt noise with signal noise ratio 0.9 to the original data sets. The three gradient estimation methods are applied to the noised head from the visual human data set and a slice of the result is taken out for comparison. Gradient magnitudes obtained from the color

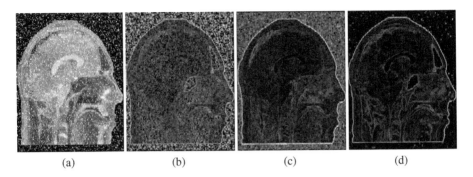

(a)   (b)   (c)   (d)

Fig. 2. The gradient magnitudes obtained from the color distance gradient (b), the Sobel operator (c) and the proposed method (d) for the noised image (a).

distance gradient, the Sobel operator and our method for the selected slice are shown in Fig. 2 (b), (c) and (d) respectively. The original image is presented in Fig. 2 (a). It is obvious that the first two methods cannot handle the noised data accurately. The color distance gradient is totally affected by the noise, getting large gradient magnitudes all over the data set. The Sobel operator can generate a relatively meaningful result inside the human head. However, the noises in the empty region, cannot be properly processed by the Sobel operator. Thanks to the filtering operations, the result of our method is hardly affected by the noise, and the estimated gradients are much better than the ones of the other methods.

We then evaluate the gradient direction through volume rendering. Figure 3 shows the rendering results of the noised leg from the visual human data set. The leg data set is noised in the same way as the head data set. Because of the presence of noises, gradient directions generated by the color distance gradient

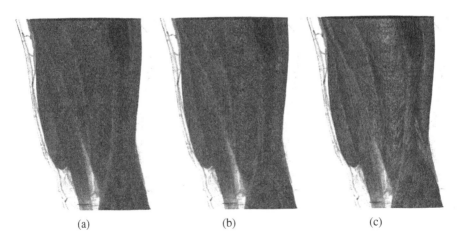

(a)   (b)   (c)

Fig. 3. The visualization results of the noised human leg data set with gradients obtained from the color distance gradient (a), the Sobel operator (b) and the proposed method (c).

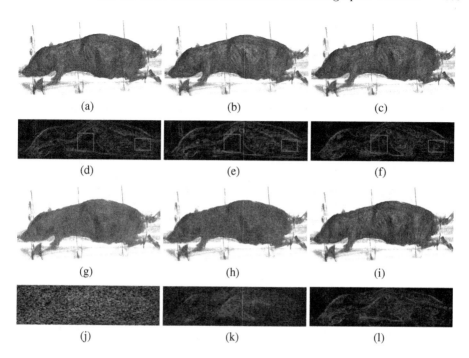

Fig. 4. Results of the whole mouse data set. (a), (b) and (c) are the rendering results based on the gradients estimated from the color distance gradient, the Sobel operator and our method, respectively. The corresponding gradient magnitudes of one selected slice are shown in (d), (e) and (f). By adding noises to this data set, the rendering results are shown in (g), (h) and (i), and the gradient magnitudes of the selected slice are shown in (j), (k), and (l). It can be seen that our method is more robust for noised data.

become irregular, and this causes less specular lights on the muscle. Although the Sobel operator does well in gradient directions, it is also affected by noises, making the result a bit more rough, which can be seen in Fig. 3(b). However, the surfaces of the muscle can be seen much more clearly in Fig. 3(c) due to more accurate gradient directions generated by our method. The global shape and local detail of the muscle can be easily perceived in our result.

We further compare the gradient directions on the whole mouse data set [15], as shown in Fig. 4. Top two rows in Fig. 4 show the volume rendering results of the original data set. Figure 4(a)–(c) are the rendering results based on the gradients estimated from the color distance gradient, the Sobel operator and our method, respectively. The gradient magnitudes of one selected slice are shown in Fig. 4(d)–(f). By comparing the two regions outlined in red in Fig. 4(d)–(f), we can see that details in these regions which can be seen in our result are missing in the results of the other two methods. After adding noise to the mouse data set in the same way as the head data set, results in Fig. 4(g)–(l) can be got.

It is clearly that the results of the three methods are almost the same for the original data set. But when the data set is noised, as results shown in the last two rows, the color distance gradient and the Sobel operator are seriously affected. By comparing the gradient magnitude results, boundaries can hardly be recognized in Fig. 4(j), (k). However, only little noises appear in the result of the proposed method. By comparing Fig. 4(c), (i) we conclude that our method is almost insusceptible to noise. Thus, our method can generate better gradient directions than other two methods.

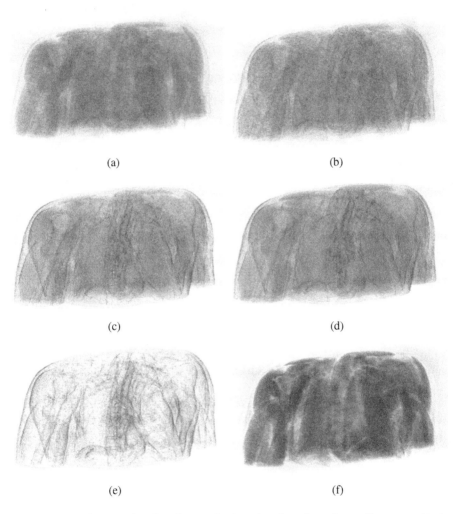

(a)   (b)

(c)   (d)

(e)   (f)

Fig. 5. Human chest rendered with transfer functions based on the gradient magnitude. The gradient magnitudes used in (a), (b) and (c) are calculated on the noised data by the color distance gradient, the Sobel operator and the proposed method, respectively. As a comparison, (d) is produced by using the proposed method on the original data. By tuning the opacities of different gradient magnitude ranges based on the result in (c), we can separate the bones and muscles in (e) and (f).

We finally compare gradient magnitudes in transfer function design, since the gradient magnitude are often used to construct transfer functions. The 2D transfer function [19], which is composed of a 1D color-based transfer function and a 1D gradient-magnitude-based transfer function, specifies the opacity to a voxel according to a combination of its color and gradient magnitude in photographic volume rendering. The color-based transfer function is fixed in our experiments. We tune the curve of the gradient-magnitude-based transfer function to generate similar results with gradient magnitudes from three different gradient estimation methods. Figure 5(a)–(c) show the rendering results of the noised chest from the visual human data set. Figure 5(d) is the rendering result based on the gradient magnitudes generated by our method on the original chest before adding noises for the comparison. The bone boundaries and the vessels are clearly displayed in Fig. 5(c), (d), but can hardly be seen in Fig. 5(a), (b). Furthermore, we tune the gradient-magnitude-based transfer function in Fig. 5(c). By setting the opacities of features with small gradient magnitudes to zero, we get the result in Fig. 5(e), in which the muscles are hided. In a similar way, we can hide the feature boundaries with large gradient magnitudes and get the result in Fig. 5(f). However, with the gradient magnitudes of the other two methods we cannot get similar results. The reason is that the gradient magnitudes produced by the color gradient distance and the Sobel operator are seriously affected by the noise, so that gradient magnitudes of boundaries cannot be easily separated.

5 Conclusion

In this paper, we proposed a novel robust color gradient estimation method for photographic volumes. The three gradient components are calculated separately in the CIELUV color space. The estimation is performed by combining the RCMG operators and lowpass filters for each gradient component. With experiments and comparisons, the proposed method is proven to be more accurate and more robust than commonly used gradient estimators in photographic volume visualization. Even when the data is noisy, a good gradient estimation result still can be got. Compared to the commonly used color distance gradient, the main limitation of the proposed method is that it takes longer time to perform the filtering operations, due to their nonlinear. However, the time spent on the calculation can be reduced to seconds thanks to GPU computing. It can be further improved by simplifying the filtering operations in future work. Since gradients can be computed in a pre-processing stage and be stored for later use, it would not be a big problem for the use of the proposed gradient estimation method in photographic volume visualization. For those high resolution photographpic volumes whose gradients are not convenient to be pre-computed, on-the-fly gradient estimation with GPU can be considered.

Acknowledgments. This work was supported in part by National Natural Science Foundation of China No. 61472354 and the National Key Technology Research and Development Program of the Ministry of Science and Technology of China under Grant 2014BAK14B01.

References

1. Correa, C., Hero, R., Ma, K.-L.: A comparison of gradient estimation methods for volume rendering on unstructured meshes. IEEE Trans. Vis. Comput. Graph. **17**(3), 305–319 (2011)
2. Ebert, D.S., Morris, C.J., Rheingans, P., Yoo, T.S.: Designing effective transfer functions for volume rendering from photographic volumes. IEEE Trans. Vis. Comput. Graph. **8**(2), 183–197 (2002)
3. Ercan, G., Whyte, P.: Digital image processing. US Patent 6,240,217 29 May 2001
4. Evans, A.N., Liu, X.U.: A morphological gradient approach to color edge detection. IEEE Trans. Image Process. **15**(6), 1454–1463 (2006)
5. Gargesha, M., Qutaish, M., Roy, D., Steyer, G., Bartsch, H., Wilson, D.L.: Enhanced volume rendering techniques for high-resolution color cryo-imaging data. In: SPIE Medical Imaging, p. 72622V. International Society for Optics and Photonics (2009)
6. Kindlmann, G., Durkin, J.W.: Semi-automatic generation of transfer functions for direct volume rendering. In: Proceedings of the 1998 IEEE Symposium on Volume Visualization, pp. 79–86. ACM (998)
7. Kniss, J., Premoze, S., Hansen, C., Shirley, P., McPherson, A.: A model for volume lighting and modeling. IEEE Trans. Vis. Comput. Graph. **9**(2), 150–162 (2003)
8. Levoy, M.: Display of surfaces from volume data. IEEE Comput. Graph. Appl. **8**(3), 29–37 (1988)
9. Max, N.: Optical models for direct volume rendering. IEEE Trans. Vis. Comput. Graph. **1**(2), 99–108 (1995)
10. Morris, C.J., Ebert, D.: Direct volume rendering of photographic volumes using multi-dimensional color-based transfer functions. In: Proceedings of the Symposium on Data Visualisation 2002, pp. 115-ff. Eurographics Association (2002)
11. Nezhadarya, E., Ward, R.K.: A new scheme for robust gradient vector estimation in color images. IEEE Trans. Image Process. **20**(8), 2211–2220 (2011)
12. Pfister, H., Lorensen, B., Bajaj, C., Kindlmann, G., Schroeder, W., Avila, L.S., Raghu, K., Machiraju, R., Lee, J.: The transfer function bake-off. IEEE Comput. Graph. Appl. **21**(3), 16–22 (2001)
13. Plataniotis, K.N., Venetsanopoulos, A.N.: Color Image Processing and Applications: Digital Signal Processing. Springer, Heidelberg (2000)
14. Roettger, S., Bauer, M., Stamminger, M.: Spatialized transfer functions. In: Proceedings of the Seventh Joint Eurographics/IEEE VGTC Conference on Visualization, pp. 271–278. Eurographics Association (2005)
15. Roy, D., Steyer, G.J., Gargesha, M., Stone, M.E., Wilson, D.L.: 3D cryo-imaging: a very high-resolution view of the whole mouse. Anat. Rec. **292**(3), 342–351 (2009)
16. Russo, F., Lazzari, A.: Color edge detection in presence of Gaussian noise using nonlinear prefiltering. IEEE Trans. Instrum. Meas. **54**(1), 352–358 (2005)
17. Sereda, P., Bartroli, A.V., Serlie, I.W., Gerritsen, F.A.: Visualization of boundaries in volumetric data sets using LH histograms. IEEE Trans. Vis. Comput. Graph. **12**(2), 208–218 (2006)
18. Spitzer, V., Ackerman, M.J., Scherzinger, A.L., Whitlock, D.: The visible human male: a technical report. J. Am. Med. Inform. Assoc. **3**(2), 118–130 (1996)
19. Zhang, B., Tao, Y., Lin, H., Dong, F., Clapworthy, G.: Intuitive transfer function design for photographic volumes. J. Vis. **18**(4), 571–580 (2015)

Edge Point Extract of LiDAR Data via Building Wrapped Circle

Yu-ze Nie[✉], Ying-lei Cheng, Lang-bo Qiu, Man-yun He,
and Pin Wang

Institute of Information and Navigation,
Air Force Engineering University, Xi'an 710077, Shanxi, China
515160842@qq.com

Abstract. In the paper, a new algorithm of extracting the edge point in point cloud is presented, which can improve the running speed with a similar result. First, a specific radius and threshold is set, and a first point is selected as the center of a circle and a wrapped circle is built. Then, count the number in the pack circle. After that, repeat the above operations for all points in the point cloud. Finally, compare the number of point in every wrapped circle with the threshold value to extract the edge point. Simulation results show that compared to alpha shape algorithm, the proposed algorithm can effectively reduce running time.

Keywords: LiDAR · Wrapped circle · Edge point · Time complexity · Extract

1 Introduction

Based on the plane detection platform, Light detection and ranging (LiDAR) is an active detection technology, which is made up by a laser scanner, global positioning system (GPS) and inertial navigation system (INS), so that it can obtain 3D spatial information of surface and ground object quickly and efficiently [1–4]. Laser pulse cannot be influenced by weather and shadow. So LiDAR can obtain a quantity of 3D coordinate information terrain rapidly by transmitting and receiving laser regardless of weather and shadow. In LiDAR system, the distance of laser to ground or object can be calculated according to the delta-T between transmitting and receiving laser, where a point cloud database can be finally obtained. Generally, LiDAR technology can work under all-weather and all-time (conditions) while providing high efficiency and abundant information, which has been widely accepted as a revolutionary technology in geographical mapping after GPS.

Data extraction and reconstruction of buildings has been the emphases and difficulties in the study of LiDAR data processing based on LiDAR. In the 3D reconstruction, as the basis of the city mapping and the establishment of 3D building model, the extraction of building's contour line is widely considered important. For simple and regular houses such as most flat-roofed buildings, after obtaining the contour line and giving its elevation information, the structure of the 3D model will be constructed directly. For two-dimensional digital images, the existing edges extraction technology has been very mature.

© Springer International Publishing Switzerland 2016
A. El Rhalibi et al. (Eds.): Edutainment 2016, LNCS 9654, pp. 403–411, 2016.
DOI: 10.1007/978-3-319-40259-8_35

However, because LiDAR raw data is a discrete, the contour structure of LiDAR data building is very difficult to extract, where the building has diversiform and complex shape with complex environment around. To extract the building outline, the key is extracting the edge points of buildings in the LiDAR data. Most of the research is conducted by using other image fusion building boundary extraction [5–7]. To extract edge points from LiDAR point cloud database after filtering [8–10] and feature point division of buildings, there are some existing algorithms widely applied, such as alpha shape algorithm, polygon fitting method [11], and Delaunay triangulation algorithm; You puts forward that the contour of buildings can be extracted by the image processing method after interpolating the laser spot twice to generate the DSM image data [12]. Literatures obtain building main direction by establishing Delaunay triangulation to extract building roof contour [13–15]; Zeng [16] put forward a method that edge points can be extracted by using the contour of Delaunay triangulation [17]. But polygon fitting method can only calculate the convex contour of overall points, and cannot extract edge point of every single building. Using Delaunay triangulation to extract contour will increase the amount of data, which will increase computational complexity. Based on alpha shape algorithm, wrapped circle algorithm is proposed to solve its slow running speed.

2   Extraction of LiDAR Building Edge Points

For LiDAR point cloud database, to extract the contour of the buildings, the building points must be picked up from the database firstly. Extracted buildings points should be showed as top view. And then using the edge points extraction algorithms extract the edge points of buildings. Finally extracted edge points will be fitted, forming contour line of the building.

A classic algorithm of extracting the contour of LiDAR point cloud database is alpha shape algorithm. Algorithm is as follows: suppose you have a point cloud data set S; and there is a radius of alpha circle rolling along the external points of the S; then the edges of the point cloud S will be well-determined by point cloud S and radius of alpha. When alpha radius is big enough, the circle will roll along the periphery of the point cloud. When the radius of alpha is small, the circle will fall into the interior of the point cloud. **As shown in Fig.** 1.

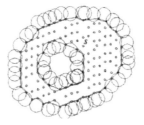

Fig. 1. The diagram of alpha shape algorithm

Shen achieves alpha shape algorithm by following methods [18]: firstly set the size of the radius as alpha; freely choose two points in the point cloud S; when the distance of two points less than 2 times of alpha (diameter of the circle), a circle can be made up by the two points and alpha; according to the position of two points and radius of alpha, the position of the circle center will be obtained; while the position of two points and radius alpha are offered, two center of circle will be obtained. One of the circle centers is the internal circle center while the other one is the external circle center; and the external circle is the rolling circle that we want; Then the distance D between the other points to the center of rolling circle can be calculated; while the distance D less than alpha, the point fall in the rolling circle; while distance D greater than the alpha, point fall into the outside of the circle. Count the number of the points that fall in the rolling circle. When there is no point falling in the rolling circle, the two points are edge points of point cloud S. Circulate above calculation until every two points are calculated, and then the edge points will be extracted.

Alpha shape algorithm has the advantage that it can not only extract internal edge and external edge well, but also different scale contour by adjust the size of the circle radius alpha. When the radius is big enough, alpha shape algorithm will extract the convex contour of point cloud database. When the radius slightly small (but greater than the average distance), the details of contour will be extracted. But it will result in higher algorithm complexity, huge amount of calculation and slower speed that alpha shape algorithm establishes rolling circle at first.

3 Improved Algorithm

3.1 Improved Algorithm Principle

As for alpha shape algorithm's shortcomings of slow speed, this paper puts forward an improved method that the edge points of the LiDAR point cloud database can be extracted by establishing wrapped circle.

With each point of LiDAR point cloud database as the center of the circle (called wrapped circle), wrapped circle can be established by setting a radius R. Count the number of the points that fall in the wrapped circle. After having filtered terrain and extracted buildings, distribution of the LiDAR point cloud database is relatively uniform. Taking rectangle as example, in the edges, there is 180° no points while serve the edge point as the center of the wrapped circle; in the corner, there is 270° no points while serve the inflexion point as the center of the wrapped circle. Therefore, according to the number of points in every wrapped circle, we can distinguish edge points from the internal points. **As shown in Fig.** 2.

We set 1.5 times average distance as radius of wrapped circle. In theory, the wrapped circle which serves the inflexion point as the center will wrap 4 points; the wrapped circle which serves edge point as the center will wrap 6 points; the wrapped circle which serves internal point as the center will wrap 9 points. In LiDAR point cloud database, distribution of the points after filtering is relatively uniform. So the wrapped circle algorithm is feasible. The feature can be used to extract the edge points that the number of every wrapped circle is different.

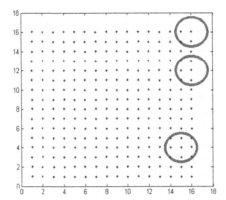

Fig. 2. The diagram of wrapped circle algorithm

Algorithm specific steps as follows:

- Step 1: Set a specific wrapped circle radius R, and the threshold H which is the number of points in wrapped circle; Do not end a page with a section or subsection heading.
- Step 2: Choose a point as the center of the wrapped circle in the LiDAR point cloud library S, with radius R;
- Step 3: Calculate the distance D from every point in S to center of wrapped circle, and count for the number N of points falling in the wrapped circle;
- Step 4: Compare every N with H, and distinguish the edge points from the internal points.
- Step 5: Circulate the step 2 until traversing the entire S.

The specific flow chart is as shown in Fig. 3.

Different from alpha shape algorithm, which use two points to establish rolling circle, wrapped circle algorithm just uses one point to establish wrapped circle. So wrapped circle algorithm decreases the data using frequency of algorithm, which can reduce the time of data processing in the circulation. In addition, the alpha shape algorithm needs to calculate rolling circle's center position, while wrapped circle algorithm does not need to do, which can simplify the algorithm a lot and improve the efficiency of the algorithm.

3.2   Analysis of Time Complexity

A LiDAR point cloud database set S with n points, main steps of time complexity analysis of alpha shape algorithm are as follows:

- While choosing two points, because algorithm must operate every two points in point cloud library, the total is $C(n,2)$, and the time complexity is $O(n^2)$;
- While solving the center of rolling circle, the time complexity is $O(a)$;

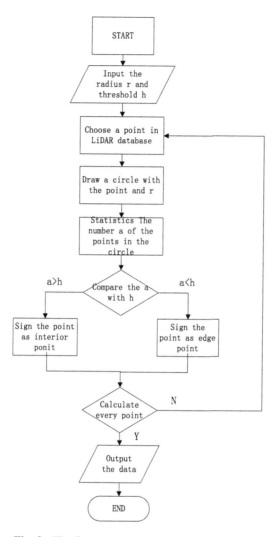

Fig. 3. The flow chart of wrapped circle algorithm

- While solving the distance from every point to center of rolling circle, the time complexity is **O(n)**;
- While judging every rolling circle, the time complexity is **O(n)**;

The relationship of the fore three steps is nested, while the relationship of the fore three steps and the last step is in series. So time complexity of alpha shape algorithm is **O(2a*n³)**.

The main steps of time complexity analysis of Wrapped circle algorithm are as follows:

- While choosing every point in S as the center of wrapped circle, the time complexity is $O(n)$;
- While solving the distance from every point to the center of wrapped circle, the time complexity is $O(n)$;

While judging every wrapped circle, the time complexity is $O(n)$; The relationship of the first two steps is nested, and the relationship of the first two steps and the last step is in series. So time complexity of alpha shape algorithm is $O(n^2)$.

Comparing alpha shape algorithm to wrapped circle algorithm, alpha shape algorithm uses two points every time the rolling circle is established, and wrapped circle algorithm just uses one point. In addition, alpha shape algorithm needs to calculate the center of rolling circle, while wrapped circle algorithm doesn't need, which can greatly reduce the computing complexity, and improve the operation efficiency of algorithm well. The time complexity of alpha shape algorithm is $O(a*n^3)$, and time complexity of wrapped circle algorithm is $O(n^2)$, which greatly improves the extraction rate of edge points.

4   Analysis of Algorithm Simulation Results

The simulation is based on the Matlab platform, and the experimental data is actual LiDAR measurement data. The experimental data is based on distribution of vertical close double row. The distance between data is different. The distance between double rows is about 1 m. The distance from double row to double row is 1.5 m. The distance of vertical point is uniform about 1 m. To alpha shape algorithm, the experiment use 1 m as the radius of the rolling circle. The experiment result is **shown in Figs. 4 and** 5. The blue points are internal points, and red points are the edge points.

Considering the complexity of the actual data, the experiment chooses 2.5 m as radius of wrapped circle. **As shown in Fig.** 6, the threshold is 9. And then using 8, 9, 10 as threshold respectively, threshold 9 is proved that can get best result of simulation. So we choose 9 as the threshold of algorithm.

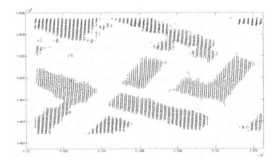

Fig. 4. The result of alpha shape algorithm

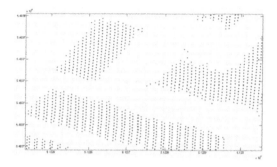

Fig. 5. The result of alpha shape algorithm

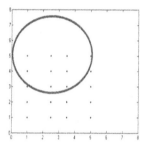

Fig. 6. The chart of wrapped circle algorithm's computing threshold

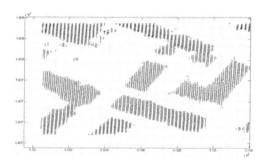

Fig. 7. The result of wrapped circle algorithm

With the 2.5 m as the radius of wrapped circle, simulation results is **as shown in Figs.** 7 **and** 8, when 9 is used as the threshold to distinguish the edge points. The blue points are internal point, and the red points are the edge points.

The experimental results show that wrapped circle algorithm can extract edge points well as similar as the results of alpha shape algorithm. And because complexity of

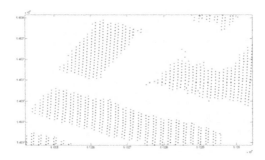

Fig. 8. The result of wrapped circle algorithm

Table 1. Comparing the time of alpha shape with wrapped circle algorithm

Numbers of points	Running time of alpha shape (s)	Running time of wrapped circle (s)
100	0.23	0.0275
600	9.571254	0.0314
1000	25.735486	0.0414
2000	102.463812	0.0646
3000	271.112137	0.1094
10000	3160.617681	0.9013

wrapped circle is simpler, the wrapped circle can operate much more quickly. The same data is computed respectively by wrapped circle algorithm and alpha shape algorithm in the same conditions. In the case of similar effect of edge extraction, the running time of wrapped circle algorithm substantially reduced, proving that the rate of edge point's extraction has improved significantly a lot. **Specific time shown in Table** 1.

According to the data in table, with the number of points increasing, the time of alpha shape algorithm increases exponentially and the time of wrapped circle algorithm increases slowly. Then gap of two algorithms' time is greater.

5   Conclusion

In this paper, the alpha shape algorithm is analyzed and the key step of limiting computing efficiency is found, i.e. the step of using two points to calculate the center of rolling circle. Therefore, wrapped circle algorithm is put forward, where every point is used to establish wrapped circle rather than two points. The simulation results show that wrapped circle algorithm can provide higher processing speed than alpha shape algorithm. However, the wrapped circle algorithm can be applied only when the data is filtered and the distribution of points is uniform.

References

1. Breniner, C.: Building reconstruction from images and laser scanning. Int. J. Appl. Earth Obs. Geoinf. **6**(3–4), 187–198 (2005)
2. Sampath, A., Shan, J.: Segmentation and reconstruction of polyhedral building roofs from aerial LiDAR point clouds. IEEE Trans. Geosci. Remote Sens. **48**(3), 1554–1567 (2010)
3. Chen, L., Teo, T., Kuo, C., et al.: Shaping polyhedral buildings by the fusion of vector maps and LiDAR point clouds. Photogramm. Eng. Remote Sens. **74**(9), 1147–1157 (2008)
4. Elberink, S., Vosselman, G.: Quality analysis on 3D Building models reconstructed from airborne laser scanning data. ISPRS J. Photogramm. Remote Sens. **66**(2), 157–165 (2011)
5. Rottensteiner, F., Briese, C.: Automatic generation of building models from LiDAR data. IEEE Comput. Graph. Appl. **23**(6), 42–50 (2003). ISPRS, Dresden
6. Huber, M, et al.: Fusion of LiDAR data and aerial imagery for automatic reconstruction of building surface. In: Workshop on Remote Sensing and Data Fusion Over Urban Areas, pp. 82–86 (2003)
7. Sohn, G., Dowman, I.: Building extracting using LiDAR DEMs and IKONS images. ISPRS Commission III, WG III/3, Stuttgart (2003)
8. Qu, Y., Cheng, Y., Qiu, L.: An improved method of extracting 3D features of building based on eight neighborhood search method. J. Air Force Eng. Univ. (Nat. Sci. Edit.) **16**(4), 66–69 (2015)
9. Zheng, W.E.I., Zhen, D.O.N.G., Qingquan, L.I., Bisheng, Y.A.N.G.: Automated extraction of building façade footprints from mobile LiDAR point clouds. Geomat. Inf. Sci. Wuhan Univ. **37**(11), 1311–1315 (2012)
10. Zhao, H., Cheng, Y., Qu, Y.: A filtering algorithm of airborne LiDAR points cloud based on least square. Sci. Technol. Eng. **14**(33), 234–239 (2014)
11. Gonzalez, R.C., Woods, R.E.: 《Digital Image Processing》, 3rd edn
12. Hongjian, Y.O.U., Lin, S.U., Shukai, L.I.: Automatic extraction of building from DSM acquired by airborne three-dimensional imager. Geomat. Inf. Sci. Wuhan Univ. **27**(4), 408–413 (2002)
13. Vosseman, G.: Building reconstruction using planar faces in high density height data. Int. Arch. Photogramm. Remote Sens. **32**(3/2), 87–92 (1999)
14. Hofmann, A.D.: Analysis of irrstructure parameter spaces in airborne laser scanner data for 3D building model generation. Int. Arch. Photogramm. Remote Sens. Spat. Inf. Sci. **35**(B3), 302–307 (2004)
15. Morgan, M., Habib, A.: 3D TIN for automatic building extraction from airborne laser scanning data. In: The ASPRS Gateway to the New Millennium, St. Louis, Missouri (2001)
16. Qihong, Z.E.N.G., Jianhua, M.A.O., Xianhua, L.I., Xuefeng, L.I.U.: Building roof boundary extraction from LiDAR point cloud. Geomat. Inf. Sci. Wuhan Univ. **34**(5), 383–386 (2009)
17. Cheng, L., Li, M., Gong, J., Shan, J.: 3D reconstruction of building rooftops from LiDAR data and orthophoto. Geomat. Inf. Sci. Wuhan Univ. **38**(2), 208–211 (2013)
18. Shen, W., Wang, L., Wang, C., Han, J.: Reconstruction of 3D building models based on LiDAR data. J. Liaoning Tech. Univ. (Nat. Sci.) **30**(3), 373–377 (2011)

TieVis: Visual Analytics of Evolution
of Interpersonal Ties

Tao Lin[1], Fangzhou Guo[1], Yingcai Wu[1], Biao Zhu[1], Fan Zhang[2], Huamin Qu[3],
and Wei Chen[1(✉)]

[1] State Key Lab of CAD&CG, Zhejiang University, Hangzhou, China
nblintao@gmail.com, guofz1234@gmail.com, ycwu@zju.edu.cn,
arthurbzhu@gmail.com, chenwei@cad.zju.edu.cn
[2] Zhejiang University of Technology, Hangzhou, China
fanzhang@cad.zju.edu.cn
[3] The Hong Kong University of Science and Technology, Hong Kong, China
huamin@cse.ust.hk

Abstract. Interpersonal ties, such as strong ties and weak ties, describe the information carried by an edge in social network. Tracking the dynamic changes of interpersonal ties can thus enhance our understanding of the evolution of a complex network. Nevertheless, existing studies in dynamic network visualization mostly focus on the temporal changes of nodes or structures of the network without an adequate support of analysis and exploration of the temporal changes of interpersonal ties. In this paper, we introduce a new visual analytics method that enables interactive analysis and exploration of the dynamic changes of interpersonal ties. The method integrates four well-linked visualizations, including a scatterplot, a pixelbar chart, a layered graph, and a node-link diagram, to allow for multi-perspective analysis of the evolution of interpersonal ties. The scatterplot created by multi-dimensional scaling can help reveal the clusters of ties and detect abnormal ties, while other visualizations allow users to explore the clusters of ties interactively from different perspectives. A case study has been conducted to demonstrate the effectiveness of our approach.

Keywords: Interpersonal ties · Visual analytics · Visualization

1 Introduction

The interpersonal tie is an important concept for edges from sociology, which describes the information carried by an edge in social networks [13]. It has been extensively studied in sociology and can be classified as strong ties and weak ties. A strong tie indicates that the nodes connected by the edge have a relatively large number of common neighbor nodes. On the contrary, a weak tie indicates that the nodes have only a few common neighbor nodes. The interpersonal ties can be continuously changing in an evolving network, where an edge has its own life cycle. For example, it is absent from the network at the beginning, then becomes a weak

© Springer International Publishing Switzerland 2016
A. El Rhalibi et al. (Eds.): Edutainment 2016, LNCS 9654, pp. 412–424, 2016.
DOI: 10.1007/978-3-319-40259-8_36

tie and gradually grows to a strong tie, and it disappears from the network at the end.

The life cycles of the interpersonal ties have significant impacts on the formation of structure, such as communities, structural holes, and local bridges, and information diffusion in networks. For example, researchers revealed that novel information often spreads out through weak ties in the dynamic networks [14]. However, the information diffusion could change if the weak ties disappear or turn into strong ties. In other words, the changes in interpersonal ties could result in fundamental changes in network structure and information diffusion. Therefore, tracking and exploring the temporal changes of interpersonal ties can not only help us detect the significant structural changes in a dynamic network, but also help us formulate hypotheses and seek the explanations for the changes. Nevertheless, the complexity of the network structure and dynamic and frequent conversion between strong and weak ties pose significant challenges in the analysis of the evolution of interpersonal ties.

Existing visualization methods explore and analyze a dynamic network mainly in the following ways: (a) draw all the snapshots of the network along the time axis or visualize the snapshots by animation [3,9,21,23]; (b) stack the snapshots of the network at each time step together, then directly visualize the network in 3D or use density kernel estimation to visualize the network in 2D [2,7,8]; (c) calculate certain metrics of the network and visualize the metrics together with the network [15,19,20]. These methods can visualize the dynamic network directly and support various analysis tasks for exploring the evolution of the network structure. However, they do not provide adequate support for the analysis and exploration of the evolution of interpersonal ties in dynamic networks because these methods mostly focus on the dynamic changes of network structure rather than the more fundamental interpersonal ties.

In this paper, we introduce a visual analysis approach for studying interaction patterns among nodes by examining the change in the strength of edges. We use strong ties and weak ties to indicate the edges of varying degrees of strength. We transform each edge into a series of strength values over time, which is denoted as a feature vector for each edge. The feature vectors of these edges are then visualized in a scatterplot view using Principal Component Analysis (PCA) to provide an overview of the interpersonal ties. The scatterplot view allows users to immediately see the clusters of the edges with similar trends of strength variation. Abnormal edges can also be easily disclosed in the scatterplot. From the overview, the users can select a group of edges and further examine their temporal changes in the strength of edges in a pixelbar chart. A layered graph is introduced to enable the users to visualize the selected edges and the connected nodes over time. A node-link diagram is also presented to show the network structure for a particular time step chosen by the users.

With this work, we make the following contributions:

- A new study of the evolution of interpersonal ties for a dynamic network and their co-evolution with the network structure and information diffusion;

- An edge based analysis framework which helps users identify edges with similar trends, compare edges with different trends, and find hidden patterns;
- An interactive visualization system that integrates four views, including a scatterplot, a pixelbar chart, a layered graph, and a node-link diagram, which allows for multi-perspective exploration and analysis.

The remainder of this paper is organized as follows. Section 2 reviews related works on dynamic network visualization and methods for analyzing time series data. In Sect. 3 we describe the measure of edge strength and the feature vector extraction method. Section 4 presents the system design. In Sect. 5, we report a use case on the Enron email dataset. In Sect. 6, we conclude and discuss future work.

2   Related Work

2.1   Network Visualization Using Graph Metrics

The statistical information of edges and/or nodes statistics can be important for understanding a network [15,16,20]. Researchers have used different metrics to characterize the network and provide useful information such as the importance of the nodes and the edges (by using, for example, centrality) [20] or other structural properties of the network such as density, modularity, and so forth [19]. Many graph visualization systems [15,20] provide the metrics to help analysts understand the overall structure of the network, or guide their attention to structurally significant nodes/edges through visual encoding and user interactions.

SocialAction [20] tightly integrates the statistical information with network visualization. Network statistics such as betweenness and centrality of nodes are sorted and visualized to facilitate the identification of important nodes. GraphDice [4] layouts the graph nodes based on some graph metric values. GraphPrism [16] utilizes a visual design that summarizes the structure of a graph by displaying multilevel histograms of some graph metrics such as degree, diameter, and transitivity. Panagiotidis et al. [19] have introduced Graph Metric Views, a technique that enriches the visualization of traditional node-link diagrams with the histograms of the graph metric values. CentiBiN [15] focuses on the computation and exploration of centrality in biological networks. Dwyer et al. [10] have presented 3D parallel coordinates that support orbit-based comparison and hierarchy-based comparison to explore and compare node centrality in networks. Zimmer et al. have introduced ViNCent [24], a system that supports interactive visual analysis of network centralities. A set of node centralities is calculated to group similar nodes.

Compared with existing work, our work focuses on exploration and visualization of interpersonal ties through the analysis of the temporal variations of the strength of edges. In particular, we aim at studying the relationship between the strong-weak tie conversion and structural changes in a network. Nevertheless, the common techniques used in existing work such as visual encoding of centrality on graph nodes are employed in our work.

2.2   Sociology Studies on Interpersonal Ties

In mathematical sociology, researchers have proposed some formal models to describe and analyze social processes and social structures in social networks [6]. The interpersonal tie is one of best-known models among the models in mathematical sociology. Granovetter [14] has introduced three states of interpersonal ties, including absent, weak, and strong, in social networks. He has also discussed the importance of weak ties in spreading novel ideas or information. In [5,17], the strength of strong ties has been extensively discussed. Friedkin [12] has described how strong ties and weak tie impact information flow in social networks.

Our work uses interpersonal ties to characterize the evolution of edges in dynamic networks. Different from the researches in mathematical sociology, our method takes the advantages of visualization and helps the user interactively analyze the temporal variations of interpersonal ties.

3   Overview

This section briefly describes the approach pipeline and user interfaces, followed by a discussion on analysis tasks for the system.

3.1   Pipeline

The TieVis system is designed for tracking, exploring, and analyzing temporal changes of interpersonal ties in dynamic networks. It consists of three components: a data processing module, an analysis module, and a visualization module. In the data processing module, the network structures are extracted from the raw data and each edge is transformed into a sequence of the interpersonal ties according to the network statistics. In the analysis module, the distances of the edges are calculated. Based on the distance, PCA is performed to determine the position of edges in a 2D plane and a hierarchical clustering algorithm is applied to determine the order of edges in 1D axis. In the visualization module, interpersonal ties and network structures are visualized. The visualization enables the user to analyze the evolution of dynamic networks intuitively and interactively.

3.2   User Interfaces

Our interface (Fig. 1) integrates five views, including a scatterplot, a pixelbar chart, a layered graph, a node-link diagram, and an information panel. It supports interactive and intuitive analysis of the evolution of interpersonal ties from multiple perspectives. In particular, the scatterplot provides an overview of all the edges in the network. The pixelbar chart visualizes the details of the temporal series of interpersonal ties. The layered graph shows the structure of the network formed by selected edges from other views at all time steps. The node-link diagram gives a snapshot of the dynamic network to show the network structure at a user-chosen time step. The information panel provides the detail information of the edges the user is interested in.

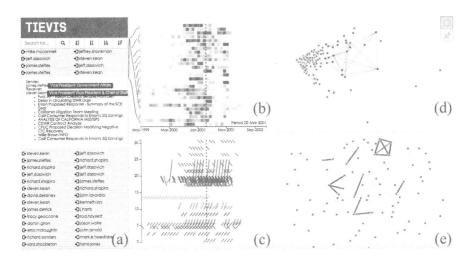

Fig. 1. Our interface includes five views. (a) a information panel; (b) a pixelbar chart; (c) a layered graph (d) a scatter plot (e) a node-link diagram.

3.3   Analytical Tasks

We identify three main analysis tasks, which should be supported by our system, to enable users to explore and understand the dynamics of the interpersonal ties in a continuously changing network interactively and intuitively.

T.1 Identify the edges with similar trends in terms of the strength of the edges over time such that users can select, group, filter, or compare different groups of ties for further analysis.

T.2 Detect the edges with abnormal variations of strength quickly to allow users to make hypotheses and seek explanations. We are particularly interested in finding the abnormal patterns because the abnormal changes could significantly impact the network structure and information diffusion.

T.3 See and explore the evolution of the interpersonal ties selected by users. Major changes of the strengthen of edges can be important for understanding various phenomenon such as the formation of structural holes and small worlds.

T.4 Analyze the co-evolution relationship between the interpersonal ties and the network structures.

4   Interpersonal Ties

Our work is based on the theory of interpersonal ties from mathematical sociology. The strength of a tie characterizes a set of the property of the tie, including the emotional intensity, the intimacy, time etc [14]. An edge in the network can have three different types of strength, which are absent, weak, and strong. In practice, the strength of an edge can be defined simply by counting the number of contacts between its two nodes. For example, in the telecommunication network, the strength of an edge linking user A and user B can be defined as the number of phone calls between A and B. On the other hand, it can also be computed by the Jaccard similarity between the neighbors of A and those of B, according to the hypothesis "the stronger the tie between A and B, the larger the proportion of individuals in the network to whom they will both be tied" [14].

It has been shown that there is a linear relationship between the two methods [11]. Therefore, we choose the first method for simplicity. The states of the interpersonal ties of an edge at each time step constitute a time series. Thus, the dynamic network can be transformed into a group of time series, and can be treated and studied as time series data. Principal component analysis (PCA) can then be used to analyze the similarity of the time series data.

5   Visualization

In this section, we firstly present the design goals of the system according to the analytical tasks and then introduce four views that are designed for multiperspective analysis of interpersonal ties in details.

5.1   Design Goals

G.1 Provide a visual summary of the dynamics of interpersonal ties to enable users to quickly identify the groups of edges with similar trends (**T.1**), and identify the patterns and outliers of the evolution of interpersonal ties (**T.2**).

G.2 Support analysis for large dataset. The design should have high scalability to support the analysis of large dynamic network dataset (**T.1-4**).

G.3 Employ timeline-based visualization to display the temporal changes of interpersonal ties and networks (**T.3–T.4**). Timeline visualization enables users to intuitively see the temporal patterns over time, and relate the temporal patterns of interpersonal ties to those of network more intuitively.

G.4 Use multiple linked views to allow users to analyze and explore the data from multiple perspectives. Because of the high complexity of the structure of dynamic networks, the designs should support multi-perspective analysis to help the user better understand the co-evolution of the interpersonal ties and network structure (**T.4**).

5.2   The Scatter Plot

The scatter plot view fulfills **G.1** by providing an overview of edges in the network based on the temporal similarity, see in Fig. 2(a)(left). The state of an edge at a time step is regarded as a coordinate in a dimension. We use Euclidean distance to measure the similarity of each pair of the high dimensional vectors, which is calculated by the following equation:

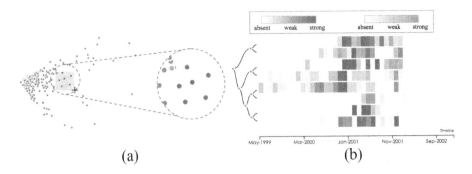

Fig. 2. (a) The visual encodings in the scatter plot. (b) The visual encodings in pixelbar chart: a dendrogram is placed on the left to show the hierarchical clustering results of edges (Color figure online).

$$d(x,y) = \sqrt{\sum_{i=0}^{n}(x_i - y_i)^2}$$

where $x = \{x_0, x_1, ..., x_n\}$ and $y = \{y_0, y_1, ..., y_n\}$. Principal component analysis (PCA) is then performed to reduce the high dimensional data into a 2D plane. This process could also be viewed as classic Torgerson's metric multidimensional scaling (MDS), which is actually done by transforming distances into similarities and performing PCA on those. In this way, dots that are close to each other in the plane indicate that the corresponding edges are similar.

The scatter plot supports two basic interactions, brushing and zoom, and is linked to other views by interactions. The zoom interaction enables the view to support network data with a large number of edges (**G.2**).When the user brushes a part of dots, the information of selected edges will be visualized in the other three views to support further analysis. Meanwhile, the linkage among the brushed edges at a certain time step will be visualized by links, as shown in Fig. 2(a)(right). The two interpersonal ties connected by a link share a common person. It could be regarded as exchange the roles edge and node play in a common graph.

5.3 The Pixelbar Chart

Design Rationale. Though the projection of edges gives an overview of edges, the details of the edge states are not shown. One way to visualize the time series data is the line chart. Another way is the pixelbar chart. A line chart shows the trend of time series directly but has a low scalability, while a pixelbar chart is not intuitive but has a high scalability. As the number of edges that appear in the network is often large, we choose the pixelbar chart.

In the pixelbar view, each edge is represented by a series of pixelbars (**G.3**). The strength of the edge is encoded by color. Light grey indicates that the edge has the lowest strength, i.e., the weakest tie, the dark grey indicates that the edge has the highest strength, i.e., strongest tie, and white indicates that the edge is absent. The color map is shown in Fig. 2(b).

The nearest-neighbor chain algorithm [18] is used to layout the pixelbars. The algorithm guarantees closer pixel bands are more similar. A dendrogram is presented in the left of the view to show the structure of a hierarchical clustering tree (Fig. 2). When the number of pixelbars is large, space is not adequate to visualize all the bars. An adaptive algorithm is applied when the total space of the pixelbars exceeds the view height. To decrease the number of pixelbars, we merge pixelbars within one cluster into a larger one which is their average. The merge result is the average of merged pixelbars. By the merging operation and the dendrogram, the pixelbar chart can visualize a large number of edges and has a high scalability (**G.2**)

5.4   The Layered Graph

Design Rationale. As the structure of a dynamic network is constantly evolving, it is necessary to show the structure information of the edges in which the user is interested. However, the life cycles of the edges are not the same, therefore the structure of the network formed by the edges are also evolving. There are three designs we have considered, including an animated node-link diagram, sequential adjacency matrix, and a modified layered graph. The animated node-link diagram is a straightforward and intuitive design, but it can not show the complete evolution process in a glance. The sequential adjacency matrix is a better choice, because it compactly visualizes both temporal and topological information. However, the modified layered graph can visualize both the temporal and topological information of the selected edges more intuitively.

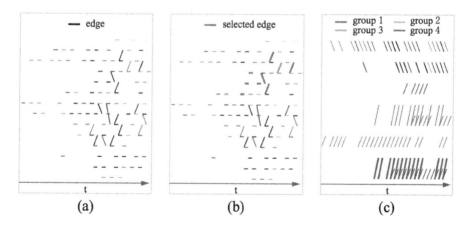

Fig. 3. The layered graph visualizes the structure of selected edges by a sequence of bi-partite networks. (a) DAG layout before time selection. (b) Mouse hovers on an edge. (c) Layout is optimized according to the group information after time selection (Color figure online).

In the layered graph view, the temporal information is encoded horizontally, as shown in Fig. 3(a). The snapshot at each time step is visualized as a bipartite network by representing source nodes and target nodes on two axes. The left axis encodes the source vertices of the edges, and the right one encodes the target vertices. Each edge is visually encoded as a link between the left axis and the right one. Then snapshots are arranged end-to-end according to the temporal sequence. Note that two adjacent snapshots share the same node order on the shared node axis. A modified Sugiyama-style graph drawing algorithm [22] is applied to optimize the node order on the axes to minimize the visual clutter within an adequately short time interval (**G.3**). When the mouse is hovering on an edge in the view, the edge will be highlighted, see in Fig. 3(b).

In order to find a balance between visual quality and performance, we decide to do the optimization hierarchically. The vertices are grouped by their connectivity, and those in the same group are aligned together.

The grouping is performed according to the connectivity of the vertices in the selected time step. The vertices of the edges connected together are regarded as in the same group. By mentioning the selected time step here, it is important to point out that the alignments are identical for distinct time steps. If the alignments are distinct for multiple time steps, it would be difficult for the analyzer to find the pattern. If edges of all time steps are considered, the connected subsets may be too large to minimize the visual clutter quickly. We optimize the alignment of the vertices in the groups and optimize the alignment of these groups. Group information is encoded by color as categorical data (Fig. 3(c))

5.5   The Node-Link Diagram

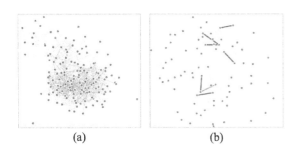

(a)   (b)

Fig. 4. The visual encodings of node-link diagram

The network structure is visualized in the node-link diagram. It helps the user locate the brushed edges in the network. Before a time step is selected by the user, the node-link diagram shows the network formed by aggregate networks at all time steps, which shows an overview of the network dataset (Fig. 4(a)). After a time step is selected, the node-link diagram shows the snapshot of the dynamic network at the time step, as shown in Fig. 4(b).

As the four views show the evolution of interpersonal ties from different aspects, including overview of similarity of ties (the projection view), temporal changes of the values (the pixelbar chart), temporal changes of structure (the layered graph view), and structural details at each time step (the node-link view), and they are highly connected by interactions, the system fulfills **G.4**.

6   Case Study

In this section, we present a case study on a dataset to demonstrate the usability and effectiveness of our method.

6.1   Data Description

The dataset is extracted from the Enron Email Dataset. The original dataset includes all the emails sent and received by 184 employees in the network. In [1], the occupations of the employees are given. We extracted 25370 emails sent among these employees from May 1999 to Dec. 2002.

6.2   Case Analysis

The Enron Corporation used to be one of the biggest energy, commodities, and services company in the world. It went bankrupt on December 2, 2001. In this case study, the analyst explores and analyzes the evolution of interpersonal ties in Enron in the period around its bankruptcy.

The analyst firstly finds the uneven distribution of density of the edges. He explores the evolution of interpersonal ties in different areas of the view and finds out that the evolution patterns are different, as shown in Fig. 5(a, b).

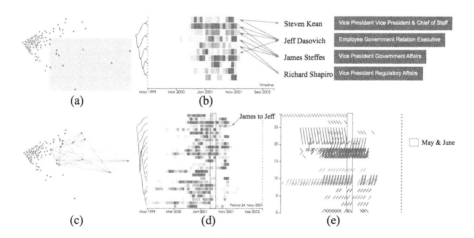

Fig. 5. (a)(b) The analyst brushes edges in the scatter plot, finds that the interpersonal ties between four people evolve similarly. Combine with their occupations, this is related to the government investigation and the bankrupt procedure. (c)(d)(e) The analyst notices the edge from James to Jeff is a strong tie on May but turn to a weak tie on June. He selects the two time step and observes the network structure in the scatter plot and the layered graph, finding out that some edges disappear on June.

He checks the edges on the lower right of the view by brushing these edges (T.1). The evolution of interpersonal ties of these edges is shown in the pixelbar chart. The pixelbars shows that the first six edges appear in almost the same period and have a similar trend of interpersonal ties (T.3). By checking the node information of these edges in the info panel by hovering the mouse on the pixel bars, he finds out that the employees linked by these edges are executives and vice presidents of Enron. He checks the occupations of the nodes and finds out the occupations include "Employee Government Relation Executive", "Vice President Government Affairs", "Vice President Regulatory Affairs", and "Vice President Vice President & Chief of Staff" (Fig. 5(b)). The occupations indicate that the employees deal business with the government, therefore the edges between them show high strength from September to November as they contact frequently during the government investigation and the bankrupt procedure.

The analyst notices that the interpersonal tie between james.steffes and jeff.dasovich is evolving regularly. To explore the relationship between the evolution of interpersonal tie and the evolution of structure evolution, he brushes many edges in the projection view. He first selects the time May-2001 when the edge is a strong tie and he notices that in the bipartite view. There are some edges missing at the next time step (June-2001) and the edge turns into a weak tie at the next time step, see in Fig. 5(d). He therefore clicks on the next time step to further explore the difference of the network structure. He finds out that there are some edges which disappear in the group, including the edges that link jeff.dasovich and steven.kean, richard shepiro and james.steffes (T.4), which reveals the relationship between the network structure around james.steffes and jeff.dasovich between the interpersonal ties of the edge (in Fig. 5(e)).

7   Conclusions

In this paper, we presented a new, interactive approach for analysis and exploration of dynamic interpersonal ties. The scatter plots together with the other four views provide an overview to detail analysis scheme, which makes it much easier for users to find interesting patterns. We demonstrated the effectiveness of our method with a case study on a dataset.

One of the limitations is that the current approach supports only small dataset analysis. Although we design the visualizations with the ability to scale to large datasets, we don't test large datasets in our system. Another limitation is that visual comparison and visual query is not well supported in the system, which makes the analysis of pattern not very convenient.

Acknowledgments. This work is supported by NSFC (61232012, 61422211, 61303141), Zhejiang NSFC (Y12F020172), and the Fundamental Research Funds for the Central Universities.

References

1. http://cis.jhu.edu/~parky/Enron/employees
2. Bach, B., Pietriga, E., Fekete, J.-D.: Visualizing dynamic networks with matrix cubes. In: Proceedings of the 32nd Annual ACM Conference on Human Factors in Computing Systems, pp. 877–886. ACM (2014)
3. Beyer, D., Hassan, A.E.: Animated visualization of software history using evolution storyboards. In: 2006 13th Working Conference on Reverse Engineering, WCRE 2006, pp. 199–210. IEEE (2006)
4. Bezerianos, A., Chevalier, F., Dragicevic, P., Elmqvist, N., Fekete, J.-D.: Graphdice: a system for exploring multivariate social networks. Comput. Graph. Forum **29**, 863–872 (2010). Wiley Online Library
5. Bian, Y.: Ringing strong ties back in: indirect ties, network bridges, and job searches in China. Am. Sociol. Rev. **62**, 366–385 (1997)
6. Bonacich, P., Lu, P.: Introduction to Mathematical Sociology. Princeton University Press, Princeton (2012)
7. Brandes, U., Nick, B.: Asymmetric relations in longitudinal social networks. IEEE Trans. Vis. Comput. Graph. **17**(12), 2283–2290 (2011)
8. Burch, M., Schmidt, B., Weiskopf, D.: A matrix-based visualization for exploring dynamic compound digraphs. In: 2013 17th International Conference on Information Visualisation (IV), pp. 66–73. IEEE (2013)
9. Burch, M., Vehlow, C., Beck, F., Diehl, S., Weiskopf, D.: Parallel edge splatting for scalable dynamic graph visualization. IEEE Trans. Vis. Comput. Graph. **17**(12), 2344–2353 (2011)
10. Dwyer, T., Hong, S.-H., Koschützki, D., Schreiber, F., Xu, K.: Visual analysis of network centralities. In: Proceedings of the 2006 Asia-Pacific Symposium on Information Visualisation-Volume 60, pp. 189–197. Australian Computer Society Inc. (2006)
11. Easley, D., Kleinberg, J.: Networks, Crowds, and Markets: Reasoning About a Highly Connected World. Cambridge University Press, Cambridge (2010)
12. Friedkin, N.E.: Information flow through strong and weak ties in intraorganizational social networks. Soc. Netw. **3**(4), 273–285 (1982)
13. Granovetter, M.: The impact of social structure on economic outcomes. J. Econ. Perspectives **19**, 33–50 (2005)
14. Granovetter, M.S.: The strength of weak ties. Am. J. Sociol., pp. 1360–1380 (1973)
15. Junker, B.H., Koschützki, D., Schreiber, F.: Exploration of biological network centralities with centibin. BMC Bioinform. **7**(1), 219 (2006)
16. Kairam, S., MacLean, D., Savva, M., Heer, J.: Graphprism: compact visualization of network structure. In: Proceedings of the International Working Conference on Advanced Visual Interfaces, pp. 498–505. ACM (2012)
17. Krackhardt, D.: The strength of strong ties: the importance of philos in organizations. In: Networks and Organizations: Structure, Form, and Action, vol. 216, p. 239 (1992)
18. Murtagh, F.: A survey of recent advances in hierarchical clustering algorithms. Comput. J. **26**(4), 354–359 (1983)
19. Panagiotidis, A., Burch, M., Deussen, O., Weiskopf, D., Ertl, T.: Graph exploration by multiple linked metric views. In: 2014 18th International Conference on Information Visualisation (IV), pp. 19–26. IEEE (2014)
20. Perer, A., Shneiderman, B.: Balancing systematic and flexible exploration of social networks. IEEE Trans. Vis. Comput. Graph. **12**(5), 693–700 (2006)

21. Rufiange, S., McGuffin, M.J.: Diffani: visualizing dynamic graphs with a hybrid of difference maps and animation. IEEE Trans. Vis. Comput. Graph. **19**(12), 2556–2565 (2013)
22. Ward, M.O., Grinstein, G., Keim, D.: Interactive Data Visualization: Foundations, Techniques, and Applications. CRC Press, Boca Raton (2010)
23. Yee, K.-P., Fisher, D., Dhamija, R., Hearst, M.: Animated exploration of dynamic graphs with radial layout. In: IEEE Symposium on Information Visualization, p. 43. IEEE Computer Society (2001)
24. Zimmer, B., Jusufi, I., Kerren, A.: Analyzing multiple network centralities with vincent. In: Proceedings of the SIGRAD Conference on Interactive Visual Analysis of Data, pp. 87–90. Linköping University Electronic Press (2012)

Author Index

Printed in the United States
By Bookmasters